The Architecture of
New York City

Also by Donald Martin Reynolds:

Masters of American Sculpture:
The Figurative Tradition from the American Renaissance to the Millennium

Monuments and Masterpieces: Histories and Views of Public Sculpture in New York City

Nineteenth-Century Art

Nineteenth-Century Architecture

Manhattan Architecture

The Ideal Sculpture of Hiram Powers

The Architecture of New York City

Histories and Views of Important Structures, Sites, and Symbols

by

DONALD MARTIN REYNOLDS

REVISED EDITION

JOHN WILEY & SONS, INC.

New York • Chichester • Brisbane • Toronto • Singapore

Library of Congress Cataloging in Publication Data:

Reynolds, Donald M.
    The architecture of New York City : histories and views of
important structures, sites, and symbols / by Donald Martin
Reynolds. — Rev. ed.
        p.   cm.
    Includes bibliographical references and index.
    ISBN 0-471-01439-7 (paper)
    1. Architecture. Modern—New York (N.Y.)   2. Architecture—New
York (N.Y.)   3. Symbolism in architecture—New York (N.Y.)
4. Buildings—New York (N.Y.)   5. New York (N.Y.)—Buildings,
structures, etc.   I. Title.
NA735.N5R49   1994
720′.9747′1—dc20   94-5705

Printed in the United States of America

10 9 8 7 6 5 4 3 2 1

In memory of my mother and father,
Helen Hughes Reynolds and James Martin Reynolds,
to whom some debts of gratitude can never be discharged.

CONTENTS

9. Fashionable Dwellings   227

10. Theaters   241

11. The New York Port Comes of Age   251

12. Art Deco Skyscrapers   275

PREFACE

This is an introduction to the architecture of New York City. It presents a compendium of histories and views of more than 120 major structures, sites, and symbols, from the seventeenth century to the present. Although this is not a comprehensive and chronological survey of New York City's architecture, the selections range from the period of colonization, when both Indian coves and trails and Dutch canals shaped the city's early terrain, to the present day, when Manhattan's towers continue to transform the city's skyline.

The book reflects a personal view of the material, from its selection to its presentation in the text as well as in the photographs, but that view is shaped by many circumstances and the work and influence of many people, to whom I owe a substantial debt.

Although it is impossible to mention them all, I would like to acknowledge some. My friend and former teacher and adviser James H. Beck, Professor of Art History at Columbia University, suggested that I write the book and made numerous observations that improved the text and the concept. Harry Cloudman, Vice-President (retired) of Macmillan Publishing Company, was supportive of the idea and instrumental in its receiving a proper forum. My editor for the first edition, Charles M. Levine, Director of General Reference Books, Macmillan Publishing Company, was responsive to the material from the very beginning and through his advice and encouragement was the guiding force in the shape and form it takes here, as well as in the earlier editions. I am also indebted to my publisher at John Wiley & Sons, Peggy Burns, for making this revised and enlarged edition possible on the book's tenth anniversary, and to my editors, Amanda L. Miller, whose care and expertise brought the book to term, and to Everett W. Smethurst, who helped initiate the project.

Joyce H. Jack edited the manuscript. Her perceptive insights into essential elements of the material, both text and illustration, and her broad editorial experience were indispensable to the focus and clarity of the manuscript. And her sense of dedication to the book contributed substantially to its success. Jane W. Low, copy editor, was attentive to every minute detail, whether technical or administrative, and was consistently sensitive to expressing every nuance of meaning. Bruce Wetterau not only copy edited the manuscript but made useful suggestions that improved the text. Jacques Chazaud and Helen Mills are responsible for the superb design of the book. Mary Reiman helped in typing parts of the manuscript, and Glady Villegas, Charles Levine's assistant, was enormously helpful at every step of the way.

I owe special thanks to my wife, Nancy Zlobik Reynolds, who not only helped to type parts of the manuscript but also made numerous constructive suggestions from the beginning.

While it is impossible to acknowledge the many individuals who have been helpful in my research, there are some who deserve special mention: Robert Rainwater, Curator of Prints, The New York Public Library; Wilson G. Duprey, former Curator of Prints, The New York Historical Society; Wendy G. Shadwell, Curator of Prints, The New York Historical Society; Kenneth Finkel, Curator of Prints, The Library Company of Philadelphia; Janet Parks, Archivist, Avery Architectural and Fine Arts Library; Dr. Joseph W. Ernst, Archivist, Rockefeller Family and Associates; Sherene Baugher, Urban Archaeologist, New York City Landmarks Preservation Commission; Marion Cleaver, Access Information Officer, New York City Landmarks Preservation Commission; Nan A. Rothschild, Assistant Professor of Anthropology, Barnard College; Patrick H. Garrow, Archaeologist, Garrow and Associates, Inc.; Joan H. Geismar, archaeologist and consultant; Diana di Zerega Rockman, Archaeologist, New York University; Warren Reiss, nautical archaeologist; Michael May, former Researcher, New York Landmarks Conservancy; Irwin S. Chanin, Chanin Management, Inc.; Philip Haller, Chanin Management, Inc.; James Pearn, Chanin Management, Inc.; Peter Entin, Theatre Operations Manager, Shubert Organization; Brigitte Kuippers, Archivist, Shubert Archives; Gerard M. Carey, Professor of Law, Seton Hall University School of Law; Robert Cavella, Buildings Design Department, City of New York; Commissioner Philip P. Augusta; Helen Barer, Lucy Jarvis Productions; Jay S. Duhl, former Editor/Supervisor, Special Events, Rockefeller Center; Timothy Allanbrook, AIA, The Ehrenkrantz Group; Larry Jay Wyman, HRO International; Guy St. Clair, Library Director, University Club; George Lefkowitz, the Old Stone House; the Municipal Offices of the City of New York, and Yusheng He.

I wish to thank those who made photographing the structures for the book not only possible but a joy: Mrs. Paul Douglas, Albert and Anne Romasco, Thomas Musto, Mrs. Sylvia Beam, Nicole Sloan, Reverend Kevin O'Brien, St. James Church; Robert Tinker, Vice-President, Empire State Building; William R. Suchanek, Superintendent of Observatories, Empire State Building; A. Robert Koenig, Superintendent, Green-Wood Cemetery; Reverend Neville C. Brathwaite, Mariners' Temple; Richard Karwoski; Richard A. Huettner, Partner, Kenyon and Kenyon; Robert Stone, artist; Israel M. Stern, Project Architect, Restoration/Renovation of U.S. Custom House; Charles R. Hinkle, Kragan and Company; Jeb Hart, Kragan and Company; Barnet Liberman, ORB Management, Ltd.; Ena Hurdle, Senior Building Custodian, City Hall; David C. Morton, architect: Roderick J. Van Leuwen, Vice-President (retired), F. W. Woolworth Company; William J. and Delores Moody; Olga Bloom, Bargemusic, Ltd.; Reverend Canon Robert J. Lewis, Church of the Incarnation; Reverend Robert M. O'Connell, St. Peter's Church; John Castagna, Maintenance and Operating Foreman, U.S. Custom House; Stephen B. Jacobs, Architect, Stephen B. Jacobs and Associates; Todd Henkels, Architect, Stephen B. Jacobs and Associates; James F. Doolan, Superintendent, Seventh Regiment Armory; Joseph Roberto, Architect, Old Merchant's House; Richard Jenrette; William L. Thompson; Richard Pierce, Public Affairs Associate, Deborah J. Greenberg, Public Affairs Coordinator, Solomon R. Guggenheim Museum; Salvator Bommarito, contractor; James Strawder, proprietor, Ferrybank Restaurant; Ben Fishbein, developer; Bernard Rothzeid, Architect, Rothzeid, Kaiserman, Thomson, and Bee; Evelyn and Edwin Sauter; Tom Loepp, artist; Laura Fischer, Office Manager, Containership Agency, Inc.; Charlene Pell, Citibank; Max Wechsler, Architect, Wechsler,

Grasso, and Menziuso; Norma Foerderer, Executive Assistant, The Trump Organization; Michael O'Keefe, owner, River Café.

I am indebted to the professional and technical staff of Modern Age Photographic Services, especially Phil Vance, Al Striano, Jorge Coste, Ben Attas, and Barbara Wyman.

Chemical Bank was generous in its support of the book with the Brooklyn Bridge Centennial Exhibition, "Remove Not the Ancient Landmark . . . (Proverbs 22:28)," and I am grateful to those at Chemical Bank who made the exhibition possible, especially Anthony G. Di Russo, Vice-President; Patti McEvoy, Assistant Vice-President; the professional staff of Creative Services; Robert I. Lipp, Senior Executive Vice-President; and William H. Turner, Executive Vice-President.

I am singularly obliged to several people, to whom this book owes much: my brother, Richard Lee Reynolds; Charles A. Sarner, physician and friend; Howard McParlin Davis, Moore Collegiate Professor of Art History at Columbia University, former teacher and long a resolute supporter; longtime friend John H. Chapman; George R. Collins, Professor of Art History at Columbia University, whose inspiration in the classroom and subsequent encouragement helped to shape my vision; Adolf K. Placzek, Librarian (retired), Avery Architectural and Fine Arts Library, Columbia University, whose generosity over the years and breadth of experience have been of enormous help; and Henry Hope Reed, Dean of the New York Walking Tour, who early on introduced me to the marvels of New York's architectural treasures.

Finally, I wish to thank my students over the past twenty-two years, whose searches and queries have repeatedly opened my eyes and mind to new riches, thereby helping to shape my own view of art and the architecture that I have photographed and written about here.

PHOTO CREDITS

Photographs are by Donald Martin Reynolds with the exception of the following:

Photographs by David Barnet, pp. 27, 29
Photograph by Kenneth Champlin, p. 211
Photograph courtesy of I. S. Chanin, p. 250
Photograph courtesy of Jack Kent Cooke, owner, p. 282
Photograph by Louis H. Dreyer, courtesy of I. S. Chanin, p. 280
Eno Collection, The New York Public Library, Astor, Lenox, and Tilden Foundations, pp. 8, 60, 93, 148
The Equitable Life Assurance Society of the U.S., p. 177
Photograph © 1993 Andrew Gordon, p. 182
Photograph by Gianfranco Gorgoni © The Equitable, p. 180
Housing & Services, Inc., New York, p. 191
Photograph by Costas Kandylis, p. 186
The Library Company of Philadelphia, p. 25
Morris Collection, Avery Architectural and Fine Arts Library, Columbia University, p. 332
Photograph by Cesar Pelli, p. 201
Courtesy of Rockefeller Center, Inc., pp. 264, 294, 298–299, 304, 310
Photograph by Schoenhals, courtesy of I. S. Chanin, p. 277
Stokes Collection, The New York Public Library, Astor, Lenox, and Tilden Foundations, pp. xii, 4–5, 49, 53, 61
Courtesy of Roderick J. Van Leuwen, p. 286
Photograph by Wurts Brothers, courtesy of I. S. Chanin, p. 274

I

Seventeenth Century:
Dutch Beginnings

New York City was born at the southern tip of Manhattan in the first quarter of the seventeenth century. Although none of the first buildings remain today, the city's development can be traced through the many irregular streets leading from the East and Hudson rivers up to the "Broad Way," as the former Indian path came to be known. Situated on a wide, unbroken ridge dominating the high ground, Broadway extended from Bowling Green (so-called because it was once fenced off as a green for the sport of bowling) northward; it was called Heere Straat by the Dutch and Great George Street by the British.

Except possibly for the Vikings, who left no record of their visit, the first European to land in New York Harbor was an Italian navigator and explorer named Giovanni da Verrazano who, in the service of France, was exploring the coast from the Carolinas to Nova Scotia in search of a passage to Asia. The major European powers sought a shorter route to the East, and they often employed explorers and navigators from other countries. According to his letter to the king (July 8, 1524), Verrazano sailed into the Narrows of New York Bay in the middle of April 1524, aboard his caravel the *Dauphine*. In honor of Francis I, Verrazano named the area "Angoleme" (Angoulême) for the principality that had been the seat of the counts of Angoulême since the ninth century. He named New York's upper bay "Santa Margarita" after the king's sister, and he called Long Island "Flora" for its rich greenery. He found a superb

Originally called the Collect or Fresh Water Pond (*facing page*), this body of water located at today's municipal center was a major Indian waterway terminal, later drained and filled.

1

natural harbor, friendly Indians (Columbus first named the native Americans "Indos" because he thought he had landed in India), fertile land, and abundant natural resources.

The harbor was deep and wide and had active currents that prevented the water from freezing. (Almost always! In the winter of 1875 ice skating on the Hudson was very good!) Since the flat terrain bordering the harbor made access easy, it was fully suitable for year-round use as a port where large vessels could load and unload. Furthermore, the harbor was sufficiently recessed to permit adequate defense. Nonetheless, Francis I did not pursue this exploration further. Why the king chose not to settle this area is obscure. Perhaps the explorations in the New World of his longtime rival, Charles I of Spain, who had enormous influence in Europe, dissuaded him. After all, Francis I's main concern at the time was to find a route to the East.

Attracted by increased interest in the commercial and political potential of the New World, a number of explorers probably approached the Narrows during the rest of the sixteenth century, but the few available records give little information about such contacts. In May 1525 Estevan Gomez, sailing for Charles I of Spain, was exploring the area from Newfoundland to Cape May and, according to his accounts, probably caught sight of Cape Cod and Sandy Hook. And in 1570 an account by Jehan Cossin of Dieppe probably describes New York's bay. But it was not until September 3, 1609, that the English explorer Henry Hudson followed the same entrance route as Verrazano and passed through the Narrows in his ship the *Halfe Moon*, with a mixed crew of from eighteen to twenty Englishmen and Dutchmen. Hudson, sailing for the Dutch East India Company during the Netherlands' golden age of colonial and maritime expansion, explored the bay area; then he entered the great North River, so-called because of Hudson's search for a northern route to India. The river was named the Hudson River, however, almost from the time Hudson explored it, despite the fact that the earliest official records of that name are found in documents of August 1614 in Amsterdam. The river has been known by many other names besides the North River, including Nassau River, Manhattas River, Great River, and Rio de Montaigne.

Hudson quickly claimed the immense natural harbor at New York for the Dutch, and one of his officers, Robert Juett, gave an account in his log of the great forests and rich land there, probably the first documented description of the area. This remarkable harbor, with its natural wealth and location along a vast and unfortified shoreline that extended from Canada southward to English Virginia, appealed to the Dutch East India Company as a base for its commercial and colonial expansion.

On September 12 Hudson proceeded up the Hudson River to what are today Albany and Troy, and to the mouth of the Mohawk River. He surveyed the entire area and met with Indians along the way. Convinced that this route led to no passage to the Orient, Hudson returned to New York Bay and rounded Sandy Hook on October 4. From his meetings with the Indians, however, Hudson discovered that a fur trade could be established with the various tribes, which prompted the Dutch to send a ship the following year (1610) to pursue this avenue of trade. Soon after (1614), Adriaen Block explored Long Island and gave Block Island its name. Then, by 1615 a few huts had been built at the tip of Manhattan Island, fortifications had been erected near Albany, and the beginnings of a lively fur trade had been established.

THE DUTCH WEST INDIA COMPANY

The Dutch established the Dutch East India Company in 1602, after Spain took control of Portugal (1580–81) and excluded the Dutch from trading with the Portuguese. Before then the Dutch had been the chief carriers of produce from Lisbon to northern Europe, and they were then forced to sail to the East themselves to continue their trade. Desirous of being free of any interference from Spain and Portugal, the Dutch sought an alternate, northern route to the East. These efforts ultimately failed and they were forced to follow the well-known route around the Cape of Good Hope to reach the Spice Islands in the East.

An outburst of independent commercial ventures in the 1590s between Dutch traders and Eastern markets led the Dutch government to combine the numerous small trading companies into one united Dutch East India Company, which could regulate trade and at the same time create a united maritime force against Portugal and Spain. The government endowed the company with great power. It was given a monopoly on trade with the East Indies and was authorized to maintain armed forces, build forts, establish colonies, make war, sign treaties, and to coin money. Its authority extended over the region lying between the Strait of Magellan and the Cape of Good Hope.

The commercial success of the Dutch East India Company produced outposts, factories, and colonies on the Malay Archipelago, Sri Lanka (Ceylon), and the Cape of Good Hope, along the Persian Gulf, on the coasts of Malabar and Coromandel, and in Bengal. The commercial potential the Dutch saw in other markets, especially in the New World, led them to expand their operations to the American and African possessions of Spain and Portugal. Thus, the Dutch

3

West India Company was founded in 1621 to establish colonies in the area extending from the Tropic of Cancer to the Cape of Good Hope and from the Arctic to the Strait of Magellan. It was to carry on trade and colonization with the same broad powers that had been granted to the Dutch East India Company. So, in colonies such as New Netherland, it had full administrative, judicial, and legislative authority.

From the outset less successful than the earlier company, the Dutch West India Company failed in its original plan to use its monopoly on the coast of South Africa to dominate the slave trade in America. Furthermore, plunder from Spanish and Portuguese galleons was disappointing, and profit had to be sought through developing colonies in America. But failures of company colonies outnumbered successes. Even though it gained solid footing in the West Indies in the 1630s, the company lost all claims to one of its major markets, Brazil, by 1661, and New Netherland (New York) fell to the English in 1664. While the Dutch East India Company grew and prospered to the end of the seventeenth century, the Dutch West India Company was forced to dissolve and reorganize in 1674–75 and never fully recovered.

View of New York (New Amsterdam); 1664. Based on a view published by Visscher, this early engraving looks north, extending from Rector Street on the west to Coenties Slip.

A "COMPANY TOWN"

Claimed for the Dutch by Henry Hudson in 1609 and then gradually occupied by traders, New Netherland was formally named in June 1623. In March 1624 the ship *New Netherland* set sail with the first permanent colonists—thirty families, mostly Walloons—who settled in Manhattan, along the Delaware River, and near Albany.

Granted trading rights and dominion from Newfoundland to the Strait of Magellan by the Dutch States General, the Dutch West India Company founded New Netherland as a fur-trading port to gather the peltry and ship it to the Netherlands. Since New Netherland was a "company town," the director general of the company was also the head of the settlement and served as governor. The settlement immediately thrived as an international trading post, but agricultural development of land beyond the coastline proceeded more slowly. Trade and commerce, then, were the primary forces directing the growth of New Netherland during its early years, and they have continued to do so into the twentieth century.

Peter Minuit, the first fully empowered resident director general, arrived in 1626 with more colonists and soon "purchased"

Manhattan Island from the Indians, although the Indians were not aware that they were selling the land. Minuit negotiated his transaction on the site of what is today Bowling Green, across from where the U.S. Custom House now stands. He gave the Indians merchandise (jewelry and cloth) valued at sixty guilders, or only about twenty-four dollars. The Museum of the City of New York today commemorates that purchase price with its annual Twenty-four Dollar Award, the highest honor it gives for outstanding service to New York City by a private citizen.

The Indians called Manhattan Island Manna-Hata, Island of the Hills; most of the hills were later leveled for landfill to extend Manhattan's shoreline. Some of the island's original hills remain, however, and include the Great Hill (134 feet), Vista Rock (136 feet), and Summit Rock (137 feet). All are in Central Park and are the three highest points of natural terrain on the island. In the naturalistic setting of the park, they convey a sense of what the island was like before it was settled.

Manhattan's first settlers were Netherlanders along with French-speaking Walloons, who were fleeing religious persecution in their homeland (now Belgium). Some stayed at the tip of Manhattan, and others went north to near present-day Albany and settled Fort Orange, named in honor of William the Silent, Protestant defender of Dutch independence.

CANALS AND STREETS

The Dutch settlers dug canals, erected mills, and built Manhattan's first dock at an inlet, footing today's Broad Street; they also constructed approximately thirty houses at the outset. Nearly surrounded by water in their homeland, the Dutch had developed a canal technology to harness the sea for survival and growth, and they employed this technology in building New Amsterdam. A number of today's streets were originally canals, flanked by walkways, enabling ships to deliver cargo. Broad Street was Broad Canal, which was filled in by the English in the 1670s. Bridge Street got its name from the bridge that crossed the Broad Canal. As maritime commerce grew, slips—wide inlets for ships to enter and unload cargo into adjacent warehouses—began to line the waterfront. Filled in later, they became wide streets, such as Fulton, John, and Coenties Slip, which retains the "slip" in its name.

An early print of New Amsterdam showed the new settlement extending along the waterfront from today's Rector Street on the west, to Coenties Slip on the east. New Amsterdam's fort was south of Bowling Green and was described in 1643 by Father Isaac Jogues, the famous Jesuit missionary to the Indians. (He is portrayed on the bronze doors of St. Patrick's Cathedral on Fifth Avenue with his mutilated hand, inflicted by the Indians he later converted.) The fort housed a stone church, the brick Governor's House, a barracks, officers' quarters, a storehouse, and a jail. The windmills portrayed may be those erected northwest of the fort around 1639—a grist mill and a saw mill. Even at that early date, New York was a melting pot. Father Jogues noted that among the community's five hundred inhabitants, there were soldiers, sailors, slaves, trappers, and artisans, and that eighteen languages were spoken.

THE FIRST BLACK SETTLEMENT

In the center foreground of the early print shown here, a crane for unloading cargo is visible near the wharf, and what was perhaps the gallows is shown nearby. On this or a similar gallows, one of New Amsterdam's first black settlers was hanged. But, miraculously, he lived to be freed, not once, but twice: first from the death penalty, and then from slavery.

A group of slaves from the Dutch West India Company were convicted of murdering a fellow slave. Since only one was to die for the group's crime, lots were drawn by those convicted and Manuel de Gerrit (called "the Giant") was hanged for the murder on January 24, 1641. But the rope broke under his tremendous weight. Since Gerrit had not been killed, he was pardoned instead. Three years later, by an ordinance of February 19, 1644, Gerrit was one of the company's slaves who, as reward for their long service, were emancipated with their wives (the children remained slaves, however) to settle and farm an area of land in today's SoHo. This, then, became the site of the first black settlement in New York.

THE STADT HUYS AND
A BUILDING STYLE

Around the harbor, a network of sinuous streets developed, and each road was lined with small shops, taverns, boarding houses, and residences. The principal street, called the Strand, was laid out along the East River shoreline in 1633; later, it was called Queen Street, then Pearl Street, because of the mother-of-pearl found in shells along the shore of the East River. It was at Pearl Street and Coenties Alley, at the end of the Long Dock, that the first city hall or Stadt Huys, as the Dutch called it, was located.

7

Built originally as the Stadts Herbergh (city tavern) in early 1642 by the Dutch West India Company, it served as a lodging and meeting place for members of the company. This building was constructed in the national Dutch style, which had matured around 1600 in the Netherlands. It had origins in Netherlandish, Renaissance, and School of Fontainebleau models, which were adapted to the Netherlanders' needs and available materials. The new Dutch style had far-reaching influence in Europe, especially in the German states and Scandanavia, and the Dutch brought it with them to New Amsterdam as well. The Stadts Herbergh was a five-story brick or stone building with end chimneys ventilating open-hearth fireplaces. It had crow-stepped gables with a steeply pitched, baked-tile roof behind and had a stone "stoep," or a small front porch (the

This 1867 lithograph shows the Stadt Huys (city hall), originally the Stadts Herbergh (city tavern), in 1679; from its inception it was the center of commercial activity.

term lingers today in English as stoop). Because in the Netherlands the water often came up to the doorway, the stoep was a way of elevating the door from the water to keep the inside of the house dry.

Early private houses (sometimes with a shop on the street-level floor) followed this same basic plan, modified in scale and materials by the owner's needs and means. Thus, the smaller private house was made either of fieldstone or wood frame faced with brick. The brick, often laid up in interesting geometric patterns, was attached to the frame of the house with decorative wrought-iron anchors (scrolls, daggers, and sometimes even the numerals making up the date the house was built). A simplified version of this device may be seen in Federal houses that still stand.

Because the houses were close together, builders had to take precautions against fires, which were always a threat from cooking, heating, washing, and forging. Tile roofs were preferred, because they would not ignite from a chimney spark, but reed—less expensive—was relatively safe and certainly an improvement over the thatching used in the earliest houses. Wood-frame chimneys were covered with plaster and raised high up from the roof to allow the air to cool any flying sparks. Nonetheless, there were still many fires, and they regularly changed the face of the city.

On February 2, 1653, New Amsterdam became a city under a charter issued by the Dutch West India Company, and a form of representative government was established. At that time, Governor Peter Stuyvesant, "Old Peg-Leg," designated the Stadts Herbergh the Stadt Huys. To signify its new official role, a cupola with a bell and handsome weather vane was erected on top of the building, as shown in the illustration. The Stadt Huys housed the local government, called the Council of Legislators, which consisted of a Schout (similar to a sheriff or bailiff in English government), two Burgomasters (similar to the English mayor), and five Schepens (analogous to English aldermen)—all dominated by the governor. It also housed courts, the jail, a school, and a firehouse.

Some years later, the formal surrender of the Dutch to the conquering British, dated August 27, 1664, "at the Fort of Amsterdam," took place in the Stadt Huys. The building was then outfitted with the royal coat of arms and served as the British city hall (Citty Howse) until October 1697, when it was declared unsafe for use. From that time, Lovelace's Tavern, or the King's House, which belonged to English Governor Francis Lovelace and which had been built in the early 1670s next door (west) to the Stadt Huys, served as one of the temporary city halls until the new city hall at Nassau and Wall streets was completed in 1701. The old Stadt Huys was demolished in the spring of 1700 and was replaced by that October;

9

Lovelace's Tavern was replaced in 1726, as the city expanded and the area changed.

A PEEPHOLE TO
EARLY BUILDING TECHNIQUES

Even though more than three centuries separate us from the construction of the Stadt Huys and Lovelace's Tavern, recent excavations (1979–82) of these and nearby sites give us a peephole to the past, showing us much about early buildings, construction techniques, and also about the people who built and occupied these structures. The artifacts found and the "features" (what archaeologists call a structure that has exterior walls) from the earliest Dutch and English settlements—when these sites were part of a fashionable residential and official area, as well as from later settlements, when commercial structures gradually replaced private homes and government buildings—help to establish a sequence of construction and demonstrate how people used the sites and built at different times.

For example, the discovery of a seventeenth-century Dutch well along with assorted Delft, ceramic ware, and clay pipes has yielded information about Dutch masonry techniques, as well as the people's standard of living. Early ceramic tableware, when compared with later objects from glass and china shops, give evidence of changes in land use. The high content of shells in the mortar of seventeenth-century foundation walls, compared with the predominance of lime in the mortar of later foundations excavated, are structural differences that may have had as much to do with the availability of materials as with the improvement of building techniques.

Archaeological digs often present puzzles, some quite difficult to solve! For example, the discovery of some seventeenth-century Dutch yellow brick at the Stadt Huys site raised questions of manufacture and use. Was it used for decorative trim on a house or was it used for paving? Was it imported for construction purposes or was it ballast? All kinds of stone were used as ballast for ships—that is, heavy objects carried to enable a ship to maintain its proper draft or trim, and to stabilize the vessel when it sailed without cargo. From such ballast, stone quarried from all over the world found its way to Manhattan and now lies beneath the ground there (which explains why sculptors are often found at construction sites). Other puzzles almost solve themselves: a stack of Belgian blocks from Maine were found in the basement of Lovelace's Tavern. While initially perplexing, the puzzle was soon explained by the discovery of a piece of a 1930s Coke bottle that was found there too. Documentation revealed that the city of New York had used the basement as a storage space during that period, and so it was assumed the blocks had been placed there for storage then.

These digs often help to explain social customs and practices of the period. Excavation of the bones of domesticated animals (including cows, sheep, and goats), oyster and clam shells, fish scales and bones, as well as remains of plants and foodstuffs, yields information about the diet and agricultural habits of the people who lived then. Moreover, some of the animal bones reveal changes in butchering techniques and thus identify ethnic differences, shifts from private to commercial practices, and changing market customs. The presence of wampum (beads used as money) at these sites illustrates the interaction between local Indians and the settlers, and also corroborates the settlers' documented use of this currency to pay their taxes, which went on well into the eighteenth century, due to the shortage of coins.

Artifacts may also help to clarify a building's use when that use departs from the norm. For example, the many clay pipes and wine and liquor bottles at Lovelace's Tavern site, along with the scarcity of ceramic tableware that usually appears in such tavern sites, raised the question of the building's function. Archaeologists concluded from this and other information that the building was probably used for meetings rather than for lodging, which would be consistent with its official function as a temporary City Hall from 1697 to 1699.

The excavation of Lovelace's Tavern and the Stadt Huys (1979–82) was the first large-scale archaeological dig in Manhattan. It was conducted under the auspices of the New York City Landmarks Preservation Commission and was sponsored by the Dollar Savings Bank; a thirty-story office building is now rising on the site. The foundation walls of Lovelace's Tavern, discovered intact (unfortunately those of the Stadt Huys had been disturbed by later construction), will be reconstructed in the plaza of the new office building directly above the original site.

AN EARLY FERRY VILLAGE

Although New Amsterdam was primarily a maritime trading center, the Dutch West India Company wanted to develop the domestic potential of the area as well. To encourage Dutch planters to farm and settle the outlying territories, long-term incentives were offered. For example, in 1638, the company offered plots of land, purchased from the Indians, between Gowanus and Wallabout bays

11

along the East River, an area (today's Brooklyn) that the Indians had already successfully farmed. After ten years of cultivation, the planter would start paying the Dutch West India Company ten percent of his production each year until his debt was retired. This arrangement, the equivalent of a homestead act, gave the tract of land its name: Bruijkleen Colonie (from two Dutch words, *bruijken*, use, and *leen*, loan) the planter-tenant was the *bruijker*.

These planters often lodged at inns or taverns in New Amsterdam until they had established their farms, and they would ferry back and forth in small boats morning and evening. Planters were thus among the first guests at the Stadts Herbergh, and a short distance to the north, innkeeper Cornelis Dircksen established regular ferry service in 1642 from his inn near Peck Slip. It went across the East River to a natural cove used by the Indians at today's Cadman Plaza West and Front Street in Brooklyn (landfill has long since replaced the cove and altered the shoreline). These two landings marked the shortest distance between Manhattan and Brooklyn and had long been boarding points in the Indians' network of waterways that connected the various tribes from New Jersey, Westchester, and Manhattan to their sacred council places and tribesmen on Long Island.

A major terminal in the Indian travel system was also located near Dircksen's Inn; settlers called it the Collect or Fresh Water Pond, and it was located just northeast of City Hall at today's municipal center. Later, drained and filled for health reasons, there is still a basinlike configuration where Fresh Water Pond once was. Northern access to the Collect for the Westchester tribes was from a stream flowing south into it through the vicinity of today's Greenwich Village. A chain of swamps and ponds, linked by streams, formed a continuous waterway westward from the Collect and emptied into the North (Hudson) River at a cove where the Indians from New Jersey landed. Another creek flowed from the Collect into a large swamp behind Dircksen's Inn, and this is where the Indian canoes entered the East River and crossed from Manhattan to the cove on the other side directly beneath where the Brooklyn Bridge now crosses the Brooklyn shore.

On that other side, the Dutch established a ferry village at the cove, also the site of a former Indian settlement, and according to one tradition called it Breuckelen or "broken land," because the irregular terrain reminded the settlers of their homeland. When the British conquered the area, they referred to both Bruijkleen Colonie and Breuckelen village as Brookland, and to the ferry as the Brookland Ferry. Thus Brooklyn began as a ferry village; it grew to become a city in 1834. By 1896, Brooklyn had annexed the adjacent settlements of Williamsburgh, Bushwick, New Lots, Flatbush,

Gravesend, New Utrecht, and Flatlands. Then in 1898, Brooklyn was consolidated into Greater New York City.

From the natural cove in Breuckelen, the Indians' major trail led to secondary roads that linked the settlements on Long Island with the Indians' principal council place. This was described by the Dutch as the "Bestvaer," or place where the wise men, or chiefs, assembled. The term was anglicized to Bedford and still designates the area today.

Dutch farmers and later the English settlers widened these Indian trails for wagon and stage roads, and their expansion continued so that today, the old Indian trails are some of our major streets and highways. Kings Highway is one good example; other settlements and even subway lines along Brooklyn's southeastern shorefront still bear Indian names. The Canarsie was named after the Canarsie tribe of the Algonquin confederation, which lived there. The Indian trail from the cove later became known as Ferry Road; it was the main traffic artery for the Dutch and English, as it had been for the Indians, from the various settlements on Long Island to the ferry by which farmers transported their produce to market, and by which the commercial and social lives of the growing communities were connected. Connections were further extended in 1741, when the Brookland Ferry became a relay station for the mail coach between New England and Virginia colonies. Some thirty years later in 1772 new life was injected into Ferry Road when a stagecoach route was established between the ferry and Sag Harbor on Long Island.

THE DUTCH FARMHOUSE

The very first dwellings the Dutch pioneers built along the coast were simply primitive shelters—dugouts covered with sod roofs, or wigwam-like structures of bark stretched over a sapling skeleton, similar to Indian dwellings. When the early settlers—planters and farmers—arrived, they built more permanent homes. The typical early settler's house was a one-room cottage with fieldstone walls on the ground floor and cedar clapboards above in the gables; the roof was thatched or shingled over heavy, hand-hewn beams steeply pitched to allow sufficient headroom in the sleeping loft built above the main room. The spacious loft also helped harbor heat rising from the hearth below, compensating for the roof's lack of insulation.

The sturdy stone walls were fireproof, and twelve to fifteen inches thick for protection against unfriendly Indians, mischievous animals, and the elements; they were also the foundations. Stones were usually quarried at the site and since they were not always uniform in size, the walls were laid up in random coursing rather than in continuous horizontal courses. Mortar was made of mud reinforced with grass and animal hair. Later, builders used sturdier mortars containing clam and oyster shells and limestone, and they "parged" their walls, a process of covering them with a thin yellowish mortar to seal them more securely from the elements; sometimes, walls were then also painted. A chimney at the end wall ventilated a large open-hearth fireplace used for cooking and heating. Small windows of four or six glass panes kept the heat in during the winter, and shutters also helped. This Dutch vernacular had a lasting influence on domestic architecture in New Amsterdam, even after the British conquered the area.

The Lent Homestead, 7803 Nineteenth Road, Steinway, Queens, shows the early Dutch settlers' masonry and carpentry practices; the fieldstone wall dates to 1729.

The Lent Homestead

The Lent Homestead at 7803 Nineteenth Road in the Steinway section of Queens is a well-preserved example of the settlers' early masonry and carpentry practices; it also illustrates how they enlarged and modernized their houses. Standing on a three-quarter-acre lot, a stone's throw from Riker's Island and facing Bowery Bay on the East River, the Lent house was originally a traditional one-room stone house built in 1729 by Abraham Lent, who was born Abraham Riker (grandson of Abraham Riker, an early Dutch settler) but who took his maternal grandfather's surname.

The addition of another room and loft later in the century doubled the house's size so that the kitchen and parlor were separated, and there was more room for sleeping and storage above. Then, between 1790 and 1810, two more rooms—this time of wood frame construction—and a central hall, featuring a dogleg staircase with mahogany railing, were added at the east end to double the size of the house again. At that time, a clapboard facade was added to unite the stone and wood frame sections harmoniously beneath a pitched roof with protruding spring eaves, which protect the front and back porches. This type of eave was introduced to New Amsterdam *c.* 1650 by Flemish farmers, who had developed the device in Europe to protect their walls of clay mortar and stone from destruction by rain.

The main entrance to the Lent house still has its original door, featuring a large wrought-iron latch, a brass knocker, and a leaded fan-shaped glass transom above. The top half of the door could be opened to admit air and light, while the bottom half was kept closed to keep animals out and children in. This double-leaf door came to be called the Dutch door and it enjoyed popularity long after colonial times.

The two eastern ground-floor rooms of 1790 and 1810 are finished in the Federal style popular at that time, and they have their original woodwork, wide-plank softwood floors, chair rails, back-to-back fireplaces with carved mantels, moulded cornices, and ample closets. The earlier fireplace in the west wing was updated by the installation of a Federal mantelpiece. The segmental arched dormers were also added later.

About sixty paces west of the house is the entrance to the Riker family cemetery. It contains more than one hundred graves, dating from the eighteenth century, of Rikers, Lents, and their relatives, a burial practice common on farms and large estates.

The Vander Ende-Onderdonck House

Settlers' houses became larger and more comfortable by the end of the seventeenth and early part of the eighteenth centuries. A good example, restored from this period, is the Vander Ende-Onderdonck House at 1820 Flushing Avenue, between Cypress Street and Onderdonck Avenue in Ridgewood, Queens. Probably built in the first decade of the eighteenth century by Paulus Vander Ende, it had a number of different owners until 1821, when it was bought by Adrian Onderdonck, whose ancestors were among the first settlers of New Amsterdam. Recent research by Bonnie Marxer and Evelyn Ortner has been revealing.

The Onderdonck House is one of the few Dutch Colonial farmhouses of the seventeenth and eighteenth centuries that remain on Long Island and is the only one of stone construction extant in this area. Moreover, the construction is of unusually high quality, suggesting the work of skilled professionals. Although it was common for landowners to build their own homes, there were professional masons, thatchers, and carpenters in the area as early as the 1660s, and the sophisticated bracing techniques used in this house, as well as the presence of Roman numerals on some of the beams (indicating a numbering system used for assembly), reveal the work of trained craftsmen.

Early Long Island had abundant forests, as was first mentioned in the log of Robert Juett, Henry Hudson's officer. Thus wood was widely available for construction, and many kinds of stone, from the varied glacial deposits, were also plentiful. While the early Dutch settlers were primarily stone builders, they also drew on native resources in developing a building type suited to their new environment; this style is exemplified in the Onderdonck House. It has a high-shouldered gambrel roof—that is, the roof has two slopes on each side and they are broken near the top of the roof—traditional to New York in the eighteenth century, and spring eaves that flare out over the front and back porches. The walls of the first floor are fieldstone, laid up in random coursing and bonded with a high quality limestone mortar, instead of the inferior and more common seashell-base mortar. Wood was used for the shingles, gable ends, and wide-plank flooring, and brick was used for the chimneys. Benches originally flanked the entrance and its traditional double-leaf Dutch door, and there may have been a stoep, even though now there is no evidence of one.

The house is rectangular in plan and has four rooms on the ground floor, two on each side of a central hall with doors at the front and back. A full cellar, with access from the outside through a bulkhead and with stone steps, houses four stone chimney foundations and wall and floor foundations. Above the first floor, a loft, reached by a ladder or boxed-in staircase, was lighted at both its gable ends by two or three small windows near the floor and by one at the apex of the gable. The loft was used for storage, as a work space, and as a children's sleeping quarters.

Soon after Onderdonck bought the house, he added dormers, one on either side of the roof, and a two-story frame wing—demolished in the 1940s—on the west side. It had a kitchen and dining room on the first floor and four rooms above. The house remained in the family until 1905, when it was sold, converted to industrial use, and subsequently suffered extensive deterioration and partial destruction. Lively community interest, fired by the spirit of the Bicentennial, contributed to saving the house. With funds from the government and the community, restoration and reconstruction began in 1980, under architect G. Cavaglieri.

When the work actually began, stone foundation walls and a cistern were discovered under what had been Onderdonck's 1820s frame addition. These may date from the 1650s, when Hendrick Barents Smith, then owner of the property, had built a house there. A hearth and brick floor were also found from a later period and were perhaps of an original shed or kitchen built just before Vander Ende began his house. It was common practice to build such a small structure for the family to live in while they built their house; sections were then added on as needed. It was impossible to save the original wood frame because of extensive charring from a 1975 fire and widespread deterioration deep into the wood beams. Therefore the house was completely photographed and existing parts were saved to authentically replicate the original structure in every possible detail, from the hand-hewn oak beams with mortise, tennon, and pin connections to the hand-split cedar shingles for the roof and gables. Even the numbering system on the beams is being reproduced. When complete, the house will be open to the public under the supervision of the Greater Ridgewood Historical Society.

The Dyckman House

The Dyckman House at 204th Street and Broadway is the only eighteenth-century farmhouse in Manhattan that remains intact. It is in an excellent state of preservation and features the traditional elements of the mature Dutch colonial style: the high-shouldered gambrel roof with flared eaves supported by slender columns; fireplaces at either end of the house for uniform warmth; entrances on the long side at the front and back; and painted clapboard end gables at the second story over fieldstone walls on the ground floor.

17

18

Front and back entrances have their original double-leaf Dutch doors, original hardware, and the rectangular transoms above.

A wide hall that extends from the front porch through the house to the back porch divides the first floor in half; the parlor and dining room open off it to the north and south. Behind the parlor on the north side lie the farm office and an adjoining bedroom; behind the dining room on the south is the sitting room. The basement is a traditional winter kitchen featuring a large brick fireplace; the rising

The Dyckman House, 204th Street and Broadway. Rebuilt in 1783 after being burned by the British *(facing page)*, it is the only eighteenth-century farmhouse intact in Manhattan. The bedroom in the Dyckman House *(below)* is maintained today with many original furnishings; most were designed to contain the warmth from the fireplace and conserve body heat.

heat warmed the floor above. A summer kitchen makes up the southern extension to the house, in which windows and doors offered needed ventilation. Composed of a single room with loft and fireplace, the summer kitchen was the first room of the house constructed, and it was here that the family lived while they built the rest of the house.

At the back of the central hall there is a narrow stairway with a simple cherrywood railing; it leads down to the basement and up to the second floor, which has two bedrooms and a storage area. A ladder leads to a garret above, used for additional storage. The two bedrooms are maintained today as they were in the late eighteenth and early nineteenth centuries, with many of Isaac Dyckman's furnishings. So here are rush-bottom armchairs (having a seat made of rushes—a hollow stemmed plant), a fall-front bureau desk or drop front—having a hinged cover on the front of a desk or secretary that may be lowered to form a writing table—washstands, samplers, and family portraits. The furniture demonstrates the practical way the settlers controlled their climate: In winter, the wing-back chairs before the hearth warmed the sitter from the front and protected back, neck, and head from the cold air flowing to the fire. The canopied beds formed small enclosures to contain the warmth from the fireplace and body heat for maximum comfort. Embers from the hearth were used to fill the foot and bed warmers, and hand-braided and hook rugs on the chestnut and oak random-plank floors helped make the rooms snug and warm.

In the garden behind the Dyckman house, boxwood hedges surround a replica of a revolutionary war hut, recalling the farm's use as a military headquarters by the patriots for a short time in 1776, and then by the Hessians and redcoats from 1776 to 1783. Following the Harlem Heights Campaign in mid-September 1776 ten thousand troops of the Continental Army were garrisoned near the house until they evacuated the region just before the Battle of White Plains on October 28. The farm was then occupied by Hessians under General Knyphausen; when the Hessians left, it remained a British defense post until the end of the war. Several hundred log cabins were built for troops west of the house; after the war, they were removed, but the replica there now was reconstructed from materials found at the site.

William Dyckman, a patriot, abandoned the farm during the war and moved up the Hudson to Peekskill, New York, until the British were defeated. Four of his sons fought and one was killed in the war. Abraham Dyckman received a military funeral with full honors, which General Washington attended.

William Dyckman rebuilt the family house in 1783, four years before he died, after the original structure, whose surviving foundations may date from *c.* 1750, was burned by the British. William was the grandson of Jan Dyckman, who came to New Amsterdam in 1661 from Bentheim, Westphalia (now in West Germany) and acquired the land upon which the house stands *c.* 1677. The Dyckman's farm grew to be one of the largest in the history in Manhattan. At one time, it extended from Fort George in lower Manhattan to beyond 230th Street and from the Harlem River to Broadway. Part of it remained in the family until 1916.

The farm was particularly well known for its cherry orchards, which were begun with black Tartarean saplings from Germany and which stood in a field opposite the house. One of the trees was saved and it grows on the present site today. Some of the Dyckman farm workers were Indians and blacks who intermarried, and their children and grandchildren continued to work the farm. Their cemetery was located to the south of the house, near an Indian village, and it continued to serve the black community until 1916.

Parts of the house were restored by the family around 1880. The back porch was reconstructed on its original foundations with hand-hewn beams from the 1780s, the roof was reshingled, exterior wood was replaced and painted, and the interior woodwork was stripped of old paint, repaired, and repainted. A replica of the original smokehouse was erected and the stonework for the old well was restored.

By the early twentieth century, the house was in poor condition, but rather than allow it to be replaced by a proposed apartment house, two of the descendants of William Dyckman, Mrs. Bashford Dean and Mrs. Alexander McMillan Welch, donated the house and grounds to the city of New York in memory of their parents, who had lived there: their mother, Fannie Blackwell Dyckman, whose grandmother was married in the house; and their father, Isaac Michael Dyckman, who had to change his name to inherit the farm. He had been born James Smith, but his mother was a Dyckman. On November 12, 1915, the city of New York accepted the gift and the Dyckman House Park and Museum was opened to the public. It has been designated both a New York and national landmark.

2

Eighteenth Century:
Georgian Architecture
and a Revolution

THE GREAT WALL
AND BRITISH OCCUPATION

As a company town, New Amsterdam had a life, values, and interests that were dictated by the world of trade. The dominant role of the governor and his handpicked associates in administrative, judicial, and legislative positions assured tight control by the Dutch West India Company over the settlement. But the autocratic climate did little to stimulate community spirit beyond commerce and trade, and a number of ineffectual governors spawned policies that sowed dissension among the colonists and that often inflamed the Indians and settlers of other nations. Moreover, the local administration's primary focus on trade and profit eventually left New Amsterdam militarily ill-prepared and vulnerable to attack.

This became significant when the Dutch possession of New Netherland was challenged by the English. In spite of the claim of the Dutch to New Netherland, which they established by discovery and settlement, the English contended the Dutch were intruders. The English claimed the same territory based on John Cabot's exploration of Newfoundland in 1497 and of Delaware in 1498 and on the crown patents for settlements from Virginia to New England in 1606 and 1620.

At the root of this disagreement was the two nations' rivalry as carriers of world trade, which led to what are called the Dutch Wars, a series of European wars between 1652 and 1678 that involved commercial relations of the Netherlands with England and France.

St. Paul's Chapel, between Broadway and Church Street *(opposite);*
1764–66. Built by Thomas McBean, it is the only intact prerevolutionary building still in constant use.

23

When the first of the Dutch Wars with England broke out (1652–54), the Dutch West India Company directed Governor Peter Stuyvesant to repair New Amsterdam's fortifications, establish tighter guardianship of the Stadt Huys, and to build a wall around the town as a defense against attack from New England. Stuyvesant also sent a commercial delegation to the English settlers in New England to work out mutually attractive trade agreements.

Stuyvesant encountered apathy and outright resistance to fortifying the town until, through legislation, he pressed the entire community into service to repair the fort and to build the wall. Harassed by limited funds and a reluctant populace, Stuyvesant rationalized that a wall around the city was unnecessary because the coastline was already adequately fortified. He therefore ordered a wall to be built from the East River to the North River, thereby enclosing the city. A trench eleven feet wide and five feet deep was dug first for the foundation of the great wall. The wall, constructed in a few weeks, was a palisade of "oaken posts" between the two rivers; it had an entrance at Pearl Street called the Watergate. The posts were thirteen feet high, twenty inches in diameter, and sharpened at the top. Larger posts were set every sixteen feet and to them were nailed split rails at the top and bottom. Ironically, Thomas Baxter, an Englishman, supplied the posts. A breastwork was constructed four feet high and tapered from four feet at the bottom to three feet at the top, which was sodded over. A ditch three feet wide and two feet deep afforded drainage and added the final deterrent to attackers. So hastily was the wall built that it required excessive maintenance and inhabitants contributed to its deterioration by stealing parts of it for firewood. Little did Peter Stuyvesant realize that, with his wall, he was laying the foundation for New York's first crosstown street, a street that would take its name from the structure. We know it today as Wall Street, the main artery of the Financial District. The wall stood until 1699 and never served its purpose. The English came by sea in 1664 and occupied New Amsterdam without firing a shot.

It is noteworthy that the sea fight between Maarten Tromp and Robert Blake in May 1652, which opened the hostilities between the Dutch and the English, is commemorated today by Louis Saint-Gaudens's statue of Tromp, which looks out over Wall Street from the top of the Custom House south of Bowling Green.

In March 1664 Charles II of England claimed the territory from the west side of the Connecticut River to the east side of Delaware Bay, and all of Long Island and other minor dependencies, and granted it to his brother James, Duke of York and Albany. Colonel Richard Nicolls, appointed by James to execute the takeover, sailed into the harbor of New Amsterdam in August with three frigates and demanded the Dutch surrender. Four more frigates soon followed. In addition, the English had a force of 2,000, Stuyvesant estimated. Faced with superior artillery, troops, and naval power, Stuyvesant, aware that a Dutch victory was impossible and that a bombardment of the city would likely burn it to the ground, surrendered on August 29, 1664. In characteristic grand style, it was noted, Peter Stuyvesant wore his silver leg for the occasion.

LANDFILL FOR
NEW REAL ESTATE

In 1684 Governor Thomas Dongan granted the city, at the request of Mayor Nicholas Bayard and the city aldermen, the land between high and low tides along the perimeter of Manhattan to raise additional revenue for the city. This device of extending the city's shoreline by means of landfill is still a popular one today. The first "water lots" (as they were called) to be sold were located across the street from the Stadt Huys.

Frederick Phillipse house; 1689. Built on New York's first landfill, it illustrates the Dutch custom of "crow-stepping" their gables and using anchor irons to affix masonry and brick to wood frames.

To create new land upon which to build their homes, wealthy merchants—the New World's aristocracy—bought the lots and filled them with soil and debris obtained by leveling nearby hills, as well as with commercial and domestic trash from neighboring shops and dwellings, and ballast dumped into the harbor from the many merchant ships that called at the port. Later, these houses were replaced by commercial buildings as business expanded and forced the wealthy northward. The archaeological excavations here have revealed layers of brick, slate, asphalt, and concrete—the foundations of buildings, one on top of the other, dating from the seventeenth to the twentieth centuries.

The lots on which 64 and 66 Pearl Street, 3 and 5 Coenties Slip, and 34 and 36 Water Street stand were owned by an early merchant prince, Frederick Phillipse, who probably purchased them from Governor Dongan, their first owner. Phillipse built a house on the property in 1689, located probably where 66 Pearl Street is now, at the corner of Pearl Street and Coenties Slip, about fifty paces southwest of the Stadt Huys. It is believed to be the house drawn *c.* 1769 by Pierre Eugène du Simitière, since in that illustration the date of 1689 was affixed to the house with anchor irons (anchor irons continued in use and can be noted in many of the Federal houses of the 1820s). Phillipse left his house and property to his descendants, and his granddaughter and her husband, Mary and Peter Jay, were probably living in that house when their son, John Jay—author of New York's first constitution and the first chief justice of the U.S. Supreme Court—was born on December 12, 1745. This house was demolished in the 1820s, along with other seventeenth- and eighteenth-century buildings on the site, to make room for the present buildings that were constructed during the commercial expansion following the War of 1812.

A MERCANTILE COMMUNITY

A few blocks north on Water Street, excavations in 1982 unearthed remnants of a mercantile community of the eighteenth and nineteenth centuries, and also revealed new information about the New York port. The block contained china and glass shops, warehouses, and a residence; the structures were eventually razed to make a parking lot which remained from 1960 until the present construction for a high-rise building began at 175 Water Street. In addition to remnants of the eighteenth- and nineteenth-century buildings' foundations and footings, archaeologists also found the remains of dry-laid stone privies and mortar-lined brick cisterns fed by wooden pipes. Since these receptacles for human waste and per-

No. 175 Water Street. Excavations in 1982 uncovered these eighteenth-century remains of dry-laid stone privies and mortar-lined brick cisterns; their proximity was no doubt a source of illness.

sonal water supply were constructed close together, some even connected by overflow pipes, this partly explains why many epidemics continued to break out well into the second half of the nineteenth century, before the germ theory was accepted.

Furthermore, cisterns and privies are among the richest sources of artifacts. After they were abandoned or, as in the case of the 175 Water Street block, when they were replaced by modern plumbing following construction of the Croton Aqueduct (1837–42), they were used as trash receptacles. With the discarded objects excavated from them and with the city documents pertaining to the buildings and their owners, archaeologists and historians can put together a picture of the site and early life there. For example, tax records, maps, histories, deeds, city directories, conveyance records, and insurance data show when and whose glass and china shop occupied a specific site, and the artifacts tell something about the nature of that shop's trade.

Some of the artifacts found in the 175 Water Street block include wheel-engraved flip glasses ("flip" was a popular drink in eighteenth-century England and colonial America and consisted of sweetened rum and beer or ale heated by inserting a hot poker or loggerhead); black basalt ware by Wedgwood; porcelain from the Orient; and delicate bud vases. These latter suggest an affluent clientele, whereas imported and locally made stoneware, pearlware, earthenware, and creamware indicate a broader based trade. The inventory of one shop, mostly imports from England, documents a wide variety of popular products used between 1794 and 1820. Some bottles bear seals with names and dates, others the purposes and origins of their contents, such as "Rowland's Magassar Oil for the Hair, Kirby Street, London."

CRIBBING THE FILL

While the excavation at 175 Water Street reveals some early structural practices and tells something about daily life in the eighteenth-century mercantile community in New York, it also demonstrates the importance of landfill as an archaeological resource and tells something about the New York seaport. Early in 1982 near the Front Street side of the Water Street site, archaeologists discovered an entire ship in a remarkably fine state of preservation! This discovery has yielded abundant information about the structural development of landfill in the eighteenth century and the nature and use of artifacts in the process.

Nautical archaeologists identified the ship as a typical two- or three-masted merchant sailing ship of *c.* 1720: eighty-five feet long, twenty-six feet wide, with a 250-ton capacity. This was the type of ship that sailed the England-Caribbean-colonial America triangle (sometimes called the rum and molasses triangle), and circumvented British taxes by stopping in the Caribbean before going on to America. Such ships carried rum, molasses, sugar, leather goods, timber, and fish. Before the revolutionary war, the islands of the Caribbean were a source, and New York City a market, for European goods, so it was common practice to tap such free ports as St. Eustatius and Montserrat for these products, which were then brought into the colonies untaxed.

Evidence that this ship was involved in the Caribbean trade includes the type of her weatherproofing; impressions of shipworms or wood bores (mollusks) from the Caribbean found in her hull planks and furring strips; and the presence in the hull of decomposed coral sand from the West Indies, used for ballast. Strained by constant service, these ships were repeatedly repaired and rebuilt until they were completely spent; their life expectancy was from ten to twenty years. After that, the derelict ships were pressed into service for the last time as landfill.

From the late seventeenth century on, water lots continued to be developed as prime real estate in New York by effective landfill

"Cribbing the Fill." To hold landfill, the frame or cribbing was made of specially built or existing structures such as piers, shown here at Water Street excavation.

technology. Customarily, wooden frames or "cribs" were either built or formed using existing structures such as piers and wharfs, to contain and stabilize the landfill material of soil and debris of all kinds in a process called "cribbing the fill" or simply "cribbing." The derelict merchant ships were ideal as giant readymade landfill cribs, and objects found aboard the ship at 175 Water Street have connected her with the landfill operation begun there around 1740 and completed by 1810. It extended the Manhattan shoreline to Front Street (parallel to Water Street), and made possible the mercantile community just discussed. The ship's position—parallel to the street—suggests she was part of the bulwark for the Front Street side of the block, and the extant footings of some of the oldest buildings rest ingeniously on the ship's deck beams, making the vessel a kind of cradle for their foundations.

Although it was common practice to crib the fill with derelict merchant ships, and even though parts of them have been unearthed along the New York shoreline before, this ship was the first one of its kind to be scientifically excavated, enhancing her historical and cultural significance, and contributing to a greater understanding of these vessels and of the landfill practices of the period in the New York port. Also, her remarkable state of preservation made her the most complete model of this kind of vessel known to date: her gun ports were intact (these ships were lightly armed for protection against pirates); her capstan was actually operable; wooden pipes still functioned; and the notches of her "monkey pole" from the cargo hatch could still support an ablebodied seaman. However, in spite of her historical value, it was deemed too costly to preserve the entire vessel. Nautical archaeologists, therefore, photographed, labeled, and measured the entire ship so that through scale drawings, it can be reconstructed on paper. Moreover, selected sections, such as her prow and beak, were removed to be preserved for cultural purposes and scholarly research. The ship was then broken up and some of her carried off; the rest remained as part of the terrain under the foundations of a new skyscraper.

TRINITY CHURCH

With the restoration of English rule in 1674 (the Dutch had retaken the city for a short time), religious toleration was extended to all faiths, and the governors began to encourage the Anglicans, who had been attending services at the fort, to build their own church. By the 1690s a group of Anglicans was able to purchase a small plot of land, at Broadway opposite Wall Street, where Trinity now stands, to build a church. Ground was broken in 1696 and the church was built with materials and labor donated by its members. In fact, in the days before Captain Kidd turned privateer, he had lent his runner and tackle for hoisting up stones for the church.

The church was officially opened on March 13, 1698. The bishop of London presented the church with its bell in 1704, but installation was delayed until 1711 when the steeple was completed. Designed in the Gothic Revival style, the church was cruciform in plan with a chancel and steeple.

Once the church members had demonstrated to the governor that there was enough support to erect and maintain a church, the governor in 1698, Benjamin Fletcher, leased the church a sizable portion of valuable land extending as far south as Bowling Green and north to around today's Vesey Street, and from Broadway to the Hudson River.

The congregation grew and the church was enlarged to accommodate its new members, so that by 1735, the structure was 146 feet long and 72 feet wide, almost twice its original size.

In September 1776 after the outbreak of the American Revolution, and following Washington's retreat across the East River from Brooklyn, a great fire swept through the city and leveled most of the buildings. Trinity was destroyed. Following the British defeat, Trinity was rebuilt on the original site.

The new church was completed in 1790 and was also designed in the Gothic Revival style. Its elegant steeple, 200 feet high, afforded a picturesque view of the harbor, the city, and the surrounding farms. That view was popular with those who had the endurance to climb up to see it. The church also boasted one of the largest Gothic windows in the United States (more than 1,000 panes of glass), and it prized its handsome marble monument to Alexander Hamilton. Structurally unsound, however, the church was beyond restoration by 1839 and had to be replaced.

It was decided to commission Richard Upjohn, well-known for his Gothic Revival buildings, to build the new Trinity on the same site as its two predecessors. The largest of the three, this structure is over 183 feet long, over 84 feet wide, and its spire is 264 feet high. The apex of the nave peaks at 64 feet and the Gothic ribs, lancet windows, and great nave arcade all work together to create lines, masses, and spaces that pull the eye and the spirit upward.

By the time the English left in 1783, following the American revolutionary war, they had pushed the city limits northward to the area of the present City Hall. But because of fire and the changing patterns of commerce, the old Dutch urban buildings have disappeared and can only be seen in contemporary prints. The English architecture of the eighteenth century is almost as mute in today's city. An eloquent exception, however, is St. Paul's Chapel.

ST. PAUL'S CHAPEL

St. Paul's Chapel, bounded by Broadway, Fulton, Church, and Vesey streets, was erected in an open field north of the city during 1764–66. Built by Thomas McBean, it is the only intact pre-revolutionary building in New York City that remains in constant use. St. Paul's is a superior example of the English church type developed by Sir Christopher Wren when he designed fifty-one London churches (and four outside the city) following the Great Fire of London in 1666.

Wren was inspired primarily by the Renaissance principles of symmetry, harmony, and revived ancient classical forms. This type was carried on by his follower James Gibbs, London's most influential church architect of the early eighteenth century, and the teacher of Thomas McBean. In fact, St. Paul's is based on Gibbs's St. Martin-in-the-Fields Church in London, which was greatly admired by the public and widely imitated by architects.

Distinguishing features of this Wren-Gibbs type, as it has been called, include the combination of a temple-front portico and steeple rising from the ridge of the roof over the principal west entrance; giant pilasters flanking the two stories of windows with "Gibbs surrounds" (the use of alternating large and small blocks of stone to surround a window or door became one of Gibbs's hallmarks and, even though used by others before, retains his name); and a stone belt course topped by a continuous balustrade.

The stone for the foundations and walls of St. Paul's was quarried from the site (where the graveyard is now), and it is called Manhattan fieldstone or mica-schist. The walls are laid up in continuous bond with native brownstone (a brown sandstone used for building), which was especially popular in the eighteenth and nineteenth centuries, used for quoins, columns, parapet, pediment, porch, and tower. The large bell, cast in London, was hung in St. Paul's spire in 1797, and a smaller bell was installed in 1866 at the centenary celebration of the chapel.

Originally, St. Paul's main entrance (west) faced the Hudson River, which at that time came up to and often overflowed onto Greenwich Street, so it was picturesquely located close to the river. The Broadway (east) portico, although part of the original design, was executed later (c. 1780s), along with the tower and steeple (1793–94), by James C. Lawrence. One of the few giant columned porches in the country at the time, this portico's colossal fluted Ionic columns support a massive pediment bearing a simple niche with a statue of St. Paul, the chapel's patron, who can be identified by his

Top of Municipal Building, Chambers Street at Centre Street; 1914.
McKim, Mead, and White, architects. A miniature version of the Choragic
Monument of Lysicrates supports a gilded statue of Civic Fame.

attributes, the sword, book, and beard. The statue is made of oak painted to simulate stone, a common practice then, and it may have been carved by John Skillin, one of New England's foremost carvers, or perhaps by Daniel Train or some other follower of Philadelphia's famous carver William Rush.

From a square base, St. Paul's tower rises to an octagonal super-structure, decorated with consoles, urns, and pediments and topped by a replica of the Choragic Monument of Lysicrates (in Athens, *c.* 334 B.C.) crowned by a gilded weather vane. In colonial times, the Choragic Monument was a symbol of special prestige; it enjoyed wide popularity through the publication of Stuart and Revett's highly influential book *Antiquities of Athens* (see Chapter 4), but especially through Thomas Jefferson's insistence on using its Corinthian capitals as the model for his new Hall of Representatives in Washington, D.C. Jefferson imported Italian sculptors from Carrara to duplicate these capitals and, when the British Rear Admiral Sir George Cockburn set fire to the Hall of Representatives and destroyed them in the War of 1812, the government replaced them with a second set carved by the same sculptor, Giovanni Andrei. These capitals are still extant and beautifully preserved in the Capitol today by the federal government.

The influence of the Choragic Monument has extended well into twentieth-century architecture in New York. If you look northeast and slightly upward from beneath St. Paul's Broadway portico, for example, you can see McKim, Mead, and White's Municipal Building of 1914, which is visible through the trees of City Hall Park, capped by a miniature Choragic Monument supporting a gilded figure of Civic Fame. The Choragic Monument was also the model for the Soldiers and Sailors Monument of 1901 at Riverside Drive and Eighty-ninth Street. Moreover, it may be seen on the tops of some of New York's apartment houses, where it is used to disguise the buildings' water towers.

Beneath the great east portico of St. Paul's, you can see the first public monument in New York to honor an American revolutionary war hero; it was erected on April 3, 1789, in honor of Brigadier General Richard Montgomery. After capturing Montreal, Montgomery, with Benedict Arnold and 1,100 volunteers, pressed on to Quebec. Their attack on December 31, 1775, ended in disaster; Arnold was wounded and Montgomery killed, one of the first patriots to die in battle. To properly commemorate the event and the hero, the Second Continental Congress requested Benjamin Franklin, then serving as a representative of the revolutionary government to the court of France, to commission an artist to design an appropriate memorial. Franklin selected Jean-Jacques Caffieri, a fashionable sculptor in Paris (who also did a portrait of Franklin).

Caffieri's design met with acclaim from critics and public alike in Paris at the Salon of 1777, where it was exhibited along with the bust of Franklin.

In the Montgomery Monument, two stone brackets support an ancient altar from which rises a broken column in rich variegated marble of pink, cream, red, and blue, supporting a funerary urn. The column is flanked by military trophies on the left and the palm branch of martyrdom and peace on the right. Behind the column rises a pyramid in low relief, a funerary image that has been traced back to Raphael, who first applied the Egyptian motif to a funerary monument in the Chigi Chapel in Rome. Under the altar, a white marble tablet carries a dedication to the dead hero.

Franklin had engravings of the monument made and distributed to members of the Continental Congress; until recently, one of these engravings hung inside on the north wall. The image is reversed, not uncommon in old prints where craftsmen rendered the image on the printing plate without reversing it from the drawing so that it would print correctly.

Montgomery Memorial, St. Paul's Chapel. This, New York's first public monument to an American revolutionary war hero, was erected in 1789 to honor Brigadier General Richard Montgomery.

The Interior

Behind the Montgomery Monument is a grand Palladian window, the triple opening window named for the great Renaissance architect Andrea Palladio, through which a glory (gilded rays approximating divine light) can be seen that hovers over the altar inside. This glory was part of the decorative program done in St. Paul's by Pierre L'Enfant, French architect and major of engineers of the Continental Army, who is best known for his city plan for Washington, D.C., and the new republic's first Federal Hall, on Wall Street. L'Enfant's chief work in St. Paul's was the glory, altar, and altar railing. From the inside, the glory shows Mount Sinai in clouds

Interior of St. Paul's Chapel. The altar, railing, and glory with gilded rays over the altar were designed by notable French architect Pierre L'Enfant.

and lightning, the Hebrew word for God in a gilded triangle, and two gilded tablets with the Ten Commandments. Beneath is the altar, the whole conveying the union of the old and the new covenants. Although the Montgomery Monument is now covered with grime and soil, scheduled cleanings promise to restore its rich colors and textures to their original beauty.

St. Paul's interior is appropriately maintained in traditional light colors with cream and gilded woodwork. It has an ample gallery, and freestanding Corinthian columns support block entablatures (echoing the continuous entablatures along the sides), from which springs the vaulting. The woodwork, carving, and door hinges are handwrought. The white and gilded pulpit is surmounted by a coronet and six feathers over the baffle, a surviving symbol of British nobility repeated in the ironwork outside. Fourteen cut-glass chandeliers, handmade in Waterford, Ireland, hang in the nave and galleries and date from 1802. The hand-carved mahogany organ case in the west gallery was built *c*. 1804.

Washington's pew in the north aisle was originally canopied. The present pew was rebuilt in this century, and in 1960 it was brought into closer conformity with the original though without the canopy. The nearby oil painting of the U.S. coat of arms, commissioned for the inauguration of Washington, may have hung next to the original pew and may be the first painting of the U.S. coat of arms.

Reproductions of Washington's U.S. flag and his Headquarters flag with thirteen stars on blue-gray background and the Bible are reminders that he worshiped here for almost two years, and that it was at St. Paul's where he was officially received after his inauguration as the first president of the United States. Cornwallis and Howe had worshiped here previously, and the pew of the first governor of New York State, Governor Clinton, is retained today in the south aisle.

Notables in the city's development since revolutionary days are commemorated in memorial tablets in St. Paul's, and many distinguished contributors to American history were buried in the church and cemetery outside. For example, on the west wall inside the main entrance, there is a monument to John Wells, leading jurist and editor, with Hamilton, of the Federalist papers. The bust, carved by New Jersey–born sculptor John Frazee, may be the first official portrait in New York carved by an American. It shows a reliance on contemporary European Neoclassical models in Wells's drapery and hair style, and in the architrave, pediment, and in the jurist's attributes (books, lamp). In place of the Classical acanthus leaf and anthemion, however, Frazee chooses indigenous plant life to surround the inscription tablet. Frazee also carved the exquisite decoration for the U.S. Custom House of 1842, at Wall and Nassau streets.

37

GEORGIAN INFLUENCE ASSIMILATED

Georgian is an architectural style that developed in England in the early eighteenth century. It was influenced by Renaissance principles and has been named Georgian for the Kings Georges (I, II, III, IV) who ruled Britain from 1714 to 1830. Also called Colonial in the New World, this style followed its English models closely at first, as exemplified by the way St. Paul's follows the Wren-Gibbs church type.

A good example of the contemporary fashionable Georgian residence is Samuel Fraunces's Tavern at the southeast corner of Pearl and Broad streets. It is a reconstruction completed by William Mersereau in 1907, of what the original may have been. The house was first built in 1719 as a residence for Etienne de Lancey, was turned into a tavern by Samuel Fraunces in 1762, and became a fashionable center of New York life in the eighteenth century. The Fraunces Tavern is distinguished as the place where George Washington stayed before he made his farewell address to his troops there, on December 4, 1783. The structure was almost totally destroyed by fire in 1837 and 1852, and by the beginning of the twentieth century, very little of the original was left. There were only some foundations and a few records, such as sketchy descriptions and an old print, when the Sons of the Revolution bought the building and started reconstruction.

Now the Fraunces Tavern is a well-maintained structure that serves the community with a restaurant, meeting rooms, and a museum. The structure itself faithfully represents the principal elements of the Georgian style. It is a 3½-story, rectangular redbrick building with a centrally placed, ornately carved Classical main doorway, which has an arched and glazed semicircular fanlight to give natural light to the inside hallway. Above the door the entablature is supported with Classical columns, and both sides of the building have three rows of double-hung windows (marking five bays in width), shed dormers, a balustrade running around the top, and double chimneys at either end. The high basement level helped to keep the house warm and dry and afforded an imposing flight of steps, with handrailing, to the front entrance.

Usually on the first floor of a Georgian residence, two parlors flanked a central hallway (illuminated by the semicircular fanlight) that extended to the back of the house and also divided the kitchen and dining room. Bedrooms, closets, and dressing rooms were on the second and third floors. Sitting rooms and servants' rooms were in the upper or attic floor.

The houses of tradesmen and professional people were two or three stories, with the kitchen and storage area in the basement. Sometimes the kitchen was in a separate building at the back of the house. The tradesman's shop, merchant's counting room, or the doctor's or lawyer's office was often located on the ground floor of his residence. Over this was the parlor or drawing room where the family gathered, entertained, and dined. Two or three bedrooms occupied the next floor above, with the servants' rooms in the attic, or above the kitchen if that was in a separate structure.

Fraunces Tavern, 54 Pearl Street. A twentieth-century reconstruction of how the original eighteenth-century Georgian residence and tavern may have looked.

SOME SIDELIGHTS
ON COMMUNITY LIFE

New York streets in the eighteenth century were made mostly of cobblestone with flat rock walks and crosswalks, and at first they were lighted, on nights when there was no moon, by a candle mounted in a lamp in front of every seventh house. Eventually, people also got into the habit of leaving their ground floor shutters open at night to help light the street outside for strollers. Because they saw that lighting the streets at night reduced crime, they pressed the Common Council for improvements in lighting. Then, of course, they were also willing to pay for improved services and even beautifying the streets. By the mid-eighteenth century, whale oil lamps on posts were tended by a lamplighter, and trees were planted for shade during the day.

New York's population grew from a total of 5,000 at the end of the seventeenth century to around 20,000 by the mid-eighteenth century, and this also brought pressure for improved public services. For example, new mid-century legislation required that all refuse be swept into the street, where it was regularly picked up. Pigs, however, were allowed to run free in the streets to eat the garbage. Good water was in short supply, but by the 1770s a circulation system, tapping a reservoir near Broadway and White Street, offered improved service for personal use as well as for fighting fires. The pillory, stocks, and gallows near the jail at what is now City Hall Park served to protect the law-abiding from the dissolute.

The arts were slow to develop in New York, where the main emphasis was on commerce and trade, compared to Philadelphia and Boston. But a stonemason or itinerant artist could carve a headstone or paint a "likeness," and there were the musicians, music teachers, and instrument makers needed to stage concerts, dances, and church services, and to encourage young talent. Moreover, traveling theatrical groups could perform in the John Street Theater, a modest wood structure near Broadway. As early as the 1730s, theatrical performances were conducted by amateurs in a store on Cruger's Wharf near the Old Slip. By about 1750 a stone building was erected on Nassau Street near Maiden Lane, where a Mr. Hallam produced English plays, featuring players from the Provincial Theater of Great Britain. Actors and plays sometimes proved provocative—after an unsuccessful attempt around 1770 by a Mr. Miller, a disappointed and irate public destroyed props and actually tore his wooden theater building down. But the John Street Theater was erected, and it continued until 1779, when it burned down. During the revolution, British officers put on plays there.

Fashionable taverns such as Samuel Fraunces's were popular gathering places for business, as well as pleasure, and popular entertainment of the day included bowling and cockfights. In the outlying areas, horse racing was common during the day, and landscaped areas wherein to stroll and listen to pleasant music had appeal in the evenings.

Although New York's priorities were primarily commercial, and it was criticized for not sufficiently encouraging intellectual life, King's College—now Columbia University—was founded in 1754 on land donated by Trinity Church near Barclay and Fulton streets. It established a level of education judged by contemporary educators as unequaled anywhere on the continent. Moreover, the public was well served by many newspapers including the *New York Journal, New-York Gazette, New-York Gazette and Weekly Mercury*, and the *New-York Gazetteer*.

THE BREAK WITH BRITAIN

By 1775 the differences between the Thirteen Colonies and Great Britain were all but irreparable. The colonists saw the Stamp Act of 1765 as taxation without representation, and the Townshend Acts (named after Charles Townshend, British chancellor of Exchequer) imposed customs duties that led to the Boston Massacre and Boston Tea Party, which precipitated the so-called Intolerable Acts of Parliament, limiting colonial government powers. The colonies' grievances, listed by the Continental Congress of 1774, were interpreted by the British Crown and Parliament as rebellious. When conciliation was judged impossible, the British General Thomas Gage dispatched seven hundred crack troops to seize the colonial military stores collected at Concord by the Massachusetts "patriots." Warned by Paul Revere (in his famous ride), William Dawes, and Dr. Samuel Prescott, about seventy minute men (named for their commitment to take the field at a minute's notice) confronted the redcoats at the town common of Lexington on the morning of April 19, 1775. Outnumbered, the minute men were dispersed when an exchange of fire, the opening engagement of the American Revolution, left eight of them dead.

The following year, two statues by English sculptor Joseph Wilton were the center of patriots' demonstrations in New York. When the newly approved Declaration of Independence was read to Washington's army there on July 9, 1776, some of his troops, along with a band of angry citizens, tore down the equestrian statue of George III (which Wilton had based on the famous Marcus Aurelius statue in Rome) on Bowling Green, where it had been dedicated six years before. The patriots melted down the gilded lead statue to make musket balls to use against the British, and they knocked off the Crown's finials from the iron fence that had been installed for the statue in 1771. Some fragments of the statue that escaped the cauldron are in the New York Historical Society. In retaliation, British troops decapitated Wilton's statue of William Pitt, Earl of Chatham (who favored repeal of the Stamp Act), standing at Wall and William Street. They also knocked off his arms, which held the Magna Charta, symbol of the supremacy of the law over the king. The damaged statue may be seen today at New York Historical Society.

WAAL-BOGHT

A short distance from the ferry landing near the present Brooklyn Navy Yard was located Wallabout Bay, which tradition holds is the birthplace of the first child of Dutch settlers born on Long Island. Because the bend of the inner harbor here reminded those settlers of a similar place in Amsterdam called Waal-Boght ("waal," an inner harbor; "boght," a bend), they gave it the same name, thereby celebrating both the new birth and the continuity of their heritage in the New World.

A century and a quarter later during the American Revolution, the bay was the scene of ignominious death and extreme suffering. More than 11,000 American patriots being held prisoner by the British died as a result of appalling mistreatment. They suffered disease, starvation, neglect, and daily floggings on prison ships anchored in the bay. They are commemorated today by the Prison Ship Martyrs' Monument, erected over the site where their bones lie buried in Fort Greene Park, nearby.

In 1802 when land around the Navy Yard in Brooklyn was being leveled, many of the bones of the dead from the British prison ships were unearthed. The public was horrified and indignant, and the Tammany Society called for proper burial and a suitable monument to honor the brave martyrs who died on the prison ships. The actual total of victims has never been documented, and the figure usually given of 11,500 is often debated. Estimates, however, range from 7,000 to 12,000 soldiers, seamen, and citizens.

John Jackson, on whose farm near the Navy Yard some of the remains were found, donated a plot of land near Wallabout Bay for a proper burial place and monument. A vault was constructed, and a burial ceremony was held. It was arranged by the Tammany Society and involved the whole city. Honor guards, contingents from New York's major societies, and dignitaries from all over attended.

On the morning of May 26, 1808, a procession began at City Hall Park in Manhattan and wound its way through the streets of the Financial District. Boats then ferried the groups to Brooklyn, where the remains were conveyed to the vault. All business was suspended for the entire day, all ships were evacuated from the slips on both the Manhattan and East rivers, bells were rung at sunrise, from noon to 2:00 P.M., and at other intervals throughout the day. It was called a day of devotion. Military salutes were fired and flags of all nations were hung at half mast, except the British flag. Eight survivors of the prison ships came from Connecticut to attend.

Once the remains were buried, plans for a monument to mark the site were soon forgotten. They were briefly revived in 1823, but by 1873 the vault that contained the remains was in deplorable condition. The remains were transferred to a brick structure in Fort Greene Park in June of that year.

In 1880 the Society of Old Brooklynites petitioned Congress for $100,000 for a monument to commemorate the martyrs. In April

The Prison Ship Martyrs' Monument, Fort Greene Park, Brooklyn; 1908. It was erected to honor the 11,500 patriots who died on British prison ships during the American Revolution.

1900 the state legislature appropriated $50,000 and, on November 14, 1908, the Prison Ship Martyrs' Monument was dedicated at Fort Greene Park. President-elect William Howard Taft delivered the oration. One of New York's leading architectural firms, McKim, Mead, and White, designed the monument, a single Doric column, 148 feet 8 inches high, supporting a bronze brazier, created by sculptor A. A. Weinman, as an eternal flame.

THE BATTLE OF LONG ISLAND AND THE "OLD STONE HOUSE"

During the revolutionary war, George Washington suffered one of his most decisive defeats in the New York area at the Battle of Long Island, where he almost lost the war during its earliest days. In his campaign against New York, the British General William Howe landed 32,000 well-outfitted troops on Staten Island in late August 1776. He was supported by a fully manned naval fleet under his brother, Admiral Richard Howe. The general then crossed over into Brooklyn where Washington engaged him with his ill-equipped army of 10,000 troops. Washington lost 1,500 men in this disastrous battle, which would have claimed more American casualties had not adverse winds prevented Admiral Howe's ships from entering the East River. Moreover, as General Howe hesitated in pressing his advantage on land, Washington evacuated his troops in small boats from the Brooklyn Ferry landing to Manhattan, under the cover of night and a settling fog.

A remarkable show of gallantry, that boosted the patriots' flagging morale, took place a short distance away at an old homestead, now called the Vechte-Cortelyou House or the "Old Stone House," located in Brooklyn near the present Fifth Avenue and Third Street, in James J. Byrne Memorial Playground. Here, the "Maryland 400" held off a superior British force from 2:00 A.M. on August 27, 1776, until well past daylight, delaying the redcoats' advance and thereby contributing to the success of Washington's evacuation across the East River. Under the command of Lord Stirling, 250 of the 400 brave Maryland contingent were killed fighting the better trained and equipped British troops under General Charles Cornwallis. The Old Stone House figured in the battle as a fortification used by the British.

The Vechte-Cortelyou House gets its name partly from its seventeenth century builder and partly from its occupant at the time of the revolutionary war. The house was built by Klaes Arents Vechte, who settled in Brooklyn in 1660 with his wife and family to farm in the Gowanus section. It was a typical two-story Dutch stone house with a loft and steeply pitched roof. The date of construction of the main part of the house—1699—was attached to one of the gables in anchor irons a foot high flanking the chimney. According to early accounts, the house faced south on the east side of old Gowanus Road about one hundred feet southwest of the present location. Peter I. Cortelyou rented the house just before the revolutionary war broke out, and his father, Jacques Cortelyou, bought it in 1790.

The house was abandoned and finally demolished *c.* 1897. But because of the historical importance of the house, the WPA, guided by contemporary sources, rebuilt it in 1934 a short distance away from its original site, perhaps with some of the stones of the original house. It served as a playground headquarters and comfort station until vandals all but destroyed the interior and defaced the exterior stonework. In 1977 the New York City Parks Department, responding to revived community interest in the house during the Bicentennial, restored it and the Old Stone House of Gowanus Association was formed to help maintain it. Now, the house has a recreation director and a variety of programs serving the members of the community, young and old alike.

THE GREAT FIRE

Following his defeat at the Battle of Long Island, Washington evacuated his troops from New York, retreating across New Jersey into Pennsylvania. The British general Howe established his winter quarters in the city. On September 21, as the British were occupying New York, a fire broke out (Tories and patriots subsequently blamed each other for it) in a wooden tavern on a wharf near Whitehall Street and swept along the Hudson River, wiping out a quarter of the city's buildings and leaving thousands homeless. St. Paul's Chapel was threatened, but the fire was stopped there due to the great amount of open space around it and because its balustraded roof allowed men to get on it and extinguish any blazes that might have damaged it.

New York remained under British rule for the duration of the war. When the redcoats were finally evacuated on November 25, 1783, celebrations were held at Fraunces Tavern, and on December 4 Washington bade a formal farewell to his troops there before resigning his commission as commander-in-chief (December 23). Six years later, on April 30, 1789, and a few blocks away at Federal Hall on Nassau and Wall streets, George Washington was inaugurated as the first president of the United States; Samuel Fraunces became his steward.

45

3

The Federal Style

The colonists' increasing rejection of English influence prior to the American Revolution extended even to English architecture. But change did not come easily or quickly in the colonies. The result was that the prevailing Georgian style, which was firmly grounded in the New World, was gradually modified to colonial tastes and needs. Finally, by the 1760s, Georgian Classical decoration was becoming more restrained in the colonies, and the Georgian plan was becoming freer as local builders adapted it to their individual needs. The restrained dignity and practicality that resulted were hallmarks of the new style that became known as the Federal style. The Federal style extended from the 1760s to the 1830s, which is the reason that period is sometimes referred to as the Federal period. Within that time, other styles inspired by Classical models emerged, which influenced and shaped the Federal style. Of particular importance to the examples selected here were Jeffersonian Classicism and the Adam style.

THE NEW REPUBLIC
AND ITS FEDERAL HALL

The oath of office was administered to George Washington in 1789 by the chancellor of the state of New York, Robert R. Livingston. Church bells pealed, the American flag was hoisted, and can-

Interior of City Hall *(facing page)*. Flying marble stairs (spiral stairs without visible support except bonding into wall) lead to a circular gallery and the governor's room.

non boomed from the Battery and ships in the harbor. Washington then walked into the Senate Chamber of the Federal Hall to deliver his inaugural address, where he was introduced to the Congress by Vice-president John Adams. Washington acknowledged the "invisible hand" of Providence guiding the new nation and pledged his support of the principles for which they had fought. Then he walked with members of his Cabinet, which included Acting Secretary of State John Jay (born only a few blocks away on Pearl Street), and New York notables to St. Paul's Chapel for a thanksgiving service.

The new Federal Hall, where the inauguration took place, was remodeled by Pierre L'Enfant from the old City Hall building of 1700–01, which had been designed by city-surveyor James Evetts and erected after the seat of colonial government had moved from the Stadt Huys in 1697. The building that L'Enfant was commissioned to remodel had special meaning for the patriots, because many key events in their struggle for independence had taken place there. In 1735 John Peter Zenger, editor of the anti-British *New York Weekly Journal,* had been tried there and acquitted of seditious libel in a landmark trial that established greater freedom of the press and broader responsibility for juries. Moreover, the Stamp Act Congress had met there in October 1765; the building was captured by the Sons of Liberty from the British in 1775; and the Continental Congress had met there also. So it was only appropriate that the patriots wanted both to preserve the building and to impart to it a new American vernacular, which these events had helped to inspire.

The Frenchman Pierre L'Enfant was a popular choice to remodel the building. A European-trained architect and engineer and a protégé of Washington, he had served on the American side in the revolutionary war, in which he had been wounded, taken prisoner, and ultimately decorated. In 1783 L'Enfant designed the medal and diploma for the Society of the Cincinnati, an influential organization of Continental Army officers (L'Enfant had even established a branch in France) named for Cincinnatus, the fifth century B.C. Roman hero, who left his farm to lead his people against an invading army and who returned to his land when they were vanquished.

After this medal, many painters and sculptors then perpetuated the image of President Washington as the new Cincinnatus—at once a symbol of liberty and national unity. Perhaps the best known of these images is the life-size statue made by Jean Antoine Houdon, Europe's leading late-eighteenth-century sculptor, for the State Capitol Building in Richmond, Virginia (1785). The bronze statue of Washington now standing in the lobby of New York's City Hall was cast from that statue. It, in turn, served as one of the models for John Quincy Adams Ward's bronze statue of Washington (1883) that today commemorates the site where Washington took the oath of office.

John Quincy Adams Ward's statue of George Washington was unveiled in celebration of the centennial of Evacuation Day, November 25, 1783. The ceremony was actually held the day after—on

The new Federal Hall of 1789, remodeled by Pierre L'Enfant, where George Washington was inaugurated as the first President of the United States.

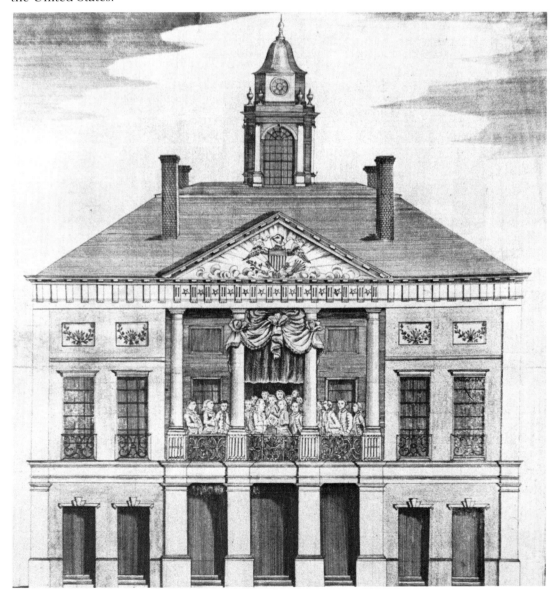

Life-size bronze statue of George Washington, City Hall; cast from original by Jean-Antoine Houdon in State House, Richmond, Virginia, 1788, commissioned by Thomas Jefferson.

rainy November 26, 1883. The band played and cannons roared, as President Chester Arthur nodded his approval to Governor Grover Cleveland, who pulled the cord unveiling Ward's great bronze statue of the first President of the United States near the place where he took office.

The 200th anniversary of Evacuation Day went almost unnoticed, except for a three-day program of events put on by the Fraunces Tavern Museum, the site where George Washington celebrated the British evacuation at a dinner party. An exhibition and performances by a fife and drum corps were part of the bicentennial celebration at Fraunces Tavern. A featured exhibit was an engraving of John Van Arsdale, nailing the American flag to the pole at Fort George during the evacuation. (As a parting gesture, the British had raised their own flag above Fort George, removed the cleats from the flagpole, and greased it to prevent the Americans from removing the British colors until the seven ships evacuating the redcoats had cleared the harbor. A resourceful soldier, John Van Arsdale, however, brought his own cleats and with surprising dexterity shinnied up the pole and replaced the British ensign with the American flag.)

The 200th-anniversary celebration of Evacuation Day was the first observance of the holiday since 1916. Once a major holiday in New York, it had already waned in popularity by then, but the United States's entry into World War I brought its demise, as Americans found themselves fighting side by side with the British against a common foe.

L'Enfant's design for the remodeled Federal Hall consists of a Doric temple portico with a balcony supported by massive pilasters that fill the space between the projecting wings of the earlier building. This composition resembles many Georgian-style buildings, except that L'Enfant opened up the gallery, employed more ample proportions, and introduced American motifs. In place of traditional Greek ornament, L'Enfant introduced thirteen panels into the Doric frieze, each with a star representing one of the original States, and added, above in the pediment, the American Eagle holding arrows and olive branch, as a symbol of power and peace. Decorative swags above the second story windows repeat the arrows and olive branch motif, and stars are carried around the tops of the balcony's four columns. Moreover, it has been noted that the monumentality of L'Enfant's cupola departs in proportion from any English or Colonial precedent and moves toward the Federal style, identified with the new republic.

L'Enfant used the national motifs of eagle and stars to create an American vernacular; in the next decade, architect Benjamin Henry Latrobe employed the tobacco leaf and ears of corn as design motifs for

51

"Corncob" capital. This uniquely American motif was used here by architect Alexander Jackson Davis in 1855 in the Litchfield mansion, Prospect Park West and Fifth Street in Brooklyn.

the U.S. Capitol in Washington, D.C., because tobacco and corn were the foundations of the country's agriculture. The influence came back to New York half a century later, and can be seen in Alexander Jackson Davis's "corncob" capitals in the Litchfield Mansion of 1855–56, located at Prospect Park West and Fifth Street in Brooklyn.

With his design for Federal Hall, L'Enfant both Americanized the Georgian style and reasserted the Classical influence to contribute to what became known as the Federal style. A Classical revival in America had been initiated by Thomas Jefferson who, with the French architect Charles-Louis Clérisseau, modeled the State Capitol Building of 1786 in Richmond, Virginia, on the famous Roman temple at Nîmes in southern France, the Maison Carée (square house) of the first century B.C. During the early years of the new republic, Roman models appealed strongly to American statesmen, artists, and builders. After all, the new government itself was patterned after the Roman republic! George Washington was the new Cincinnatus, and Jefferson's and Clérisseau's State Capitol Building was the first statehouse in modern times to be called a capitol and to accommodate a republican senate.

It is noteworthy that Clérisseau's contribution to the Classical tradition in America is not restricted to this building alone. He had been the mentor of Robert Adam, whose publications, based upon his study of ancient Roman architecture, included *Ruins of Spalatro* (1764) and *Works in Architecture* (with his brother James; volume 1, 1773; volume 2, 1779; volume 3, 1822). These works exerted a formative influence on American building of this period.

In addition to L'Enfant's remodeled Federal Hall and his decorations for St. Paul's Chapel, he also designed the Federal House in

Philadelphia, and made the plan for the nation's capital in Washington—inspired in part by Versailles, and in part by English examples of urban planning. The federal government was moved from New York to Philadelphia in 1790, and then on to Washington, D.C., in 1800, to be closer to the southern states. Unfortunately, L'Enfant's gracefully remodeled Federal Hall in New York was demolished in 1812, and the site is now commemorated by the Federal Hall National Memorial, which was built as the Custom House in 1842. The National Park Service maintains the building as a museum with exhibits related to the American Revolution to illustrate the significance of the site. For example, the suit and accessories Washington wore at his inauguration are displayed along with part of the iron balcony from L'Enfant's old Federal Hall. John Peter Zenger's printing press is also exhibited and demonstrated there.

CITY HALL: MUNICIPAL LANDMARK

In need of new facilities and more space, the Common Council, meeting in L'Enfant's remodeled building, proposed a competition for designs for a new city hall in 1800, and Joseph François Mangin

City Hall, Broadway and Park Row; 1802–11. Mangin and McComb, architects. Print shows early methods of paving and pigs allowed in the street to eat garbage.

and John McComb, Jr., won. The site chosen was the old City Common of the English, located at that time north of the city on elevated ground across from the Brick Church of 1767, which had been designed by John McComb's father, John McComb, Sr. The foundation stone for City Hall was laid on September 26, 1803, and the building was completed in 1812—a superb example of the rich variety of Classical expression embraced by the Federal period.

The two-story building is rectangular in plan, with projecting east and west wings and an attic over a rusticated basement. It was originally constructed of white Massachusetts marble, except for the brownstone used for the basement and the north facade, where builders said no one would see the cheaper material. The roof was covered with copper, surrounded by a marble balustrade, and a cupola rose from it supporting a colossal figure of Justice with her attributes, sword and scales. The statue was created by Irish sculptor John Dixey and installed *c.* 1818.

City Hall's cupola was elevated in 1831 to make room for a clock with an illuminated dial and a bell of six thousand pounds, which still faithfully chimes the hour, even if its tone now lacks its original clarity.

Inside City Hall, a pair of flying marble stairs (that is, spiral stairs without visible support except the juncture with the wall) leads to a circular gallery on the second floor, which is railed and floored with marble. The floor repeats the diamond pattern used below in the lobby. A coffered dome with glazed skylight springs from ten Corinthian columns surrounding a central rotunda. The mayor's office is on the first floor and the public hearing rooms are on the second.

In 1814 a governor's room was established in City Hall, following the tradition of the two previous city halls. The governor's room was used for official functions, such as a reception for Lafayette in 1824. Two presidents were laid in state outside these rooms for New Yorkers to pay their last respects—Abraham Lincoln on April 24 and 25, 1865, and Ulysses S. Grant on August 8, 1885. The room is now maintained as a showcase for historical furnishings, such as Washington's writing desk from the earlier Federal Hall, and historically important portraits, including some commissioned by the Common Council: George Washington (1790), George Clinton (1791), Alexander Hamilton and John Jay (1805).

Although the respective roles of the two architects of City Hall have long been a matter of discussion, modern scholarship largely credits Mangin with the design of the building, except for the cupola and some details and interior features. McComb is believed to have handled construction of the building and design of the cupola and some of the interior elements. This conclusion is supported by the appearance of Mangin's name ahead of McComb's in the competi-

A coffered dome with skylight inside City Hall springs from Corinthian columns surrounding a central rotunda; note refined detailing of swags and rosettes.

The governor's room was added to City Hall in the nineteenth century and was used for official functions such as Lafayette's reception in 1824.

City council chamber, City Hall. Note superb artistry in the handsome brackets along the ceiling, the relief work of the gallery, and the ceiling plasterwork.

Detail of plasterwork, City Hall. Note the elegant Adamesque characteristics —boldly relieved bracket set against delicate Classical moulding, each detail precisely articulated.

Board of estimate room,
City Hall. The influence
of leading British
architect-designer Robert
Adam is shown in the
semicircular interior
forms and meticulous
detailing.

Governor's room (detail,
pilaster flanking
fireplace). Here,
American motifs mix with
Classical orders in the
stars, swags, and torches
of liberty in the ceiling
moulding.

57

tion drawings and by the style of the building, which is drawn mainly from eighteenth-century French models. Mangin, who probably came to America to escape the French Revolution, had worked with France's leading architect, Jacques Ange Gabriel, on the Place de la Concorde in Paris. Some scholars believe that McComb's name alone is on the cornerstone of the building because Mangin and McComb were no longer associated when the building was actually built. The exact contribution of each may never be known for certain, but it has been observed that McComb's meticulous execution of the design retains the French refinement of Mangin's design.

McComb, son of a successful Colonial architect, was among the last of the builder-architects after the revolutionary war. His inspiration came largely from the English tradition and the works of those figures including William Chambers, James Paine, and Robert Adam. The James Watson House at No. 7 State Street (1793–1806), attributed to McComb, is a superb example of a Federal style mansion, while also carrying the curved colonnade and exquisite detailing inspired by the English models.

City Hall has suffered a good deal of damage during its 170 years of service to the community. The tower and attic were destroyed in 1858 by a fire, caused by fireworks set off during the celebration of the laying of the Atlantic cable by Cyrus W. Field. Restoration was supervised by Leopold Eidlitz and was based upon the drawings of Mangin and McComb. Over the next forty years as city government changed, so did the configuration of office and meeting spaces in the building and, through a succession of alterations, the building lost much of its original decoration.

At the turn of the century, when Greater New York was established, incorporating the five boroughs, City Hall underwent a general restoration based on the drawings and plans of its original architects. Among the features that are particularly noteworthy are the combinations of American motifs of star and swags with Greek forms in the governor's room, recalling L'Enfant's "American Order" in the old Federal Hall Building. Moreover, John Dixey's original wood statue of Justice was faithfully duplicated in copper for greater permanence.

In the early 1950s it was apparent that age, weather, and chemical action on the surface of City Hall had produced a general deterioration that threatened the building's very existence. However, public sentiment supported the herculean task of saving the structure, which was called the Renascence of City Hall. Under the Department of Public Works and their architects Shreve, Lamb, and Harmon, master masons, carvers, modelers, and plasterers—the last of a dying breed—came together and, using techniques that go back to the Middle Ages along with modern ingenuity, they encased the building in new stone, exactly duplicating Mangin's and McComb's original marble columns, capitals, Classical urns, and mouldings in Alabama limestone. They also replaced the old brownstone basement with Missouri red granite. Some 15,000 individual stones were secured to the old structure by hand with bronze rods; the north facade was also faced with limestone like the rest of the building, because people do see it now!

MANGIN AND McCOMB

Other buildings designed and built by Mangin and McComb in the late eighteenth century are also noteworthy. Mangin's versatility enabled him to adapt to prevailing styles as well as innovative modes. His Park Theater, which opened in 1798, was a brick building plastered over to look like the local fieldstone used in St. Paul's Chapel across the park. A pediment and pilasters echoing the chapel's Georgian portico were originally planned but never executed. The theater had an elegant lobby, a coffee room on the second floor, and a lyre-shaped auditorium that would accommodate 2,500 people. It was hailed as a triumph by the public, and such leading actors of the day as Edwin Forrest, Edmund Kean, and Junius Brutus Booth were featured there. The interior burned in 1820, and was restored the following year; then, the theater was totally destroyed by fire in 1848.

Mangin's Old St. Patrick's, 1815, located at 260–264 Mulberry Street between Prince and East Houston, has been called the first example of the Gothic Revival in New York; even though Gothic ornament had been used before, this was the first time that an architect consciously tried to apply Gothic design and structure to a modern building. Mangin's model was Notre Dame in Paris, which is impossible to see in it now, because his building was never properly completed. It was almost totally destroyed by fire and the restoration of 1868 did not follow Mangin's original design. All that remains now of his work—the walls—suggest only the enormous scale (120 feet long, 80 feet wide, and 100 feet high) of the projected building.

McComb's works were equally as interesting. Even though he followed primarily in the English tradition of Gibbs, Adam, and Chambers, his buildings reflect a wide range of European influences, and they reveal a versatile sensibility with a high level of refinement and good taste. A good example is the West Battery (now Castle Clinton National Monument), a fort he built between 1807 and 1811; it had a counterpart, named Castle Williams (after its builder, Lt. Col. Jonathan Williams, a nephew of Benjamin Franklin) on Governor's Island, duplicated from McComb's West

West Battery; 1807–11. John McComb, Jr., architect. Built as a fort, it has served many purposes including Castle Garden, the concert hall where P. T. Barnum presented Jenny Lind in 1850 *(shown here)*.

Battery in 1811. The two forts were designed to defend the approaches to the Hudson and East rivers, and they were equipped for battle during the War of 1812, but neither ever saw combat. Called McComb's most original work, the West Battery invites comparison with some of Europe's leading eighteenth-century models.

Although the West Battery's interior has been gutted, its walls remain intact and have served the city of New York in many roles. As Castle Garden from 1823 to 1855, it was the famous concert hall where promoter P. T. Barnum presented the Swedish Nightingale, Jenny Lind, who captured the hearts of New Yorkers in 1850. In 1855 Castle Garden became the Immigrant Landing Depot, but it was closed in 1890, reopening in 1896 as the New York Aquarium (until 1941). Threatened with destruction by the Battery Park underpass, the remains of West Battery were saved in 1946 by congressional designation as a national historic monument. During the Bicentennial its interior was transformed by the National Park Service into an exhibition area relating the history of the West Battery and its environs. The battery's counterpart on Governor's Island, Castle Williams, was converted into a military prison in 1912.

Government House, originally; 1790–91. John McComb, Jr., and James Robinson, architects. This superb example of the Federal style tastefully combines Georgian, Jeffersonian, and Adamesque features.

Government House, whose facade was probably designed by McComb, was a superb example of the Federal style mansion, tastefully combining Georgian, Jeffersonian, and Adamesque features. Built by carpenter and master builder James Robinson in 1790 for George Washington as the country's first presidential mansion, it was located on almost an acre of elevated land facing the north-south axis of Broadway across from Bowling Green. The mansion was three stories high with shed dormers and high chimneys, and it had a two-story projecting portico supported by four Ionic columns, elements identified with Jeffersonian Classicism. The columns, however, were Adamesque in their slender lightness. Above the roofline, the Classical pediment contained the Arms of the State (in place of Jefferson's circular or semicircular window), supported by life-size personifications of Justice and Liberty, which were carved in low relief and were painted white against a light blue ground. This provided an elegant contrast with the forceful redbrick walls, clean white moulding, and boldly projecting cornice. The mansion was seven bays wide with a pedimented central doorway, which was flanked by slender windows with cap moulding at the first floor and pedimented lintels at the second floor. The mansion also had a high rusticated basement. Echoing the main facade at the sides, a Georgian pedimented roof capped four slender pilasters flanking rectangular windows. The light mouldings and refined detailing of the mansion reflect the influence of Adam.

Since the Government House was built as the presidential mansion (and later became the Custom House), when the capital was moved to Philadelphia it became the Governor's mansion. In the print depicting the mansion *c.* 1796, the Watson House on State Street, which still stands, may be seen on the right; No. 6 was occupied by James Watson in 1794. The house at the left was on property formerly owned by Frederick Phillipse, a loyalist whose lands were confiscated and sold by the commissioners of forfeiture.

THE FEDERAL ROW HOUSE

McComb designed and built many types of buildings, including houses aplenty. On Harrison Street in New York, you can see examples of McComb's Federal houses of 1828 (restored), moved from their former Washington Street location, which was also where McComb lived. These are carefully preserved examples of the Federal row house in New York; they had two-story brick facades with double dormers, three bays across, an entrance at the side reached by stairs with railings, cornice with fascia board beneath, and windows with sills and moulded lintels. Often they had a passageway separate from the house entrance that led from the street to the backyard, which was used for horses and the like. From twenty to twenty-five feet wide and two rooms deep, the New York row house was more compact than its Boston counterpart, and less severe than the domestic dwelling in Philadelphia. (Moreover, they were usually built in twos and threes.) As a practice, builders would build the houses together, connected by common sidewalls and forming a continuous group. These were therefore called row houses, and the builder would often live in one while he rented or sold the others.

A number of authentic Federal houses (unique for the number and quality) exist in the Charlton-King-Vandam Historic District. The district is within the area bounded by MacDougal Street, Vandam Street, and King Street and was bounded on the west by the Hudson, which came up to Greenwich Street when these houses were built in the 1820s. It was the site of elegant Richmond Hill, one of the wealthy estates of the colonial and post-revolutionary war periods. The Georgian mansion was built in 1767 for British Major Mortier and, situated atop a one-hundred-foot rise amidst a garden landscaped in the English eighteenth-century tradition, the mansion overlooked the Hudson. During the American Revolution, Richmond Hill served briefly as Washington's headquarters, was subsequently the vice-presidential mansion for John Adams, and finally became Aaron Burr's residence.

Burr planned to develop the estate for private housing, but he was forced to leave New York following his duel with Alexander Hamilton; so he could not complete the project. Finally in 1817 John Jacob Astor purchased the six-acre estate from Burr, and laid it out according to the recently adopted Randel Plan.

As New York's population continued to grow, the city expanded northward. By 1790 New York's population was 30,000, growing at a rate of about ten percent a year, so that early in the nineteenth century the city's population was approaching 100,000. To plan for the northward expansion, the only direction in which New York

Vandam Street. This unbroken row of Federal houses illustrates the style's characteristic variety in doorways, painted brick facades, sills, and lintels.

could grow, as well as for orderly development of the city, a commission was formed by an act of the legislature, April 3, 1807.

The commission saw its role as a historic one that would mark an end of old New York and the beginning of a modern city. After debating the advantages and disadvantages of the various alternative plans for urban expansion—elliptical, circular, rectangular—they decided that a rectangular plan was best suited to New York. Rectangular lots were most compatible with straight-sided and right-angled houses, which were the cheapest to build and the easiest to live in. The commission employed surveyor John Randel, Jr., to survey the city and to lay out an appropriate plan. The Commissioners' Plan, or Randel's Plan, as it is also known, resulted in the so-called grid plan that dictated New York's subsequent expansion.

The plan was accepted in 1811, and it established a basic grid of avenues and streets: twelve avenues (running north-south), each one hundred feet wide, were to extend from the East River to the Hudson River (running parallel to the rivers); and streets, sixty-five feet wide (except for selected crosstown arteries, seventy-five feet wide, that crossed Broadway), were to start at Houston Street and run parallel from east to west, crossing the avenues to form the grid.

When development began, Richmond Hill Mansion was moved to the southeast corner of Charlton and Varick streets, where it was used as a theater. The hill itself was leveled and the lots sold to local builders, who built in the prevailing Federal style. By 1829 most of the houses were completed. Homes in later styles were built on lots developed later, or where the original Federal houses burned down. The first tenants in these Federal row houses were prosperous builders, lawyers, and merchants, who worked with the markets, wholesale establishments, and shipping firms, which lined the wharves nearby at the Hudson and which dealt largely in produce from New Jersey and Staten Island.

One of this neighborhood's distinguished citizens was Clement Clarke Moore, perhaps best remembered today for his Christmas poem, "A Visit From Saint Nicholas," but in his own time he was renowned as a Classical scholar. He lived at the corner of Charlton and MacDougal streets and in the 1830s, converted his family estate, Chelsea, into a residential development—from Twentieth to Twenty-eighth streets and from Eighth Avenue to the Hudson (at that time about Tenth Avenue)—that kept the name and is today a historic district.

The size of the Federal houses was dictated by the standardized lot of twenty to twenty-five feet wide by ninety to one hundred feet deep; they were two or three stories high, were built with red brick, and had a steeply pitched roof and pedimented dormers. Most were three bays wide and had an entrance to one side with a stone stoop and iron railings, a high basement, and shallow front yard enclosed by an iron fence. A passageway at the side of the house led from the front to the backyard. It had a separate entrance with a window above for light. The flatness of the plain, white-stone sills and lintels contrasted with the elaborate doorway, whose recesses and moulding were designed to create rich shadows.

The parlor was on the main floor in front in the standard Federal house, with a bedroom or the dining room right behind, connected by sliding or hinged double doors, so that the two rooms could be joined to make a suite. When the hinged doors were open, they folded back to conceal recessed closets placed between the two rooms; the interior window shutters folded away just as neatly. The kitchen, family room (where breakfast was usually served), and wood or coal storage room were in the basement, and the second and third floors were for family bedrooms, closets, dressing rooms, and sitting rooms. The attic bedrooms were for servants and were lighted by the dormers. A sewing room on the top floor was often lighted by a skylight. The fireplaces had beautifully carved marble mantels, which became simpler at each floor. Richly modeled plaster moulding was an important decorative feature for walls and ceilings (later ceilings have either covered over or replaced original ceilings in some of these houses still standing). Plaster craftsmen got their designs for cornices, medallions, and the like from pattern books. In the back of the house, there was usually a porch, suppported by columns, and there were often planted gardens. The privy was connected to the house by a covered walkway and was serviced by the "honey wagon" from the alley. The alleys were frequently lined with shops, stables, or servants' quarters.

Charlton Street Federal Houses

Built in 1826–27 and carefully maintained today, No. 25 Charlton Street is the only house on the block that retains its original passageway, with its elliptical window above the door for light, from the street in front, to the garden in the back, reached through a handsome double-leaf Dutch door installed by the present owner. It also has the only extant stable on the block. In 1829 a carter who owned the house built the stable near the alley for his horses. The sturdy brick and fieldstone building is still in excellent condition and even retains its great iron hook for lifting hay to the loft. Although the interior of the stable has been converted to domestic use, four narrow windows on either side identify the eight stalls that used to stand within. Edna St. Vincent Millay once lived in the house (she also lived at No. 75½ Bedford Street, called the narrowest house in Greenwich Village).

65

The Federal-era passageway from the backyard at No. 25 Charlton Street *(left)*. It served horses and carts; the double-leaf Dutch door is a later addition.

Stable behind No. 25 Charlton Street *(below)*. Built in 1829 by a carter for his horses, it retains the original hoisting hook and slender side windows for stalls.

Parlor and bedroom doors, No. 25 Charlton Street *(left)*. Large hinged doors served to separate or join the two parlors, as well as bedrooms and sitting rooms, in Federal houses; they concealed smaller closet doors.

No. 25 Charlton Street *(facing page)*. Built in 1826–27, it has a typical Federal doorway and stoop with a separate door to backyard passageway lit by the elliptical window above.

67

A few doors west on Charlton Street is another remarkable Federal row house, particularly noteworthy for its sensitive and sophisticated restoration. No. 37 (its twin No. 39 stands next door) Charlton Street was built in 1827 by John Gridley, a carpenter-builder, and was rebuilt in 1829 following a fire, about which little is known. A third story, added after 1913 (the owner has a photograph of that date that shows the house with its original dormers), along with other modifications and many coats of paint, eventually obscured the house's original Federal style and decorations.

Financier and collector Richard Jenrette bought the house in the 1970s and restored its brick exterior, as well as its structural and decorative detail throughout. Among the specialists he retained for the work were Edward Vason Jones, late architect to the White House; painter Robert Jackson; and David Flaherty, specialist in plasterwork. The carpets were designed by Scalamandre and custom-made at the Wilton Looms in England.

As many as twenty-nine coats of paint were removed from woodwork, which now reveals the clean, crisp detail of its superlative carving. You can see the precise fluting and delicate moulding of the white Ionic colonettes and entablatures that surround the main entrance, now unveiled after generations of obscurity. The play of light and shade across the colonettes, cornices, and varied planes of moulding, set against slender recessed leaded sidelights and broad transom, enhances the sculptural qualities so characteristic of the Federal doorway.

Inside, the Classical order is repeated in the parlor and combined with indigenous motifs; all has been restored to its original clarity. Ionic pilasters flank a Belgian black marble mantel and the deeply paneled double doors that separate the parlor and dining room. Above the door frame and continued in the woodwork of the adjoining dining room is the richly carved acorn motif, so popular in New York during the Federal and Greek Revival periods. Once again it is clear, crisp, and distinct and this sharp-edged purity of small-scale decorative motifs illustrates the influence of Robert Adam on the Federal style. His major followers in this country, the

No. 37 Charlton Street. The parlor *(top)* has mahogany-paneled double doors that separate it from the dining room; the fireplace is black Belgian marble. In restoration, many coats of paint were removed to reveal the superlative detailed carving around the door and door frames *(bottom, left)*. The stairway *(bottom, right)* has typical Federal elements: window with rosettes on landing, simply turned handrails, and delicately carved stringers.

New England architects Samuel McIntire and Charles Bulfinch, popularized Adam's translations of late Roman art, which were inspired in part by the excavations of Herculaneum and Pompeii. Architect Bulfinch's follower, Asher Benjamin, propagated the clean-cut Adamesque forms through his pattern books, widely used by the carpenter-builders. The plaster medallion for the chandelier in the parlor was reproduced by David Flaherty from contemporary patterns, and compares favorably with the finest examples extant.

Besides restoring a fine New York row house to its former Federal splendor, the owner has selected furnishings, paintings, and sculpture that are both appropriate to the period, and that reflect his personal taste and close ties to his native state of North Carolina. Thus, the carpet in the library on the second floor is a replica of the carpet in North Carolina's old House of Representatives. A bust of North Carolina Judge William Gaston by Robert Ball Hughes (1834) was replicated by David Flaherty for the house.

Vandam Street Federal Houses

On the north side of Vandam Street is an unbroken row of Federal houses which illustrates their characteristic variety in door-

The Federal passageway to the backyard at No. 11 Vandam Street *(left)* has been converted to a modern driveway. The building's original brick vaulted storage room with stone steps *(right)* has been preserved and is still in use.

Clapboard exterior on the back of No. 17 Vandam Street, which faces a deep garden, is another example of Federal construction.

ways, painted brick, sills, and lintels, thereby retaining the feeling of the early nineteenth-century neighborhood, in spite of later modifications. For example, No.'s 9 and 11 have their passageways to the backyard or garden, and their street-level doors with windows above, still intact. No. 9 retains its authentic Federal facade, except for the later main entrance. The passageway at No. 11 is used as a driveway now and a modern garage stands near the alley. Tasteful modifications to No. 11 include an Italianate cornice and brackets, and a later doorway. The house has its original marble mantels, and its brick-and-mortar-lined storage room in the basement is still being used. To the west a few doors, No. 17 has its original narrow door, flanked by Classical colonettes. It is the only house on the block with clapboard exterior on the back facing a deep garden, another example of Federal-style construction.

THE PATTERN BOOK

As New York grew and the building market expanded, the carpenter-builder relied more and more on specialists to draw up plans and designs, which he then executed. Moreover, English pattern books, an important source of builders' designs, became more numerous and diverse. These were artisans' manuals and illustrated digests of the great buildings and ideas of the world's leading architects from antiquity through the Renaissance to the modern era. In additon to the manuals of Batty Langley, Abraham Swan, and Isaac Ware, which had served the Colonial builders before the American Revolution, the illustrated volumes of William Paine, James Paine, and the Adam brothers enriched this body of material toward the end of the eighteenth century.

At the turn of the nineteenth century, a new wave of publications came out that at once exerted fresh influence on the builders and designers, inspiring some gifted Americans to publish their own volumes of high quality. Peter Nicholson's books, which were full of decorative and structural detail and information, were among the best illustrated of the English pattern books, and they were widely imitated. Moreover, Nicholson had a strong influence on the American pattern books, especially the first one, *The Country Builder's Assistant* by Asher Benjamin of 1797. A host of others followed and were published by such designers as Edward Shaw, Chester Hills, John Haviland, Owen Biddle, and Minard Lafever.

Lafever was one of the most competent and successful of the new breed of American designers, and the extraordinary popularity of his builders' guides rivaled even the prestigious European publications. Trained as a carpenter in upstate New York, he was a self-taught architect. When he arrived in New York City in 1828, he worked as a draftsman for different builders, and the next year he published *The Young Builder's General Instructor* (1829) followed by *The Modern Builders' Guide* (1833) and *The Beauties of Modern Architecture* (1835). He has been called the greatest designer of architectural decoration in America in his time.

Certainly, he was the most influential. His designs became so widely adapted that buildings have been attributed to him that were not actually his, such as the Seabury Tredwell House, called the Old Merchant's House, located on Fourth Street between the Bowery and Lafayette. For this house, the models for the main entrance and some of the cornice ornament are found in Lafever's *The Young Builders' General Instructor;* the columns and door connecting the

Front doorway, the Old Merchant's House. Its richly decorated design came partly from a contemporary "pattern book" by New York designer Minard Lafever.

The Old Merchant's House,
29 East Fourth Street. Built in
1832, it is larger than earlier
Federal houses, with a more
elaborate doorway.

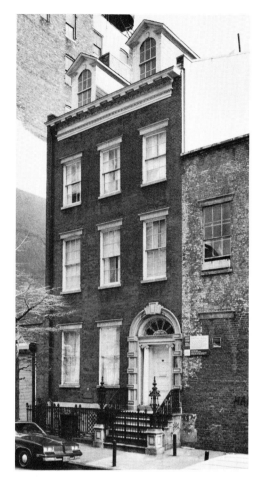

Dining room, the Old
Merchant's House. Occupied
by the same family for a
century, it uniquely records
changing tastes in home
furnishings.

parlor and dining room come from *The Modern Builders' Guide;* and some of the plasterwork is based on models from *The Beauties of Modern Architecture.*

THE OLD MERCHANT'S HOUSE

The Old Merchant's House displays the distinguishing characteristics of the late Federal house. It is built of red brick, three bays wide, three stories high with steeply pitched roof with dormers, and it has an elaborately carved doorway, a stone stoop, and a high basement. Fine ironwork at the railings includes caged newels and anthemion finials. These late Federal row houses are larger and simpler than those of the previous decade, and the clean, crisp, character of the plaster and wood detail carries a rich variety of Greek motifs influenced by the Greek Revival.

Carpenter-builder Joseph Brewster built the house (his portrait hangs in the family room in the basement) and lived in it from April 1832, when he finished it, until 1835, when he sold it to Seabury Tredwell, a wealthy merchant. At that time, farmland lay to the north, and from their windows the Tredwells could see the farms where they bought their produce. Tredwell's daughter Gertrude was born in the house in 1840, and she died there in 1933 in the same bed. The furnishings today are as she left them, except for worn carpeting and drapery, which have all been faithfully reproduced. In addition there is an abundance of clothing, personal effects, and table settings, which are all correctly displayed.

Thus, the house remained occupied by the same affluent family for a century. It was well maintained, and practically the only changes were in the furnishings. Consequently, it is a rare example of a late Federal house that has not been altered, and it uniquely records the changing tastes in home furnishings of the nineteenth century. Moreover, the house demonstrates how creations of the Victorian era were suitably adapted to the earlier Federal-style architecture.

When Gertrude died a nephew, George Chapman, bought the house and opened it to the public in 1936 as a historical society museum, governed by a board of trustees. Now open to the public on Sundays and by appointment, it is impeccably maintained.

THE COUNTING HOUSE

Federal and Georgian elements were combined in much of the commercial architecture of the eighteenth century. This is particu-

75

Counting houses on Schermerhorn Row. These four-story brick buildings
(seen on the right) were built with loading-and-storage areas below and
counting rooms above.

larly evident in the storage and warehousing buildings along the
East River, which were based on the English counting house, itself
derived in part from the seventeenth-century English market halls.
Some of the best examples are in Schermerhorn Row, along the
south side of Fulton Street near the river. This is a row of six counting houses built in 1811 for Peter Schermerhorn, a leading merchant, shipowner, and chandler; subsequently he leased them to
individual merchants.

In Schermerhorn Row you will see four-story brick buildings in
Flemish bond with a loading and storage area below and counting
rooms on the second floor, which were reached by iron stairways on
the front of the buildings (no longer extant). Their Federal windows
with plain stone lintels are still well preserved. Rusticated Georgian
archways, which opened off the dock into the unloading area, have
all been replaced by later alterations, except for the brownstone
archway at the east end of the row. High-pitched Georgian hip roofs
of slate served the practical purpose of housing the hoist apparatus
for lifting cargo. The gabled dormers were added later. Tall chim-

neys, some of which may still be seen, were built to prevent fire, and fire laws required extended party walls, also still visible, to keep flames from spreading across the rooftops.

By 1814 the Fulton Ferry from Brooklyn was landing at Schermerhorn's wharf, enhancing the value of his row, and the area was thriving. Shops multiplied and business increased; a market opened across the street from the row in 1822, and the Fulton Fish Market opened on South Street in 1835. The commercial shift to the Hudson at mid-century, however, left a temporary void in the entire area. This void was soon filled by the fishing industry, whose members took over the vacant warehouses, counting houses, and shops. Later in the century, the area began to decline as the commercial focus of the city moved away from the seaport, and the buildings were gradually abandoned. Finally, they were threatened with demolition until community and government interest brought about a program of preservation for the area.

Designated a local (1968) and national (1972) landmark, the South Street Seaport Historic District, bounded approximately by Dover, Pearl, South, and John streets, is now owned by the State's Office of Parks and Recreation. A full-scale restoration of its architecture is underway. With a budget of $350 million, New York City, New York State, the Rouse Company (which developed and operates Faneuil Hall Marketplace in Boston and Harborplace on the Baltimore Waterfront), and the Seaport Museum have introduced a commercial and cultural program to assure the survival of the district. The $350 million project combines the new with the old to preserve the area's significant architecture and to make the area commercially successful. The first phase was completed in July 1983. It included a new Fulton Fish Market Building, housing markets for fresh produce, cheese, meat, and poultry; Museum Block, which utilizes restored buildings that date from 1797, and new structures; and Schermerhorn Row, the row of restored counting houses with shops and restaurants on the ground floor and residential lofts above. Cultural programs are to include South Street Venture—a multimedia presentation relating the history of South Street, regular exhibitions at the Seaport Gallery, concerts on Pier 16, and regularly scheduled walking tours.

The rest of the project is to be complete by summer of 1984 and will feature a three-story Victorian-style pavilion, promenades, and a grand arcade with more than one hundred shops and restaurants. A thirty-four-story office building, going up on Fulton Street across from Museum Block, will be managed by a subsidiary of the Rouse Company, and will attract more business to the area.

4

Nineteenth Century: Greek Revival

By the early part of the nineteenth century, builders and architects in search of a style more "American" and less dependent upon Roman models turned toward Greek forms, which were becoming more fashionable for a combination of reasons. The eighteenth-century excavations at Herculaneum and Pompeii—featured prominently in the contemporary press—had increased the world's awareness of ancient Rome and Greece. German art historian and antiquarian J. J. Winckelmann's publications at mid-century gave new insights into the "noble simplicity and calm grandeur" of Greek art and architecture, and the widely celebrated removal of some architectural sculpture from the Acropolis (the Elgin Marbles) to England in 1806 by Thomas Bruce, seventh earl of Elgin, exposed scholars, architects, and the public as well to more of the wonders of Classical Greece.

Americans liked to identify themselves with the enlightened civilization of ancient Greece (America was the "new Athens") with its democratic system of city-states and its respect for human liberty. They also felt a kinship to modern Greece in its war for independence against the Turks, and this interest found its way into works of American and European artists. Vermont sculptor Hiram Powers, working in Florence, produced the white marble statue *Greek Slave,* which became world famous. It portrays a Greek virgin in chains being sold at public auction by the Turks; purity personified, she was called an "unveiled soul" (as Powers wrote to Elizabeth Bar-

Federal Hall National Memorial, Wall and Nassau streets *(facing page).*
Begun in 1833 as the U.S. Custom House, this Greek Revival building
now serves as a museum.

rett Browning). So popular was the statue that Powers carved six replicas of it, four of which are in the United States now; the last one (and the only one with manacles instead of chains) is in the Brooklyn Museum on permanent exhibition. From her Florentine retreat in Casa Guidi, Elizabeth Barrett Browning saluted the *Greek Slave* as an artwork confronting worldwide serfdom, a reference to the slavery issue in the United States as well as the war in Greece. But the English poet whose song for Greek independence most poignantly touched the hearts of the Americans was Lord Byron, who died of a fever in 1824 while serving with the Greek rebels.

Further, *The Antiquities of Athens* (first volume 1762, second volume 1789) by Scottish architect James "Athenian" Stuart and English architect Nicholas Revett played an integral part in this Greek Revival, exerting its pervasive influence largely through the pattern books of the period. "Athenian" Stuart received his nickname by building the first Greek Revival temple in Europe at Hagley Hall in Worcestershire, England (1758), then by duplicating the Choragic Monument of Lysicrates at Shugborough Park in England. He and Revett traveled to Athens to make accurate drawings of the ancient monuments; they actually measured every architectural detail, which gave their publication authenticity and authority. *The Antiquities of Athens* offered one of the first trustworthy records of Greek architecture of the fifth century B.C., and its large and detailed illustrations, supported by precise measurements, served as reliable patterns for architects and patrons alike.

EARLY DESIGNS

In 1818 architect William Strickland, who had studied under Latrobe in Philadelphia, designed what has been called the first mature Greek Revival building in the United States—the Second Bank of the United States in Philadelphia—and he based it on Stuart and Revett's illustrations of the Parthenon. The finest extant temple front in New York that was inspired by the Parthenon is the U.S. Custom House, built between 1833 and 1842. It was subsequently the Sub-Treasury Building (1862–1925), and is now the Federal Hall National Memorial, designed by Ithiel Town and Alexander Jackson Davis. Made of Westchester marble, the Federal Hall National Memorial is an amphiprostyle structure—that is, it has porches at either end, no columns along the sides, and massive squared piers to take the place of the absent columns. At the front and back, it has eight Doric columns, each thirty-two feet high and five feet eight inches in diameter.

Rotunda, Federal Hall National Memorial. The two-story rotunda is sixty feet in diameter, supported by Corinthian columns, pilasters, and connecting walls.

The interior plan of Federal Hall National Memorial draws on both Greek and Roman models and was modified by English architect William Ross when the building was constructed. American sculptor-builder-architect John Frazee probably drew the working drawings for the building and executed the exquisite detailing, while Samuel Thomson supervised construction. From a massive ring vault supported by thick Tuscan piers, a central rotunda, sixty feet in diameter, springs two stories and has a low dome supported by Corinthian columns, pilasters, and connecting walls. Meticulously crafted detail is picked out in blue, white, and gold; the design motifs of bead and reel, anthemion, acanthus, and dentil mouldings enrich the surfaces.

Ithiel Town and Alexander Jackson Davis were among New York's most successful and influential architects of the early nineteenth century; well trained, highly imaginative, and enormously energetic, they produced an abundance of sophisticated work in various styles, extending beyond the Greek Revival. Town came out of the New England builder-architect tradition. Trained in Boston, where he probably studied with Asher Benjamin, author of America's first pattern book, he gained fame and fortune as the inventor of a highly successful truss (support system) for bridges, and won recognition for Classical as well as Gothic designs in Connecticut. One of the founders of the National Academy of Design in New York, Town was dedicated to the establishment of an American architecture. Toward that end he opened his library of architectural books and engravings to the public and subsequently designed a building in New Haven to house it.

Davis was from New York and had earned a reputation as an able draughtsman and designer before becoming Town's partner in 1829. He was a founding member of the American Institute of Architects, collaborated with numerous architects, and worked in various styles.

American pattern books propagated the faith in Greek design. The first American pattern book to carry plates of the Greek orders, published the year Strickland designed his Second Bank, 1818, was *The Builders' Assistant* by John Haviland and Hugh Bridport. Many handbooks followed to illustrate the flexibility and practical application of the simple forms, grand scale, and restrained ornament of Greek architecture to domestic, institutional, and commercial uses. Among the most influential pattern books in the spread of the Greek Revival were those of Minard Lafever, and they had a profound influence on the Greek Revival row house. The Greek Revival style succeeded the Federal in row house construction in the 1830s.

WASHINGTON SQUARE NORTH

Built between 1829 and 1833, the houses east of Fifth Avenue on Washington Square North were conceived as a single unit of two complementary rows of fashionable houses, No.'s 1–6 and 7–13, to occupy the entire block. This unit is the finest extant example of early large-scale row house planning in New York. The developers, three socially prominent and successful merchants, John Johnston, James Boorman, and John Morrison, leased the land from the philanthropic Sailors' Snug Harbor for one hundred years and built a block of houses that at once attracted wealthy residents and influenced contemporary home builders.

John Johnston (No. 7) and James Boorman (No. 13) were partners in the import-export business, and John Morrison (No. 9) was also involved in foreign trade. They served on various boards and were associated with cultural and charitable causes. For example, Johnston was a founder of New York University, and his son John Taylor Johnston was the first president of the Metropolitan Mu-

Washington Square North, Greenwich Village. These Greek Revival row houses were called "the Row" when built; they housed prestigious leading citizens.

seum of Art. Boorman was a benefactor of organizations for orphans and the blind. The other residents were among New York's leading bankers, merchants, and community leaders, and their conservative style of life was well served by the architecture of "the Row," as it was reverently called. The design united conventional row house construction with the new Greek Revival style.

Probably built according to an overall design by the popular architect Martin Thompson (each owner then selected his own builder who conformed to the master plan), the Row combines the traditional Federal construction of red brick in Flemish bond with the new Greek Revival style expressed in Classical forms, large proportions, and simple decoration. Unlike the Federal row house, usually built in twos and threes, the entire block of the Row is unified by a continuous redbrick facade; an unbroken entablature with projecting cornice (alas, originally capped at the roofline by white balustrades, now long gone); grand porticoes; and continuous iron fencing enclosing shallow gardens which were like extensions of Washington Square Park across the street.

Within this overall unifying design, there were differences in each house that both enhanced the distinction of the Row and satisfied each resident's sense of individuality. These differences extended to the use of either Doric or Ionic orders, as well as to different lintel mouldings, ironwork design, and door panels. For example, Doric columns flank the entrance of No. 4 and its door has a single full-length panel (more characteristic of the Greek Revival); its ironwork features the anthemion and Greek key or fret, and pointed moulded lintels surmount the window openings. No. 7, on the other hand, has Ionic columns flanking its door and the door is multipaneled. Its ironwork has the same motifs as No. 4, but they are more elaborate and the lyre design flanks the entrance gates; over the windows, there are cap moulded lintels rather than pointed.

The proportions of the entrances of the two rows are also different, but this had less to do with aesthetics than it did with lot sizes. The entrance porticoes of No.'s 1–6 are narrower than those of No.'s 7–13, because the latter row originally stood on eight lots that were merged into seven wider ones, which is evident by once more comparing No.'s 4 and 7.

Johnston lived at No. 7 until he died there in 1851, and the house remained in the family until 1935. Samuel Thomson, a well-known builder, owned No. 4, which he built (he probably built others on the block as well) just before he was appointed to supervise construction of Town and Davis's prestigious new Custom House. Another architect prominent later in the century, Richard Morris Hunt, lived two doors away at No. 2.

The grand entrances are the most striking feature of the Row's facade. White marble balustrades (except for No. 12, which has wing walls without balustrades) lead to deep entrance porticoes with massive entablatures supported by grand, freestanding fluted columns and richly carved capitals. In the door enframement beneath, the orders alternate. At No. 4, for example, large Doric columns support the entablature, but a pair of engaged Ionic colonettes on either side of the door itself support the transom beam and frame the elegant sidelights. At No. 7, large Ionic columns support the entablature, but paired Doric pilasters support the transom beam and frame the slender sidelights.

Delicately carved egg and dart, leaf and dart, and dentil mouldings, as well as the ironwork—all somewhat obscured now by many coats of paint—are nonetheless elegant settings for the massive and

No. 4 Washington Square North. Doric columns flank this entrance, and window lintels are peaked; the ironwork palmette motif is characteristic of Greek Revival.

No. 7 Washington Square North. This entrance is flanked by Ionic columns, and window lintels are cap moulded; two elaborate lyre-panels mix with ironwork palmettes.

diminutive structural elements juxtaposed within those deep entrances. Regrettably, the replacement of the black-and-white diamond-patterned marble walks, which once led from the iron entrance gates to the white marble steps, has diminished the original grandeur of the approach to these stoops. But the aura of refinement the Row enjoyed in the nineteenth century is visible even today through the veils of paint and age, showing in the rich materials, tasteful detail, and superb craftsmanship of these portals.

The Row's Greek Revival interiors conformed basically to the Federal style floor plan. Dining room, kitchen, and storage area were in the basement, front and back parlors were on the first floor, and bedrooms, servants' rooms, and utility spaces occupied the upper floors. The scale and decoration, however, differed noticeably from the earlier houses. The Greek Revival basement was larger, producing a higher stoop at the front entrance, and the rooms above had higher ceilings with correspondingly higher windows. The stairways were moved from the back of the house to the center, and were lighted by a skylight surrounded by decorative plasterwork. Arched niches in the walls at the landings where stairways turned, used later for flowers and statues, allowed space for moving furniture up and down and prevented damage to the plaster walls. Greek motifs decorated doorways, windows, ceilings, cornices, and fireplaces and were carved (wood) and modeled (plaster) with simplicity and clarity.

Some alterations at the end of the nineteenth century and later have interrupted the unity the Row enjoyed when it was new. No. 3 was rebuilt by architect J. E. Terhune in the Queen Anne style in 1884 and was known as the Studio Building. Its very high ceilings have attracted some of the city's best-known artists over the years: William Glackens and Ernest Lawson of the Ashcan School; more recently the American Realist Edward Hopper lived and worked there. Even though the facade of the Studio Building is brick, nothing else relates it to the earlier houses. Its greater height breaks the otherwise unifying cornice, and its terra-cotta decoration is incompatible with the earlier Classical moulding and simpler carvings. The elaborate Queen Anne doorway further separates it from the restrained style of the neighboring buildings.

Less disruptive, yet still noticeable, is the uniformly higher cornice from No. 7 through 13, raised in 1939 when those dwellings were remodeled into a modern apartment house with its main entrance from Fifth Avenue. The original facade of the Row was retained, but the attic story was elevated to accommodate modern higher ceilings; it was faced on the exterior with white stucco to continue the line of attic windows of the earlier buildings. Ten years later, the east end, No.'s 1–6, was leased to New York University until the year 2002 and currently serves as administrative space for the university.

In spite of the numerous alterations, loss of the white stone balustrades from the roofline, and replacement of black-and-white diamond-pattern marble walks, the Row still retains a touch of the "genteel retirement" that Henry James discovered in his grandmother's house at No. 18 Washington Square North, west of Fifth Avenue. (He was born nearby at No. 27 Washington Place, which he described in his novel *Washington Square.*)

WASHINGTON MEWS

Behind the Row on Washington Square North were deep yards, stables, and a cobbled private street, originally designed as an access to service the stables and the houses. The mews, a British term for a stables and service area, extends from Fifth Avenue to University Place, running parallel to the Row, and is now tastefully converted into a small residential block, Washington Mews, leased to New York University in 1949 by Sailors' Snug Harbor. The stables were first built along the north side of the mews behind the vacant Eighth Street lots, allowing deeper gardens for the Row residents. Because this was a fashionable area, it was stipulated in leases that stables were permitted only for private use.

Later in the century, as Eighth Street developed, the Row residents built stables on the south side of the mews. The most representative example of these that substantially retains its original appearance is No. 15. Built in the early 1850s and converted to a residence in the early twentieth century, its brick cornice and dentils survive and, although the opening for the carriage door has been filled in with windows and a modern door, its original configuration is still intact. On the north side of the mews, the only extant example of a stable whose brick facade has not been stuccoed over is No. 52. The opening for the stable door is still visible, even though the door was replaced with windows in 1918, when the stable was converted to a residence. The quaint coachman's entrance (to his apartment above) just east of the stable door still remains.

In this century, a row of ten two-story houses with studios facing gardens, was built on the south side of the mews and was designed in harmony with the converted stables. A brick entrance at the west end on University Place has iron gates flanked by arched pedestrian gateways and suitably isolates this charming hamlet from the city's noise and traffic.

SAILORS' SNUG HARBOR

Once the farm of Robert Richard Randall, the land upon which the Row and Washington Mews were built had originally been intended for an entirely different purpose. Having no heirs, Randall left his twenty-one-acre farm and assets for a "Sailors' Snug Harbor" to maintain and support "aged, decrepit, and worn-out sailors." This was an appropriate way, he felt, to honor the sea trade, whence came the family wealth. Robert Randall's idea had two closely linked sources of inspiration—tragedy in the life of his father, Thomas Randall, and British philanthropy.

Thomas Randall, who came to New York from Scotland in the 1740s and made a fortune privateering during the French and Indian Wars, lost both his father and his firstborn son to the sea in tragic accidents. Consequently, as a founding member of the Marine Society of the City of New York, formed under a charter granted by George III, he helped to shape the society's benevolent aim of providing assistance to indigent shipmasters and their widows and orphans. The Crown's support of such assistance originated with the Royal Hospital at Greenwich, founded in 1694 and dedicated by William and Mary to aged seamen. This hospital has been called the only institutional precedent for Randall's Sailors' Snug Harbor.

By the early nineteenth century, the city had already extended to the edge of Randall's farm; therefore, the trustees of his estate decided to purchase the Isaac Hausman farm on the north shore of Staten Island for the Snug Harbor and to develop the land in Manhattan to generate income for the trust. Thus the land was leased for housing and became the Row. Sailors' Snug Harbor opened on August 1, 1833, with thirty-seven sailors in house; it served the maritime community on Staten Island until the mid-1960s, when the buildings received landmark status and were purchased by the city of New York. The trustees then moved the institution to Sea Level, North Carolina, new home of the "Snugs," as the retired seamen are called. During the Bicentennial, plans to use the buildings on Staten Island for cultural and community purposes were initiated.

Over twenty buildings make up the complex of Sailors' Snug Harbor; they date from the 1830s to the early twentieth century and are in a variety of architectural styles. The five Greek Revival buildings behind the entrance gate that face Richmond Terrace are particularly noteworthy because the grouping is rare, and the buildings are of high-quality design, construction, and materials. Minard Lafever was commissioned to design the project. The central building, the first one constructed, was the Administration Building, erected

Sailors' Snug Harbor, Staten Island. These temple fronts, designed as a home for retired sailors, make up a remarkable complex of Greek Revival buildings.

by Martin E. Thompson (1831–33), for which Lafever had based his design upon the Temple of Ilyssus, illustrated in Stuart and Revett's *Antiquities of Athens*. The remaining four buildings were designed to harmonize with it and to suggest a row. Rectangular in plan, the Administration Building is a two-story structure with attic, Classical pediment, and high basement, and its stone octastyle (eight-columned) portico with Ionic columns is approached by a flight of stone steps extending the width of the temple front.

The year after the Administration Building was completed, a monument was raised to Robert Randall in front of the building, and his remains were brought from St. Mark's in the Bowery and buried beneath it; then willows were planted around the monument. In 1839 a marble bust of Randall was installed in the main lobby of the building.

CUSHMAN ROW

In the early nineteenth century fine residential housing was developed in the Chelsea area. Cushman Row, No.'s 406–418 West Twentieth Street, is a handsome row in the Greek Revival style that is remarkable for its state of preservation and instructive when compared with the Row. While at Washington Square North the attic was raised during later renovation, it remains intact at Cushman Row, accurately demonstrating the Greek Revival proportions that lend a distinctive sense of height to the individual houses. Moreover, the cast-iron laurel wreaths that frame the attic windows are superb examples of a popular Greek Revival decorative motif, and they are but one illustration of the block's fine ironwork, most prominently displayed at the entrances to these houses.

In 1813 Clement Clarke Moore inherited Chelsea, the family estate, from his grandfather, Captain Thomas Clarke, who had purchased the land in 1750 and named it after the Chelsea section of London. In conformity with the Commissioners' Plan of 1811, Moore developed (*c.* 1830) the land into a residential complex of row houses built around a central landscaped square, which was the focal point of the neighborhood. He donated the square to the General Theological Seminary (where he taught Classical languages). Inspired by the Row at Washington Square North, Moore required that each house have a front yard or garden ten feet deep (the Row's were twelve feet deep), which related the houses to the

Cushman Row, West Twentieth Street, Chelsea. Don Alonzo Cushman built this Greek Revival row in 1840, when cast-iron laurel wreaths were a popular decorative motif beneath cornice.

The oldest house in Chelsea (the building second from right), No. 404 West Twentieth Street, shows Federal proportions; at its left an Italianate apartment house built in 1897 is named "DONAC" after Don Alonzo Cushman.

landscaped square for the seminary. Moore stipulated that the gardens in Chelsea must remain unobstructed "forever." That stipulation has long since been disregarded. In fact, Moore's Chelsea no longer exists. It has been transformed, piece by piece, by such developments as New York's first elevated railroad on Ninth Avenue, the legitimate theater along Twenty-third Street, and commercial and industrial developments around the piers. However, there are substantial sections of Chelsea that still retain its original flavor and provide a glimpse of an earlier time. Cushman Row is one of those notable exceptions.

Cushman Row takes its name from Don Alonzo Cushman, a friend of Moore's, who built the row, as well as other houses in Chelsea. Of them the most notable was his mansion and landscaped garden—between Twentieth and Twenty-first streets on Ninth Avenue—which faced the seminary and which was celebrated in the book *Cushman Chronicles, a Tale of Old Chelsea.* Cushman, who descended from a Pilgrim family, came to New York City from upstate New York and made a fortune in the dry goods business. He lived in Greenwich Village until he bought land in Chelsea the year Washington Square North was completed. He began his celebrated mansion and row soon after, when he devoted himself more fully to real estate and banking. A founder of Greenwich Savings Bank, he also served as its president.

Instead of the Row's marble balustrades, iron railings flank the Cushman Row stoops with vertical panels resting on each step, beneath a plain handrail and continuous Classical scroll. Each panel carries a mirror-image palmette design that was especially popular in Chelsea, and the bottom palmette nearest the street is replaced by a mud scraper for shoes, much needed before streets were paved. (Mud scrapers are common with Federal houses as well.) Although most of the original exquisite iron candelabra-type newel posts have been removed, a few remain (No.'s 416 and 418) showing pineapple crowns (symbol of hospitality) supported by Greek motifs. And behind the handsome iron gates with anthemion cresting are some of the shallow gardens that were planted when the row was built in 1840.

Cushman Row stands next to the oldest house in Chelsea, No. 404 West Twentieth Street. Even though its size, Federal-style proportions, and still extant clapboard sidewall betray its earlier date of 1829–30, alterations have attempted to relate it to the style of houses built later. The entrance now carries Greek Revival pilasters, albeit in wood rather than stone; the wrought ironwork continues the design consistent with the row; and the roof was raised to bring it into alignment.

Next door at No. 402 is a Classical Revival apartment house of 1897 that C. P. H. Gilbert designed for Angelica B. Faber, a Cushman descendant. As if in graceful deference to Moore's stipulation that the gardens be left unobstructed "forever," a concave bay makes a suitable transition from the facade of No. 404 to the sidewalk in front of the apartment house. Moreover, the name of the building, "DONAC," which is inscribed above the entrance, is an acronym of Don Alonzo Cushman's first name and the initials of his middle and last names.

COLONNADE ROW

Colonnade Row, 428–434 Lafayette Street in Greenwich Village, designed by Alexander Jackson Davis and built by Seth Geer in 1833, is a version of the Greek Revival row house as a monumental streetscape. Part of Colonnade Row still stands across the street from Joseph Papp's Shakespeare Festival. Two other rows contemporary with Colonnade Row that also embodied the concept of the

Colonnade Row, 428–434 Lafayette Street; 1833. Tall white marble
Corinthian columns screened nine elegant houses designed by Alexander
Jackson Davis; the four houses remaining today are sadly in neglect.

monumental streetscape, but which are no longer extant, were
DePauw Row on Bleecker Street—large houses unified by end and
center pavilions—and two rows of stone houses on either side of the
street at LeRoy Place.

The most notable features of Colonnade Row were its two-story
Corinthian columns, built from radiant Westchester marble above a
massive rusticated basement and connected at top by a projecting
bronze cornice that extended across the nine houses. Entrances
were slightly above street level. Doric columns flanked the doorways,
which were illuminated by candelabra-type cast-iron lampposts, of
which one remains (at No. 434). Davis originally designed roof gardens with vine-covered pergolas; however, they were never executed. The principle of repetitive Classical forms, creating a facade
screen facing the street, is one that became popular with Greek
Revival builders.

Colonnade Row was known at the time it was built as Lafayette
Terrace, after the Marquis de Lafayette, for whom the street was
also named. Built for the wealthy, Colonnade Row housed such
prominent families as the Vanderbilts, Astors, and Delanos; Washington Irving often wintered there. It enjoyed fame as the most
elegant row in New York until the 1860s, when the growing commercialization of the neighborhood forced the wealthy tenants
northward and brought about the conversion of the row to cheap
dwellings and shops. Finally, at the turn of the century, five of the
houses at the south end of the row were razed to make way for the
Wanamaker warehouse.

5

Temples of Commerce and Houses of Industry

NEW HOMES FOR INDUSTRY

The application of the Greek Revival style to public buildings enhanced the images of industry and government by identifying them with the benevolent and enlightened institutions of antiquity. Moreover, some of those temples of commerce set new standards of excellence and opulence for modern architecture, such as Martin E. Thompson's Second Merchants' Exchange Building, 1825–27, modeled partly on illustrations in Stuart and Revett's *Antiquities of Athens*. On Wall Street between William and Hanover streets, the building was a massive rectangular cube with a facade of white Westchester marble. The front featured an elevated basement supporting a portico of two stories, a huge entablature, and an attic. The grand front entrance was recessed behind a screen of four Ionic columns, each twenty-seven feet high and weighing eighteen tons. These columns were carved *en de lit* ("in the bed"), that is, carved of a single piece of marble from the quarry bed to leave the natural textures of the marble undisturbed and continuous, rather than of many pieces (drums) stacked one on top of the other. The whole was topped by a communications cupola to house a telegraphic apparatus.

Inside, five rooms opened off an elliptical rotunda eighty-five feet long, built to accommodate auction sales and shipping and stock negotiations. Winding stairs flanked the rotunda to the second-story gallery, the attic-story meeting rooms, and the cupola, where mes-

The Merchants' Exchange, 55 Wall Street *(facing page)*. Isaiah Rogers designed this Greek Revival building (1836–42) with Ionic columns; above it, McKim, Mead, and White's addition (1905–07) with Corinthian columns doubled the building's height.

sages were transmitted and received by semaphor through relays with Sandy Hook, southeast of the Narrows in New York Bay.

The ideals of the new American republic were reflected not only in this architecture, inspired by antiquity, but also in its public statuary, which followed the European Neoclassical style. In statues, America's founders and heroes wore the drapery of antiquity, but they carried the attributes of the new nation.

One of the earliest examples of the new sculpture was a portrait statue commissioned to stand in Thompson's Merchants' Exchange Building. This was a fifteen-foot-high statue in Carrara marble of Alexander Hamilton, portraying him in a toga draped over the left shoulder and holding a rolled parchment, the certificate of membership in the Cincinnati Society. Executed by Robert Ball Hughes, Royal Academician from London, the head was based upon a portrait bust by Giuseppe Ceracchi, an Italian sculptor, well-known during the revolution for his busts of leading patriots. The most familiar likeness of Hamilton even today, it was popularized by sculptors who made a business of reproducing in various media, and at affordable prices, famous busts of prominent people. (Plaster, painted to look like marble, was the cheapest medium; locally quarried stone was higher priced; and imported marble was the most expensive.) One sculptor, John Dixey, who also did the statue of Justice atop City Hall, made many replicas of Ceracchi's Hamilton, and the marble copy he donated to the New York Historical Society is believed to be the model for Hughes's statue of Hamilton for the Merchants' Exchange.

The Hamilton statue was widely acclaimed, and through its models it had broad influence, but it had a short life. Unveiled on March 28, 1835, it was lost only nine months later, in the great fire of December 17, 1835, which destroyed Thompson's magnificent building, along with more than six hundred other structures in one night. An example of Thompson's work may still be seen, however, in the Westchester marble facade of his United States Branch Bank, later home of the U.S. Assay Office, built originally on the site of the present 30–32 Wall Street and now erected in the Metropolitan Museum of Art's American Wing. Although it is less ambitious than the Merchants' Exchange, the careful detailing of Classical motifs and the unconventional proportions distinguish it.

Following the great fire of 1835 one of the leading architects of the period who had recently arrived in New York, Isaiah Rogers, was commissioned to build another Merchants' Exchange on the same site (1836–42). Nothing like his building had yet been seen in America for uniting monumentality, simplicity, excellence in detailing, and practical engineering. The portico of twelve granite columns rises almost forty feet high, screening an enormous recessed porch that rises three stories. The entire exterior is granite, and through insulated floor construction—pioneered in the mills of England—and a caissoned brick dome, Rogers created a fireproof building that still stands today.

The trading room (now the banking room) is a rotunda eighty feet in diameter, its grand scale enhanced by four sets of paired Corinthian columns at the four principal compass points, which screen bronze and iron balconies, behind which walkways carry the traffic of each floor. The building served as the Custom House from 1863 to 1899; then, when it became the headquarters for the First National City Bank (now Citibank), it was remodeled and three more floors were added, doubling its height.

This addition was designed in 1905–07 by McKim, Mead, and White and was constructed between 1908 and 1910. To retain the Classical flavor, the architects followed the ancient laws of superposition—that is, orders ascended from Doric to Ionic to Corinthian, from heavier to lighter proportions and dimensions, from what the ancients perceived as massive, masculine forms to lighter, feminine ones. Thus, above Rogers's Ionic Order, McKim, Mead, and White's Corinthian soars correctly.

The interiors were finished in 1914. Rogers's original design was altered to provide banking and office spaces, and the skylight was covered over. Unfortunately, the view of the great Corinthian columns was partially eclipsed by the addition of balconies.

A MODERN HOTEL
FOR NEW YORK

Rogers, who began his career as a carpenter, was originally brought to New York from Boston to build a hotel, the Astor House (1832–36), on the site between Barclay and Vesey streets on Broadway. He made a reputation for himself in 1828–29, when he built the Tremont House in Boston. This was America's first modern hotel and it broke away from the Colonial tradition of the eighteenth-century inn, by employing modern technology and a new architectural style. In the Greek Revival style, the Tremont House had one hundred rooms and offered indoor plumbing for toilets and bathrooms on the first floor. It boasted ample stairs and spacious rooms, elegant public rooms, and a formal dining room. Its plan and elevation—a rectangular block of granite four stories high —as well as its simplicity, luxury, and technological advances made it the talk of the day and even the subject of a popular book by W. H. Eliot, *A Description of the Tremont House* (1830).

The Astor House Hotel in New York was built on the same plan by Rogers, but on an even grander scale, and with greater refinement and luxury. And, instead of using a temple front consisting of freestanding columns supporting a grand pediment over a deep portico, more common then and used in the Tremont House, Rogers followed a temple front type popular in New York at the time. This type was well exemplified in the churches of St. James, between St. James Place and Madison Street in lower Manhattan, and St. Joseph, at Sixth Avenue and Washington Place in Greenwich Village. A simple pair of classical columns frame the entrance and support a colossal entablature. Refinement of detail was the hallmark of the Astor House, which boasted improved technology as well. Whereas the Tremont House had inside plumbing only on the first floor and in the basement, water was pumped to a tank on the roof of the Astor Hotel, making it possible to install plumbing throughout! This provided bathrooms and toilets on every floor—a sensational innovation which helped transform hotels.

Rogers was hailed as establishing a new standard of hotel design, both in this country and in Europe, with these two buildings. He continued to build modern hotels and, over three decades, he built some of this country's greatest ones: the Charleston Hotel in Charleston, South Carolina (1839); the St. Charles in New Orleans (1851); and the Burnet House in Cincinnati (1850), for example. The six-hundred-room Maxwell House in Nashville, Tennessee (1854–60), was the last hotel he built; its name at the time conveyed the epitome in elegance and taste, and it lingers today in the name of the coffee served there.

Joel Cheek, founder of Cheek-Neal Co., one of America's leading coffee producers in the nineteenth century, formulated a special blend of coffee for the Maxwell House, which it served exclusively and which was marketed later under its name. When Cheek-Neal Co. was incorporated into the General Foods Corporation, Maxwell House soon became a bestseller, as it remains today. It is probably the only coffee whose slogan was written by a president of the United States. When Theodore Roosevelt was visiting the Hermitage, Andrew Jackson's old home and where they served the Maxwell House blend, he was asked if he would like a second cup. "Delighted!" he said. "It's good to the last drop!"

THE COUNTING HOUSE REVISITED

The Greek Revival gave rise to what some historians see as a new commercial building type. Although modeled after the counting house (as described in the section on Schermerhorn Row), it trans-

Coenties Slip converted warehouses, at Coenties Slip and Pearl Street; 1829–58. The tallest building in the row extends through the width of the block to face on two parallel streets: Pearl Street view is seen above; the Water Street facade is seen right. These buildings stand on New York's first landfill and represent an innovative warehouse design.

formed the earlier type of building into a structure that was simpler and ampler, to satisfy the growing needs for more storage space and more efficient display area.

While this new building type was probably developed by Uriah Cotting in Boston between 1810 and 1820, Ithiel Town is traditionally credited with introducing it to New York in 1829, with his design for Lewis and Arthur Tappan's Store at 122 Pearl Street, which no longer stands. That same year, however, one of these stores, or counting houses, that still stands was built a short distance away, at No. 3 Coenties Slip. It was followed immediately by another next door to it at No. 5 Coenties Slip, and then three others next to them, which means they were built, along with Town's building, to a common model or models, as noted by Theodore Prudon and Timothy Burditt in their recent research in this area. Indeed, these new counting houses became so common that their gradual disappearance under the wrecker's ball in this century went almost unnoticed until recently. Now they are scarce, and the group at Coenties Slip is unique. The group's importance is further enhanced because they stand on the site of New York's first landfill, as discussed previously.

These five buildings at Coenties Slip were built between 1829 and 1858 so they reflect the changes in style during that period. Then, as the East River port became less prominent with the shift of maritime commerce to the Hudson on Manhattan's West Side during the second half of the century, these buildings underwent a succession of alterations that continued into the twentieth century, as they were adapted to the ever-changing face of commercial life along the seaport. Now their original and restored architectural elements comprise a tangible historical record of their physical development from construction through to the early years of this century. That record is easily readable in such physical evidence as the different patterns of brickwork and other building materials used.

The main principle of Greek architecture—the post and lintel system—was never more neatly and effectively applied than in the new counting house style.

The buildings were three or four stories high, built of granite piers with heavy entablatures at the ground floor and brick walls above; windows had granite or brownstone sills and lintels, and the building was capped with a projecting cornice over a simple fascia. The ground floor of the new counting house, ample and airy, was used for selling, display, and some clerical functions, while the upper floors were simply large, open spaces for storing quantities of merchandise. Goods were carted from the ships to the loading docks by horse and lifted by hoists to the upper-floor storage areas.

No. 3 Coenties Slip, built in 1829, was originally four stories high, recently revealed by research. It was raised to five stories be-

No. 3 Coenties Slip. Star anchors secure walls to joists; early Flemish
bond brickwork (short and long sides of bricks alternate in each row) can
be seen in lower wall.

tween 1865 and 1870. In 1884 the window openings and floors were raised in line with No. 5 next to it, and the existing iron cornice was installed across the facades of the two buildings. Further uniting the two in 1920, doorways, leading to a common staircase (no longer extant), were cut through the party walls at each floor. The star anchors, securing the walls to the joists (as in the seventeenth-century houses these buildings replaced), are still visible and were probably added at that time.

The difference between the earlier facade and the later addition is particularly noticeable in the brickwork. The earlier handmade brick of 1829 (machine-made brick was introduced early in the 1830s) is less consistent in size and more porous and uneven in texture. The bonding patterns differ, too; the earlier brick is laid up in Flemish bond (stretcher and header alternate), the later in American common bond (row of headers and from four to six rows of stretchers).

The brownstone sills may date from 1829 but the granite lintels are from 1884, when the window openings were raised to make them larger (letting in more light) and more modern. It has recently been discovered that originally, the facade was not painted, then in c. 1879 it was painted a light color. In 1886 it was painted red, when it was united to the building next door. The windows were six over six (that is, six panes above six panes) double-hung sash in the original buildings. By mid-century, two over two pane windows were fashionable, and by the end of the century, one over one. All these changes are retained in the building exteriors, which consequently read like a book expressing the historical sequence of changing motifs in the block.

No. 5 Coenties Slip is five stories high as originally built in 1833, and it faces Coenties Slip and Water Street. In 1884 the Italianate pressed-iron projecting cornice with brackets replaced the original Greek Revival cornice, making No.'s 3 and 5 appear to be one building. The original redbrick facade is laid up in Flemish bond with granite sills and lintels. There are alterations at the ground level from different periods; for example, the neo-Colonial door with leaded fanlight dates from c. 1920, and the other doors date from the 1970s. Those involved in the restoration of these buildings feel that there was originally an entrance at the corner on the Water Street side, where you can see the stone has been worn down, probably by foot traffic.

No. 36 Water Street, next door to No. 5 Coenties Slip, has had the fewest alterations of all five buildings. This may be due to the continued ownership of the property by the Van Cortlandt family until 1919. The building is five stories with granite trabeated storefront three bays wide, supporting a redbrick facade with granite sills

No. 66 Pearl Street also has a facade on Coenties Slip, where a neo-Grec cornice with sharply incised floral motif was added in the late 1870s.

and lintels, capped by a moulded brick cornice over a simple fascia. While its shutters were removed in 1892, a close look reveals that some of the fixtures still remain, and the original cornice was altered early in this century, which can be seen in the modern extruded brick. The building has retained its natural redbrick color.

Around the corner from Coenties Slip on Pearl Street is another variation of the new counting-house-type warehouse. No. 64 Pearl–No. 34 Water Street is a single building running the width of the block; it replaced two previous buildings in 1858. The building is six stories high with mirror-image, cast-iron Italianate storefronts (bearing the founder's mark, T. B. Richards, on Perry Street, weathered but still visible), and brick facades with granite sills and lintels capped by projecting iron Neoclassical cornices. Thirty-six Egyptian Revival cast-iron columns support the upper floors but are now enclosed, because of fire regulations. The sixth floor was added in 1912—a fact revealed by the different bonding—and the original shutters have been removed, evident from the fixtures yet remaining. In 1927 an elevator was installed in the existing hatchway. The original loading docks are intact on the Water Street side; those on Pearl Street have been replaced. The paneled doors on both storefronts have been restored and fold back into I beams. The facades were painted white originally, changed subsequently to green, and then brown.

With the demolition of the Pearl Street Elevated in 1950–51, expansion in the Financial District accelerated, and by the early 1970s, high-rise office buildings had sprung up in the area, setting new records for commercial floor space and expense. For example, at 55 Water Street, across the street from the Coenties Slip buildings, Emory Roth and Sons erected (1972) the largest privately financed office building in the world. Consequently, the old buildings were threatened with destruction to make way for a parking lot, until they were granted national (1977) and local (1978) landmark status. They were finally purchased in 1978 for restoration and rehabilitation by Coenties Slip Preservation, Inc., a wholly owned subsidiary of the New York Landmarks Conservancy.

The buildings were expected to be financially self-supporting after restoration, so the conservancy leased them to the Coenties Slip Apartments Co., developers. The developers in turn retained the architectural firm of Stephen B. Jacobs Associates to design and execute the transformation of the properties to residential use. One

Apartment, Coenties Slip. During conversion the architects retained the original brick walls where possible, as here.

of the numerous proposals for the site was a reconstruction of the old Stadt Huys, a plan that is on display in Fraunces Tavern at the other end of the block.

By the late 1970s when restoration began, the buildings were in extremely poor condition. There was practically nothing left of the interiors except the cast-iron columns and brick party walls, that is, the wall separating two adjoining properties, and much of the exterior brickwork was unstable. Nonetheless, the architects accomplished the restoration mostly with existing brick from the old buildings. Dilapidated sections were dismantled; then the brick was cleaned and reused. When necessary, however, brick was custom-made. The original party walls were saved and may be seen in some of the apartments, and the cast-iron columns were saved but have been enclosed in fireproof material to conform with fire regulations. Approximately 70 percent of the joists had to be replaced, along with 30 percent of the cornice work. Special craftsmen duplicated historical details, and much of the hardware had to be found to match the original.

The five buildings were converted into forty-two rental apartments, with shops along the street, common lobby and elevator, and the addition of glassed-in penthouses, which were set back from the roofline in order not to interfere with it. Historically, as these buildings have been adapted to the commercial realities of each successive age, the architects saw these penthouse additions as an appropriate solution to keep the buildings financially viable. A landscaped park is planned for Coenties Slip, and it will enhance the view and offer a promenade near the shore.

6

Churches: From Temple Fronts to Statue Columns

ew permanent churches were built in New York until well into the eighteenth century. During both Dutch and English rule, an atmosphere of religious toleration slowly developed, as long as religious observance did not disturb the status quo. But the community was primarily oriented toward trade and commerce, and any building erected usually related to these interests. By the end of the eighteenth century, however, following the American Revolution, the numerous faiths represented in New York began to exhibit a greater sense of community, especially during such ever-present crises as fever epidemics and the like. Gradually, churches were built, and the spirit of cooperation among the various denominations continued with these constructions. Of course, members of these other denominations had helped in securing land and materials and in the actual construction of the first Trinity Church building on Broadway as early as the 1690s.

By the 1820s church building was keeping pace with the rest of construction in New York. James Fenimore Cooper wrote to his wife from the Broadway Hotel in 1824, "New York is rich in churches, if numbers alone be considered . . . at least a hundred and maybe more." By 1835 New York had approximately 150 churches and several synagogues, and by the 1850s the city counted 250 churches of every conceivable denomination.

Among the most notable churches from the 1830s that are still standing, several share important architectural characteristics that

Interior of Church of the Incarnation *(facing page)*. Characteristic of the English Commissioners' church type, with open nave and side aisles, clerestory windows (at top of arches), high vault, and short chancel.

were derived from earlier buildings and that had widespread influence. For example, Greek temple fronts and Greek decorations were combined with the Wren-Gibbs-type design, as exemplified in St. Paul's Chapel discussed earlier (Classical portico with steeple rising from the ridge of the roof over the principal entrance, and giant pilasters flanking the two stories of windows with Gibbs surrounds).

THE MARINERS' TEMPLE AND
ST. JAMES CHURCH

One temple-front style is called the *distyle in antis*, because it has a portico of two round columns between two square piers like pilasters. Because the piers terminate a wall, they are called *antae* and because the two columns (*distyle*) are placed between them, they are said to be *in antis*. The vestibule is recessed behind the paired columns *in antis*, and the entrance to it may be placed between the columns, as in the church of St. James at St. James Street, between St. James Place and Madison Street in lower Manhattan; or behind them, as in the Mariners' Temple, at 12 Oliver Street (corner of Henry Street), and in St. Joseph's Church, at Sixth Avenue and Washington Place. In this temple-front style for churches, orders were interchangeable and considered suitable with any entrance arrangement.

This enormously popular temple-front style was introduced in New York by Ithiel Town and Alexander Jackson Davis in their Presbyterian church on Carmine Street, which no longer stands. Fortunately, there are a number of extant examples of the type that show the flexibility and creativity it afforded the builder.

Both the Mariners' Temple and St. James Church had beginnings in previous sites. The Mariners' Temple Baptist Church was founded early by the New York Domestic Missionary Society, to serve the sailors that congregated from the busy East River. The first church was built in 1795 at 234 Cherry Street, where it was incorporated as the Mariners' Temple. An active church, it soon attracted immigrant populations, organized Swedish, Italian, Latvian, Russian, and Chinese congregations, and exported the Baptist movement to Scandinavia. When steamships replaced sailing vessels and the Hudson River became the scene of New York's main port, the sailors left, commercial centers shifted, and the area became economically depressed. The church then turned its attention to the poor and homeless. Today, two Baptist congregations worship there: the Mariners' Temple Baptist Church and the Chinese Baptist Mission, which holds services in Chinese.

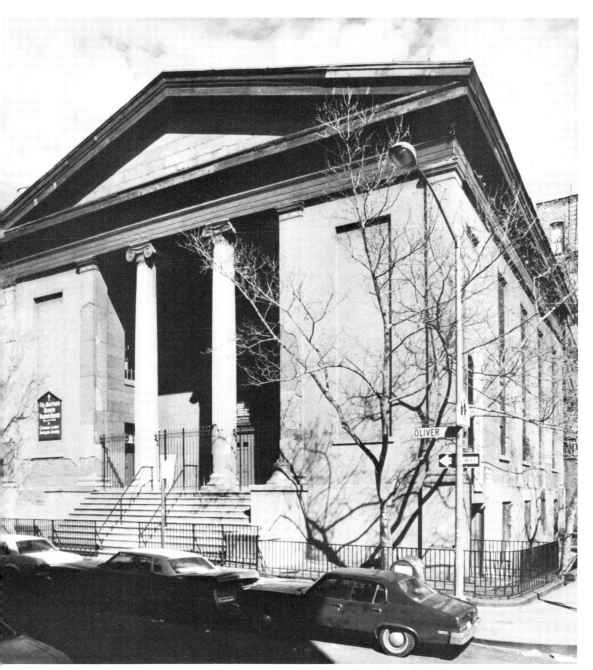

Mariners' Temple, 12 Oliver Street; 1842. Attributed to Minard Lafever, architect; vestibule is recessed behind Ionic columns *in antis*.

St. James Church, 32 James Street; *c.* 1835. Attributed to Minard
Lafever, architect; another variation of the temple-front design
popularized by Town and Davis.

St. James Roman Catholic parish had its origins in Christ Church on Ann Street (a converted Episcopal church, built in 1794, but no longer standing; the Catholic congregation kept the original name). The church served a large number of Irish immigrants in its early years, and the annual celebration of St. Patrick's Day in Christ Church parish was the forerunner of New York's now-famous St. Patrick's Day parade. When the parish outgrew Christ Church, part of the congregation moved to the present site of St. James Church, which was named after the apostle St. James, not the street where it is located. The street was named for James Debrosses, a successful distiller.

Like the Mariners' Temple, St. Joseph's (1833), at Sixth Avenue and Washington Place, attempts to relate the temple front and Georgian features closely. Georgian quoins replace Classical pilasters at the corners and the round-headed windows of the sidewalls are repeated in the facade. Moreover, the Doric frieze above the columns continues around the sides of the building. The central entrance is recessed behind the paired Doric columns, and the two side entrances, at right angles to it, reinforce the continuity of the sidewalls, which appear to fold around and into the facade.

On the other hand, St. James Church (*c.* 1835) on St. James Street, perhaps by Minard Lafever, has paired Doric columns *in antis*, and the facade has a plain entablature and pediment. Over the three entrances are square-headed windows and meticulously carved entablatures carrying rosettes and the scroll anthemion design, favorites of Lafever, and one of the reasons the church has been attributed to him. The design has dignity and shows restraint, another characteristic of Lafever's buildings.

Churches, like houses, were often altered, a fact that can be easily seen when comparing the interior of the Mariners' Temple, which has had few changes, and St. James Church, which has had many. Even though the plasterwork and woodwork are now deteriorating, the interior of the Mariners' Temple, also attributed to Minard Lafever (1842), is largely intact.

Two sets of enormous Corinthian columns repeat the arrangement of the building's facade (whose columns are Ionic) and define the elevated stage with lectern. Smaller Corinthian colonettes, echoing the great columns, support the gallery extending around the south, east, and west sides of the hall. Subtle combinations of dentil, egg and dart, leaf and dart, and bead and reel moulding enrich the acanthus leaf corbéls and capitals beneath the galleries. Crystal chandeliers hang from decorative plaster motifs, and the elaborately decorated ceiling is both remarkable and characteristic of Minard Lafever's designs. In Georgian fashion, tall clear-glass windows along the sidewalls and a light-toned interior create abundant and

111

Interior of Mariners' Temple. Attributed to Minard Lafever; the ceiling medallion *(facing page)* is characteristic of his exquisite designs. Small Corinthian colonnettes support the gallery *(above)* extending around the south, east, and west sides of the hall.

uniform illumination, and the lightly colored mahogany-trimmed pews act as a foil to the ceiling medallion.

The ceiling, as mentioned, is a *tour de force* in craftsmanship. Its central medallion resembles a small Classical rosette enlarged a thousand times; it is set like a jewel against a great coffered wheel. Between the wheel spokes the design is picked out with carefully framed simpler rosettes, and the design reverberates outward like rings in an agitated pond, covering the entire ceiling with a geometric pattern that emphasizes the organic forms of the central medallion. Its detailing is made up of multiple layers of wavy oblong fronds and lacelike petals that are intertwined with tightly curled leaves in a rich floral pattern. The varied configurations of light and shade in this design are enhanced by the crisp and immaculate execution of the plaster work.

113

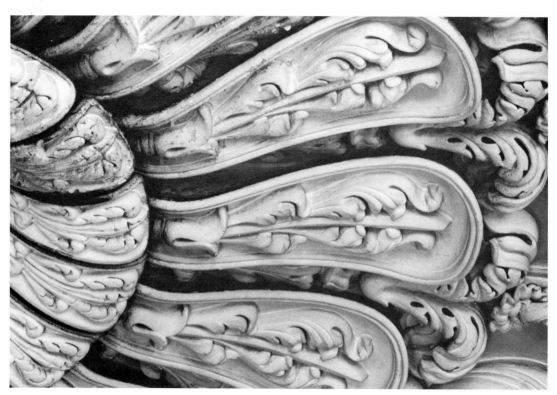

Mariners' Temple:
detail of ceiling
medallion. Like a small
Classical rosette
enlarged a thousand
times, the work
contains richly
modeled, undulating
organic forms.

St. James Church;
1835. Still intact is the
rich stone inlay work of
Greek Revival floral
design in maroon,
black, and tan hues.

St. James's interior was originally similar to the Mariners' Temple, but it has had many alterations, and now it conveys an entirely different spirit. In five renovations between the 1850s and 1927, the original clear-glass windows, light-colored interiors, and crystal chandeliers gave way to stained glass, darkly painted surfaces, and modernized illumination. Around 1927 the present white marble altars were installed, and during the 1940s the original wooden altar rail was replaced with the present marble balustrade and a movable pulpit was donated from a private residence. (In 1977 the sanctuary was modified further according to the Vatican II liturgical reforms.) Also in the 1940s the galleries on the east and west walls were removed. The design on the remaining south gallery front has been traced to Lafever's *The Beauties of Modern Architecture*, one of the reasons the church has been attributed to him. Another Lafever feature is the granite main doorway with its delicately scrolled lintels. A remarkable decoration that has survived is the rich stone inlay work of Greek floral design, in maroon, black, and tan tones, that forms a border along the sidewalls of the body of the church.

GRANDEUR IN GRAY GRANITE: ST. PETER'S ROMAN CATHOLIC CHURCH

St. Peter's Roman Catholic Church, by John R. Haggerty and Thomas Thomas, built in 1838, was long attributed to Isaiah Rogers because of its grandeur and exquisite detailing. It represents another variation of the Greek temple front applied to the Wren-Gibbs body, this portico being supported by six Ionic columns with an entablature and pediment above. Located at Barclay and Church streets, the church was reopened in September 1981, after being closed for repairs for several years. In the oldest Roman Catholic parish in New York, the present St. Peter's replaced the first church, a Georgian building constructed on this site in 1785, but which partially collapsed in 1836.

St. Peter's was the first Catholic church in New York built in the Greek Revival style. In its pediment there is a niche carrying a statue of St. Peter; it is carved in the Baroque style characteristic of the ship's figurehead tradition, which was popular at the time. The facade on Barclay Street and the west wall on Church Street are faced with gray granite; the east wall is obscured from public view and therefore its raw brick wall remains unfaced. High slender square-headed windows along the sidewalls are capped by smaller rectangular windows that once admitted light through decorative grilles, which are now enclosed. The grand proportions that distinguish the exterior of St. Peter's are echoed in the spacious interior, whose

St. Peter's Roman Catholic Church; 1838. Original white plaster walls—
now painted green—were articulated by pink stone, fluted pilasters, and
a gilded ceiling.

original plain white plaster walls were articulated by pink stone,
fluted pilasters, and a gilded ceiling, now painted a dark green and
picked out with occasional gilding. The dark colors and stained-glass
windows which replaced the original clear glass create a dark interior quite different from the original one, which had an abundance
of natural illumination reflected throughout.

Even though the white plaster and some of the marble of St.
Peter's interior has been painted over, the superbly carved and modeled detailing is still intact. There is a rich variety of elegant detailing
and Classical motifs in the mouldings around the ceiling, the great
crystal chandeliers, and the black-and-white marble altar. Moreover,
beneath an elegant broken pediment and flanked by niches, fluted
pilasters, and statuary, a black-and-white marble tabernacle repeats
the Ionic colonnade from the portico and forms the centerpiece of
St. Peter's Baroque altar, which fills the sanctuary wall.

Above the tabernacle is a Crucifixion scene, one of three paintings by Mexican artist José Maria Vallego, donated to the first St.

Peter's church by the Spanish legation. In gratitude to Charles III of Spain and his chargé d'affaires in New York, Don Diego de Gardoqui—who was instrumental in establishing the first church on the site and in raising funds for its construction and decoration—the trustees of St. Peter's reserved the front pew in perpetuity for His Majesty's Legation. That pledge was restated in a formal ceremony in 1976, as part of St. Peter's observation of the U.S. Bicentennial celebration.

A bronze plaque on St. Peter's facade commemorates Pierre Toussaint, a parishioner and one of New York's leading citizens in the early nineteenth century. Although blacks made up approximately 20 percent of New York's population at the end of the eighteenth century, they were mostly slaves and therefore had little opportunity to participate in community affairs. Pierre Toussaint was a notable exception. Freed by a family that had fled the slave uprising in Haiti in 1787 and settled in New York, Toussaint became a successful hairdresser and a wealthy philanthropist. He distinguished himself for his range of charities, for ministering to deserted plague victims and for helping needy students, newly freed slaves, and worthy institutions. Some 2,000 manuscript pages in the Schuyler archives of the New York Public Library document the enormous range of Toussaint's philanthropy and his contribution to the city's less fortunate. At his funeral on July 2, 1853, St. Peter's overflowed with people from all walks of life who had come to pay their last respects to the former Haitian slave and prominent citizen and benefactor of New York.

DISTINGUISHED REPOSITORY:
CHURCH OF THE INCARNATION

To serve the fast-growing population north of Greenwich Village, Grace Church—which had consecrated its new building at Eleventh Street and Broadway by James Renwick on March 7, 1846 —established a mission chapel at Twenty-eighth Street and Madison Avenue soon after. The chapel became an independent church in 1852 under the name the Church of the Incarnation. Then, as its congregation grew, the church bought land at Thirty-fifth Street and Madison Avenue and commissioned architect Emlen T. Littell to build a more commodious structure for the growing number of parishioners. The cornerstone was laid on March 8, 1864, and the new Church of the Incarnation was consecrated on April 20, 1865. It houses painting, sculpture, and decoration by leading artists and designers of the nineteenth and early twentieth centuries.

117

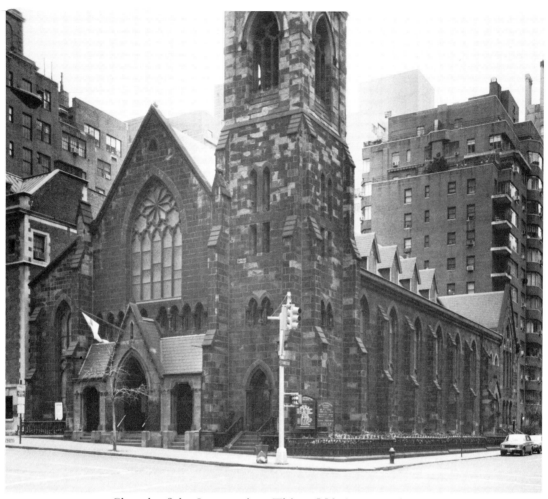

Church of the Incarnation, Thirty-fifth Street and Madison Avenue; 1865. Emlen T. Littell, architect; distinguished both for its architecture and its refined interior decoration and artwork.

The design of the church was based upon the Commissioners' church type, which was developed in England in the early nineteenth century. The name refers to the Commission of the Church Building Society in England in 1818 to build modest, attractive, and serviceable churches for the many small communities in the remote areas of England that were springing up during the height of the industrial revolution. They featured a narthex, an open nave with side aisles, and a short chancel. In the Gothic Revival style, they had steeply pitched roofs, towers, and a clerestory.

The Church Rebuilt

Incarnation was destroyed by fire in 1882, except for the tower and walls. David Jardine, a well-known architect at that time, was commissioned to rebuild the church following Littell's original design, but enlarged the building by lengthening the nave, adding a transept to the north for additional pews and a gallery, and deepening the chancel for an additional entrance in the south wall. The corner tower is now as Littell designed it, with a spire, but the spire was not added until 1896, when it was erected according to the plans of still other architects, Heins and LaFarge. In 1929 the base of the tower was converted to a chapel and the original opening into it was filled with a stained-glass window.

The building is of a vermiculated brownstone with lighter sandstone trim. Its shallow porch, beneath a steeply pitched slate roof, leads to the three portals of the main entrance, which are aligned with the three aisles beyond the shallow narthex. The Gothic Revival skeleton of piers, colonettes, and pointed arches is carried out in walnut and ash framing around plaster panels. The furniture is in walnut, ash, and chestnut, and the warm, rich tones of these woods combine appropriately with the intimate interior illuminated by the LaFarge and Tiffany glass.

Colonettes with leafy capitals support the pointed arches over the doorways. Above the entrances, the gable is pierced by a great rose window supported by slender lancets. The main entrance on Madison Avenue is sixty feet wide and the facade on Thirty-fifth Street is one hundred feet wide. Along Thirty-fifth Street, pier buttresses define the bays and frame a series of especially fine stained-glass windows, portraying cycles and events from the life of Christ in the New Testament and key figures and events from the Old Testament. While the religious narrative is consistent, the windows are by different artists. They were executed by renowned American artists, including John LaFarge and Louis C. Tiffany and internationally distinguished European artists Sir Edward Burne-Jones and William Morris of England, leaders in the Arts and Crafts Movement, who were especially committed to medieval art as an embodiment of the values of a more spiritual age.

Painting and Sculpture

John LaFarge also painted the chancel murals portraying the Adoration of the Magi, and the altar is by Heins and LaFarge, who designed the Grace Church Clergy House and the apse, choir, and crossing of St. John the Divine, the prestigious Episcopal cathedral. Moreover, one of America's leading architects, H. H. Richardson designed the Henry Eglinton Montgomery Memorial, in honor of the church's second rector; noted American sculptor Augustus Saint-Gaudens modeled the portrait cast in bronze. Saint-Gaudens's brother, Louis, designed the baptismal font. He also designed fig-

119

ures for Cass Gilbert's Custom House and the two angels in the chancel of the Church of the Ascension at Tenth Street and Fifth Avenue.

Launt Thompson executed the marble-relief memorial to Admiral Farragut, portraying the likeness of Farragut in a medallion resting on the prow of his ship, the *Hartford*. Thompson, who in 1869 married Marie L. Potter—sister of Henry Codman Potter, rector of Grace Church and later bishop of New York—was a superb portrait sculptor and by the 1870s had distinguished himself through busts of poet William Cullen Bryant (1865), Hudson River School painter Sanford Gifford (1871), and America's leading portrait painter Charles Loring Elliott (1870). Thompson's bust of Bryant, exhibited at the National Academy in 1865, was acclaimed, and it served as the model for Herbert Adam's statue, which is now in Bryant Park (1911). Another fashionable sculptor, Daniel Chester French, designed the oak chancel rail and executed the bronze portrait bust of the third rector, Arthur Brooks, for his memorial.

THE INTEGRITY OF A STYLE: ST. THOMAS CHURCH

As the Church of the Incarnation came from Grace Church as a mission, so St. Thomas's congregation came partly from that of Grace Church (the old Church at Rector and Broadway), partly from Trinity at the head of Wall Street on Broadway, and partly from St. George's Church on Beekman Street.

St. Thomas's first building was erected in 1824 at Broadway and Houston Street and was one of the first Gothic Revival buildings in New York. When it burned down in 1851, it was immediately replaced by a building in the same style. By the middle of the next decade, the church had outgrown its building and purchased a site at Fifth Avenue and Fifty-third Street.

Richard Upjohn's Trinity Church, along with James Renwick's Grace Church in the 1840s, had been the major monuments in inaugurating the Gothic Revival in New York. Therefore, it was especially noteworthy that Upjohn was commissioned to build the new St. Thomas. It was also one of his last buildings. The cornerstone was laid on October 14, 1868, and the church opened on October 6, 1870. On August 8, 1905, fire leveled the building, except for the tower, and the firm of Cram, Goodhue, and Ferguson was commissioned to rebuild the church in the Gothic style, for which they were well known.

On November 21, 1911, the cornerstone was laid and although on October 4, 1913, the congregation celebrated its first services

St. Thomas Church, Fifty-third Street and Fifth Avenue; 1911–16.
Architects Cram, Goodhue, and Ferguson were inspired by the Gothic
cathedrals of Europe in their design.

there, the building was not completed until 1916. By that time, Cram, Goodhue, and Ferguson had dissolved their partnership, and Bertram Goodhue completed St. Thomas Church.

The Embodiment of a Building Tradition

While the Church of the Incarnation was modeled after the English Commissioners' churches, St. Thomas was modeled after the great Gothic cathedrals of medieval France, known for their soaring spaces, great masonry skeletons, and elegant decoration. The body of the church extends the full width of the property for an ample nave, and open side aisles; it is 100 feet wide and 214 feet long, over 30 feet higher than Incarnation, almost twice as wide, and more than twice as long. St. Thomas is faced with limestone on the exterior and a light-colored sandstone inside.

Unusual for the period, the building is completely of masonry construction, although it was subsequently reinforced at points with steel. At the time this church was built, architects more commonly combined the latest technological advances in steel skeleton construction with historical styles, as in Cass Gilbert's Custom House from a few years earlier. Thus, a modern skeleton was built, which was then clad in masonry carved in Renaissance, Classical, Romanesque, Gothic, or Empire dress. Not so with St. Thomas's architects, who believed in the integrity of a style. If it was going to look Gothic, it had to be Gothic. St. Thomas, then, was built in the tradition of the great Gothic cathedrals, with the stone columns, walls, and buttresses all performing their respective structural functions.

The great square tower, at the corner of Fifth Avenue and Fifty-third Street, rises fifteen stories and projects a remarkable silhouette to the three approaches, south, north, and east. It houses twenty-one bells for carillon playing. Massive pier buttresses project like welcoming arms and frame the main entrance reached by a long flight of steep stairs. The wide, main portal and the two small entrances flanking it on the north and south reflect the interior disposition of its space. A wide nave creates a dramatic sense of openness, from which the entire body of the church can be seen, and the narrow, intimate side aisles, neither neglected nor subjugated, are open to the grandness of the nave.

The sculpture program of the main entrance was planned from the beginning, but it was not executed in stone until 1963. It combines local and regional figures important to St. Thomas's with traditional figures and symbols that have universal significance. As in cathedrals of old, the patron saint of the church stands in front of the trumeau (the stone pier supporting the tympanum in the center of the entrance) between the two entrances. St. Thomas is shown at

St. Thomas Church (entrance). Figures of the apostles, like the statue columns on great European cathedrals, flank the main entrance.

the moment of recognizing the risen Christ. Flanking the saint are six of the apostles, three on either side, like the statue columns on the great Gothic cathedrals. Above, the other six apostles are portrayed, along with Mary Magdalen and Martha. Christ the King is in the center flanked by Mary and John the Baptist. Panels and archivolts carry symbols of the sacraments, gifts of the Holy Spirit, and scenes from the life of St. Thomas.

The horizontal row of figures just above the archivolts portray saints of the early church and, above the rose window, the row of saints portrays figures responsible for the spread of the church from England to America and New York. The great rose is surrounded by the traditional tetramorph, symbols for the four Evangelists, carved in low relief. Above the main double doors are dark wooden panels, carved and gilded in relief, showing the four church buildings that the congregation has occupied since it was organized early in the nineteenth century.

The south portal is the bride's entrance, over which is portrayed the marriage feast at Cana and figures and motifs celebrating the sanctity of marriage as a sacrament. The north portal repeats the medieval practice of showing the patron holding a model of the building. Here, the rector at the time the church was built, Dr. Ernest M. Stires, holds the model in his hands. In Gothic Revival architecture, this practice is also found in commercial buildings, as in the case of Cass Gilbert, who is portrayed, holding a model of the Woolworth Building, in the lobby of the building.

The figures on the buttresses portray such major thinkers and leaders as Augustine, Ambrose, Athanasius, and Chrysostom—saints of the East and West—symbolizing unity, continuity, and the significance of unbroken tradition. Based upon Gothic tradition, the program was developed and tailored to St. Thomas Church by Canon Edward N. West and Bertram Goodhue. It was designed by the sculptor Theodore Barbarossa and carved by Rochette and Parzini.

The Interior

The narthex, as originally planned, carried symbols relating past and present through spiritual and physical symbols: the four elements, earth, air, fire, and water; four angels with emblems of sacrifice; and symbols of the four seasons, winter, summer, spring, and autumn. These still remain; however, the narthex was redesigned in the 1940s to commemorate those who served in World War II and the principles of peace. Mosaics of peace symbols and inscriptions ornament the floor in rare and variegated marbles, and an altar of peace stands at the north end.

Unfortunately, in 1961 glass was used to replace the oak-paneled screen that divided the narthex and nave, which altered the architects' original idea for the illumination of the nave. However, except for the back of the nave, the architects' intended effect has not been totally impaired.

The clerestory windows are eighteen feet wide and thirty-two feet high and were made by Whitefriars in London. They portray fruits of the Holy Spirit expressed through traditional biblical characters interacting with historical figures in the life of the American church. As an example, in the window celebrating meekness, Christ, Moses, St. Augustine, and St. Stephen are portrayed along with William H. Hare, first Bishop of South Dakota. Between the narthex and the chancel, a low parapet is decorated with eight mosaics. The four on the south side portray the church in its familiar symbols as ship, lighthouse, gateway, and kingdom of God. On the north side, the symbols treat key events in American history. In the memorial to World War I, actual stones were brought from the bombed Rheims cathedral and arranged here to represent the cathedral in the mosaic. The oak pulpit is surrounded by carved portrait statues of famous preachers, including a number from the New York church. Above, on the sounding board, Old Testament prophets and their prophecies make up a richly carved frieze, and symbolize the foundations of the message preached there.

The architects planned for the altar screen or reredos to be the main focus of attention inside. It was designed by Bertram Goodhue with sculptor Lee Lawrie, who were influenced in part by the screen by Augustus Saint-Gaudens that was in the former church. The reredos covers the entire west wall of the chancel above the main altar, some eighty feet high. More than sixty figures are arranged in niches, panels, and groups that emphasize the central theme of Thomas's discovery expressed in his cry, "My Lord and My God." Everything revolves around this theme. From the Old Testament, for example, figures express the messianic prophecies such as Isaiah's "Behold, a virgin shall conceive and bear a child," and its fulfillment in the New Testament is illustrated in the *Te Deum* that salutes "the King of Glory."

Three stained-glass windows admit a warm light that rakes across the smooth texture and ivory tone of this panoply of figures, niches, and reliefs, accenting them in mysterious colors and rich chiaroscuro.

A fitting foil to the light key of the reredos is the exquisite wood carving of the dark oak chancel. The kneeling rail, choir stalls, and altar rail are ornamented with rich carving. Moreover, images of famous organists embellish the organ case, and angels, carved in oak and holding host and chalice—symbolizing communion— frame the bronze grill of the altar rail.

125

7

Cast-Iron Buildings,
Their Legacy,
and the Palazzo Style

Although the use of metal in building goes back to Greek and Roman architecture, its application to commercial building in the eighteenth and nineteenth centuries was the result of the demands of the industrial revolution. It began in England, then spread throughout Europe and the United States. Iron was used as early as the 1770s to support galleries in churches (e.g., St. Anne's Church, Liverpool). Then in 1792 W. Strutt used vertical iron supports to carry timber beams in his mills at Derby and Belper. Soon after, mills all over England were being built with a rudimentary form of iron skeleton construction throughout, which meant that the weight of the building was supported by the metal frame rather than by load-bearing walls. This structural innovation had far-reaching effects on commercial building in England and abroad and contributed ultimately to the most revolutionary architectural achievement since the Gothic cathedral—the skyscraper.

Builders and architects quickly recognized the advantages of cast-iron construction. Cast iron was less expensive than traditional building materials. Moreover, prefabrication (standardized interchangeable parts made in quantity at a foundry and assembled on the site) was quickly making cast-iron construction even more economical. However, the complexity of some structures required that they be assembled first at the foundry, where each piece was numbered to assure correct and rapid reassembly (by matching the numbers). The structure was then disassembled, shipped in parts, and

Formerly McCreery's Dry Goods Emporium, Eleventh Street and Broadway *(facing page);* 1868. John Kellum, architect. Converted to modern apartments in 1972, the building is picturesquely sited at a bend in Broadway.

reassembled at the construction site. Foundries made every conceivable kind of structure. From domestic dwellings to churches and palaces, and from lighthouses to mills and warehouses, iron buildings were manufactured in England and shipped all over the world. Moreover, pattern books were available from the foundries and served as catalogs of designs from which clients could order.

Decimus Burton and Joseph Paxton in the 1830s and 1840s in England further advanced iron-frame construction by their designs for conservatories. For example, Paxton devised a ridge-and-furrow system·in his glass-cage-like greenhouses for the duke of Devonshire's collection of exotic plants. Each plate of glass fit into troughs (made of wood first, then later, metal) and each unit of glass and metal was standardized and could be reproduced rapidly and cheaply. Thus the entire structure was essentially composed of a replication of that single standard unit.

Paxton's great Crystal Palace of 1851, the building for the first World's Fair, was constructed on this principle and was the largest and most spectacular prefabricated building constructed up to that time. Made entirely of this ferrovitreous construction (combining glass with metal skeletal construction), it was over 1,800 feet long and more than 70 feet wide; so Douglas Jerrold of the English magazine *Punch* christened it "the Crystal Palace." Soon after it was erected, most every major city in the world constructed its own version of the Crystal Palace. New York's was built in 1852 next to the site of the present New York Public Library at Forty-second Street and Fifth Avenue, at Reservoir Square, but it was destroyed by fire in 1858.

NEW YORK'S EARLY PIONEERS IN CAST IRON

James Bogardus and Daniel Badger were the major innovators in popularizing cast-iron architecture in New York. Bogardus introduced the cast-iron facade that was also a load-bearing wall. Before that, cast-iron fronts in New York had been hung like great curtains in front of traditional brick and wood structures. In 1850 Bogardus patented an all-iron building, after being influenced by what he had seen in Europe between 1836 and 1840. In Bogardus's early buildings, there was no attempt to conceal the building's structural frame. Hence, the structural functions of the vertical supports and horizontal beams that made up the skeleton frame of the building were revealed in the simple grid form (or nondirectional pattern) of the entire facade, which was surprisingly similar to the modular patterns of twentieth-century skyscrapers.

The taste for European architectural styles replaced the functionalism of the early designs by Bogardus, who was neither an architect nor an engineer, but a manufacturer and inventor. The new designs obscured the simple functional lines of cast-iron facades and replaced them with Renaissance and Classical forms at first, and then more elaborate decorations as the century progressed.

THE PALAZZO STYLE

The first of the great commercial palaces in New York that was to establish the Italian palazzo style for commercial buildings was also America's first great department store: A. T. Stewart Dry Goods Store. Designed by the architect John B. Snook (the architect for Cornelius Vanderbilt's elegant Grand Central Station), the building was completed in 1846, and it stands at 280 Broadway between Chambers and Reade streets.

The Italianate palazzo reached maturity over the next decade, and one of the earliest surviving examples is the Cary Building (1857) at 105–107 Chambers Street, extending through the block with an almost mirror-image facade at 89–91 Reade Street. It was hailed not only for its elegance, but for being the largest and most complete store of its kind as well. The architects were Gamaliel King and John Kellum, partners during the decade of the 1850s when they achieved great stature as major shapers of the new commercial architecture to which the Cary Building contributed enormously with its palazzo features. Five stories high and eight bays wide, the entire wall surface was cast-iron and painted white to imitate rustication. Ground-up pieces of marble and stone were often mixed with the paint to give the surface the appearance and texture of masonry. Some of these facades are so deceptive that only by applying a magnet to the surface can the true material be known. The facade is crowned with a heavy bracketed cornice and large triangular pediment. Within the pediment is a large cartouche enclosing the words "Cary Building." Each bay is composed of paired Corinthian columns supporting a simply moulded arch with raised floral keystone. Most of the capitals on the north facade have been stripped of their acanthus leaves, a mutilation which is instructive. One can see how the capitals were bolted onto the columns, leaf by leaf.

Originally, the ground floor of the Cary Building was composed of high and wide display windows flanked by Corinthian columns with Corinthian piers at either end and, even though it has since been modified, the piers and six of the columns still survive (slender cast-iron supports took up less space than the massive masonry piers, leaving more room for display). Furthermore, the original rolling iron shutters, one of Daniel Badger's early innovations, can still be pulled down over the windows on both north and south facades. The Cary Building is a noteworthy example of the collaboration between foundry and architect. Its facade was cast by Badger's Architectural Iron Works and may even have been designed by Englishman George H. Johnson, Badger's principal designer.

Cary Building, 105–107 Chambers Street and 89–91 Read Street; 1857. Gamaliel King and John Kellum, architects; an early cast-iron palazzo, painted white to look like marble or stone.

CAST-IRON ELEGANCE

Another of Badger's masterpieces is the cast-iron work in the E. V. Haughwout Building (J. P. Gaynor, architect) at Broome and Broadway, the elegant emporium of Eder V. Haughwout, merchant in cut-glass, silverware, clocks, and chandeliers. This and the Cary Building are the oldest surviving cast-iron palazzi in New York. The building is important too for its Otis elevator: Elisha Graves Otis's invention of a safety device to prevent an elevator from falling made the passenger elevator safe and initiated a great industrial enterprise. Otis installed his first practical safety elevator in the Haughwout Building, and it is still in use.

Although cast-iron facades were often textured and painted white to look like cut stone, giving their pediments, entablatures, and Corinthian columns the appearance of carved marble, American ingenuity often modified these Classical, Renaissance, and Baroque forms in adapting them to a building's function. For example, the "sperm candle" column was inspired by the European Baroque colossal order, in which columns and pilasters rise several stories to unify a facade. But as American architects, founders, and builders applied the device to nineteenth-century commercial architecture, the columns became more slender and elongated, which reminded people of the familiar candles made from the oil of sperm whales—thus the name. The design was used in both cast iron and stone. For example, the sperm candle columns at 388 Broadway are in marble, whereas those at 55–57 White Street (by John Kellum) are cast-iron painted and textured to look like marble.

John Kellum's cast-iron architecture demonstrates the successful application of the founder's art and the structural principles pioneered by James Bogardus. When Kellum left his partnership with King and set out on his own in 1859, the second A. T. Stewart Building at Broadway and Ninth Street was one of his first major undertakings. Not only was it elegant and the largest cast-iron building in New York, but it was built on one of New York's most fashionable shopping promenades. Kellum extended the use of cast iron beyond the facade and used it in the structure itself. The building later became Wanamaker's and was destroyed by fire in 1956. The name of the apartment house that now occupies the site, the Stewart, is the only reminder of the great cast-iron building that once stood there.

Kellum and Stewart became fast friends and Kellum built Stewart's palatial residence, the "Marble Palace," at Thirty-fourth Street and Fifth Avenue (northwest corner). It was demolished in 1901,

131

except for two of its pedestals, which today flank the steps of Our Lady of Lourdes Church (1904) at 467 West 142d Street.

Two blocks north on Broadway, at the northwest corner of Eleventh Street, Kellum built another cast-iron palazzo in 1868, the James McCreery and Co. Dry Goods Emporium, a building that has been saved and converted to modern apartments. Deterioration and damage by fire in 1971 had threatened the building with demolition. As part of the new design, the cast-iron columns throughout the building were retained and now appear in hallways, sleeping lofts, kitchens, and other unexpected places.

McCreery's store is picturesquely sited at the point where Broadway bends to the northwest. Therefore, it can be seen from lower Broadway at a great distance. Kellum dramatized that view by an ingenious device. When the architects began replacing the glass in the sixteen-foot-high windows, they found that contrary to standard practice, each bay was a slightly different size. The window frames decreased by one inch in width with each frame, proceeding north along Broadway from Eleventh Street, creating the illusion that the Broadway facade is longer than it actually is. Kellum had exaggerated the linear perspective by progressively diminishing the width of each window to create the illusion of greater length, thereby enhancing the picturesque view of this emporium.

While the principles of cast-iron construction and the palazzo style were highly compatible in producing some of New York's great emporiums, their influences were also widespread. For example, the combination of cast-iron construction with the passenger elevator contributed to the birth of the elevator building of the 1870s in New York and ultimately to the modern skyscraper. And the union of skeleton construction with monumental stonework in the palazzo style produced some of New York's most elegant private and public buildings, well exemplified in three of its private clubs and one of its most publicized courthouses.

CLUBS

Clubs in New York had their beginnings in taverns and coffee houses during the colonial era. Poets and artists would assemble at one, politicians at another, and merchants at still another. The wealthy would meet in their own homes on a regular basis.

New York's club buildings are an impressive architectural expression, a permanent record in stone and steel, of a significant sector of New York life. Three of these clubs—the Metropolitan Club, the University Club, and the Racquet and Tennis Club—individually, as well as collectively, are particularly noteworthy. Together, they represent at once a striking commentary on the design of New York's fashionable clubs and the work of one of New York's most important architectural firms: McKim, Mead, and White.

The Metropolitan Club, One East Sixtieth Street, and the University Club, One West Fifty-fourth Street, illustrate McKim, Mead, and White's work in their heyday, a time when all of the partners were still living. The Racquet and Tennis Club, 370 Park Avenue (between Fifty-second and Fifty-third streets), shows the continuity of their influence on the second generation of the firm. These three clubs reflect the Beaux-Arts tradition of relying on historical styles to build for the present. Further, they are all in the palazzo style that was also popular with some of the great cast-iron commercial structures of the period and which inspired the Villard Houses (finished 1886) and the Boston Public Library (1887-95)—commissions that were important in establishing the reputation of McKim, Mead, and White, and which made a great impact on the architecture of the time. Moreover, the palazzo style had been adapted to clubs in England a half century earlier, and that appealed to fashionable patrons in the United States.

Elegance Born of Conflict:
The Metropolitan Club

The Metropolitan Club was born of a dispute that arose during the 1880s between two factions of the Union Club (founded 1836), over the governing process and the admission of new members. The dispute led members of the older contingent, including J. P. Morgan, Cornelius Vanderbilt, and Robert Goelet, to break away and found their own club early in 1891, which became known as the "Millionaire's Club." The members built their new clubhouse on Fifth Avenue at Sixtieth Street, a most fashionable site, with a one-hundred-foot front along Fifth Avenue facing Central Park. The view prompted some members to suggest the name Park Club; other members, inspired by the English clubs and the view, wanted to call it the Spectator.

The new building was to be of marble and in the Italian palazzo style, following the tradition of the famous English clubs. In order not to interfere with the view of the park along the Fifth Avenue facade, the main entrance, originally planned for Fifth Avenue, was changed to the Sixtieth Street side at the south end of the site. The main lounge then occupied the full one-hundred-foot expanse parallel to Fifth Avenue and took full advantage of the view. Moreover, its location at the corner provided a view of the south, overlooking Grand Army Plaza, as well. A courtyard recessed from Sixtieth Street

133

The Sherman Monument, Fifty-ninth Street and Fifth Avenue; 1903. McKim, Mead, and White, architects; Augustus Saint-Gaudens, sculptor, shows William Tecumseh Sherman on his march to the sea led by a winged Victory. The Metropolitan Club (seen on the right), built in the popular palazzo style in 1893, was called the "Millionaire's Club."

provided a convenient area within which carriages could approach the main entrance through a high wrought-iron gate.

The lines of the building are clean and fine and the proportions monumental. Three stories surmount a rusticated basement and are capped by an enormous cornice projecting six feet from the facade. The rich elaboration of Classical moulding—incorporating egg and dart designs, dentils, and strong modillions in marble and copper—denotes a fitting climax to the restrained surfaces of the facade, whose smooth marble face is pierced by rectangular windows surrounded by restrained moulding.

The entrance to the vestibule is located to the west of the courtyard, convenient to the grand lounge. The vestibule is vaulted in light Guastavino tile, opening up the entrance dramatically to the splendid entrance hall sheathed in various marbles. The lavish interiors bear a striking contrast to the restrained exterior. Leading decorators, artists, and artisans were commissioned to decorate the interior. French Baroque ceiling paintings, ornamental plasterwork, and colorful murals were designed by Gilbert Cuel. The American painter Edward Simmons, who had studied under some of the leading masters in France, executed murals, and the woodwork throughout was crafted by leading artisans. The east wing, which houses the Canadian Club, was added in 1912; architect Ogden Codman has tried to adopt the spirit of the earlier structure.

For Literature and Art:
The University Club

In 1865 the University Club was organized to promote literature and art by maintaining a library, reading room, and art gallery. For many years, its members met at the Jerome Mansion at Twenty-sixth Street and Madison Avenue. In 1896 when they required additional space, they commissioned McKim, Mead, and White, who were also members of the club, to design the new building at the recently available site at Fifth Avenue and Fifty-fourth Street. The firm had achieved prominence not only from their buildings, but also through their dominant role in the World's Columbian Exposition of 1893 in Chicago, which did much to establish the use of Classical and Renaissance forms for urban architecture and town planning.

Completed in 1899, the building occupies a site extending 100 feet along Fifth Avenue and 140 feet along Fifty-fourth Street. In the palazzo style and faced in granite, the University Club is organized along the same lines as some of the great Florentine palaces of the fifteenth century, including Alberti's Rucellai Palace and Michelozzo's Medici Palace. The club's nine floors are organized horizontally into three colossal tiers, articulated by great arched windows with carved keystones; above each window is a smaller rectangular window. On the Fifth Avenue facade, a grand balcony with bronze railings, supported by large, carved brackets, projects at the base of the second tier; a smaller balcony appears at the upper tier. The building is capped by an enormous cornice carved with lions heads, egg and dart mouldings, and a chorus of scroll brackets.

An enormous arch frames the main entrance on Fifty-fourth Street, flanked by colossal Doric-type columns with drums of alternating rustication and carrying the club monogram and initials of various schools. The columns support a giant entablature, with a Doric-type frieze of triglyphs and metopes. The head of Minerva is carved by sculptor Charles Niehaus into the keystone.

Even though both the Metropolitan and University clubs are in the palazzo style and were completed only five years apart, each has its individual character. The University Club's entrance, for example, is more robust, and its symbolic carving and decoration expresses its distinct role. The club seal, designed by artist Kenyon Cox in 1896, is carved above the main entrance. Two youths shake hands in friendship: one holds a tablet inscribed "Patria" and the other the torch of learning. Behind, in the center, a model of Pallas Athena stands on a Classical altar, symbolizing the arts and sciences. At the top of the seal, inscribed in Greek, are Aristotle's words, "In fellowship lies friendship." The theme is repeated inside the building in a marble relief by sculptor Charles Keck above the fireplace of the atrium.

Inside the University Club, the atrium opens off the vestibule and its vaulted ceiling rests on great, green Irish marble columns with bronze capitals. A vaulted ambulatory is distinguished by its rich marble and mosaic decoration. White Norwegian marble surrounds set off the doorways with distinction, and the floor is paneled in Italian and Vermont marbles. Roman symbols decorate the frieze and east and west doorways in this room.

The reading room, the library, and the dining room all reveal the richness and variety of the decorations. The reading room extends the length of the Fifth Avenue facade. Its deeply paneled and gilded ceiling is supported by colossal pilasters and its marble doorways are richly carved. The Italian walnut woodwork and deep red velvet walls enhance the elegance of this grand space.

The library occupies the second floor, and the collection contains 130,000 volumes; it is strongest in biography, history, and literature. A vaulted central hall is surrounded by alcoves, and the card room and the chess room open off it. Statues of Augustus and Demosthenes and busts of Aeschylus, Euripedes, Sophocles, Plato, Socrates, and Homer surround the room. Above the doorways are

University Club, Fifty-fourth Street and Fifth Avenue; 1899. McKim,
Mead, and White, architects, did much to establish the use of Classical
and Renaissance forms for urban architecture, as expressed in this great
Florentine Renaissance palazzo.

bronzed busts of Sir Isaac Newton, John Milton, John Locke, Julius Caesar, William Shakespeare, Jean Jacques Rousseau, Benjamin Franklin, and Sir Walter Scott. Henry Siddons Mowbray, who is well remembered for his murals in the New York Public Library and in the J. P. Morgan Library, was commissioned to adapt the Renaissance master Pinturicchio's murals in the Vatican's Borgia apartments to the University Club's library ceiling. Completed in 1904, the murals portrayed personifications of the Liberal Arts, images from the Old and New testaments, figures from ancient mythology, and representations of great figures from ancient and modern literature.

The dining room occupies the third floor. It is a long room, with stately oak pilasters and columns supporting its thirty-seven-foot high, richly ornamented gilt ceiling. It still has a loggia, over the entrance, that was originally used for musicians. This was a feature of the Villard Houses also. Later decorative additions to the room include Allyn Cox's murals of six of America's earliest universities (Harvard, William and Mary, Yale, University of Pennsylvania, Princeton, and Columbia) painted in 1967.

Private dining rooms, offices, and apartments are located on the upper floors. The original grill room, billiards room and bar, and the ladies dining room have received different designations over the years; and the mezzanine was converted to the tap room in 1933.

The Continuity of a Style:
The Racquet and Tennis Club

The Racquet and Tennis Club Building was erected in 1918 on Park Avenue between Fifty-second and Fifty-third streets soon after the new Grand Central Station was completed (1913). With the electrification of trains and the subsequent covering of the great cut down the center of Park Avenue for the New York Central Railroad tracks, the area became fashionable and resulted in the building of luxurious apartment buildings. St. Bartholomew's Church acquired its Park Avenue site in 1916, and Bertram Goodhue brought McKim, Mead, and White's magnificent facade (inspired by the famous Romanesque portal of St. Gilles du Gard in southern France) from the old church on Madison Avenue and East Twenty-fourth Street to the new building, which he completed in 1919.

Although the Racquet Club was designed and executed in the decade following the deaths of White and McKim, it retains the characteristics of the firm's works established in their time. That continuity of style was due largely to the fact that William Symmes Richardson, the firm's designer of the Racquet Club, had studied at the École des Beaux-Arts and had been White's assistant.

The Racquet and Tennis Club, Park Avenue between Fifty-second and Fifty-third streets; 1918. Designed by William Symmes Richardson of McKim, Mead, and White, it features a pattern of crossed racquets in *architecture parlante*.

The Racquet Club was organized in 1875 as an athletic and social club. In 1891 it moved from the building at 55 West Twenty-sixth Street and occupied 27 West Forty-third Street, a neighborhood it shared with the Century, the Columbia, the Harvard, and the New York Yacht clubs. However, the appearance of tall buildings and the accelerated commercialization of the area, resulting from the northward expansion of the city and the development of Grand Central, led the club to seek a new location.

Robert Goelet, one of New York's wealthiest citizens, offered to build the new building on land he owned on Park Avenue between Fifty-second and Fifty-third streets and to lease the land and the building to the club. The site was still conveniently located, and fashionable Park Avenue was quite a suitable location. His proposal was accepted on June 27, 1916, and the building was completed two years later and opened on April 15, 1918.

The club's exclusive position is expressed by the elegance and grandeur of its building as designed by McKim, Mead, and White. Sited to be seen from near and far, the building is visible on three sides because of the generous width of Park Avenue, two lanes of roadway separated by a landscaped center strip. The club occupies

139

the entire block front on Park Avenue and rises massively five stories in three tiers in Renaissance palazzo fashion, with the colossal stone blocks of the basement level boldly sculpted. Racquets are carved into the Corinthian capitals of the columns supporting the arches, a light and appropriate touch of *architecture parlante*, and the club seal is inscribed on a giant cartouche above the central arch. The arch form is borrowed from several well-known Florentine palazzi and goes back to some of the great abbeys and churches of the tenth and eleventh centuries.

It has been suggested that the University Club of San Francisco (1910) may have influenced the Racquet Club design. The New York Club's facade is framed by massive quoins pointed in the same fashion as the voussoirs of the arches, at once stabilizing and unifying the design. A stone balustrade caps the building above its cornice, which boldly projects over a terra-cotta frieze with square-headed attic windows and a decorative pattern of racquets. Tennis and squash courts occupy the upper floors, where natural light is abundant. The lounges, dining room, and library occupy the second floor, where the ball lounge opens out onto the great loggia above the sidewalk. The arched openings flanking the main entrance on Park Avenue provide expansive display areas for commercial spaces that provide revenue for the club's maintenance.

The proportions of the building are scaled to the avenue, further integrating it with its site. The height of the facade is approximately the width of Park Avenue, and the width of the building is equal to twice the height, proportions that the architects used to impart a sense of stability and permanence to the structure. The impression of solid mass produced by the club's stable proportions is enhanced by the bold handling of the arch motif and the exquisitely carved stonework. Arches are repeated in the north and south walls over entrances to the vaulted driveway behind.

THE NEW YORK CITY COURTHOUSE

By the 1850s, with the expansion of the city and its local government, there was a pressing need for more space to house courts, juries, county clerks, the district attorney, and the like. At first, the call was for a new City Hall, but by 1860 the city's leaders had decided to build a new courthouse behind City Hall on a historically important site that had served public and civic functions alike from New York's early years.

This site had initially served as a grazing and public meeting place north of New Amsterdam during the Dutch occupation. It became the "Common" in the 1680s under British rule, and this was

140

where public floggings were administered and where the stocks stood as constant reminders to lawbreakers. It was also the site of perhaps the first cemetery for blacks in New York. The first public almshouse was erected there in 1738 (demolished 1797), and City Hall now stands on the site. Slightly to the east, a jail was built in 1757–59 (now demolished).

In 1795–96 a second almshouse was built where the Tweed Courthouse now stands, and later it housed cultural institutions including the Academy of the Arts, the New York Historical Society, and one of New York's first museums (John Scudder's American Museum). In the nineteenth century, the building was converted to offices and courtrooms and was used until 1857, when it was razed. Just east of it stood the rotunda on Chambers Street, which was built in 1817–18 (demolished 1870) to exhibit artist John Vanderlyn's great popular panorama of the palace and gardens of Versailles. Panoramas were very popular in the eighteenth and nineteenth centuries; they derived from the *Eidophusikon*, which was developed by Philippe de Loutherbourg in France and England in the eighteenth century and combined realistic landscapes and seascapes with sound effects to convey wind, seas, and avalanches.

New York City Courthouse, Chambers Street between Broadway and Centre Street; 1872–76. Kellum and Eidlitz, architects. Designed in the palazzo tradition, its grand stairs were removed when the street was widened; also called the "Tweed Courthouse."

The rotunda was circular, built of brick and stone, and fronted on Chambers Street. It was fifty-three feet in diameter and forty-five feet high. Its main entrance was a Classical portico with massive entablature supported by columns and a grand pantheon-like dome with skylight crowning the central space within. There, the spectator climbed stairs to a central platform to view the panorama that completely surrounded him. Besides Vanderlyn's Gardens of Versailles, covering some 3,000 square feet of canvas, other popular panoramas exhibited in other less elegant halls included views of Mexico and the Battle of Waterloo. The rotunda included an art gallery, and public sculpture was important as well at this time.

The public had wanted an equestrian monument to George Washington ever since the George III monument had been pulled down at Bowling Green during the American Revolution. Therefore, Enrico Causici, one of the Italian sculptors imported by Benjamin Henry Latrobe and Thomas Jefferson to complete the U.S. Capitol decorations, was commissioned to execute an equestrian statue of Washington, which was erected at the south end of today's City Hall Park. Executed in plaster, it was installed on July 4, 1826, but funds were never raised to cast it in bronze, and it was removed by April 25, 1831.

Boss Tweed's Courthouse

The New York City Courthouse got its nickname, "Tweed Courthouse," from "Boss" Tweed, who dominated the city and county for a decade from 1861 to 1871. Because of the graft and corruption of Tweed's organization—popularly called the "Tweed Ring" by *Harper's Weekly* cartoonist Thomas Nast—the building, which was budgeted at $4.5 million, cost more than $9 million.

William Marcy ("Boss") Tweed, the son of a chair manufacturer, got his start in 1848 when he helped to organize the volunteer fire company American Engine Company No. 6. It adopted the emblem of the Snarling Tiger, which Thomas Nast later used as the Tweed Ring's monogram. Fire companies were often stepping stones to political positions and power in those days and, through Engine Company No. 6, Tweed began a rapid rise in local politics. In 1861 he became chairman of the Democratic Central Committee in New York. This gave him enormous influence that he used to become head of the committee on the new courthouse. Then for almost ten years, Tweed and his associates methodically and flagrantly defrauded the taxpayers of large sums of money by manipulating agreements with contractors on the courthouse project. Some of the abuses were more notorious than others; Andrew J. Garvey, for example, a grand marshal of Tammany Hall, was dubbed the

"Prince of Plasterers." His bills for the plaster work on the building amounted to almost $3 million in just two years. There was enough carpet purchased (at least, transactions recorded that purchases were made) to cover City Hall Park three times, and some of the carpet suppliers did not even exist. The marble for the building was quarried from Tweed's own quarries in Sheffield, Massachusetts, or from those in Eastchester which he controlled.

Finally, in the summer of 1871 Tweed's empire fell. When the Ring's bookkeeper was killed in a sleighing accident in January, a county auditor replaced him and released enough conclusive evidence from the comptroller's files to *The New York Times* to send Tweed to jail and destroy his organization. The breakup of the Tweed Ring interrupted construction work on the building until 1876. The first principal architect, John Kellum, also died in 1871 and was replaced by Leopold Eidlitz, whose ideas are reflected in the later additions.

The Architects and Their Plans

Architect Thomas Little was commissioned to draw up the original plans in 1859, and on September 16, 1861, ground was broken. Architect John Kellum had joined Little early on, and Kellum soon took over as architect for the building, adding a dome and rusticated basement to Little's plan, along with other modifications. Kellum's plan was influenced by the English architect Sir Charles Barry's Traveller's Club (1830–32) and Reform Club (1838–40) in London, both done in the Italian palazzo style especially popular in cast-iron architecture in New York. George Dance's Mansion House of 1735 in London also influenced Kellum's design in the character of the Corinthian columns supporting the triangular pediment of the entrance portico.

Another more immediate influence on the new courthouse was Thomas U. Walter's U.S. Capitol Building in Washington, D.C., under construction from 1851 to 1865. Kellum's plan for a dome for the courthouse building was not carried out, though guidebooks to New York of 1869 stated that a dome was to surmount the finished building, which would resemble the U.S. Capitol dome. This was not unusual, because most government buildings in the late nineteenth century followed Walter's design.

The building was organized along a rectangular plan, 250 feet wide by 150 feet deep, with the main entrance on the long north side facing Chambers Street. East and west wings extend from a central block with a grand portico accenting the main entrance.

The portico is composed of four Corinthian columns supporting a colossal entablature and crowning triangular pediment. Origi-

143

nally, the stairway extended well beyond the present Chambers Street curb line and afforded a ceremonial approach to the entrance portico, another feature borrowed from the U.S. Capitol Building. The destruction of the stairway in 1942, when Chambers Street was widened, has left the building looking awkward without a proper front, but the engaged Corinthian columns that still flank the entrance are reminders of what the facade looked like in its original state.

The building rests on a granite base and is faced with smooth ashlar marble that clads its brick load-bearing walls. Stately windows repeat the Classical motifs of the main portal. Lintels are supported by consoles on paneled pilasters, and moulded sills rest on corbels. Originally, striped awnings were installed over each window, a detail criticized by *The New York Times* in 1871.

New York City Courthouse: south wing. The round-arched windows and chevron moulding show in Eidlitz's section (on the left); Kellum's earlier Classical detail is on the right.

Behind its four-story facade, the building houses more than one hundred public rooms, courtrooms, offices, and utility rooms arranged symmetrically around a central octagonal rotunda that rises five floors over a full basement to a glazed skylight. Kellum designed this octagonal well in cast iron and plaster with Classical detail. On the second floor, cast-iron brackets, baseboards, and balustrade retain the sense of fluid space, uniting balcony and passage areas with the stairwell. The Classical detail is continued in the structural members, as well as the cast-iron niches set against plaster walls. These niches once displayed memorial busts of former justices. Kellum's marble tile floors contribute a rich stability to the appearance and the structure. The colorful encaustic tile flooring in the south wing reflects a different sensibility, that of another architect.

After the death of John Kellum and the suspension of construction during the Tweed Ring trials, Leopold Eidlitz was commissioned to finish the building. Eidlitz was one of America's leading architects. From Prague, he had studied in Vienna and had come to New York in 1843 where he joined Richard Upjohn, leading protagonist of the Gothic Revival here. Eidlitz's buildings included St. George's Church on Stuyvesant Square (1846–48) in the Romanesque Revival style and St. Peter's in the Bronx (1855) in the Gothic Revival style. In 1875, the year before the Tweed Courthouse commission, he collaborated with Henry Hobson Richardson and Frederick Law Olmsted on the State Capitol Building in Albany. His principal contribution was the Assembly Chamber, done in Gothic Revival with medieval detail, polychromatic materials, and vaulted ceiling, which resembles his work in the Tweed Courthouse.

The South Wing

Eidlitz was responsible for the south wing of the courthouse and the rotunda and its skylight. The south wing was originally to be a portico similar to that of the main facade, but financial restrictions and the need for more office space produced the present structure.

The wing is four stories high and three bays wide. The marble is of a different kind and the decoration reflects a blend of medieval and Classical models, rather than more purely Classical ones. This is particularly evident in the round-arched windows and the chevron moulding. Walking by the facade along the path behind City Hall provides an ideal comparison between the original Classical style and the more eclectic later one, especially noted from this vantage point where the walls of the old and the new meet. In the mind of the medieval-oriented architect, this juxtaposition was in no way an unhappy one. After all, the great medieval cathedrals were

145

often built in many campaigns that extended over several centuries, each addition reflecting the current style.

Eidlitz's preference for medieval forms is especially apparent in the third floor. Round arches and blind arches are supported by sturdy round stone columns with leafy capitals. The walls are laid up in red, black, and tan brick in varying patterns to complement the gray stone columns, and the skylight was glazed in stained glass to enhance the medieval flavor. Eidlitz filled in Kellum's spaces, enclosing the rotunda with arcaded brick walls, and glazed the skylight with red, blue, green, and amber panels depicting floral motifs and animals. Eidlitz's brick walls separate the various spaces—rotunda, stairways, passages—in contrast to Kellum's fluid interpretation which unites them.

Unfortunately, Eidlitz's ideas of color and texture as expressed here have been obscured because the surface has been painted gray, the columns have been marbleized (painted to look like marble), and the stained glass has been removed from the skylight. Consequently, neither Kellum's airiness nor Eidlitz's fantasy are evident today in the courthouse building.

Some of the individual rooms offer more reliable records of the two quite distinct sensibilities that went into making this unique and magnificent monument. For example, room 201-2 in Eidlitz's south wing retains the many-colored encaustic tile (red, blue, beige, white, and black) in geometric patterns with foliated borders. Stone arches, carved ceiling panels, and a large carved stone fireplace preserve the medieval quality of Eidlitz's conception. Moreover, such details as the octagonal bases of the columns relate individual components to the central space, the octagonal rotunda, and reflect the underlying unity of the building despite its eclectic character. The octagon also appears in the floor tiles.

There are many ornamental riches still retained in the building, even though the stucture has suffered deterioration over the past years. For example, Kellum's cast-iron door enframements with pilasters, bracketed cornices, pediments, and the like, are still intact in many of the spaces, especially on the second floor. Fine wooden doors are preserved throughout the building, some with etched-glass panels with the city's seal. Much of the original hardware—door handles, escutcheons, locks, and decorative hinges—is in surprisingly fine condition.

Doors, with the stepped paneling that Eidlitz favored, remain, as does the handsome staircase with its Gothic rail on the third floor winding up to the mezzanine in the south wing. Kellum's moulded iron baseboards, ceiling ornament of plaster medallions, original vent grilles, and stone baseboards preserve the sense of the courthouse's early elegance.

Of all of Kellum's rooms, numbers 308 and 316 are the most elaborate. High cove ceilings and window frames are topped with cartouches and carry stepped foliate bases. Flat mantels are supported by pilasters with inset colonettes. Room 303, moreover, has an unusually well-preserved arched fireplace, and its oak doors, with original decorative brass, are still in place.

THE ELEVATOR BUILDING

The union of metal skeleton construction, designs employing iron and glass as major building materials, and the passenger elevator produced the modern skyscraper and satisfied the nineteenth century's fast-growing need for more commercial space in areas where available land was limited. Although the term "skyscraper" has its origins in Italy in the thirteenth century, referring to the new heights buildings had reached there (towers exceeded heights of modern fifteen-story skyscrapers), in modern times it refers to tall buildings of steel-skeleton construction equipped with high-speed elevators.

The greatest growth in the modern skyscraper's early development took place in Chicago following the famous fire of 1871, which decimated the city that had become America's mid-continental shipping center. Skyscraper design offered Chicago speed, efficiency, and economy in rebuilding and, over the next two decades, produced virtually a new city of steel and stone.

The earliest skyscrapers were the so-called elevator buildings of the 1870s in New York. Since people would not walk up more than five flights of stairs, the advent of the passenger elevator now made the upper stories as desirable as lower ones, and opened the possibility of building to new heights. Although these early elevator buildings were not of skeletal construction throughout, they combined height with the elevator and introduced the compositional principles that became an integral part of skyscraper design well into the twentieth century.

The First Skyscraper Designers
and Their Legacy

George B. Post's Equitable Life Assurance Building, 1871; his Western Union Building, 1873–75; and Richard Morris Hunt's Tribune Building, 1873–75, were the earliest mature examples of elevator buildings. In the Western Union Building (where AT&T's 195 Broadway building stands) and the Tribune Building (where Pace University stands across from City Hall Park), Post and Hunt intro-

The Tribune Building (demolished); 1873–75. Richard Morris
Hunt, architect. A first in elevator buildings, it stood east of City
Hall Park; from it came the bronze statue of Horace Greeley now
standing near City Hall.

duced innovative designs that shared a common organizational principle. Above the basement level and below the roof, the floors were unified structurally and visually by a similarity of formal treatment that made the building appear to be divided into a base, shaft, and capital, as in a Classical column. This tripartite organization remained a dominant principle of skyscraper design well into the twentieth century and even figures in today's postmodern designs.

The metal skeleton soon replaced masonry, making it possible to build on a site of almost any size without taking up much space for foundations and walls. Regulations governing the new skeleton, or "cage," construction replaced the laws of masonry building, which had required thickening of walls at the bottom as the building rose higher. The thinner walls permitted by the new code allowed more usable floor space and more window area.

The first tall buildings, in which cage construction was fully developed, were in Chicago in the 1880s. New York's building codes impeded development of the new building type until 1892, when new legislation made greater provision for skeleton construction. Then development in New York began to move ahead rapidly. It was in Chicago, also during the late 1880s, that "curtain wall" construction was introduced, wherein the outer walls of the front of the building carried no support load but acted simply as curtains of brick and terra-cotta, keeping the weather out.

THE CHICAGO SCHOOL

The skyscraper in Chicago at this time began to reflect its skeletal construction externally, in a grid pattern recalling that which James Bogardus had pioneered with his cast-iron fronts in New York in the 1850s. The internal structure, then, of vertical supports and horizontal beams, dictated the external form. This was a guiding principle expressed later as "form follows function," which dominated commercial architecture in Chicago. Its functionalism and antihistoricism became hallmarks of the Chicago School, comprising those architects who practiced the new mode.

One of the foremost figures of the Chicago School was Louis Sullivan, who was Frank Lloyd Wright's master and whose Bayard-Condict Building (1898) at 65 Bleecker Street is the only completed building by Sullivan in New York. Its thin curtain wall, reflecting its skeleton, and the slender colonettes within each of the five bays emphasizing the building's verticality, were considered radical for their time. It is ironic that the principles of design, which Sullivan employed in his Bayard-Condict Building and which New York's building codes resisted, had actually been pioneered a half century

The Bayard-Condict
Building, 65
Bleecker Street;
1897–99. Louis
Sullivan, architect,
was the foremost
figure of the
Chicago School of
architecture and
teacher of Frank
Lloyd Wright.
Angels *(below)* are
exquisitely detailed
beneath the cornice
and surrounded
with rich Art
Nouveau terra-cotta,
in which Sullivan
excelled.

before, only a few blocks south in New York's grand cast-iron ware-houses, shops, and emporiums. The same principles laid the foundations for the "glass cage" on Park Avenue that opened a new era in skyscraper design—the Lever House (1952).

THE GLASS BOX THAT SACRIFICED COMMERCIAL SPACE

The twenty-four-story Lever House is a simple arrangement of rectangular slabs over a light and airy space. A glazed and masonry vertical slab rests on a one-story mezzanine, a horizontal slab, supported by square piers, above a garden at the ground level, which extends to the public sidewalk. An open well over the garden admits light from above and permits a view from below of sky and buildings. The third floor is recessed, setting off the tower from the mezzanine. The top three floors of the tower, housing machinery and equipment, are also visually set off by a horizontal band in the curtain wall, so the whole building retains a reference to the traditional skyscraper design of base, shaft, and capital.

By utilizing only 25 percent of the available air space for its tower, Lever House introduced a new relationship between the skyscraper and its urban setting that has had many imitators. Moreover, the building as a symbol is linked with the visionary architecture of the nineteenth century. An innovation in *architecture parlante*, Lever House is a gigantic advertisement for making "cleanliness commonplace," which was William Hasketh Lever's stated goal as inscribed on a steel plaque on the building. The building itself provides a product demonstration everytime it is cleaned; the glazed curtain walls that surround Lever's slab on three sides are washed down (negotiated by movable scaffolding invented for this function) with the same product Lever markets to clean windows and kitchen fixtures in the home (Handy Andy was used first).

Lever House was the first major building of its designer-architect, Gordon Bunshaft, of Skidmore, Owings, and Merrill (partner, retired). Bunshaft studied architecture at the Massachusetts Institute of Technology, where he was an admirer of Mies van der Rohe. Before joining Louis Skidmore in 1937, he worked with Raymond Loewy and Edward D. Stone in New York.

Innovative design and rich materials are hallmarks of Bunshaft's buildings, and one of his aims has been to promote an architectural vernacular appropriate to his time. His Manufacturers Hanover Trust Building (1954, New York) applied the glass cage to bank design, and the W. R. Grace Building (1973, New York) and the 9 West Fifty-seventh Street Building (1974, New York) introduced the

151

Lever House, 390 Park Avenue; 1952. Designer Gordon Bunshaft
created a glass box *(facing page)* that sacrificed commercial space and
opened a new era in skyscraper design. The glass and stone slab building
rests on giant stiltlike pillars or pilotis *(above)*, creating an open space for
pedestrian circulation.

View from southwest corner of 140 Broadway. Gordon Bunshaft uses
Isamu Noguchi's red cube at 140 Broadway (1969) and Jean Dubuffet's
treelike sculpture (seen in the right background) at Chase Manhattan
Plaza (1961) to relate the two buildings to their environment.

sloping facade as a new solution to the setback to satisfy zoning regulations. As a variant on the blank box, Bunshaft's National Commercial Bank (1982, Jeddah, Saudi Arabia) is an immaculate travertine tower from the outside. An equilateral triangle in plan, it surrounds a central environment with seven floors of glass-walled offices protected from direct sun by deep loggias.

Although best known for his skyscrapers, Bunshaft has said, "I like architecture you don't have to lie on your back to see," which is exemplified in the H. J. Heinz Company plant (1952) in Pittsburgh and the headquarters for the Connecticut General Life Insurance Company (1957, now CIGNA Corporation) in Bloomfield. The Connecticut General Life complex of modern glass cages is adapted to a 250-acre landscaped garden, complete with sculpture and a lake, that is reminiscent of the picturesque tradition. It became influential as a suburban office building type. The American Institute of Architects gave the complex its first honor award in 1958, and numerous other citations have included those from the American Association of Nurserymen and *Administrative Management Magazine*.

The importance of environment applies to his urban projects as well. Although the design for the Chase Manhattan and its plaza (1961, New York) was dictated largely by zoning considerations, aesthetic ones were also significant in relating the plaza to the surrounding area. To emphasize that, Bunshaft favored a vantage point from the southwest corner of 140 Broadway—above which the glazed black tower of the Marine Midland Bank (1967) rises from an ample plaza—where Isamu Noguchi's red perforated cube dramatically punctuates the space. Looking eastward into the Chase plaza, Jean Dubuffet's great treelike sculpture, installed after 140 Broadway was completed, is placed on the axis of Cedar Street, thereby visually uniting these two sites.

Some Highlights of the Past Forty Years

THE GLASS BOX TRANSFORMED

The Secretariat Building of the United Nations, 1950, was New York's first glass curtain wall. The design has been attributed to Le Corbusier, and the commission was the work of an international committee of architects headed by Wallace K. Harrison, one of the architects for Rockefeller Center.

From the Secretariat Building, it was a short step to Lever House (1952) in which the glass cage was applied to a commercial skyscraper. The glass box and open space of the Lever House were to have a longlasting influence on New York architecture. Six years later (1958), Mies van der Rohe, the famous Bauhaus architect, built the Seagram Building in New York, a glass box sheathed in bronze and marble, as the epitome of elegance. The richness and perfection of the Seagram Building could not be replicated; consequently, in the 1960s, the glass box moved in different directions.

Citicorp Center, United Nations Plaza, and the World Trade Center represent the variety of alternatives to the glass box that architects in New York explored in the 1970s. Citicorp Center of 1977, designed by Hugh Stubbins and Associates, was not only an innovative design, but its success was instrumental in bringing about a wave of commercial construction on the East Side. Its great fifty-four-story tower with its distinctive sloping roof, wrapped in a light-colored aluminum skin, rests on four giant piers above a sunken plaza that leads to subway and shops. Reminiscent of Philip Johnson and John Burgee's IDS Center in Minneapolis (1972) in which huge towers of glass surround an enclosed court, Citicorp Center features a retail atrium, the Market.

Kevin Roche and John Dinkeloo's United Nations Plaza of 1976
represents a practical attempt to adapt the glass box to surrounding
structures. The result is a remarkable sculptural form of glass and steel
whose shape shifts from every vantage point as it advances and recedes at
different levels, interpenetrating neighboring structures to the north,
south, east, and west of it. Its skin of blue-green glass picks up the tones
of the Secretariat Building to the east. The slice taken off its southeast
corner echoes the building it faces to the south, a device that has practical
advantages. The angle produced by the slice, for example, creates a more
accessible entrance to the hotel and a more ample walkway beneath the
glass canopy, which gently flares at the base of the Plaza's immaculate skin.

The World Trade Center, 1976, by Minoru
Yamasaki and Emery Roth and Sons follows the
city-within-a-city concept pioneered at
Rockefeller Center but scaled to a new height of
110 stories. Its underground complex of retail
outlets and transportation has enjoyed success.
However, the plaza has been less manageable
for the public. Even though sculpture dots its
enormous expanse, the scale of the plaza is
nonetheless overwhelming, and the thousands
of people who work at the "Twin Towers"
prefer the seemingly shorter underground walk.
Intense wind currents created by the towers are
an added deterrent to pedestrian traffic. Yet the
height has dramatic appeal. Visitors to the top
floors, for example, are still amazed at looking
down on a jetliner flying by beneath them.

The towers create spectacular silhouettes and
relationships to their surroundings, which are
best appreciated from distant vantage points.
Views from the tops of nearby skyscrapers, for
example, reveal the dramatic sculptural
properties of the twin towers and the plaza
nestled beneath them. Singularly engaging are
the views from neighboring boroughs,
exemplified here in the glimpse of the World
Trade Center from the entrance to Green-Wood
Cemetery in Brooklyn (top, right). Here, the
sun's reflection radiates from the flattened
corner of the tower and animates the new
colossus of the Manhattan skyline.

In addition to new heights, the twin towers
introduced technological innovations to
skyscraper design. The skin, for example,
actually bears much of the building's weight.
The conventional skyscraper's steel skeleton
carried the weight of the building to its
foundations, and its cladding hung like a curtain
to keep the bad weather out. But the World
Trade Center towers depart from this
convention, reintroducing the load-bearing wall
(right). Structurally, then, the walls of the towers
resemble the sides of a corrugated box. The new
elevator system made it possible for large
express cabs to carry passengers to sky lobbies at
which point passengers could transfer to local
cars, thereby reducing the number of elevator
shafts needed and saving space. The sky lobbies
are reflected on the surfaces of the towers as
light horizontal bands.

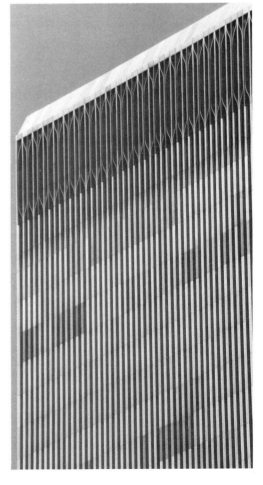

A crisp and elongated motif of ogival arches
surrounds the base and top of each building.
These arches frame the natural light that enters
the main lobbies, but the tops of the arches are
clipped off inside by the mezzanine floors. This
visual interruption distorts the otherwise
dramatic neo-Gothic-like effect.

COMPATIBILITY AND ADAPTABILITY

Some recent skyscraper designs have been criticized because they ignore their surroundings. Eli Attia and Associates' building at 101 Park Avenue, for example *(left)*, a fifty-story tower sheathed in dark glass, is set diagonally on its site and presents an irregular profile, with shapes, textures, and colors that do not repeat the neighboring structures. Attia's irregular shapes that create "wings," or shifted corners, however, provide eight corner offices per floor, with views of the neighborhood and New York's skyline. Although the grand scale of the main entrance to the ninety-foot-high lobby on Fortieth Street is unlike anything nearby, the steps of its deep granite plaza are staggered to conform to the rising hill upon which the building is located, creating easy access to the spacious plaza. Wide granite benches provide ample seating and the fountain and trees further enhance the plaza space. Moreover, the secondary entrance on Forty-first Street has a seventy-foot-high lobby with restaurant and shopping arcade.

Philip Morris World Headquarters (across the street from 101 Park Avenue), 1983, by Ulrich Franzen *(facing page, top),* has a modest twenty-six floors. Franzen's design is a straightforward and recognizable adaptation of a structure to its urban setting. Because the building faces two major thoroughfares on a corner site, Forty-second Street running east and west and Park Avenue running north and south, his challenge was complicated by the presence of the viaduct south of Grand Central Station. The viaduct gives the north-south artery a two-story configuration facing the east facade of the Philip Morris building. Moreover, the high and vertically oriented contemporary buildings along Park Avenue contrast with the low-rise Grand Central Terminal and its neighbors that dominate the area along Forty-second Street, two thoroughfares, then, with two quite different structural and visual characters. To complicate the challenge further, a branch of the Whitney Museum of American Art was to occupy the ground floor of the new Philip Morris headquarters. Franzen adapted his building to this site by simply creating two distinct facades, each shaped by what it faced.

By placing the main entrance of the
Whitney Museum on Forty-second
Street, Franzen could create an
elegant and colossal portico *(above)*
compatible with the great triumphal
arch and Beaux-Arts temple design of
Grand Central Station facing across
the street. The windows and
spandrels above, arranged in
horizontal bands, echo the low-rise
orientation of the neighboring
structures. The Forty-second Street
facade is capped by a loggialike
design that repeats the three giant
stone piers at the entrance below,
thereby creating a well-proportioned
postmodern adaptation of the
Classical tripartite skyscraper
elevation. The Park Avenue facade
(right) combines the high basement,
dictated by the Forty-second Street
entrance, with a window treatment
above that emphasizes verticality.
Square windows are set back from
alternating bold and slender piers.
Above, a band of five rectangular
openings, capped by a broad masonry
fascia and moulded cornice, is aligned
with the Forty-second Street loggia.
The basement is divided into two
horizontal levels by a line that echoes
the roadbed of the viaduct south of
Grand Central Station, which faces it.

The Solomon R. Guggenheim Museum, 1956, by Frank Lloyd Wright *(left)*, remains a tour de force in combining adaptation to a site with artistic independence. The rectangular base of the exterior and the textures of its walls conform the structure to New York's grid and the surrounding buildings. Within is the spiral ramp that Wright designed as early as 1943. He designed and executed numerous structures, incorporating innovative uses of the circular and spiral forms, which include the Greek Orthodox Church (1956), Wauwatosa, Wisconsin; the V. C. Morris Gift Shop, San Francisco (1948); houses for his sons in the 1940s and 1950s; and most notably the Herbert Jacobs House, 1948, Middleton, Wisconsin.

Height, skeletal construction, and the passenger elevator have defined the skyscraper since its birth in the nineteenth century. Within that triad, what the human spirit and imagination have produced has been compared to the great Gothic cathedrals of the Middle Ages. As there is enormous variety in the medieval cathedral so is there in the modern skyscraper, evident in those being built today. One can stand at the corner of Fifty-sixth Street and Madison Avenue, for example, and look up and see three of today's most famous postmodern towers come together overhead like the poles of a gigantic wickiup *(right):* Philip Johnson's AT&T Building, Edward Larrabee Barnes's IBM Tower, and Der Scutt's Trump Tower. These three buildings are ingeniously interconnected physically as well, thereby creating a covered space between Fifth and Madison avenues and from Fifty-fifth to Fifty-seventh streets.

The AT&T Building (near completion) is inspired in part by Romanesque and Gothic forms as well as other familiar historical styles, including Renaissance and eighteenth-century elements. Within the traditional skyscraper elevation of base, shaft, and capital, Johnson has carved out of textured pink granite a base with an arched entrance six stories high. The building is capped with a broken pediment like a bonnet top; that is, a broken arch top common in cabinet furniture between 1730 and 1780. Identified with Thomas Chippendale's use of the motif, Johnson's top has been called a "Chippendale top."

At the rear entrance, a mid-block arcade will be covered by a quarter arch, similar in shape to a Gothic flying buttress, which will provide a covered walkway from Fifty-fifth Street to Fifty-sixth Street. This covered street will lead directly to IBM's covered plaza across the street north.

The three-story-high lobby is groin vaulted and faced with pink granite. The gold-leafed vaulting appears as a great canopy for the colossal gold-leafed figure of Evelyn Longman's "Spirit of Communication," the telephone company symbol, better known as "Golden Boy," the statue that stood atop AT&T's headquarters at 195 Broadway (for which it was designed) and now stands in the center of the new lobby. A massive pink-granite arcade separates the main lobby from an elevator narthex. Oversize bronze-paneled elevator cabs behind marble-arched elevator entrances spirit you up three floors to the sky-lobby reception area, also groin vaulted but lower and broader and faced with white veined marble. From the sky lobby wide hallways and ample stairways lead to conference rooms, offices, elevator banks, and service areas. The grand proportions of these spaces and the exquisite white marble facing are reminiscent of the interiors of AT&T's offices at 195 Broadway designed by William Welles Bosworth.

The IBM Building, 1982, across the street from AT&T is a five-sided forty-three-story tower, clad in dark green granite and green-tinted glass. While its main entrance, a shifted corner at Fifty-seventh Street and Madison Avenue, has been criticized for the absence of any visible support, the device provides a large and convenient covered space. Amenities for the public include a fine arts and science exhibition gallery, a plaza garden, retail shops, and an enclosed street *(pictured below)*.

The plaza garden and street are ingeniously combined so that there is no loss of space, each one flowing into the other. The street, extending through the building from Fifty-sixth Street to Fifty-seventh Street, is covered by a wide illuminated ceiling, one story high.

Although Europe has had covered streets for many centuries, such conveniences have been rare in the United States and have only recently begun to become popular in New York (in part, because the New York City Planning Commission offers developers zoning incentives for such so-called public amenities). One notable exception, however, is the covered walkway of the New York Telephone Company building at 140 West Street between Barclay and Vesey streets, designed by Ralph Walker of Voorhees, Gmelin, and Walker, in 1926, which is still in excellent condition *(pictured above)*. When it was built, the Washington market was across the street, and many telephone company employees shopped there. The covered sidewalk afforded them welcome protection and enriched the architectural form of the street. Guastavino vaulting is used, and Walker took care to relate the decoration of the walkway to the market; fruit, vegetables, and wildlife are carved in the limestone trim *(left)*.

Some imaginative conversions
of old structures have recently
produced successful covered
spaces. For example, the old
Mills House, 1896, at 160
Bleecker Street in Greenwich
Village, built by famous
architect Ernest Flagg for poor
gentlemen, became run-down
and was converted to
apartments in 1976 by
Wechsler, Grasso, Menziuso,
architects. A pair of decorative
paved courtyards, with
lampposts and planters,
covered by skylights are part of
the two atria that replaced the
earlier sixty-foot-square air
shafts *(pictured above)*. Balcony-
hallways *(right)* wrap around
three sides of the eleven-story
rectangular space and overlook
the light and airy courtyard.
The architects' use of the
atrium design in their
conversion inspired the new
name for the building, the
Atrium.

THE ATRIUM

One of the most popular architectural forms to enhance public spaces recently is the atrium. Although the form goes back to antiquity, early Christian times, and the Middle Ages, modern atria differ from the early models, and the term is broadly applied. The Roman atrium was an inner court in a private house. It was rectangular and open to the sky. The Christians adopted the form as an open, usually colonnaded, court in front of their churches.

Today's atria in New York are shaped by their purpose and zoning incentives, as well as by aesthetics. Citicorp's Market (*above*) is a retail atrium three stories high with gourmet shops, restaurants, boutiques, bookstore, and a home-decorating store. The skylight provides abundant natural light, tables and chairs are available to the public, and concerts are a frequent attraction.

Chem Court (*facing page, top*), Chemical Bank's glass-enclosed atrium at 277 Park Avenue, the bank's world headquarters, extends from Forty-seventh Street to Forty-eighth Street along the front of the building. Designed by Haines, Lundberg, Waehler in 1982, the atrium replaced the open concrete plaza of the building's original 1965 design of Emery Roth and Sons. It is an attractive lobby space featuring a picturesque blend of colorful flowers, tropical trees, exotic plants, and cascading pools. The design is by landscape-architect Mark Morrison, and the display is changed seasonally by GLIE Farms.

Chem Court is enclosed by a three-story-high greenhouse of insulating glass set in aluminum framing to maintain proper temperature control. The entrance is paved in dark gray granite, the same stone used for the planters, which are connected to a submerged irrigation and fertilizing system.

The Trump Tower atrium at Fifty-sixth Street and Fifth Avenue *(right)* was designed by Der Scutt of Swanke, Hayden, Connell, and Partners. Six balconied floors extend around three sides of the atrium that faces a five-story illuminated waterfall cascading down a wall of red marble and overlooking a dining area below. Shops, boutiques, and specialty stores open off the balconies and their extended walkways. All the visible surfaces are faced with rich materials, mostly warm red marble or bronze surfaces, either reflective or transparent, which gives the atrium the appearance of being larger than it is. Live piano and violin music and uniformed doormen contribute to the Trump Tower's distinct character. The atrium features a shopping arcade that connects with Bonwit Teller department store and IBM's garden plaza, an amenity that allowed more floor space for the tower above, which pays for the atrium space.

The sixty-eight-story mixed-use tower for retail stores and luxury apartments has an irregular silhouette, somewhat similar to that of 101 Park Avenue, created by a succession of setbacks that provide more corner spaces and a greater variety of views of the city.

Equitable Center, Seventh Avenue between 51st and 52nd streets, Edward Larrabee Barnes, architect, 1985. Photo: Tim Hursley © The Equitable.

EQUITABLE CENTER:
PARADIGM OF "INVESTMENT REAL ESTATE"

Equitable Center is one of the largest and most comprehensive collaborations of architecture, urban planning, and public art since Rockefeller Center, built more than 50 years ago, which it emulates and of which it is an extension. It consists of two corporate towers, a through-block galleria, an atrium, a museum, shops, plazas, restaurants, below-ground concourses, a theater and art galleries, and corporate collections of painting and sculpture.

The center was born of Equitable's need to develop its real estate holdings on the West Side. The company leveled the declining properties along Seventh Avenue between Fifty-first and Fifty-second streets, such as the old Abbey-Victoria Hotel, and raised a new tower in 1985 west of its former headquarters building at 1285 Avenue of the Americas. The first major corporation to build its headquarters on Seventh Avenue, The Equitable Financial Companies converted the entire block from Fifty-first to Fifty-second streets and from Avenue of the Americas to Seventh Avenue into the cultural complex it has christened Equitable Center.

The center was planned to improve the character of Seventh Avenue and act as "a magnet attracting people from Seventh Avenue and Avenue of the Americas and an anchor for development in the area." Soon after the center opened in 1987, Equitable had already enlarged that anchor with the improvement of its own properties adjacent to the center. Renovation of the old Taft Hotel across the street south of the center on Seventh Avenue between Fiftieth and Fifty-first streets produced Executive Plaza, a luxury hotel-condominium complex. The facades of City Squire Hotel to the west and the Sheraton Centre to the north of Equitable Center were cleaned and both hotels were renovated.

Equitable Center is the first development to link Avenue of the Americas and Seventh Avenue through the total integration of architecture, public art, and urban planning. It therefore extends the commercial and cultural life of Rockefeller Center another block westward and is a tribute to John D. Rockefeller's vision.

Rockefeller Center and the West Side

On November 1, 1939, when John D. Rockefeller drove a silver rivet in the steel skeleton of the U.S. Rubber Company Building (now Simon & Schuster Building) on Sixth Avenue marking the completion of Rockefeller Center, a new concept in urban planning was celebrated, and the future of the West Side was assured. When

169

the center was begun in 1931 (see Chapter 13), few people shared Rockefeller's vision that tawdry Sixth Avenue, obscured by the "El" (until 1939), its buildings covered with grime from soot-belching locomotives, could one day be a thriving revenue-producing thoroughfare. Yet, the designers of Rockefeller Center succeeded in extending Fifth Avenue respectability to Sixth Avenue, and by 1973, the wall of high rises on the west side of Avenue of the Americas confirmed Rockefeller's confidence in the commercial potential of the West Side.

Faintly echoing the lines of Rockefeller Center's original complex of buildings, the new slabs and their sites were also shaped by the zoning regulations of 1961, and they feature fountains, plazas, and walkways, the so-called amenities that provide the public with light and air and the developers with additional rental space. Those slabs west of Avenue of the Americas, however, lack the unified design of architecture, public art, and urban planning that characterizes Rockefeller Center. Now with the comprehensive plan of Equitable Center, those principles of organization and design that made Rockefeller Center a commercial and aesthetic success are being employed once again. Equitable Center not only provides a model for unification of the slabs along Avenue of the Americas but also is a guide for commercial expansion westward.

America's First Skyscraper

In addition to reviving the principles of innovative planning established by the designers of Rockefeller Center, Equitable continues its practice of supporting progressive architectural design, a tradition that goes back to the nineteenth century. Equitable's first building at 120 Broadway (1868–70), by distinguished architect George B. Post, was also America's first skyscraper. Twice as tall as the average commercial building at the time, it rose 130 feet. By realizing the possibilities of the passenger elevator, the Equitable Assurance Society Building became the first building to break the height barrier to commercial architecture, and the skyscraper was born.

Post's building was destroyed by fire in 1912, but Equitable had rebuilt on the same site by 1915. Architect Ernest R. Graham's design for Equitable's new headquarters was another first. Graham provided his client with 1.2 million square feet of floor space on almost an acre of land, an unprecedented exploitation of a site, which produced a colossus undreamed of before. It also produced a panic that contributed to New York City's first comprehensive zoning regulation just one year later. Faced with the possibility of even larger buildings, terrified New Yorkers were convinced that one day the city would be without light and air—isolated and strangled by ever-higher walls of stone. So the city adopted what became known as the "setback law," which produced the "wedding cake" or "ziggurat" skyscraper style that prevailed from the 1920s to the 1950s. Based on the width of the street, a building would set back at specified intervals, which would not only admit light and air to the street but also create a uniform facade or street wall.

In 1924, Equitable moved its headquarters to 393 Seventh Avenue, next door to the new Pennsylvania Hotel (now the Penta Hotel), to become a part of McKim, Mead, and White's new and distinguished classical precinct surrounding the celebrated and elegant Penn Station, whose waiting room had been fashioned on the Baths of Caracalla of ancient Rome. The same pioneering spirit prompted Equitable's move to 1285 Avenue of the Americas in 1961 to be among the first corporations to extend Rockefeller Center west of Avenue of the Americas. The noted architectural firm of Skidmore Owings and Merrill designed a glass box for Equitable's new headquarters, which influenced skyscraper design along Avenue of the Americas in the 1960s and 1970s. The building was incorporated into Equitable Center in 1985 and re-named the PaineWebber Building for Equitable's major tenant.

In the Rockefeller Tradition

As Rockefeller Center had to change the character of Sixth Avenue in the 1930s to attract and hold tenants who would pay the rents that the center needed in order to prosper, so Equitable Center set out to change the character of Seventh Avenue in the 1980s to achieve the same ends. Its architects have employed some of the same devices employed at Rockefeller Center to accomplish this.

As the RCA Building tower, the centerpiece of Rockefeller Center, was extended west to provide Sixth Avenue with an elegant facade (called RCA Building West), bringing Fifth Avenue respectability to the west side, so Equitable raised its new tower on Seventh Avenue west of its 1961 building on Avenue of the Americas to push the commercial frontier another block west. Recalling Rockefeller Center's shop-lined corridors and concourses, but on a grander scale, Equitable Center's architects designed an 800-foot-long covered street lined with shops and galleries set off with lattices and mahogany paneling that links the lobbies of the new tower on Seventh Avenue and the PaineWebber Building on Avenue of the Americas. The covered street intersects a through-block galleria between Fifty-first and Fifty-second streets, where an escalator leads to the lower concourse that connects the two buildings with Rockefeller Center and the subway.

As Rockefeller Center was the product of a battery of leading architects, designers, and artists of the 1930s, so Equitable Center was shaped by a cadre of leading talents of the 1980s. Skidmore Owings and Merrill renovated and modernized its 1961 building for PaineWebber; Edward Larrabee Barnes designed the new tower and art complex on Seventh Avenue; and Kohn Pedersen Fox Conway designed the executive floors above the 34th floor.

Equitable's New Tower

Barnes's 51-story tower rises nine stories above the old headquarters and is set off by an eight-story wing to the east and a five-story wing to the west facing Seventh Avenue. Its ziggurat top with triumphal arches creates a new identity on the Manhattan skyline. Enhancing the tower's distinction, the base of the building on the Fifty-first and Fifty-second streets sides are set back ten feet, thereby widening the sidewalks, recalling Rockefeller Center's wide sidewalks, an innovation in the 1930s. The widened sidewalk is of pink granite in a thermal finish, which creates a distinctive texture that extends from Seventh Avenue to Avenue of the Americas uniting Equitable's sidewalk with PaineWebber's urban plazas.

Skidmore Owings and Merrill's 1961 open spaces on the north and south sides of the PaineWebber Building have been redesigned by sculptor Scott Burton as Urban Plaza North and Urban Plaza South to provide accommodations for people to meet. Urban Plaza South is furnished with permanently installed stools and tables of green granite, like a sidewalk cafe in sculpture. At the southeast corner of the plaza, teak benches provide additional seating and a park-like accent to the space. The benches line triangular planters that are filled with Sargent Weeping Hemlock trees selected by landscape architect Kevin Gerard. Rectangular benches of green granite in Urban Plaza North are arranged randomly, which creates an informal space that encourages sociability within the otherwise congested cityscape.

In keeping with zoning regulations, Equitable's new tower on Seventh Avenue sets back from the side streets at the twelfth, thirty-fourth, and fiftieth floors in fourteen-foot increments, echoing the setbacks of the RCA and International buildings in Rockefeller Center. Barnes's flat grid of limestone and polished Brazilian red granite picks up the limestone towers of Rockefeller Center and the blond brick bands of City Squire Hotel to the west and the Sheraton Centre to the north, and blends with the clean lines of the PaineWebber Building to the east.

Double floors, each one two feet higher than the office floors, are located at the setbacks to accommodate corporate and mechanical functions and at the same time to enhance the tower's design. The windows of the double floors are recessed, which creates the illusion of rows of colossal piers whose alternating vertical accents of light and shade serve to unite the two floors and to articulate the setbacks. This sculptural device provides the spectator with a visual transition at each setback, relating the building to the Art Deco towers that populate the West Side.

The higher windows of the double floors extend along the front (west) and back (east) facades of the tower to reflect the side street setbacks, a subtle reference to the ziggurat-style skyscrapers common on the West Side. Rows of colossal piers along the sidewalk at the base of the building echo those at the setbacks above, unifying the tower and establishing a monumental scale at ground level.

Crowning the front and back facades, triumphal arches reflect the great vaulted spaces within for private and public corporate functions atop the tower. Originally, the openings were designed to be simple oculi (round openings, literally eyes), but triumphal arches opened up the wall more amply in order to provide the abundance of natural light those corporate spaces needed.

The Equitable Assurance Society and Public Art

Equitable developed an art program that would enhance its prestige, unify the complex, and attract tenants, a device it called "investment real estate," in which Equitable, its tenants, and the public alike benefit. Its $7 million art program includes painting, sculpture, design, and restoration and extends to Equitable's atrium, the through-block galleria, PaineWebber's urban plazas, Palio Restaurant, Equitable's health club, the lobby of the First National Bank of Chicago, and Equitable's fifteen dining rooms and corporate spaces. Moreover, twin galleries that flank the atrium and face Seventh Avenue feature exhibits of contemporary art and gallery talks free for the public.

Roy Lichtenstein's "Mural with Blue Brushstroke," and Scott Burton's "Atrium Furnishment" set the tone of the atrium and provide the visitor with a transition from monumental to human scale in the five-story-high skylit atrium.

A grand stairway from the atrium leads to the underground 495-seat theater/auditorium, also accessible by elevators, for film, concerts, and drama.

"Atrium Furnishment" is a forty-foot semicircular bench in polished green marble with onyx and lights. It faces a circular pond also of polished green marble containing various water plants. An arc of tropical conifers picks up the shape of the bench, an 11-inch wide broken circle of polished bronze set into the floor frames the bench

173

Equitable Center, view into atrium with Roy Lichtenstein's "Mural with Blue Brushstroke" and Scott Burton's "Atrium Furnishment." Photo: Tim Hursley @ The Equitable.

and the pond, and occasional square red granite pavers surround the circular enclosure.

Lichtenstein's "Mural with Blue Brushstroke" relates Equitable Center to its urban context through a complex iconography of inter-related forms and images. On entering the tall atrium of the center, Lichtenstein's mural (68 feet high and 32 feet wide) dominates the wall facing Seventh Avenue just as the great sixteenth- and seventeenth-century frescoes and altarpieces command their spaces in Renaissance and Baroque churches. Lichtenstein has acknowledged his debt to Renaissance and Baroque art, especially in the way the mural is divided into an upper and a lower realm—"like heaven and hell," he mused, relegating Matisse, Leger, Kelly, and Johns to heaven and Braque and Stella to hell.

The mural is an homage to Pop Art, and it celebrates Equitable Center as a link between Rockefeller Center and the city's commercial expansion westward. Borrowing details from a selection of paintings by such modern masters as Leger, Braque, and Matisse, Lichtenstein illustrates the origins of Pop Art in cubism and collage and its dialogue with the abstract and figural traditions. The figure at upper left with ball is from Fernand Leger's "The Dance," the balustrade silhouette at lower center from Georges Braque's "The Balluster," and the fernlike form at the center edge to the left is from Matisse's "Music."

Lichtenstein's own pioneering role in the Pop Art movement is surveyed and celebrated in references to his "Knock Knock" in the doors at the bottom center, "Placid Sea" in the radiant sun at the top, and "Still Life with Red Wine" in the orange at the lower center of the composition. The isolated abstract painting at lower left is from his "Artist's Studio—Foot Medication."

Lichtenstein acknowledges the influences of his contemporaries —Frank Stella, in the protractor at the lower right from "Dove of Tanna," Jasper Johns, in the fractured cubes from "End Paper," directly above the protractor, and Ellsworth Kelly, in the green rectangle at upper right from "Red Blue Green." Willem De Kooning's "Greece on 8th Avenue" is the source of the great blue brushstroke that gives Lichtenstein's mural its name.

A picture frame, architectural molding from a building in lower Manhattan, and a contemporary advertisement remind the spectator that the stuff of Pop Art is the reproduction of everyday objects from advertisements and comic strips. It is through just such an enlargement, a woman's hand holding a sponge, that the meaning of Lichtenstein's mural emerges. The hand with sponge appears to wipe away part of the mural and reveal windows behind the canvas on which the mural is painted. It is as if the band of windows in the atrium extends behind the mural and can now be seen as the hand wipes away the mural.

The mural's windows repeat the windows of the galleries' twin facades on Seventh Avenue and pick up the ribbon windows of the Sheraton Centre facade across the street, visible through the atrium skylight. Lichtenstein's revelation is not only that the architect's treatment of the windows is a way to unify his tower and relate it to the surrounding architecture. These gridlike windows also reveal the influence of the Bauhaus on the tower's design, a reference to the architect's orientation. Edward Larrabee Barnes studied architecture at Harvard with Marcel Breuer, who had studied and taught

175

at the Bauhaus. Lichtenstein has spoken of how the architecture of a building for which he designs a mural can provide him with forms he uses to compose his murals. The same principle connects Lichtenstein's mural with the art program at Rockefeller Center.

The hand wiping away the mural echoes sculptor Lee Lawrie's "Wisdom Interpreting the Cosmic Forces of Sound and Light" above the entrance to the RCA Building. The sweep of Wisdom's compass across the clouds is repeated in Lichtenstein's swipe of the hand with sponge wiping away the mural, and De Kooning's blue brushstroke that partially frames the swipe and that gives Lichtenstein's mural its name repeats the cloud shape Lawrie uses in the RCA Building relief.

Lichtenstein's rectangular format, individual panels, unusually wide range of color, and the Leger figure from which the sun radiates relate his mural to Lawrie's colorful International Building limestone panel above the entrance at 25 West Fiftieth Street in which Mercury surveys mankind's progress from feudalism to capitalism and enlightenment through the arts, sciences, and technology. Above Mercury at the top of Lawrie's open relief, a radiant sun serves as the face of a clock, and narrative elements are arranged in panels beneath.

Lichtenstein frames the detail of the hand wiping away the mural to reveal the windows behind with a classical Greek column on the left and De Kooning's blue brushstroke on the right from his painting, "Greece on 8th Avenue." The mural faces toward Eighth Avenue. The only thing related to ancient Greece there was the now demolished Adonis Theater, between Fiftieth and Fifty-first streets, which was then scheduled for demolition to make way for another high rise. Looking through Lichtenstein's windows from the other side and gazing westward, the Adonis was clearly visible then. Directly beneath the windows is the closed door from Lichtenstein's painting "Knock Knock" (the words were deleted in the mural against the artist's wishes). The door is the threshold on Seventh Avenue of the ideas begun at Rockefeller Center and embodied in Equitable Center that will continue to move westward, symbolized by the razing of the Adonis Theater.

"America Today"

Roy Lichtenstein's "Mural with Blue Brushstroke" makes formal and symbolic connections between Equitable Center and Rockefeller Center. "America Today," the mural by Thomas Hart Benton that stretches for ninety-five feet along the wall of Equitable Center's north corridor, establishes a thematic connection between the two art programs. In fact, Benton was one of the artists considered to

"City Building," *America Today,* Thomas Hart Benton, painter, 1930. From the collection of the Equitable Life Assurance Society of the U.S.

paint murals for Rockefeller Center, but "American Today," the mural that Equitable has called a keystone in its art program, decided the jury against Benton because his realism was "too strident."

"America Today" was unveiled on January 15, 1931, in the New School for Social Research at 66 West Twelfth Street. Commissioned for the third-floor boardroom of Joseph Urban's celebrated Art Deco building of 1930, it depicts life in the 1920s in nine panels that wrap around the thirty-foot-square room. A tenth panel was added in 1931 over the entrance to the boardroom. Joseph Urban, architect of the Ziegfeld Theater (1927–28) and scenic designer for the Ziegfeld Follies and the Metropolitan Opera, wanted a mural that "didn't stay on the wall." The restrained moldings and clean lines of Urban's boardroom provided the perfect setting for Benton's writhing figures played out against his undulating landscapes, panoplies of cityscapes, and industrial settings. Paired windows overlooking the New School garden and cove lighting concealed by the ceiling molding provided the illumination that set Benton's scenes in motion like tableaux vivants, whose figures recall those of the Ashcan School or urban realists. "America Today" was an immediate success and had a profound influence on the extensive mural program sponsored by the WPA in the 1930s. It marked the immediate rise of Thomas Hart Benton's career.

"America Today" captured the spirit of the country during a decade of promise, from the street scenes of the big cities to the regional panoramas of the farming belts and from the territorial expansion of the Midwest to the technological might of industrial centers.

Two panels, "Deep South" and "City Building" were on either side of the boardroom, facing each other, and in that position illustrated America's move from the country to the city, from primitive to advanced technology. The crowning achievement of that transition from rural to urban development for Benton was the skyscraper. Benton concurred with historians and chroniclers of social change who recognized the skyscraper as the most significant architectural form since the Gothic cathedral. In Benton's view, it was "the first effort of the American spirit to give itself an original monumental expression."

By the time Benton finished the mural, he was struck by the reality of the Great Depression, so he painted the tenth panel, which he placed above the boardroom entrance. This narrow horizontal panel portrays four pairs of hands in friezelike fashion against the image of a poorhouse in the background. The hands of the destitute reach out for bread and coffee while the hands of financial manipulators clutch fistfuls of dollar bills. "Outstretching Hands," as Benton called the panel, underscores the painter's criticism of the inequalities of capitalism that he felt produced the Depression. Because this panel is not organically linked to the others and was an afterthought of the artist, it is exhibited on the opposite wall in Equitable's north corridor.

Benton's mural portrays the social conditions of the 1920s and celebrates the country's anticipation of a better tomorrow through technology and industrialization. Rockefeller Center's program embodies a similar theme. A principal difference is that Benton's imagery is tied more closely to the everyday world and his figures are portrayed in an earthy strident realism, whereas the imagery of Rockefeller Center is more idealized. While Benton portrays farmers, straphangers, circus acrobats, bartenders, and factory workers, Rockefeller Center's program features Prometheus, Atlas, Wisdom, Truth, and personifications of virtue and power. Even such historical figures as St. Francis of Assisi and Abraham Lincoln have the status of mythological figures in the Rockefeller Center program.

Serendipity and Restoration

Equitable's purchase of "America Today" may be called a case of corporate serendipity. After the mural's unveiling in 1931, the boardroom was eventually converted to a classroom, and the murals were subjected to soil and damage. Thomas Hart Benton himself restored the mural in 1957 and again in 1968. By the 1970s, the mural was again in need of restoration, but the New School could no longer afford to maintain the mural and exhibit it properly. So, they looked for a buyer. In 1984, the office of the Mayor and private citizens interested in the preservation of the city's heritage sought a home for Benton's masterpiece. It was at that time that Equitable was purchasing art for the new center. When they learned of the availability of "America Today," it seemed like just the right addition to the center.

The mural needed extensive restoration before it could be installed, which required a thorough analysis of its composition and structure. Research by conservators at the Williamstown Regional Art Conservation Laboratory into Benton's technique of egg tempera, the medium in which the mural was painted, and their examination of the paint surface and the board on which the mural was painted produced a substantial body of technical information necessary to restore the mural. At the same time, an extensive study by art historians of the origins of the commission and of Benton's ideas related to it and expressed in the mural revealed an aspect of Benton's art that had been either overlooked or inadequately studied.

Long acknowledged as one of America's foremost Regionalist painters of rural life in America, Benton emerged from this new research as a canny social critic of the industrialization of America whose mural "America Today" had a profound influence on the mural movement in America in the 1930s. Recognizing the value of this new information to conservators, art historians, specialists in related fields, and the interested public, Equitable funded a catalogue to provide those groups with a permanent record of the conservational and art historical research on the mural. Equitable also funded a colloquium at Williams College in 1985 to encourage scholarly discussion of the mural, and it funded an exhibition there to acquaint the general public with the project.

Art and Space

Three environmental works in Equitable Center are remarkable for their power and their variety. The swimming pool in the Equitable Center health club, entered at the foot of the escalator from the galleria, features a mosaic tile mural seventy-two feet long and

179

Detail of *Palio*, Sandro Chia, painter, 1985. Photo: Gianfranco Gorgoni © The Equitable.

twelve feet high by Valerie Jaudon. (Jaudon's subway gates at the Lexington Avenue and Twenty-third Street station and her design for Police Plaza have received critical acclaim.) Running almost the full length of the pool area, thin black lines create a web of arcs, diagonals, right angles, and dotted lines against a field of blue and aquamarine grids. The clean lines against the simple but pure color field combine to create an almost serene environment.

For the bar in the Palio Restaurant designed by Raul de Armas of Skidmore Owings and Merrill just off the galleria, Florentine painter Sandro Chia re-created the centuries-old horse race in Siena, Italy, for which the restaurant is named. The pageantry, drama, and color of the biannual event is spread over the four walls of the bar's intimate space above the wainscoting so that the entire drama from the opening parade, to the race, the award ceremonies, and the ritual victory celebration can be seen from any place in the bar without interference. Every square inch of the mural is covered with animated figures, period costumes, heraldic banners, and flags.

Chia's colorful palette is dominated by a wide range of reds, and his figures virtually dance in the subtle lighting of the bar.

Agnes Denes was commissioned to create an environment for the entrance lobby to the First National Bank of Chicago's New York headquarters just off the galleria. Literally with mirrors and light, she transformed the small lobby into a world of limitless space. Bronzed mirrors panel the walls to create a muted illusion of infinity. Plantings at the elevator and a security desk at the entrance to the space appear to float beneath the tour de force of the design, its ceiling mural—"Hypersphere: The Earth in the Shape of the Universe." Etched in 144 frosted glass panels is a map of the earth in which the continents are re-shaped into the configuration of Einstein's universe. The map is illuminated from behind the glass, and the fixtures that bind the panels together are visible. The effect is of a grid through which the visitor sees Einstein's universe miraculously floating above, which heightens the sense of infinity.

Equitable has extended its commitment to art beyond the art program for its public spaces. Through favorable rents and corporate assistance, Equitable encouraged the formation of the Arts Resources Consortium at Equitable Center to support artists. It consists of Volunteer Lawyers for the Arts, Center for Arts Information, and the American Council for the Arts. Free legal assistance, information on grants, insurance, loft space, and arts resources are available to artists at the consortium. The New York branch of the Archives of American Art, whose mission it is to collect and preserve archives relating to the visual arts in America, also has its offices at Equitable Center.

AMERICAS TOWER

As Equitable Center extended commercial life west of Rockefeller Center to Seventh Avenue, the fifty-story Americas Tower, constructed in 1991, at 1177 Avenue of the Americas extends Corporate Row south from Rockefeller Center to Forth-fifth Street. Occupying the last available full blockfront on Avenue of the Americas, from Forth-fifth to Forty-sixth streets on the west side, Americas Tower acts as an anchor to the great row of office buildings that includes Exxon, McGraw-Hill, Time & Life, and PaineWebber. Its link to Rockefeller Center is underscored visually by Swanke Hayden Connell's design. Echoing the Art Deco setbacks of the center's great limestone piles, unlike the sheer slabs of Corporate Row, Americas Tower is clad in alternating bands of Finnish coral granite, tinted glass, and gray aluminum spandrel panels. Its tapered crown,

Americas Tower, 1177 Avenue of the Americas, Swanke Hayden Connell, architects, 1991. Photo © 1993 Andrew Gordon.

Americas Tower, National Sculpture Society Gallery, 15th floor.

Below, view of lobby.

182

Worldwide Plaza, view toward Eighth Avenue.

visible from Long Island, the Fifty-ninth-Street Bridge, and La Guardia airport, asserts its place on the West Side skyline with rare distinction. Samba pink granite plaza-like sidewalks extend around the building's perimeter, and a blend of thermal and polished granite floors and walls, dramatic lighting, and burnished steel and glass appointments enhance the tower's three-story-high museumlike lobby, home of The Lobby Sculpture Gallery.

A corporate/arts partnership between the National Sculpture Society and KG A&A Corporation, owner of Americas Tower, in the spirit of Rockefeller Center and Equitable Center, the gallery is a permanent showcase for year-round revolving exhibitions by Americas Tower and the National Sculpture Society. The society, which has its headquarters and gallery on the fifteenth floor of the building, was founded in 1893 and is the oldest organization of professional sculptors in the United States.

SYMBOL OF SOCIAL CHANGE

The commercial press westward took on a social role in the 1980s. The Worldwide Plaza complex, a 49-story office tower adjoined to a 39-story condominium, a group of five- and six-story condominium townhouses, a movie theater, retail spaces, and an

Worldwide Plaza, Eighth to Ninth Avenues, West 49th to West 50th streets, office tower, Skidmore, Owings, and Merrill, 1989; apartment tower, Frank Williams, 1989.

Worldwide Plaza, view of movie theater and condominium tower and town houses.

underground garage, on the site of the old Madison Square Garden, has been called a symbol of social change that is taking place in the Clinton preservation district. Located just west of the theater district and Times Square, from Eighth Avenue to the Hudson River, from Forty-third to Fifty-seventh streets, it includes much of the old Hell's Kitchen neighborhood, where crime and destruction continue to impede development. William Zeckendorf, Jr., agreed to renovate 132 units of low- and moderate-income apartments in return for developing the complex. The renovations are judged inadequate by some tenants, and critics complain that upgrading the neighborhood through the development of Worldwide Plaza is driving out the poor and increasing the homeless population in New York City.

Worldwide Plaza was not the first effort to infuse new life into the Clinton neighborhood. Manhattan Plaza, for example, designed by David Todd Associates in 1977, a subsidized rental complex of 1,688 apartments attracting many theater people, was conceived to generate redevelopment of the district at its southern end along Theater Row. With its 45-story twin towers, Manhattan Plaza acts as an anchor to the district, whose buildings above Forty-third Street are restricted by zoning to seven stories in height.

185

The Strand, Tenth Avenue and 42nd Street, Costas Kandylis, architect, 1988. Architect's model.

THE STRAND

Against that backdrop, a 41-story condominium was erected in 1988 at Tenth Avenue and Forty-second Street in the midst of Theater Row. It was therefore dubbed by its creator, Arun Bhatia, a Bombay-born engineer, the Strand at West Cross to recall the Strand in London's West End, famous for its theaters.

The Strand occupies a 25,000-square-foot site directly west of Manhattan Plaza. To capitalize on the panoramic views of the Hudson River and the surrounding open vistas, Bhatia's architect, Costas Kandylis, designed a tower soaring above the low-rise buildings around it, cut at the corners in a diamond shape and set at a 45-degree angle, breaking away from the traditional north-south axis. Each unit's wraparound windows, with balconies integrated into the diamond shape of the building, provide the tenant with multiple views and a sense of spaciousness not found in traditional rectangular configurations. Some apartments command views of 270 degrees.

At the base of the tower, commercial frontage respects the street wall and lines up with the sidewalk, while a triangular landscaped plaza at the corner articulates the residential entrance. Kandylis's stepped crown of colored horizontal banding is a logical resolution to his tower's formal and tonal accents. With its vertical spine and alternating bands of glass and modulations of red brick, Kandylis's skin recalls the great Art Deco towers of the 1930s. He was particularly conscious of the McGraw-Hill Building of 1931 by Raymond

Hood on West Forty-second Street with its green terra-cotta tower and strong vertical accent, and the Starrett-Lehigh Building also of 1931, by R. G. and W. M. Cory, the great beige pile of banded glass and brick on West Twenty-sixth Street.

GENTRIFICATION AND SOCIAL DIVERSITY

As with Worldwide Plaza, the tall tower is a symbol of William Zeckendorf, Jr.'s forays into gentrification in Union Square also. In exchange for building a 625-apartment condominium and office complex, the city of New York renovated Union Square Park, driving out the drug dealers and returning the park to the people. Four towers, completed in 1987, rise from a six-story street wall, facing Union Square Park. Landscaping, subway kiosks, luminaires, and paving opened up the park. A green market three days a week attracts people to the park, who are willing to pay inflated prices for produce, flowers, pastries, and refreshments, which provides another mode of continuous use by a neighborhood elite.

Community groups in dialogue with city officials and developers, however, are lobbying to retain a social and ethnic diversity in the neighborhood and to develop moderate- and low-cost housing. The greatest impediment to workable solutions here appears to be the sheer number of community groups that converge in the Union Square area, which produces unending jurisdictional conflicts on all matters, including housing. Adjacent to seven neighborhoods, with representation of five community boards, three congressional districts, and four senate districts, it is little wonder that consensus in housing issues is difficult to achieve.

A twelve-story apartment house on East Thirteenth Street for homeless and low-income families tied in with the development of a retail complex on adjacent Fourteenth Street may serve as a model for the area. Called Genesis Apartments at Union Square, it includes medical care, day care, recreation, and counseling for tenants, and is funded by the city and state and sponsored by Housing Enterprise for the Less Privileged (HELP), a nonprofit organization. The project is not without its critics, however, who oppose the project. They say it is an illegal use of public money, which would be better spent purchasing and restoring existing apartments. In spite of legal action, Genesis management expects the project to be completed by 1995.

Numerous groups in the city, with private, state, local, and federal assistance in various combinations, are improving neighborhoods through renovation, restoration, and rebuilding for low-income families, as well. For example, in Brooklyn, the Southside United

187

Zeckendorf Towers, 1 Irving Place, from 14th to 15th streets at Union Square, Davis, Brody, and Associates, 1987. Consolidated Edison's majestic clock tower and World War I memorial, once clearly visible from Union Square Park, is now almost totally eclipsed by Zeckendorf's towers.

Green Market at Union Square Park, Barry Benepe, architect and planner, 1987.

327 St. Nicholas Avenue,
formerly P.S. 157, 126th
Street and St. Nicholas
Avenue, Charles B.J. Snyder,
architect, 1896–99;
converted to moderate- and
low-income housing, 1980s.

Housing Development Fund Corporation, popularly known as Las
Sures (Spanish for Southside), has renovated more than 1,000 abandoned derelict buildings in the Williamsburg section, manages
1,100 others, and at the end of 1993, had 157 new units under
construction.

At One Hundred Twenty-sixth Street and St. Nicholas Avenue,
P.S. 157, vacated in 1975, was renovated and converted into moder-
ate- and low-income housing in the late 1980s through a joint venture of New York State, the Harlem Urban Development Corporation, and New York City's Department of Housing, Preservation,
and Development. Tenants are exposed to some of the riches of architectural history. The building, designed by Charles B. J. Snyder,
was erected between 1896 and 1899 in a Renaissance Revival style.
Of limestone, terra-cotta, and light gray brick, historians have noted
that the gables and dormers and general massing of the five-story
building recall the riches of French and Flemish design of the sixteenth century.

In East Harlem in the closing months of 1993, El Barrio's Operation Fightback renovated three derelict buildings, producing forty-
five new low-income units, and completed renovation on four other
buildings of thirty-seven units. Moreover, the city's Housing, Preservation, and Development agency selected Fightback to manage an
additional four rehabilitated city-owned buildings.

El Barrio's Operation Fightback was the outgrowth of a community battle against local drug dealers. In 1983, a group of concerned
residents of East Harlem, in conjunction with local elected officials,

189

succeeded in recapturing tenements from entrenched drug dealers, and in 1985, El Barrio's Operation Fightback was incorporated to continue its work. Under its executive director Gus Rosado, Fightback has expanded its range of services to East Harlem families and individuals to include building management, rehabilitation, and a range of social services. Its Pleasantville Youth Center, for example, opened in November 1993, at 320 Pleasant Avenue in a building that Fightback had renovated. Its first project was a multidisciplinary program of science and art, produced by The Monuments Conservancy in cooperation with the American Museum of Natural History and the Erick Hawkins Dance Foundation. An anthropologist, dancers, sculptors, and historians of art and dance introduced a group of fifth- and sixth-graders to fundamental concepts of the human figure and its expression in the arts of dance and sculpture. Continued instruction in the arts and the humanities will be part of its ongoing program.

"The Castle"

Restoration of an old Beaux-Arts mansion in 1989 also revived the building's original mission—to care for needy children. Situated above the valley of Macombs Dam Park and Yankee Stadium at 936 Woodycrest Avenue near Jerome Avenue in the Bronx, the building was built in 1902 to the designs of William Burnett Tuthill, best known as the architect of Carnegie Hall. This great pile of gray stone and brick with terra-cotta ornament and imposing dormers set in a grand mansard lacking its original copper crestings was built by the American Female Guardian Society and Home for the Friendless as a home to provide medical, spiritual, and educational care for destitute children. Following the society's move to Rockland County in 1974, and a succession of owners, the building fell into disrepair until Housing and Services, Inc. and Highbridge Community Life Center, Inc., with assistance from the city of New York, purchased the building and renovated it as Highbridge Woodycrest Center, Inc., to provide a residential health care facility in uplifting surroundings for families with children as well as single adults with HIV illness. "The Castle," as it is called in the neighborhood, has 19 two-bedroom apartments, 23 single rooms, on-site primary health care, dining room, children's day care center, activities room, and a Japanese garden, designed by landscape architect Barbara Schaedler and executed by landscape gardener Lou Contini. Through sensitive design, restoration architect Donald Sclare was able to retain much of the original architectural ornament and the mansion's grand staircase, while meeting the state's health code.

Highbridge Woodycrest Center, 936 Woodycrest Avenue, near Jerome Avenue, Bronx; formerly, American Female Guardian Society and Home for the Friendless, William Burnett Tuthill, 1902; restoration, Donald Sclure, architect, 1989. Photo: Housing & Services, Inc.

Highbridge Woodycrest Center, Tuthill's original staircase, during restoration; staircase has been retained. Photo: Housing & Service, Inc.

Queens Landmark condominiums, originally Bulova Watch Factory, 62-10 Woodside Avenue, between 62nd and 63rd streets, Queens; erected by Arde Bulova, 1926; converted to condominiums, Ralph Wuest, 1985.

The Character of the City Expressed in Its Conversions

There is hardly a building type in New York City that has not been converted into a new use. A sampling illustrates the variety of New York City's conversions and the artistry and originality that often come into play in their conception. While many conversions sensitively retain the historical character of the original structure, there are those that destroy it. The old Bulova Watch factory at 62-10 Woodside Avenue in Queens, for example, built in 1926 by Arde Bulova, was converted into apartments and retail space in 1989, its ornament emasculated and its famous clock tower removed.

That same year, architect Kenneth Halpern, in a playful mood, converted the old World Champion Sports Corporation building at 110 Clifton Place in the Clinton Hill neighborhood of Brooklyn into cooperative apartments and renamed it the Ping Pong Apartments, a reference to the paddles and tables that used to be manufactured there. The 1924, four-story concrete and steel building purchased at a municipal auction in 1981 now houses 33 cooperative apartments with twelve- to fourteen-foot high ceilings and floor-to-ceiling windows.

The old and revered Keith-RKO Prospect Theater on Ninth Street in the Park Slope section of Brooklyn, built in 1914 as a vaudeville theater, was converted to a movie house as vaudeville died out, and the theater closed with the advent of television. Then, with

Ping Pong Apartments, entrance facade, formerly World Champion Sports Corporation, 110 Clifton Place, Brooklyn, 1924; converted to apartments, Kenneth Halpern, architect, 1981.

Ballet Hispanico, entrance facade; originally, carriage houses, 167-169 West 89th Street, Frank Rooke, architect, 1892; converted to ballet studio, Buck and Crane, architects, 1989.

the revival of Park Slope, the theater underwent two major conversions. In the 1960s, the auditorium, except for the stage, was converted into a supermarket, and in the 1980s, the rest of the theater was converted to condominiums.

The Ballet Hispanico of New York City rehabilitated and converted two carriage houses at 167-169 West Eighty-ninth Street near Amsterdam Avenue. The Romanesque Revival buildings that originally served the wealthy owners of nearby mansions were designed by architect Frank Rooke in 1892. Buck and Crane, architects, sensitively converted the stables and living quarters of the old carriage houses into studios, dressing rooms, and office space for the dance troupe. Completed in 1989, the project was part of the West Side's urban renewal effort, begun in the late 1950s and extending from West Eighty-seventh to West Ninety-seventh streets and from Amsterdam Avenue to Central Park West, which combined new construction with the renovation and rehabilitation of existing structures. Supported by government, corporate, and private donors, low- and middle-income projects were financed to maintain the area's social and economic fabric.

The Archives Building was converted in 1988 to a mixed-use facility by architect Avinash Malhotra. Constructed by the United States Government in 1899 as a warehouse for federal archives, it was designed by Willoughby J. Edbrooke, William Martin Aiken, and James Knox Taylor, in the Richardsonian Romanesque style and clad in red brick with stone trim. Enormous round arches frame the display windows at ground level and provide tenants at the seventh floor with cathedral-like views of the surrounding cityscape and the Hudson River to the west. In designing the lobby, Judith Stockman installed 1890s brass fittings to give the space a period accent.

Covering the entire city block bounded by Greenwich, Barrow, Washington, and Christopher streets, the building, re-named the Archive, is eleven stories high, has 479 apartments, a supermarket, and other retail and commercial establishments, as well as an elevated sun deck on the roof, and a recreation area in the courtyard created by an atrium which was carved out of the center of the building, as part of its conversion to residential and commercial use. It is noteworthy that a year following the Archives Building conversion, the brick-clad Consolidated Edison records warehouse built in 1931 in the midst of the old jewelry district at 157 Hester Street, was converted to a jewelry exchange and 81 condominium apartments.

A pair of garment warehouses, six stories high and ten bays wide, at 20-26 Greene Street, were combined and converted in 1990 to 24 commercial condominiums attracting lawyers, architects, and the like. Because they are in the heart of SoHo, the most distinguished cast-iron district in the country, it is fitting that the architect,

The Archive, main entrance, east side.

The Archive, originally the Archives Building, Greenwich, Barrow, Washington, and Christopher streets, Greenwich Village, Willoughby J. Edbrooke, William Martin Aiken, and James Knox Taylor, architects, 1899; converted to apartments, Avinash Malhotra, architect, 1988.

The Rouss Building, 555 Broadway, Alfred Zucker, architect, 1889; converted to office center, 1989.

Arpad Baksa and Associates, retained the twin facades, which are outstanding examples of late nineteenth-century cast-iron design. Originally designed by Samuel A. Warner in 1880, the two warehouses were in excellent condition at the time of conversion except for a few broken pieces, and the addition of a stoop that shortened the bases of the ground floor piers. (John Sniffen is listed by the New York Landmarks Preservation Commission as the carpenter for the two buildings. He is best known to New Yorkers as the builder of the carriage houses on East Thirty-sixth Street, which have been converted to professional and residential use as Sniffen Court.)

The flamboyant entrepreneur Charles Broadway Rouss, who came to New York City from Virginia following the Civil War penniless and $50,000 in debt, amassed a fortune in thirteen years, which he celebrated in 1889 with a monument to his achievement—555 Broadway. Designed by Alfred Zucker as a mercantile building on the street whose name Rouss appropriated, the building is a rich combination of granite and cast iron. Ten stories high with two stories of attics, to the north and to the south, and twelve bays wide, located in SoHo, the building was converted into an office center in 1989 on its hundredth anniversary to attract architects, engineers, advertising agencies, and the like, an appropriate tribute to Rouss's

The Rouss Building, frieze bearing Rouss's name.

philosophy: "Pluck adorned with ambition, backed by honor bright, will always command success, even without the almighty dollar."

The facade of the old Grand Central Post Office by Warren and Wetmore served as the expansion base for a new mixed-use office tower, designed by David Childs of Skidmore Owings and Merrill and completed in 1992. The lantern atop the building was not finished until 1993, and it was then illuminated.

While the interior of the Post Office was gutted, the facade was restored to preserve the historic nature of the street wall near Grand Central Terminal. The first four floors and some mechanical rooms are occupied by the Post Office, and the rest of the building is an office tower. The Post Office's historical ornament, such as postal cages and grillage, was all preserved by the New York State Office of Historic Preservation.

Childs picked up the classical elements of the Beaux-Arts Post Office for his tower and developed a logical composition of squares, verticals, horizontals, and arches fundamental to the classical tradition; thus, in drawing on the past, he created something new. Celebrating the historic nature of Warren and Wetmore's building, Childs built on cues from their design. The strong corners and punched windows below, for example, are repeated at the attic level, and the intersecting diamond pattern around the windows below are picked up in the paving pattern in the lobby, as well as in the rotating squares and metal appendages at the top of the building, calling out the detail of the old Post Office facade below and articulating the new building's tripartite composition of base, shaft, and crown.

As the workplace has become more complicated through advanced technologies and increasingly sophisticated management systems, clients by necessity are becoming more involved in building design; consequently, not only do their staffs include more and more specialists in architecture, engineering, and construction, but the new buildings are also better suited to the clients' specific needs. Thus, a major tenant for the new tower, a prestigious law firm, needed special elevators, reinforced floors for its library, file room, computer center, and a package conveyer to its receiving room, as well as provisions for a maze of wires and conduits for its ten floors of lawyers' offices. Cooperation between client and architect from the early stages of planning through to completion of the tower not only assured a successful design but also affected the final appearance of the tower.

In many conversions, the original integrity of the building is beyond reclaiming. The vaulted lecture and exhibition hall and the great library, for example, of Grosvenor Atterbury's Russell Sage Foundation Building of 1915 at the southwest corner of Twenty-second Street and Lexington Avenue did not survive conversions into apartments in 1975 and 1988. Fortunately, however, the building's distinguished palazzo skin remains intact. Its cyclopean rustication, great arched entrance and windows at the street level, and elaborate cornice that caps the nine-story palazzo recall such Renaissance landmarks as Michelozzo's famous Medici-Riccardi palazzo of 1445 in Florence.

Grosvenor Atterbury's association with the Russell Sage Foundation extended to his collaboration in 1913 with the landscape architect Frederick Law Olmsted, Jr., on Forest Hills Gardens in Queens, a model housing project that produced a picturesque neighborhood of winding streets, landscaped enclaves, and romantic vistas, reminiscent of John Nash's Blaise Hamlet in Bristol, England, a century earlier, that adapted the rustic cottage to modern housing. (The Russell Sage Foundation was established in 1905 by Margaret Sage in the name of her late husband, the famous financier, to help make the world a better place.)

Renovations sometimes even create new neighborhoods—almost incidentally. Hudson Square, for example, has yet to find its way into the *AIA Guide to New York City*. Bounded by West Street, West Houston, Avenue of the Americas, and Canal Street, this office district emerged in the 1980s as resourceful ad agencies, production houses, architects, and the like sought proximity to the financial

Gramercy Towers, originally
Russell Sage Foundation
Building, 4 Lexington Avenue,
Grosvenor Atterbury, 1914,
1919; converted to apartments,
1975.

Gramercy Towers, north
entrance.

district at cheaper rates, by renovating the old printing plants and warehouses in the area.

With the closing of the old French Renaissance Hotel Martinique (by Henry J. Hardenbergh, 1897) at 53 West Thirty-second Street, which had become a welfare hotel, and the construction of A&S Plaza in the 1980s, the area around Herald Square, after the closing of Gimbel's, was revitalized.

RTKL Associates of Baltimore created a vertical mall out of the old Gimbel's department store in 1988, called A&S Plaza at Greeley Square, 1275 Broadway, between Thirty-second and Thirty-third streets. The first major department store in Manhattan in twenty years, it includes a 300,000-square-foot branch of Abraham and Straus department store, 125 specialty shops and food concessions, and 330,000 square feet of showroom space for children's clothing. The office tower was added in 1989 by Emory Roth and Sons.

RTKL broke through each level of the old Gimbel's store to create a basement-to-roof atrium. Shops are situated off the center court, and the department store's selling floors open onto the atrium. An ideal location, the mall is a block from Penn Station and directly above a transportation hub where three subway lines and the PATH train system meet. With Macy's as the nexus, Herald Square is a retail neighborhood crowded with shoppers seven days a week.

A&S Plaza, originally Gimbel Brothers Department Store, at Greeley Square, between 32nd and 33rd streets on Broadway, D.H. Burnham & Company, architects, 1912; converted to mall, RTKL Associates, 1988; office tower, Emory Roth & Sons, 1989.

A&S Plaza, detail of basement-to-roof atrium.

The World Financial Center, Battery Park City, Cesar Pelli, architect, 1982, sketch by the architect with the World Trade Center towers in the background.

A NEW CONTEXT FOR LOWER MANHATTAN

Battery Park City is a ninety-two-acre landfill extension of Lower Manhattan's Hudson River shoreline. The result of a master plan drawn up in 1979 by Cooper Eckstut Associates, and the product of federal and local government working with architects and private developers, it incorporates commercial, residential, and recreational development. Moreover, $250 million of its revenues have gone toward low- and middle-income housing in New York City. Tenants started moving in in 1982, and now Battery Park City's population is 7,000 with projected occupancy of 25,000.

The character of Old New York is echoed in Federal and brownstone references that architects have captured in the townhouses and apartments that cluster around vest-pocket parks animated by contemporary public sculpture that invite tenants and visitors alike to use the space. The esplanade that terminates in the South Cove provides the public with panoramic views of Miss Liberty and the Hudson River.

The revolutionary urban design concept of Rockefeller Center spawned Battery Park City's commercial area, the World Financial Center, begun in 1982 and completed in 1988, designed by architect Cesar Pelli. A pair of nine-story octagonal towers flanking Liberty Street create a formal gateway to the center, which occupies 13.5

201

The World Financial Center, the grand staircase, Winter Garden.

acres and is composed of four office towers rising from 34 to 51 stories, the Winter Garden, and a 3.5-acre landscaped public plaza.

The hub of the World Financial Center is the Winter Garden, an 18,000-square-foot courtyard ringed with restaurants and shops and enclosed by an enormous vault of glass, 125 feet high, 120 feet wide, and 200 feet long, which recalls Joseph Paxton's Crystal Palace for England's world's fair of 1851. The Winter Garden serves as a meeting place for the entire complex, and it is not uncommon for pedestrian traffic to reach 35,000 people an hour. To the east, the Winter Garden connects the complex with the World Trade Center through an enclosed bridge over the West Side highway, and to the west, its crystal grid provides the visitor with a panorama of the Hudson River.

Visitors enter the Winter Garden from a grand baroque staircase that descends to a grove of native American palm trees, ninety feet tall, that were specially selected for their hardiness and the way they enhance the view of the Hudson River. Geometric floor patterns in different kinds of marble relate the scale of the palm grove to the space, and the variegated tones of the marble enhance the courtyard's granite and marble walls.

The Winter Garden features dance and music programs free to the public, which is predominantly people from the financial district

The World Financial Center, Dow Jones & Company Building and Oppenheimer & Company Tower, view from the public plaza.

but includes tenants and tourists, as well. Entertainment ranges from the Vienna Boys Choir and the Basel Ballet to a troupe of Siberian dancers and the Herbie Hancock Trio.

Pelli's four towers surround and define the public plaza, the heart of the waterfront edge. They step down from the World Trade Center's twin towers to the east, and their bulky silhouettes capped by ancient forms rising 34 to 51 stories provide the context for Yamasaki's heretofore lonely twins, which now form a backdrop to Pelli's towers. Drawing on the ancient dome of the timeless Egyptian mastaba, step pyramid, and pyramid for the tops of his towers, Pelli's historical forms act as foils to Yamasaki's squared-off shafts of the World Trade Center and introduce a new era to Lower Manhattan's skyline.

Through his remarkable surfaces, Pelli establishes his towers as "responsible citizens of the ground and sidewalk," while celebrating their poetry as "idealized buildings of the sky." As the towers rise from their granite-sheathed bases that house shops of all kinds, the proportion of windows to granite increases at each setback until the tops of the towers are reflective glass skins. The effect is particularly ethereal when large puffs of clouds are driven across the sky. Their reflections against the glass towers make the towers appear transparent, as if the clouds are passing behind them. The tops of the towers are clad in copper, which in time will weather to the familiar lime-sherbet green that characterized Manhattan's Golden Age of skyscrapers from the Woolworth Building to the Art Deco confections of the 1930s.

WHITHER THE GREAT WHITE WAY?

With the demise in the 1960s of the great movie palaces that sprang up along Broadway in the 1920s, the stage was set for the mixed-use glass boxes of the Post Modern creations of the 1970s and 1980s that soar above the buildings they replace along the great White Way. The 42-story office tower at 1585 Broadway, for example, occupies the entire westerly blockfront of Broadway between Forty-seventh and Forty-eighth streets. Designed by Gwathmey Siegel and Associates for Solomon Equities, the building's curtain wall is an assemblage of blue-green glass, translucent white glass, mirror glass, silver-grey aluminum panels, and polished stainless steel. The design presents a modulated stepped base, which relates the building's mass and silhouette both to pedestrian scale at the street level and to the Times Square skyline, a transitional shaft, and an extended articulated top. The architect's intention was to create a "modern skyscraper that has a compelling silhouette and a dynamic and multiple scale presence."

Kevin Roche John Dinkeloo and Associates' design for 750 Seventh Avenue at Times Square, on the other hand, occupies a narrow island site, but its design mix of ancient forms and modern materials makes its distinctive mark on the Times Square horizon. A helical tower articulated by staggered setbacks recalls the construction ramps for the pyramids of ancient Egypt and the stepped construction of the ancient ziggurats of Mesopotamia, thereby avoiding the static image of stacked diminishing boxes. Roche and Dinkeloo's tower resolves the building's vertical thrust dynamically in a capping spire that pulls the building's core northward on the cityscape. Ceramic coated glass calls out the tower's horizontal and vertical grid, and the vision panel is expressed with a dark gray reflected glass.

To retain the distinctive color and character of Times Square, bathed in neon since the 1920s, a city ordinance of 1987 established design regulations requiring the new towers to incorporate "super" signage. Thus, a 120-foot-high neon display covers the facade of Embassy Suites Times Square, the 43-story hotel at Forth-seventh Street and Broadway designed by Fox and Fowle in 1989, while Spectacolor, the computerized wall of lights carrying advertising announcements, hangs from 1 Times Square and continues to dominate the triangle at Forty-third Street.

Space-age technology now promises to transform at least one of the new towers into a megalomaniacal display, if the project is ever realized. The developers of the 44-story tower at 1540 Broadway plan to provide advertisers with a video wall 150 feet wide and 30 feet high, composed of 375 video screens. The video wall will offer

Crowne Plaza Hotel, 1601 Broadway, north of 1585 Broadway to the left; Alan
Lapidus bestows a touch of this father's (Morris) Miami Beach architectural glitz
on the area.

205

1585 Broadway, office tower, Gwathmey Siegel and Associates, architects, 1989; Crowne Plaza Hotel, 1601 Broadway, Alan Lapidus Associates, architects, 1989; 750 Seventh Avenue, office tower, Kevin Roche, John Dinkeloo and Associates, 1989 (easy to locate—at Seventh Avenue and 50th Street).

advertisers virtually countless permutations for their clients' messages, limited only by their imaginations. Even if the project fails, the "super" signage ordinance augurs a new age of glitz for Times Square in the twenty-first century.

Preservationists took heart when the threatened auditorium of the famous Palace Theater was saved. Although the building that housed the theater facing Duffy Square was razed, its landmarked auditorium was preserved and incorporated into the new Embassy Suites Times Square. Designed by Kirchoff and Rose in 1913, the Palace Theater was built as a vaudeville hall and served later as a movie theater. Then, from the 1960s, it was one of Broadway's largest legitimate theaters, seating 1,701.

In spite of this new construction, developers, architects, and public officials cannot seem to make up their minds what to do with Times Square, the crossroads of the world. The options for the district include perpetuating its "exuberant vulgarity" with increased signage through modern technology, transforming it into a more economically successful center via tall towers, or letting it find its own level through zoning incentives. New York City's world famous entertainment district seems to be moving in the direction of a mixture of all these.

After a decade of planning and debate, a redevelopment plan for Times Square was agreed upon by New York City and state officials in June 1988. The plan included four office towers from 32 to 57 stories in height called Times Square Center, a merchandise mart, a hotel, the restoration of nine historic theaters along Forty-second Street, and a multimillion-dollar restoration of the Times Square subway station. Opponents to the plan, however, included civic groups, architects, critics, and some local politicians, who vehemently opposed especially the size and design of the towers of Times Square Center, which they felt would restrict light and air. Many preservationists were upset about the possible loss of 1 Times Square Plaza, originally the Times Tower, which would have been razed had the plan materialized. The triangular 25-story office tower, which was erected by the *New York Times* in 1904 and ushered in the New Year (becoming an annual event), was originally clad in an ornate Italian Renaissance terra-cotta skin that was replaced in 1966 with an antiseptic marble sheath and now carries Spectacolor.

Times Square Center was designed by Philip Johnson and John Burgee in the spirit of Rockefeller Center, according to Johnson, and would have carried "crested mansards, entrance arcades, and stone appliqués—to create the buzz image that substitutes upscale marketing for the art of architecture," according to Ada Louise Huxtable, former architecture critic for the *New York Times*.

A faltering real estate market coupled with critics' growing resentment over the design of the towers led to fundamental revisions of the entire plan. Even though an interim plan for Forty-second

"Super" signage occupies entire south facade of the Renaissance Hotel, 714 Seventh Avenue, Costas Kandylis, architect, 1992; towers of 1585 and the Crowne Plaza Hotel visible at left.

Street has now been developed by the New York State Urban Development Corporation (UDC) and the city's Economic Development Corporation, the future of the area cannot be predicted. The interim plan for Forty-second Street consists of a set of design guidelines to be enforced by the UDC. The design team, headed by architect Robert A. M. Stern and graphic designer Tibor Kalman, has proposed wide-ranging guidelines including security grilles, a "billboard park," a fountain of advertising, theatrical lighting, and commercial displays of all kinds employing the latest technologies to perpetuate the colorful and glitzy character of Forth-second Street. It could be that the future of Forty-second Street will be determined independently of Times Square, whose future is anything but clear.

THE MUSEUM OF MODERN ART AND THE "HUMANIZING ELEMENT"

Faced with an eroding endowment and a growing collection of art housed in cramped quarters, the Museum of Modern Art, nearing its fiftieth anniversary, took measures that not only solved its financial and exhibition problems but also changed the image of the country's most important museum devoted to modern art.

Founded in 1929, MOMA opened in rented space in the old Heckscher Building, now the Crown Building, designed by Warren and Wetmore and constructed in 1921. The building itself is historically significant as the first building built according to New York City's innovative zoning laws of 1916. MOMA rented six rooms for galleries, offices, and a library in the building. The museum was founded by three women who had been avid collectors of modern art since the Armory Show of 1913—Abby Aldrich Rockefeller, wife of John D. Rockefeller, Jr., Lillie P. Bliss, heiress to a textile fortune, and Mary Sullivan, wife of a wealthy attorney. They formed the core of a committee of some of New York City's most powerful people. Other members of the founding committee were industrialist A. Conger Goodyear, art historian Paul J. Sachs, editor Frank Crowninshield, and philanthropist Josephine Boardman Crane. Goodyear's enthusiasm for modern art had cost him his trustee seat at the Albright Gallery in Buffalo. Sachs, a member of the Sachs family of investment bankers, was a professor of art history at Harvard, Crowninshield was editor of *Vanity Fair,* and Crane had been a founder of the Dalton School. Alfred Barr, Jr., professor of art history at Wellesley College, was the first director, a post he held until he had differences with MOMA's president Stephen C. Clark, Jr., in 1943, after which he was curator of collections until 1967, when he retired.

MOMA moved to space in the Rockefeller townhouse at 11 West Fifty-third Street in 1932, and in 1939 opened the doors to its own building on that site. It was dedicated by the president of the United States, Franklin Delano Roosevelt. The seven-story building was designed by Philip L. Goodwin and Edward Durell Stone in the International Style and remains its finest example in New York City. To some sensibilities, the new building with its white marble and glass sheath was an intrusion on a block of low-rise brownstones and Beaux-Arts townhouses. Even though the setback of Goodwin and Stone's facade respected the cornice line of the residential architecture at mid-block, to some critics its white cubic skin was an affront to the brownstone, swags, and foliations of the quiet side street. The intrusion was prophetic of MOMA's future growth at that site. New Yorkers, then, had no way of knowing that fifty years later, some of their sons and daughters would be fighting MOMA's expansion once again as the museum set about to raise a 55-story condominium tower above it and to demolish a distinguished Beaux-Arts townhouse built for financier George Blumenthal next door to it at 23 West Fifty-third Street by Richard and Joseph Hunt, sons of one of America's most important and respected architects, Richard Morris Hunt.

In 1936, MOMA acquired four buildings adjacent to the museum and the following year occupied temporary headquarters in the Time & Life Building at 14 West Forty-ninth Street in Rockefeller Center, while its new building was erected on the original site. At the same time, John D. Rockefeller, Jr., donated the site that became the Abby Aldrich Rockefeller Sculpture Garden, designed by Philip Johnson in 1953. The Grace Rainey Rogers Annex (also designed by Philip Johnson) had opened at 21 West Fifty-third Street two years before.

In 1953, MOMA acquired the brownstone at 27 West Fifth-third Street and, in 1956, the museum acquired the George Blumenthal residence. The distinguished Beaux-Arts townhouse served first as offices and then as the museum's bookstore. When the Whitney Museum of American Art moved to 945 Madison Avenue in 1963, MOMA acquired the Whitney Museum Building at 20 West Fifty-fourth Street, now part of the Lillie P. Bliss International Study Center.

Under growing pressure to exhibit the world's most important collection of modern art, the museum commissioned Philip Johnson to design the expansion. On May 25, 1964, the enlarged MOMA opened: two new wings, an enlarged sculpture garden, the Edward

Steichen galleries and photographic study center, the Paul J. Sachs Galleries for drawing and prints, and the Philip L. Goodwin Galleries for architecture and design. Mrs. Lyndon B. Johnson dedicated the enlarged spaces.

Over the years, rising costs and what now seems to be questionable fiscal management began eating into the museum's endowment. Meanwhile, the museum had developed the single most important collection of modern art in the country, but it could only exhibit 19 percent of its permanent collection, while people were coming in ever-growing numbers to see a fraction of what the museum officials felt they should be seeing. By the 1970s, it seemed that the museum's options were limited and its directive clear. It would be a violation of the museum's trust to sell off works of art to pay for expansion and maintenance and was a short-term solution at best. It was clear that the museum should expand its facilities to exhibit more of its collection and to achieve long-term financial stability.

The financial success of the residential condominium in Olympic Tower on Fifth Avenue and East Fifty-first Street nearby proved to the trustees that the neighborhood would support a condominium, and they had the air rights over the museum to develop such a venture, which would help to reduce the museum's deficit, but what about long-term solvency?

MOMA reasoned that if the taxes from the condominium (Museum Tower) could.be. applied to the museum, that would be a way to generate regular income for the maintenance of the museum and its collection. But nonprofit institutions cannot enter into such negotiations. MOMA, therefore, proposed state legislation to establish the proper instrument. Under the New York State Cultural Resources Act of 1976, the Trust for Cultural Resources collects tax equivalent payments from Museum Tower and dispenses them to the museum.

The cost of the tower and the museum expansion were covered by a capital-fund-raising campaign by the museum. Museum Tower Associates purchased the air rights over the new wing and the existing museum properties and the tax equivalency payments provide the museum with what has been called a "continuing endowment."

That solution increased the museum's endowment to a realistic level and generated sufficient income to do what the museum is supposed to do—collect, care for, exhibit, and instruct. How successful MOMA's financial solution will be in the future remains a question. Financial and legal specialists have noted perhaps the primary potential problem—the tax equivalency payments. It is to the

Museum of Modern Art facade (modified), 11 West 53rd Street, Philip Goodwin and Edward Durrell Stone, architects, 1939.

Museum Tower apartments, 21 West 53rd Street, Cesar Pelli and Associates, architects, 1985. Photo © Kenneth Champlin.

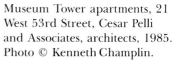

Cesar Pelli's expansion into MOMA's sculpture garden.

advantage of the developer to keep them down and to the museum to keep them up.

There were critics who argued against MOMA's solution on philosophical grounds—a museum of art should not be in the real estate business. Others were unhappy with the intrusion into the neighborhood of a tower at mid-block on a side street and the demolition of a remarkable Beaux-Arts townhouse by distinguished American architects. They insisted that one of the aims of zoning had been to retain a low cornice line at mid-block in residential areas. Furthermore, the removal of the Blumenthal residence, a superb example of Beaux-Arts design, for the tower violated one of the principles for which MOMA stands, preservation of urban design and distinguished architecture. Furthermore, the New York City chapter of the AIA had encouraged retaining the Blumenthal residence. There was a further problem. The plan for the tower initially called for eliminating the museum's original 1939 facade, a solution totally unacceptable to preservationists, architects, and critics alike. Goodwin and Stone's International Style facade was, therefore, retained but altered. The facade is not only New York City's finest example of the International Style but also a monument marking the site of the style's christening. It was in an exhibition in 1932 at MOMA in which Henry Russell Hitchcock and Philip Johnson first used the term International Style and thereby gave the style its name.

The distinguished architect Cesar Pelli, who at the time (1977) was dean of architecture at Yale University, was selected to be the architect for the tower and for the museum expansion, which were completed in 1984. The concrete-frame Museum Tower features a multi-colored glass curtain wall with patterned mullions, tinted vision glass, and eleven shades of spandrel glass. The sleek polychromatic tower is designed to suit its urban context. Pelli's museum expansion included 30 percent more curatorial space, an auditorium, two restaurants, and the bookstore. His design more than doubled the amount of exhibition space while it retained the intimate quality of the galleries that MOMA's first director, Alfred Barr, had introduced and which the curators were adamant to preserve. Since most modern art before 1945 was small and meant to be seen in an intimate space, the galleries were designed accordingly, to accommodate Barr's informal and asymmetrical arrangement of works, which Pelli sensitively retained.

A sore spot with critics of Pelli's design was its encroachment on the sculpture garden, a favorite oasis with New Yorkers for its sunny setting—a unique enclave in the midst of the metropolis. Pelli's expansion included a restaurant at the east end and a glass-enclosed escalator on the north wall of the old wing and the south face of the garden. Not only was the sculpture garden thereby reduced in size by thirty feet but Museum Tower now placed it in shadow, like a vest-pocket park in the canyons of the Financial District. Not considered one of Pelli's most successful designs, some critics have likened it to a shopping center.

By its fiftieth anniversary, MOMA successfully garnered its enormous resources to achieve financial solvency and to exhibit its collection more fruitfully. The museum needs now to draw on its formidable resources to address the most important aspect of museum life in the twenty-first century—education. In 1920, Sir Herbert Read wrote, "without the creative arts, there would have been no advance in myth or ritual, in language or meaning, in morality or metaphysics." Fifty-five years later, George Heard Hamilton, when he was director of the Sterling and Francine Clark Art Institute in Williamstown, Massachusetts, recalled Sir Herbert's words in calling art "the primary humanizing element in the development of human consciousness."

MOMA has always supported museum education and even pioneered the field in its early years. Scholars have noted, for example, that MOMA, under Alfred Barr's direction, created the first serious catalogues dealing with the modern movement. Indeed, museum catalogues all over the world have ever since become major reference works in all periods of art history.

Museum education in the twenty-first century must not only continue to develop and refine sophisticated scholarship but must also reach out to the fast growing populations of the culturally deprived, through that "humanizing element" unique to art. The same creativity and extensive resources that MOMA used to solve its financial and exhibition problems on West Fifty-third Street can be used to extend the museum's cultural riches to New York City's other boroughs. That outreach could take the form of branch museums, similar to the Whitney Museum of American Art's expansions, or tie-ins with the city's public and private schools, as well as with historical societies and other cultural institutions. It could follow already existing multidisciplinary programs such as The Monuments Conservancy's program in East Harlem (see p. 190), with funding coming from foundations, the corporate world, and the private sector. Such an outreach program would extend MOMA's cultural riches as a "humanizing element" to areas of greatest need.

214

8

The Tallest Building in the World, 1913-30: The Woolworth Building

At 7:30 on the evening of April 24, 1913, President Woodrow Wilson pressed a button at the White House in Washington, D.C., that officially opened the Woolworth Building in downtown New York City. All the lights of the building went on, an orchestra struck up *The Star Spangled Banner* at a dinner for the architect (with 825 dignitaries in attendance) on the twenty-seventh floor, and a telegraphic announcement of the event went out across the ocean to the Eiffel Tower (the only structure that was taller) and to all the ships at sea. Dubbed the "Cathedral of Commerce" by a noted divine of the day, the Woolworth Building remained the tallest building in the world until 1930.

The idea of the Woolworth Building originated with the need to provide space for the Irving National Bank and a headquarters for Frank Winfield Woolworth's chain of five-and-ten-cent stores. Moreover, the tallest office building in the world would be a colossal monument to Frank Woolworth's achievement and a fitting landmark for the city of New York.

Woolworth wanted a Gothic building with a tower and lots of windows (there are more than 5,000) arranged so that the interior spaces could be subdivided into large or small offices with each, no matter how small, having adequate natural light. He chose Cass Gilbert, an architect with an outstanding reputation for building modern architecture in the historical mode.

The Woolworth Building, 233 Broadway *(facing page);* 1913. Cass Gilbert, architect. "The Cathedral of Commerce" is a modern steel skeleton clad in ivory-colored terra-cotta in the Flamboyant Gothic style; it was the tallest building in the world.

Pointing out that it would be impracticable to construct an authentic Gothic building, Gilbert suggested using Gothic detail which would give the desired effect. Later, he confided that a major challenge was to make the building picturesque because of the business emphasis on the utilization of all possible space; this limited projections and recesses that architects use to create definitions of light and shade, which were characteristic of the picturesque tradition that Woolworth liked.

In order to achieve the desired sculptural and tactile effects, Gilbert chose Flamboyant Gothic tracery and decoration of the late fifteenth and sixteenth centuries, which allowed great flexibility with almost limitless ornamental possibilities. Combined with appropriate color, this allowed him to accent and enrich the shadows and to define the main lines of the building, satisfying both Woolworth, the client, and himself, the architect. Ten years later, Gilbert professed, "It was . . . an honest endeavor to express in exterior form the function of the building and the fact that it was a steel structure not a masonry structure."

CLAD IN TERRA-COTTA

Cass Gilbert designed the Woolworth Building to be faced with architectural terra-cotta, a building material particularly suited to the structural needs, as well as to the decorative requirements of the building. Fifty-two of the fifty-five stories (793.5 feet high at Barclay Street side, highest point) above the three-story stone basement are clad in terra-cotta, which sheaths the steel frame and withstands fire, rain, frost, and the destructive chemicals in the atmosphere of the city. And it is a material that is easily cleaned. The terra-cotta on the building is a clay composition, pressed in plaster molds, coated with ceramic color and fired in a muffle kiln at approximately 2,250 degrees Fahrenheit. Its partial vitrification enables terra-cotta, when properly constructed and backed up, to bear great weight. In the case of the Woolworth Building, the backing is brick, particularly serviceable because almost any brick can be used as long as it is not too soft or absorbent. The terra-cotta units are attached by means of metal anchors, hangers, rods, and bolts.

Terra-cotta's plasticity and its adaptability to color handling allows an enormous range of modeling and tonal possibilities in the execution of decorative features, thus making it specially suited to Cass Gilbert's Gothic designs. The subtle modeling and tonal combinations of the building's exterior reflect the architect's thorough knowledge of his materials and an awareness of their decorative potentials. From the third story to the roof, the entire facade on all elevations is architectural terra-cotta.

THE SHAFT: COLOR AND LIGHT

The basic color of the shaft of the building is a matte cream glaze, varying in tone from light to dark. The vertical lines of the facade are emphasized by diagonal projections, which dramatically catch the light and cast shadows. These lines are broken by belt courses at five-story intervals and buff panels between the window courses modeled in Gothic ornament, against backgrounds of blue, green, golden yellow, and sienna. Besides the different colors used, the slight natural tonal variation in the terra-cotta medium (no two pieces are identical in color) imparts a scintillating vitality to the surface. In order to maintain an appearance of overall uniformity in tone, the colors increase in density gradually from the bottom of the building to the top. This is necessary because the intensity of natural light increases uniformly upward as there is less interference from surrounding structures. (Now the effects are muted by the surrounding buildings.) Thus, while the tone of the terra-cotta at the fourth floor appears to be of the same density as the tone of the terra-cotta at the upper floors, it is actually lighter. Similarly, the decorative relief is progressively bolder and more deeply undercut in the upper stories to create uniformity of light and shade.

Between the twenty-sixth and twenty-seventh stories the vertical lines are interrupted by panels of dark green bronze, and the twenty-seventh story is finished with an intricately modeled canopy. Darker color tones combine with the deeper undercutting to accentuate the natural shadows and give a greater sense of depth. This visual treatment serves as a transition from the shaft of the building to the tower with its flying buttresses, pinnacles, projecting grotesques, and other intricately modeled ornament. This wealth of modeling in the upper stories, seen from below, creates the illusion of delicate lacework culminating in a profusion of diaphanous forms which make the topmost part of the tower appear to merge with the atmosphere.

An inner court of the building is enclosed on three sides, and its twenty-five stories are faced with lustrous, instead of matte cream, terra-cotta; the greater reflection of light resulting helps to give the appearance of overall uniformity in tone of the terra-cotta facing.

THE TOWER: A WONDROUS VIEW

At the twenty-ninth story the tower begins, flush with the Broadway front and the inside court walls, and inset from the two side

217

elevations (from Park Place on the north and Barclay Street on the south). At the forty-second story, the tower is inset on all four sides (from the Broadway side as well; the building fronts on Broadway and extends nearly two hundred feet west), and at the forty-eighth story it is inset again and the tower plan changes from square to octagonal, with turrets and pinnacles rising at the four corners from the spaces created by the transition (three were decorative and the one at the northeast corner encased the smokestack; recent restoration has modified them all). From the fifty-second story, the roof slopes to the fifty-fifth story and the crowning pinnacle.

The roof rises 125 feet and is sheathed in ornamental copper in the late Gothic design. Problems were posed in executing this work at a height which up until then had not been attained. New reckonings with wind pressure required additional bracing, which had to be concealed for aesthetic reasons. At the same time, the height presented new dangers to the workers and to pedestrians below (Gilbert was very proud that there were no fatal casualties), requiring special kinds of scaffolding and outrigging devised to meet the specific problems involved in reaching the new heights. The darkened roof has been denigrated as "charcoal Gothic." When new, it was gilded by a new process in which rolls of gold leaf in sixty- to seventy-foot lengths were applied to the ornamental copper sheet by means of a machine that conformed the gilding to every contour without tearing the gold leaf. It took forty men four months to cover the 40,000 square feet of the tower and the lower roof.

The gilded apex and the colors that Gilbert selected for the exterior were carefully calculated to blend the tower with the subtle atmospheric nuances of blue and gray skies and to lend the illusion of even greater height to the building. For many years, an observation gallery at the fifty-eighth story afforded the sightseer what was called "the most wondrous view in all the world."

THE DECORATION: A UNIQUE COLLABORATION

The Atlantic Terra-Cotta Company was awarded the terra-cotta contract for the Woolworth Building on June 12, 1911, for $265,000. The terra-cotta was made at their Perth Amboy, New Jersey, plant, which had been inaugurated in 1878; they were one of the major pioneers of the terra-cotta industry in America.

The customary manner of working with the terra-cotta supplier was for the architect either to indicate in general terms what he wanted by means of drawings, sketches, or models in varying degrees of finish and detail, or to employ the modeling department of the factory to execute the designs. The terra-cotta companies preferred the latter because it was more profitable for them and they had control over the work from start to finish; they claimed this assured a higher level of work. Cass Gilbert sought the best of both systems and selected his own modelers to work in Atlantic's factory.

On July 7, 1911, Gilbert appointed John Donnelly and Eliseo V. Ricci of the sculpting firm of Donnelly and Ricci to do the terra-cotta designs, as well as the entire range of ornamental design work, from iron elevator fronts and bronze, wood, and plasterwork, to the elaborate main doorway on Broadway and granite ornamentation. They were also commissioned to execute the special decorative marble of the first, second, and third floors in the lobby. The amount of their contract was $11,500.

THE NAPOLEON OF COMMERCE

The depressed arch that frames the main entrance on Broadway is cut into the massive granite base of the building and carved with rich ornamental quotations from medieval and ancient models. Twenty of Donnelly and Ricci's animated figures set into the face of the arch follow its continuous contour and resemble the *Labors of the Months* carved on the facades of Gothic cathedrals in France. At their apex is an owl symbolizing wisdom, night, and industry, an image repeated above the arch on either side and hovering protectively over the single initial "W," taken from Mr. Woolworth's stationery (in Gothic script).

Beneath the monogram, two Classical figures recline along the top of the arch: Mercury on the left, wearing his winged helmet, symbolic of commerce, and Ceres on the right, goddess of grain. A broad, flat arch shading these figures connects two exquisitely carved, but empty, niches that flank the giant portal. A statue of Frank Woolworth was to be carved by Daniel Chester French, noted American sculptor, for one of the niches. It was never executed, however, and no one knows why. Whose figure was intended for the other niche is equally obscure. Perhaps Cass Gilbert, or Napoleon; Woolworth was known as "the Napoleon of Commerce."

Two months following the opening of the building, a visit to Napoleon's Palace at Compiègne gave Woolworth the inspiration for furnishing his private office. Patterned on Napoleon's Empire room, the office still serves the chairman of the board of the F. W. Woolworth Company. Although remodeled, it retains the wall panels of green marble from northern Italy, with pilasters in a darker tone surmounted by gilded Corinthian capitals (in the style of the Empire room).

Woolworth Building: main entrance (details).
Architect Cass Gilbert used salamanders as the
symbol for the transmutation of iron and clay
into steel and terra-cotta *(top, left)*. One of the
carved archivolts from the main entrance that
frames the Broadway entrance depicts the
harvesting of corn *(top, right)*. The owl *(bottom,
right)*, symbolizing wisdom and industry, is a
recurring image; here it hovers over the initial
"W," taken from Mr. Woolworth's personal
stationery.

Main entrance, Woolworth Building *(facing
page)*. Granite carvings are taken from
medieval and antique models; animated figures
surround the main archway, flanked by two
niches above coiled salamanders.

Objects reflecting Woolworth's regard for Napoleon have been assembled, along with company memorabilia, in an engaging display in a small exhibition area immediately adjacent to the twenty-eighth floor reception room. Included are Woolworth's mahogany desk (7'6" x 3'9") with bronze mounts and green leather top edged in handtooled gilt; his Empire lamps with gold figures of Victory over the top; a bronze equestrian statuette ink well (Napoleon astride); and a life-size bronze bust of Napoleon as Julius Caesar on a mahogany pedestal.

Coiling salamanders, used symbolically in the ornamentation of the building, support the two mysterious niches that flank the main entrance. The salamander in the ancient world, believed to be unharmed by fire, became the symbol in alchemy for the transmutation of baser metals into gold. Gilbert used the lizardlike creature in the Woolworth Building as the symbol for the transmutation of iron and clay into steel and terra-cotta, the two basic structural components of the building. On the occasion of the tenth anniversary of the building, Cass Gilbert stressed that the style in which the decoration was carved is Flamboyant, meaning "flamelike," to describe the tracery that is shaped like tongues of flame. Thus, the image of the salamander and the style of Flamboyant Gothic are symbolic of the elements that produced the building: flame and heat.

Crowning the main entrance, in the center of the moulding that connects the two niches mentioned earlier, is a great American Eagle, looking south as if in grateful tribute to the U.S. Custom House, which was built by Cass Gilbert in 1907 and which was the commission that brought him to New York to stay. Beyond the elaborately carved main arch, a simpler one opens onto the lobby and is crowned by a pelican—the bird which loves its young so dearly that it sustains them with its own blood by pecking open its breast.

THE LOBBY:
ITS SYMBOLS AND ORIENTATION

The distinctive carving style of the animated figures of the main entrance is repeated in the lobby in a series of brackets or corbels. Twelve plaster brackets, tucked away in archways and beneath decorative cornices, are carved in caricatures of men who were involved in the construction of the building in various capacities. These figures were the work of Thomas R. Johnston, of Cass Gilbert's firm. Each man, in medieval tradition, is represented with his particular "attribute," which describes his role in the building. For example, Cass Gilbert is shown holding a model of the building, and Mr.

Woolworth Building. This corbel *(above, left)* by Thomas R. Johnston in the main lobby shows Cass Gilbert—the architect—holding a model of the Woolworth Building. Another corbel *(above, right)* by Thomas R. Johnston in the main lobby shows Frank Woolworth paying for his building with nickels and dimes, since he paid for its construction with cash.

Grand arcade and stairway *(right)*. The illuminated stained-glass ceiling of the Woolworth Building is framed by animated polychromed figures that caricature aspects of the retail business.

Woolworth is in the act of paying for his building with his nickels and dimes. Woolworth laughed heartily when he saw the sculpture and ordered it never to be removed. It was a most appropriate image of Woolworth; he had paid for the building as it was being built—all $13 million—and there was never a mortgage. But his direction to preserve the caricature was motivated as much by his respect for Cass Gilbert, because the coin he holds between thumb and forefinger reveals a profile that is not found on any U.S. currency. It appears to be the profile of Cass Gilbert.

Gilbert's image is equally charged with "submerged symbolism." The object he holds, in true medieval fashion (like the bishops who are portrayed holding their cathedrals in medieval Europe), is probably not the Woolworth Building, but a model of the building that he persuaded Woolworth to have executed for exhibiting at trade fairs in Europe. It cost $6,000 and was a small functioning replica of the Woolworth in which the metal construction was visible, the elevators worked, and every detail including the heating and ventilation systems were articulated. The model was partially destroyed by bombing in World War I and then completely demolished by bombs in World War II, while it was being exhibited in Europe.

Another engaging feature of the lobby is the series of spirited corbels along the carved cornice, beneath a coffered and illuminated stained-glass ceiling that extends over the great marble staircase of the grand arcade leading into the Irving Bank. These many colored figures, exaggerated and contorted in their movements, caricature a variety of the merchandising aspects of the five-and-dime business. For example, these animated figures hold up various items for sale in the Woolworth stores, such as pans and shirts. Others lampoon the business: a figure losing his shirt demonstrates the warning "caveat emptor."

The lobby is covered with glass mosaics and rich marbles from here and abroad. Images, in the two lunettes on the second floor overlooking the lobby, portray tributes to American commerce and industry and, characteristic of Cass Gilbert, an almost undetectable detail in the oculis of the mosaic dome in the center of the lobby orients this fantasy of light and color to the real world—a compass points due north, which interrupts the symmetry of the design. The building conforms to the shape of the city block, but the mosaic compass in the eye of the lobby dome obeys the laws of nature. By this device, Cass Gilbert, then, orients the Woolworth Building to the world of the city and commerce, as well as to the larger world of the cosmos.

This lobby dome, with its merging pendentives, was probably inspired by the Mausoleum of Galla Placidia, an early Christian building in Ravenna, Italy, which Gilbert apparently could not afford to admit. While the building was given the appellation "the Cathedral of Commerce," Gilbert denied any ecclesiastical inspiration for its structure. Instead, he said that a number of medieval civic buildings with towers were studied but not copied, and included the Halls of Middlesburg and Alkamaar in Holland, the City Hall in Brussels, and the Hotel de Ville in Compiègne. His was a commercial building, not an ecclesiastical one.

The Woolworth Building's location was of supreme importance, it was noted in 1913. Nine entrances faced upon three streets; it was near City Hall, the Municipal Building, the Brooklyn Bridge, the post office, the courts, the banking center, and the subway system. No better location was available to a tenant. Today it still attracts tenants, as well as tourists.

THE CATHEDRAL OF COMMERCE

It was S. Parkes Cadman, the first of the great radio preachers in America, who christened the Woolworth Building "the Cathedral of Commerce." Reverend Cadman's favorite view of the Woolworth Building was glimpsed from the Brooklyn Bridge at dusk. The "grandiose effect," he wrote, "is beyond the brush of Turner to paint or the eloquence of Ruskin to describe." When Cadman wrote these words in 1917, the world was locked in global conflict. He tried to give the country a symbol of hope. "The Cathedral of Commerce," he said, referring to the Woolworth Building, was "the chosen habitation of the spirit in man which, through means of exchange and barter, binds alien people into unity and peace, and reduces the hazards of war and bloodshed."

The Woolworth Building was the tallest building in the world from 1913 until the Bank of Manhattan Company and the Chrysler Building went up in 1930. It remains one of the most distinguished skyscrapers in the world. Its architect, Cass Gilbert, achieved a rare balance by uniting the advanced technology of the steel skeleton with Gothic forms, adapted to contemporary design. Recently restored to its original beauty (at greater cost than to build the building), the building's decoration tells the story of its architecture in a fruitful way.

Of the many praises that have been sung in honor of Cass Gilbert's achievement, one is particularly suitable even today. In 1921 a reporter in *The Times* of London wrote, ". . . the Woolworth Building will be New York's fame. . . . A growing city built on a narrow peninsula is unable to expand laterally, and must, therefore, soar. The problem was how to make it soar with dignity, and the problem has been solved. . . ."

9

Fashionable Dwellings

THE DAKOTA

The Dakota (1884), on Seventy-second Street at Central Park West, was the first truly great luxury apartment house in New York City. The idea of the affluent sharing a common roof had been introduced by Richard Morris Hunt in 1869 with his Flats on Eighteenth Street just east of Irving Place, which were based on Parisian models and were the first examples of gracious apartment living in New York. Alas, they no longer survive.

Nothing on the scale of the Dakota had ever been tried before; furthermore, the building was so far from the center of the town that many predicted its failure and dubbed it "Clark's Folly." Edward S. Clark, its owner and developer, was the flamboyant president of the Singer Manufacturing Company, makers of the Singer Sewing Machine, a household word in America. Others said his great apartment house was so far north that it was in "Dakota Territory" (thus its name). Nonetheless, Clark, who did not make sizable investments lightly, believed that the relentless press of the city northward would justify his venture. Furthermore, the West Side Association, of which Clark was an active member, was promoting the development of row houses above Seventy-second Street in order to maintain a harmonious appearance in the neighborhood and uniform high quality in its housing.

The Dakota's location was well calculated: Seventy-second Street is a major artery, the first one-hundred-foot-wide street above Fifty-ninth Street, and the Dakota stands on the crest of the West Side plateau, picturesquely situated on the highest part of the city over-

The Dakota, Seventy-second Street and Central Park West *(facing page)*; 1884. Henry J. Hardenbergh, architect. New York's first great luxury apartment house was named for the Dakota Territory because it was so far from the town center.

looking the entire island of Manhattan. Long Island Sound and the hills of Brooklyn were within view, as were the Orange Mountains, the Palisades, and the Hudson River. Clark's commitment to the upper West Side was not limited to the Dakota alone; he also purchased land, adjoining the Dakota, between Eighth and Ninth avenues on West Seventy-third Street. He built twenty-seven row houses on this land. Then he built a power plant in the basement of the Dakota which was powerful enough to supply the electricity for not only the apartment house, but for his other twenty-seven houses as well.

Clark commissioned Henry J. Hardenbergh, one of New York's finest architects, to design his new apartment house. Hardenbergh's plan was a masterful achievement in practicability, elegance, and beauty, and he took full advantage of the building's site (as he did with the Plaza), a characteristic of his work.

Almost square in plan, the Dakota is approximately two hundred feet wide across the main facade on Seventy-second Street; massive pavilions seven stories high with steeply pitched roofs, adding two more stories, comprise the four corners of the building. Between them, slightly recessed cubes are surmounted by steeply pitched roofs at right angles to those crowning the pavilions. The main entrance on Seventy-second Street is a two-story archway, originally designed to accommodate carriages, with an iron gate opening into a groin vaulted vestibule. Another set of iron gates opens into an enormous "I"-shaped court within, where carriages assembled. Automobile traffic is prohibited because the below ground courtyard for delivery cannot sustain the weight of modern vehicles.

A boldly projecting terra-cotta cornice with diaper pattern runs around the entire building between the second and third floors just above the apex of the main entrance archway. Four stories above, a continuous projecting balcony girds the building, and the two coursings divide the surface of the building vertically in a two-to-one ratio. This proportion creates a consummately stable structure for the panoply of stepped dormers, chimneys, finials, pediments, and crestings that animate the magnificent slate and copper roof. Strong vertical elements at the center of each pavilion and the central panel of each facade unite the three great layers of salmon-colored brick (a new shade just developed successfully at that time) and olive-colored Nova Scotia sandstone trim, picked out with warm terra-cotta ornament. A good cleaning is needed to unveil the rich tones of this remarkable structure.

The color and pattern the architect used creates a handsome silhouette for a prominently sited structure. The building was constructed of materials whose tones complement each other and soften the shadows created by the deep recesses of cornices, windows, and balconies cut into the heavy walls of salmon brick, olive trim, and terra-cotta decoration. Moreover, from a distance, the energetic pattern of light and shade created by the ornamental treatment of the wall openings lightens the appearance of the mass of the building. It is only upon close inspection that the enormity of the structure is apparent, an enormity that results from the commodious design of the apartments and facilities within.

Services, Facilities, and Interiors

Four passageways lead from the courtyard to the interior of the building. From the ground floor, where walls are wainscoted in rare marbles and paneled in fine woods, four elegantly wrought bronze staircases and luxuriously fitted elevators lead to the upper floors. Two fountains in the courtyard serve also as ventilators and skylights for a large basement below. Surrounding the subterranean space were tenants' storerooms, a laundry, kitchen, pantry, and bake shops. Hardenbergh introduced service elevators at the backs of the apartments. It is noteworthy that the original steam radiators still heat the building. In the Dakota's early years, permanent tenants and transient guests enjoyed gardens and croquet and tennis courts that extended west 150 feet from the back of the building.

The structure of the building is load-bearing walls with steel arches, and the floors are over eighteen inches thick, specially constructed of earth and concrete for acoustical insulation. Its thick masonry and brick walls keep the rooms remarkably cool in the summer and snug in the winter.

The Dakota was originally divided into eighty-five suites and each had from four to twenty separate rooms. A typical parlor measured twenty-five by forty feet. Ceilings were fifteen feet high on the first floor, diminishing to twelve feet on the eighth floor. Libraries, reception areas, and dining rooms were paneled and wainscoted in fine woods, such as mahogany and oak, and the suites were furnished with carved buffets, mantels and mirrors, tiled hearths, open grate fireplaces, and parqueted floors. Almost every room of the eighty-five apartments was equipped with a wood-burning fireplace, and until recently all had their original brass andirons, tongs, and shovels. Kitchens were faced with Minton tile and marble wainscoting, and the spacious bathrooms were elegantly appointed and featured porcelain bathtubs. There were also playrooms, gymnasiums, servants' quarters, and large storage areas.

The building was designed to accommodate hotel guests as well. Public dining rooms to serve them on the first floor are fitted out with inlaid marble floors, baseboards and ceilings of hand-carved English quartered oak, ornamented with bronze relief.

THE PLAZA HOTEL

The first Plaza Hotel was designed by George W. DeCunha and was begun in 1883. However, the builders ran out of money before it was finished and, when New York Life Insurance Company foreclosed in 1888, McKim, Mead, and White was retained to redesign the interior. The hotel opened on October 1, 1890, was eight stories high and had four hundred rooms to let for people of fashion. It was named for its location at the Fifth Avenue Plaza at Fifty-ninth Street; the plaza originally served as a clearing for carriages entering Central Park from the east and thus prevented the blocking of traffic on Fifth Avenue and Fifty-ninth Street. By the 1860s the plaza had been extended a block south to Fifty-eighth Street. It was renamed Grand Army Plaza in 1923.

By 1902 the Plaza Realty Co. had bought the hotel and commissioned Henry Janeway Hardenbergh to design a new, bigger structure. Hardenbergh had already built the city's first luxury apartment house—the Dakota—and the American Fine Arts Society Building (1892; now, the Art Students League) in the French Renaissance style at 215 West Fifty-seventh Street. From the outset, Hardenbergh noted the advantage of the site, which faced the broad open plaza. Any building on the site would be seen from many points of view.

Completed in 1907, the new Plaza opened on October 1, as the first Plaza had, but the "New Plaza Hotel," as *The New York Times* called it, had eight hundred rooms, five hundred baths, private suites of from fourteen to seventeen rooms, marble fireplaces, crystal chandeliers, two floors of public rooms, marble staircases, and ten elevators. Even though it has added rooms (300 of them in 1921) and made numerous alterations at various times since then, the hotel remains unique for its distinctive charm and elegance.

In the French Renaissance style, the Plaza Hotel is eighteen stories high, composed of brick and marble, and has two principal facades, the north, 275 feet wide, and the east, 200 feet wide.

The building is organized along Classical lines of base, shaft, and capital. A two-story marble rusticated basement and a row of balustraded balconies, beneath a boldly projecting coursing, make up the base. From this base rise eight stories in smooth yellow brick, which are capped by two transitional floors of balustraded balconies. Above these floors are a massive cornice and a mansard slate roof of five floors with gables and dormers and copper cresting. The centers of both north and east facades are recessed, and rounded towers make up the north and south corners.

The Plaza Hotel, Fifty-ninth Street and Fifth Avenue; 1907. Henry J. Hardenbergh, architect. Built of brick and marble in the French Renaissance style, the Plaza remains unique for its distinctive charm and elegance.

When the hotel opened, the festive champagne porch opened off a lobby restaurant and faced the great open plaza. During the expansion in 1921, however, the porch was removed and the restaurant was converted into the present lobby and Fifth Avenue entrance, which extends the full width of the recessed facade.

The Interior: Elegance and Charm Preserved

Although the interior of the Plaza is substantially the same as it was originally, some significant changes have been made over the years. In 1907 the tea room (called the palm court since the 1930s) had plate glass walls, columns of green stone and violet marble from Italy, Chinese cachepots, and mirror panels. All of these features remain. The original Tiffany glass-domed ceiling, however, was removed in the 1940s, unfortunately, when the floor above was remodeled.

The rose room, or Fifty-eighth Street Restaurant, became the Persian room in 1934 following Prohibition. Fortunately, the Fifty-ninth Street entrance lobby has retained its original marble walls and decorative detail. Moreover, the Fifth Avenue Café—at the northeast corner of the building and looking out on Central Park across Fifty-ninth Street—was remodeled and renamed the Edwardian room in 1955. But it has since been restored to its former dark wood paneling, red damask, and beamed ceiling.

West of the Fifty-ninth Street entrance, the oak bar has its original paneled walls of British oak and the now famous murals—painted in the 1940s by "Ashcan School" artist Everett Shinn—of three night scenes around Grand Army Plaza. One scene, showing the Pulitzer Fountain (before the changes were made), is over the bar; another of the Plaza at the turn of the century shows the hotel in the right foreground, with the Cornelius Vanderbilt mansion in the background, where Bergdorf Goodman's Department Store is today. The third mural shows Central Park as it looked from the hotel on a winter night.

Shinn, a magazine and book illustrator as well, also painted a series of eighteen murals for the Balasco Theater on West Forty-fourth Street about 1907, when the Ashcan School of New York realists were first being recognized. The oak bar murals represent a return to that form of painting after a lapse of several decades. The oak room, next to the bar, lacks its original decorations, but has been refurbished. The ballroom, the next flight up at the northwest end of the building, was two stories high and was replaced in 1921. That space was converted into offices during the expansion.

Grand Army Plaza Design and Statuary

The design of Grand Army Plaza, which evolved from Olmsted and Vaux's Central Park plan, was discussed and debated at numerous times from the 1860s. In 1903 Augustus Saint-Gaudens's equestrian statue of William Tecumseh Sherman, the Civil War hero, was erected at the north end of the plaza, which was considered an appropriate site for the monument.

The bronze Sherman statue stands on a polished pink granite pedestal ornamented with three bronze wreaths. The pedestal, set three steps above the island, was designed by McKim, Mead, and

Pulitzer Fountain, Fifty-eighth Street and Fifth Avenue. Joseph Pulitzer, at his death in 1911, left $50,000 to the city of New York to build this fountain near the Plaza entrance to Central Park.

White. The general sits on his horse with the reins in one hand, his hat in the other, and his cape fluttering behind. Winged Victory strides ahead of him on foot, holding a palm branch, emblem of death, in her hand and wearing a billowing Greek mantle. A fallen pine branch on the ground beneath the horse symbolizes the devastation of Sherman's march through Georgia.

In 1911, Joseph Pulitzer died and left fifty thousand dollars to the city to erect a fountain—"like those in the Place de la Concorde, Paris, France"—near the plaza entrance to Central Park. After some debate, however, the Art Commission of New York City convinced the Pulitzer estate that the Plaza should be conceived as an entity. In the Beaux-Arts tradition of urban planning, it was decided that Grand Army Plaza should have a formal accent to retain the form of a boulevard, which would emphasize the residential aspect of the site and protect it from excessive commercial encroachment. A competition was held for an appropriate design, and the project was awarded to Thomas Hastings of Carrère and Hastings, a British Academy-trained architect whose New York Public Library Building at Forty-second and Fifth Avenue remains as one of the crowning

233

achievements of his career and one of New York's finest architectural monuments.

It was then decided trees were to be planted along the east side of Fifth Avenue and the south side of Fifty-eighth Street, to enclose the site and establish its boundaries. Two symmetrical islands would form focal nodes at the extremities of the plaza's north-south axis interrupted by Fifty-ninth Street. The Sherman Monument already occupied the north island (it was moved about sixteen feet to bring it in line with the axis). The Pulitzer Fountain was planned to occupy the southern node.

The Pulitzer Fountain sculpture was designed by sculptor Karl Bitter, who had long been an advocate of the overall plaza design. Therefore, his fountain was conceived for this site. It is called the Fountain of Abundance, and shows Pomona, protectress of fruit trees and therefore identified as Goddess of Abundance, atop a fountain of five concentric tiers of Hautville stone. Pomona holds a basket of fruit, and cornucopias on either side carry the theme of abundance. She is turned, as though distributing the fruit. Within the top basin, a low pedestal is decorated with four carved masks that spout water and support the statue.

The figure of Pomona is based on Giambologna's sixteenth-century Boboli Gardens Venus in Florence. Bitter was killed in 1915, when struck by an automobile, so the figure was finished by Karl Gruppe and Isidore Konti. In 1970 the fountain was altered so that instead of the water flowing from a concealed ring around the base of the statue, it now flows through the four masks decorating the base.

The two islands are semicircular, reflecting the shapes of the two monuments. Planting and stone stanchions and benches reflect their shape, too. Walks, patterned stone pavements, and colorful flowerbeds, bordered by green and low shrubs, complete the design. Although the effectiveness of the north-south axis of the plaza is diminished by the open space to the east at the General Motors Building (which would be corrected by the originally planned trees), the main character of the plaza remains little changed from the original design.

THE VILLARD HOUSES

The Villard Houses were born of their owner's desire to have a private and quiet residence reminiscent of the great palaces of his native country, Bavaria. They were informed by the architect's taste for Renaissance models and inspired by his patron's desires. Recent work by William Shopsin and Mosette Broderick has yielded new material and perceptive insights into the patron, the architects, and the period.

Ferdinand Heinrich Gustav Hilgard came to America when he was eighteen years old and changed his name to Henry Villard for reasons that are uncertain, though speculated to be either to avoid conscription or to dissociate himself from the large immigrant population. Henry Villard then settled in Illinois and worked as a newspaper reporter for English and German language newspapers. Through his association with one of his cousins and with Abraham Lincoln, he became an ardent abolitionist and married Fanny Garrison (Helen Frances), daughter of the famous abolitionist William Lloyd Garrison. Villard later studied finance and supervised the U.S. holdings of a group of German businessmen. Through his astute dealings in railroad mergers and stock manipulation, he amassed substantial wealth and moved to New York.

In 1881 he bought a plot of land, 200 feet long and 175 feet deep, on Madison Avenue opposite the recently completed St. Patrick's Cathedral to build houses. He originally wanted a building surrounded by a garden, to assure privacy and quiet, and a fountain in the center like some of the great European houses he had seen outside the cities of his native land.

Villard's brother-in-law was married to the sister of the architect Charles Follen McKim, who was a friend of the Villards and who had done some work for Mrs. Villard on the Villard house at Dobbs Ferry. These interconnections influenced Villard's choice of McKim, Mead, and White to design his new house. One of the firm's most gifted architects, Joseph M. Wells, was responsible for the design. Wells had worked in Boston with several architects and in New York with the famous Richard Morris Hunt before joining McKim in 1879. Wells and Villard became good friends during the course of this project, and its success contributed to the firm's winning the Boston Public Library commission. Apparently the only disagreement the two men ever had was over the facade material. Wells wanted limestone, but Villard wanted brownstone because it was less ostentatious and more conservative.

The principal source of architectural influence for the Villard houses was the Cancelleria in Rome, the late fifteenth-century palazzo that was at the time believed to have been the work of Donato Bramante, the first of the great High Renaissance architects (credit for the design is still debated). It was a highly influential building during the revival of Renaissance models that was popular at the time Wells was developing his design for the Villard houses.

An Urban Plan

Wells's design combines elements from the Cancelleria with the European Palace plan (built on three sides around a garden with iron gates surrounding the whole). When Villard bought his land, St. Patrick's across the street had a square English Gothic east end with the archbishop's residence a projecting wing on the south, and the rectory a projecting wing on the north. Although James Renwick, architect for St. Patrick's, had intended to build the great four-hundred-foot spire of the Lady's Chapel, funds ran out. Therefore, when Villard was ready to build his house, facing his land from St. Patrick's was a picturesque plot enclosed on three sides by the cathedral's east end (the open side along Madison Avenue faced Villard's property), the archbishop's house, and the rectory. Wells designed Villard's courtyard to be almost identical in size to that of St. Patrick's across the street, and aligned the Villard wings with those of St. Patrick's, thereby creating an impressive expanse of greenery that, while divided by Madison Avenue, nevertheless united the urban plan. Villard wanted six houses; his was to be the largest and the others were to be sold. Villard's house is on the south side of 451 Madison, sixty feet north from Fiftieth Street with its entrance on the courtyard, and one hundred feet deep along Fiftieth Street.

Wells's open courtyard allows a view of the arcaded portico of the central part, which is based upon the arches of the Cancelleria, even to the decorative medallions between the arches. However, Wells eliminated the Cancelleria's gallery overlooking the courtyard and used projecting balconies at the second story on the north and south wings instead. The facade on the courtyard appears at first to be of one house. However, Wells uses quoins (the stones at the corners of a building) at the second, third, and fourth floors to show the divisions of the houses. This device in no way interferes with the coherence of the facade but it allows each house its individuality. By creating a unified facade on the courtyard, the building looks like one large Italian palazzo, a monumental design.

The houses are all different in dimensions and plan. Villard's is the largest and most grandiose, but he did not enjoy it for long. In 1884 his empire crumbled, and he left the house never to return, even though he soon recovered substantial wealth.

A Modest Mansion

While the interiors appear elaborate today, Villard's house was not considered to be at all ostentatious in his time. On the first floor, Villard had a triple parlor, a large hall, grand music room with balcony, huge dining room, and pantry. Below this he had a basement-service area with bath, wine cellar, and billiard room. Moreover, leading artists were retained for the decoration: Augustus Saint-Gaudens, sculptor; Francis Lathrop, painter; LaFarge and

Tiffany for artistic glass; and David Maitland Armstrong for mosaics.

The decorations were all supervised by the architect, but each room had its own designer, in order to achieve variety contained within an overall design. Thus, the Renaissance style prevailed throughout, and other styles and periods were included, a coherence that had great influence at the time when combinations of chinoiserie, Gothic, and Moorish forms were common. Stanford White did the main hall and dining room. The entrance leads up a short marble stairway through a barrel-vaulted vestibule, with colorful mosaic, into the grand main hall. The room is covered with rich mosaic and elegant flooring, and its walls are of Mexican marble inlaid with panels of Siena marble. The fireplace has a marble mantelpiece, and above it there is a low relief in warm marble of a woman with child and the inscription "PAX" by Augustus Saint-Gaudens. Saint-Gaudens and White also collaborated on the zodiac wall clock on the main landing. The landing now leads up to the new hotel lobby. The houses have recently been restored and are part of a new hotel that rises above and around them.

A two-story music room was designed for Sunday afternoon concerts and had a balcony for the musicians, reached by a hidden stairway behind. Saint-Gaudens inserted into the north and south walls plaster casts (five on each wall) of the Renaissance master Luca

Originally the Villard Houses, now the Helmsley Palace Hotel, 451–455 Madison Avenue; 1884. McKim, Mead, and White, architects. Designed by gifted Joseph M. Wells, these town houses are united to appear as a great Italian palazzo; the inspiration was partly the Cancelleria in Rome.

della Robbia's marble "Cantoria," the singing angels from the sacristy of the Cathedral of Florence. They illustrate the 150th Psalm praising God in his firmament and the angels appear with trumpet, lyre and harp, timbrel and dance, strings and pipe, and sounding cymbals. Although the room was designed for a movable ceiling to be lowered and raised to adjust acoustics, it was never installed.

The dining room is designed in a rich combination of woods and marbles, and its decoration combines the folk and classical past with appropriate timeless symbols. The furnishings are in richly carved English oak with mottoes carved in panels in German, French, English, and Latin. Panels of stylized floral designs are inset with mythological paintings related to feasting by Francis Lathrop. The fireplace, symbolic of man's first gathering place for warmth and food, was designed by Augustus Saint-Gaudens and carved in warm red marble. Above it are the crouching personifications of Joy, Hospitality, and Moderation. At the sides, there are niches with dolphins and basins with indoor fountains which spouted the Croton. The fireplace has been moved several times, but since 1980 it has been the focal point of the lobby of the new hotel erected behind and above Villard's houses.

THE ALICE AUSTEN HOUSE

The Alice Austen House, also called "Clear Comfort," is named for the granddaughter of John H. Austen, a successful New York dry-goods auctioneer. The house has gained fame because its owner became one of America's leading photographers. Alice Austen produced more than 7,000 photographs over a fifty-year period. They represent a compilation of her views of the world she knew from the 1880s until the Great Depression of 1929, and offer a very personal view of one aspect of the picturesque in America. Her photographs are housed in the Staten Island Historical Society, of which she was a longtime member.

An uncle, a Danish sea captain, introduced her to photography in the 1880s and at the same time, another uncle, a professor of chemistry at Rutgers College, taught her how to develop her photographs. Born to wealth, she developed her photography as a hobby, while taking a prominent role in the cultural and social life of Staten Island, as a prominent member of the local historical society, garden club, and antiquarian society. Although she lost her inheritance in the Depression and died penniless in 1952, Alice Austen lived to see her photography recognized by critics and the public alike. John Constable, the great English Romantic landscape painter, often said that it was the Suffolk countryside (now called

"Constable country") around him that made him a painter. So too it was "Clear Comfort's" picturesque setting that contributed to the formation of Alice Austen's personal and distinctive view of one very moving aspect of the American scene, which she recorded with remarkable artistry.

The house and site that contributed to this artist's body of works dates from early times. The Alice Austen House is a characteristic example of the Dutch Colonial house with successive additions to accommodate larger and more affluent families. The central section facing the Narrows was built *c.* 1691–1710, a one-room farmhouse with a large fireplace and high chimney, gabled roof, and sloping eaves. The house was added onto *c.* 1700–30 at the south end. Its great wooden, hand-hewn beams and wide-plank flooring are still intact. A stone out-kitchen (apart from the main house) with fireplace and bake oven in back, built before the American Revolution, was subsequently joined to the main house.

By the nineteenth century, the house was part of a one-hundred-acre farm. In 1835 the farm was incorporated into a larger tract of land along the Narrows, roads were built, and land was subdivided for residential development. In 1844 John H. Austen, Alice's grandfather, bought the house and an acre of land around it. Two years later, Austen added a room at the north, changing the plan from an "L" to a "T" shape, modernized it with Gothic dormers, and added Gothic ornament that remains today. The Gothic cresting that animated the ridge line of the roof unfortunately has been removed; the scalloped shingles have also been replaced.

The Gothic Revival additions have been attributed to James Renwick, a friend of Austen and a well-known pioneer and practitioner of the Gothic Revival in New York. He was finishing his famous Grace Church at Broadway and Eleventh Street in 1846, about the time these modifications to Austen's house were probably made. Another room with porch above was added *c.* 1880. The grounds were landscaped during the nineteenth century according to the picturesque tradition, capitalizing on the magnificent view of the Narrows running parallel to the front of the house. Through Alice Austen's photography, the long sweep of the terrace down to the Narrows became a legend in its own time, for both its view and its siting. Cultivated gardens were planted in the back of the house and by the 1880s ivy grew full over the front of the house in picturesque fashion.

Alice Austen came to the house to live in 1868, when she was two years old, and remained there until 1945, when she lost the house and moved to the city farm colony. It is hoped that the house, which has fallen into disrepair, will be restored and one day open to the public.

IO

Theaters

THE LYCEUM THEATER:
A NEW PLAYHOUSE

With the opening of Charles Frohman's Empire Theater at Fortieth Street and Broadway in 1893, and Oscar Hammerstein's Olympia on Broadway between Forty-fourth and Forty-fifth streets two years later, a new theater district was inaugurated. It was quickly built up by such major builders as Irwin and Henry Chanin, called the "Chanins of Broadway," and such major producers as J. J. and Lee Shubert, and Klaw and Erlanger. On April 19, 1904, Longacre Square (named after the district in London) became "Times Square" with the naming of the new subway stop at Broadway and Forty-second Street that connected the West Side with Grand Central Station. This stimulated further commercial growth in the new entertainment center.

Theaters were often a family business; Charles Frohman's brother Daniel, who headed up the country's leading repertory group, moved his Lyceum Theater Company from its old site (demolished) on the west side of Fourth Avenue in the twenties to the new theater district uptown. On October 16, 1902, he laid the cornerstone for his new Lyceum playhóuse, placing thirteen bricks from the old theater in the new foundation at 149 West Forty-fifth Street to symbolize the continuity of its traditions. Frohman opened with his repertory group on November 2, 1903, with *The Proud Prince*, starring his old friend and supporter, E. H. Sothern. Finally, when repertory theater gave way to plays of long-run engagements, Frohman stopped producing plays, but he continued to run the theater.

The Lyceum Theater, 149 West Forty-fifth Street *(facing page);* 1903. Herts and Tallant, architects. The Beaux-Arts facade includes colossal Baroque columns and ornate theater masks on the attic frieze.

Frohman's Lyceum was a *tour de force* in elegant and practical design. The combination of innovative mechanical technology, rich and commodious spaces, and Frohman's successful management made the Lyceum one of the most successful and profitable theaters on Broadway.

Under the supervision of Daniel Frohman, the Lyceum was designed by architects Henry Beaumont Herts and Hugh Tallant, who would go on to build the Folies Bergère theater at 210 West Forty-sixth Street (later renamed the Helen Hayes and recently razed) in 1911. Both architects had studied at the prestigious École des Beaux-Arts in Paris. The combination of Beaux-Arts rationality and Frohman's insistence on a modern practical building resulted in a structure that satisfied the needs of contemporary production and which actually improved the overall theater craft.

Everything Under One Roof

All the activities and services required to produce a play were successfully housed together for the first time in the Lyceum Theater, which is actually two buildings back to back. The five-story building with marquee and rich Beaux-Arts facade on West Forty-fifth Street houses the vestibules and auditorium, a rehearsal hall, and Frohman's penthouse apartment. Behind it, rising eleven stories, is a loft building that housed special reception areas for notables, large storage areas for scenery and equipment, mechanical fixtures, a costume room for cutters and seamstresses, a carpentry shop, and studio with north light for painting scenery, which was large enough to accommodate four backdrops at any one time. The room is thirty-five feet high and one hundred feet deep. Its entire north wall from floor to ceiling is glass, to provide an abundance of natural light. Slots in the floor permit lowering flats directly onto the stage. Moreover, dressing rooms accommodated two hundred people, and each dressing room was equipped with its own bathroom, an innovation at the time the theater was built.

The theater extends through the entire block from West Forty-fifth to West Forty-sixth streets, and the two-buildings-in-one function as a unified plant. For example, the entire first floor of the facade of the loft building on West Forty-sixth Street was an entrance that opened into a wide passageway that led directly onto the stage (it has since been altered). This provided direct access to the stage from the street to admit horse-drawn carriages, vehicles of all kinds, and menagerie.

The stage is eighty-nine feet wide and thirty-seven feet deep, with an addition of forty feet at the rear so that a scenic production depth of seventy-four feet was connected to the passageway and street. The stage proper was movable; as constructed with a series of elevators it allowed an entire scene, or any part of it, to be lowered or raised instantly and an auxiliary stage, or bridge, to be either placed over it or removed just as quickly (such devices were developed in the eighteenth century at Versailles for setting tables for large banquets, thereby eliminating annoying food odors). Moreover, these bridges could be placed at various angles to make terraces, cliffs, lakes, or whatever to create the atmosphere desired. The original apparatus is still intact, but it has been boarded up and is no longer used.

Closer Contact Between Actors and Audience

Frohman insisted on a wide auditorium to bring the audience closer to the stage, and through the elimination of posts, tie rods, and massive piers, nothing interferes with the view of the stage. Moreover, all lighting is indirect, so actors can see the audience and the audience's sight lines remain uninterrupted. There are not even any chandeliers to interfere with the production. The reporter for *The New York Times*, reviewing opening night, said of the lighting, "When the stage is temporarily darkened for transformation of scenes red electric lights pour a dull light upon the audience and prevent that nerve thrilling obscurity which women abhor." Further comfort was provided by a sophisticated heating and cooling system that provided a complete change of air in the auditorium every six minutes.

The color scheme of the Lyceum's interior approximates tones of autumn foliage and runs from deep yellow to warm red and brown. These tones are maintained in the furnishings throughout. For example, the seats were originally covered in a dark yellow Cordovan leather (since changed). The foyer is of Maryland marble, a warm eggshell color.

A Picturesque Experience

James Wall Finn, who distinguished himself by doing paintings for the house of Stanford White, a residence of Anna Gould, and the St. Regis Hotel, painted the two lunettes in the theater's entrance foyer. One is a portrait of Sarah Siddons, the famous English actress of the late eighteenth century, well known for her marvelous voice and for famous portraits of her by Sir Joshua Reynolds and Thomas Gainsborough. The other painting shows the renowned eighteenth-century actor and producer David Garrick in a smiling pose delivering his famous words, "Tragedy is easy enough, but comedy is a serious business." Finn also tinted the three figures over the pros-

243

cenium, representing Pallas Athene, the goddess of Wisdom and patroness of the arts, accompanied by personifications of Music and Drama—beautiful complements to the classically inspired facade.

The facade is of limestone ornamented with bronze crestings at the top. There is a massive rusticated basement with arched canopy and rising above it are colossal fluted and banded Corinthian columns, which frame two-story arched windows and support a massive entablature with a boldly projecting cornice. Above each leafy capital, ornately carved theatrical masks are set against the smooth attic surface. Above the entablature a broken balustrade encloses the balconies in front of three pedimental windows of Daniel Frohman's penthouse, now housing the Shubert archives. Ornate oval dormers pierce the mansard above and illuminate what was once the rehearsal hall.

The entrance has three vestibules, leading into the main foyer, which are done in marble selected to match that of the Parthenon. Elaborate portals mark the entrance into the auditorium, and marble-encased steel staircases lead to the balcony foyer and smoking rooms. Additional stairs and elevators lead to service areas and Daniel Frohman's suite. Frohman's library is a reproduction of David Garrick's famous library. A concealed window at the floor of the library opens into the ceiling of the auditorium which allowed Frohman to survey the entire stage from his suite. Moreover, by means of a special telephone line, he had instant contact with the stage manager at all times.

The Lyceum's Legacy

The Lyceum has enriched many magic moments in the theater. Charles Laughton began his American stage career at the Lyceum in 1931 in *Payment Deferred,* Ethel Barrymore played Nora in Ibsen's *A Doll's House* (1905), and even in the years following World War II, when the Lyceum's star began to fade, it still had bright moments, as when Judy Holliday starred in *Born Yesterday* (1946). Under Shubert management since 1952, the Lyceum has received landmark status, the interior has been refurbished, and the Frohman suite has been restored. The suite houses the Shubert archives which are now being catalogued.

THE MOVIE PALACE
AND THE ATMOSPHERIC THEATER

During and following the Great Depression, the union of movies and vaudeville brought the American public a respite from the fears and hardships of difficult times. Moreover, the great palaces in which they were presented became an integral part of that entertainment.

The atmospheric theater was developed by John Eberson, an Austrian architect who designed the first one in Houston, Texas, in 1923 (the Majestic, demolished). A domelike ceiling was painted blue with small, blinking electric lights arranged like stars in heavenly constellations spread across the sky. A special machine projected an illusion of clouds drifting across the sky to make the scene more realistic. Painted panels with exotic landscapes and buildings of foreign lands were mounted on the walls of the auditorium. And balconies, gazebos, parapets, and fountains added to the illusion of exotic places.

Several atmospheric theaters still exist in New York City, and are in varying states of preservation. The Loew's Paradise on the Grand Concourse (between 184th and 188th streets), also by Eberson (1929), retains the blue sky, twinkling lights, and moving clouds. However, it is now divided into two theaters, Paradise 1 and Paradise 2, so the total "atmospheric" effect no longer survives.

Another of Eberson's theaters, the Loew's Valencia at 165–11 Jamaica Avenue in Queens, became the Tabernacle of Prayer for all People, after the Loews Corporation gave it to the Congregation in 1977. Because it is used for public worship services, it has escaped partitioning. Moreover, the stage has been restored and accommodates the congregation's three-hundred-member choir, which broadcasts from there to forty-two states throughout the country. Decorative changes include the transformation of nude nymphs above the proscenium into winged angels.

The Loew's Valencia opened in 1929 and was decorated in a Spanish Baroque style, with murals in turquoise, red, blue, and gold that depict seventeenth-century Spanish towns behind authentic balconies and framing balustrades. Across the blue dome of the firmament, sixty-five feet up, tiny stars twinkle from the Big Dipper, and other familiar constellations.

The two-story vaulted entrance hall and lobby are still intact and the Baroque decoration of the auditorium is carried through in the woodwork, plasterwork, and chandeliers of the lobby, creating a palatial atmosphere. Its facade of patterned yellow brick and colorful terra-cotta trim is framed by massive pilasters and is accented with exuberant cherubs. The marquee and free-standing ticket booth are intact.

The Walker Theater at 6401 Eighteenth Avenue in Bensonhurst, southwestern Brooklyn, was designed in 1928 by Charles A. Sandblom and now operates as a neighborhood movie theater. Its interior is almost entirely intact. Its floating dome with twinkling stars and clouds is illuminated by the original lighting system and its Wurlitzer organ is fully operable.

The Loew's Pitkin in Brooklyn at 1501 Pitkin Avenue is now the Hudson Temple Cathedral and was erected in 1925 by one of the most prolific architects of the great movie palaces of the 1930s and 1940s, Thomas Lamb. He built them in all the major cities in the United States, largely for his major client, Marcus Loew.

Lamb came to New York as a youth from Scotland and studied engineering at Cooper Union. He later became one of the few architects who specialized in theater architecture. His early theaters, the Regent Theater (1913) at 116th Street and Seventh Avenue and the Cort (1912) at 138 West Forty-eighth Street, for example, followed Classical and Renaissance models. However, in his atmospheric theaters, he relied on more decorative and ornamented Baroque forms, as in the Keith Flushing RKO of 1928. Lamb's style

Keith Flushing RKO Theater, Northern Boulevard and Main Street, Flushing; 1928. Thomas Lamb, architect. One of the few remaining atmospheric theaters: in its prime the auditorium's Spanish facades were silhouetted against a simulated sky with twinkling stars and moving clouds.

Keith Flushing RKO Theater. On the mezzanine, the waiting room is distinguished by an elaborately carved wooden ceiling above gilded spiral columns and moorish arches.

for this has been dubbed "Mexican Baroque," which is more properly a version of Churrigueresque, a florid Spanish Baroque style named after the Spanish architects José, Joaquin, and Alberto Churriguera.

The End of a Tradition

Now divided into three theaters, the Keith Flushing RKO is one of the few great atmospheric movie palaces to survive. The auditorium walls carry mural panels of Spanish facades rendered in painting, gilded plaster, and wood, whose tops are silhouetted against the clear sky of the ceiling, creating a convincing illusion of a peaceful setting in the open air.

The vestibule is two stories high with arches supported by gilded spiral columns beneath an azure blue vault simulating the sky. The fountain, which was originally in the center of the vestibule, has been replaced by a candy concession. Staircases at either end of the vestibule lead to the mezzanine, which has an elaborately carved wooden ceiling. Original iron and tile work, terra-cotta, and gilded plaster mouldings survive in the lounges.

The Keith Flushing RKO opened as a subscription theater—that is, season tickets were sold and the shows, which featured vaudeville and films, were changed weekly.

The "K" in RKO stands for Benjamin Franklin Keith, who started out in show business as a kind of medicine man with a circus in New Hampshire. He met Edward Franklin Albee in Boston, who was a circus promoter too, and they collaborated there in producing Gilbert and Sullivan musicals for the masses. The B. F. Keith Theater Circuit resulted from this partnership in the 1880s, and then Keith and Albee started "continuous vaudeville" theaters, where you could go in any time and see a show, and built the country's largest vaudeville chain.

Keith and Albee built theaters in all the major cities of the country. As movies became popular, they also became respectable when associated with vaudeville, and so Keith and Albee offered the double bill, which opened the way for subscription theater and season tickets, as at the Keith Flushing RKO. Through a succession of mergers with other chains or circuits, the B. F. Keith Theater Circuit became RKO, the Radio-Keith-Orpheum circuit, and many of their theaters were the atmospheric type.

From Nickelodeon to Palace

When movies first began, "the silents" were shown in what amounted to small shops called nickelodeons, equipped with a projection booth, a screen, and seats. They had a door to come in and one to go out that flanked a ticket booth in the center. Eventually, to attract attention, the nickelodeons put blinking lights around an overhanging panel outside and used this as a means of announcing the movie that was playing.

As movies improved technically, they became more popular with the public and consequently more attractive to the theater entrepreneur, who gave movies respectability by combining them with vaudeville in a graciously furnished theater.

Perhaps the major force in giving respectability to movies was Samuel L. Rothafel, better known as "Roxy," who combined vaudeville with movies in beautiful theaters. His Rialto Theater, which opened in 1916, was designed by Thomas Lamb. Built three years after the famous Woolworth Building, dubbed the "Cathedral of Commerce," Roxy called his Rialto "The Shrine of Music and the Allied Arts." Then when he opened the largest movie theater in the world—the Roxy, named after him, at Fiftieth Street and Seventh Avenue—he called it the "Cathedral of the Motion Picture," since it had twisted columns supposedly modeled after Bernini's great bronze columns for the Baldacchino in St. Peter's in Rome, alas not a cathedral but a basilica!

Thus the theater became increasingly important and transformed its interior space into something not of this world, something exotic, exciting, and highly desirable. Marcus Loew, proprietor of the famous chain of theaters, knew where the appeal really was: "We sell tickets to theaters, not movies." Movies and vaudeville progressed hand in hand until the changes in economics and live entertainment separated them, and the great movie palaces became America's leading form of entertainment.

II

The New York Port
Comes of Age

Through new technology and innovative services in shipping, the New York port grew with unprecedented speed in the nineteenth century. For example, on January 5, 1818, the *James Monroe*, a packet ship of the Black Ball Line, left South Street at 10:00 A.M. in a blizzard and thus introduced regularly scheduled packet service between New York and Europe. Until then ships, like the ferries, left port only when they were full and the weather was good. Now, full or not, good weather or bad, these durable square-rigged liners set sail punctually at the appointed time and reached a European port such as Liverpool in three weeks. This made it possible for the first time to guarantee merchants the delivery of their goods, and thereby revolutionized commercial shipping.

By mid-century the faster clipper ships, which could cut as much as six weeks off a trip from New York to San Francisco, had replaced the packets and in the process had captured the hearts and imaginations of the public. Their grace and engineering inspired Horatio Greenough (America's first internationally known sculptor, who preferred "Greek principles" to "Greek things") to proclaim that the makers of our great yachts were nearer to Athens than those who would bend Greek temples to every use! But the clipper ship era was a short one. The first American clipper, the *Rainbow*, was built near Fourth Street at the East River in 1845, and the last clipper built in America was the *Twilight* from Mystic, Connecticut,

Grand Central Station *(facing page)*. The circumferential plaza goes around the terminal building and over Forty-second Street, allowing traffic to move freely in all directions.

launched in 1857. The only American clipper still extant is the *Snow Squall* (1851), and she survives only as a fragment in the Falkland Islands, where she was recently discovered as part of a pier in Fort Stanley Harbor.

The advent of transatlantic steamships with greater capacity and the completion of the Panama Railway in 1855 signaled the end of the clipper ship era. Moreover, as the larger steamers needed a deeper and wider harbor, so the Hudson River replaced the East River as the New York port. Profoundly important to the further development of the New York port and American trade was the opening of the Erie Canal in 1825, which united the inland resources of the country with the eastern seaboard and international markets. The Erie Canal was considered the most successful transportation system in America until the opening of the interstate highways network of the 1950s. The railroads further contributed to the growth of the New York port through the development of American transportation and commerce: from the many short lines both along the seaboard and inland that sprang up, beginning in the 1820s, to the great transcontinental railroads, beginning with the Union Pacific in 1869, and then with the standardization of commercial rail passage in the 1880s.

THE U.S. CUSTOM HOUSE: SYMBOL OF A NEW ERA

By the opening of the twentieth century, the importance of the New York port to the economic prosperity of the United States was fittingly illustrated in the erection of the new U.S. Custom House across from Bowling Green. *The New York Times* called it "a great Temple of Commerce." The customs service had grown enormously since July 4, 1789, when Congress passed the first tariff bill to raise revenue for government expenses by collecting duties on all foreign imports from ships docked in New York Harbor. Revenue from imports grew to become the main source of the federal government's income until 1913, when the Federal Income Tax was introduced.

The foreign imports generating this income were directly tied to the issue of the United States's broadening economic interests throughout the world. Beginning in the 1880s, the United States was increasing its foreign trade and naval force until by 1900, it had become a significant world power with a strong navy and with a manufacturing capability to compete with the most advanced industrial nations anywhere.

The United States was ushered into the forum of world politics and power by its victory in the Spanish-American War. The Treaty of Paris between the United States and Spain, signed on December 10, 1898, freed Cuba, ceded Puerto Rico and Guam to the United States, and surrendered the Philippine Islands; now the U.S. was inextricably involved in the affairs of Latin America and the Far East.

New Symbols and a New Look

Commodore George Dewey's victory over the Spanish fleet in Manilla Bay on May 1, 1898, won with his Asiatic Squadron of modern cruisers and gunboats, established the United States as a major power in the Pacific and was seen to symbolize America's new role as a world power. Dewey's victory and triumphant return were commemorated in a great triumphal arch erected on Twenty-third Street where Madison Square and Fifth Avenue meet. The arch was constructed for his visit to New York City in the summer of 1899 and was made of staff (impermanent material built with plaster, such monuments were not meant to be permanent). It was designed by architect Charles Lamb after the Arch of Titus; Frederic Wellington Ruckstull was in charge of the sculpture program for the arch, which was sponsored by the National Sculpture Society. Major sculptors of the period participated, and the arch's theme was America's military power dedicated to peace. An attempt to have the arch reconstructed as a permanent monument in stone failed. Remnants of the arch, however, were salvaged following the festivities by J. Kennedy Tod, a banker, for his estate near Stamford, Connecticut.

Theodore Roosevelt, who had resigned as assistant secretary of the Navy to help organize the First U.S. Volunteer Cavalry for service in Cuba, became a national hero in the war when he led his famed "Rough Riders" up Kettle Hill (alas, not San Juan Hill). The nation's strength and influence throughout the world grew under Roosevelt (president, 1901–09), to which his knowledge of and commitment to maritime affairs contributed substantially. As a young New York State Assemblyman, Roosevelt had published a history of *The Naval War of 1812* (1882), and as president in 1903, he deployed U.S. Navy ships at Panama to assure the success of its revolt for independence from Colombia and thereby made possible the construction of the Panama Canal. The year the U.S. Custom House in New York was completed, Roosevelt sent the "Great White Fleet" (most of the U.S. Navy) on a world cruise as a show of U.S. naval strength.

The customs service, at the turn of the century, was not just running out of space in the old Merchants' Exchange Building on Wall Street; it also needed a new home to look like what it was—an

253

U.S. Custom House, at Bowling Green; 1907. Cass Gilbert, architect.
"A Great Temple of Commerce" that combined a steel skeleton with
elaborate Beaux-Arts cladding.

extremely important and highly visible arm of the government's maritime and economic body. Furthermore, it was felt that the building should be up-to-date, with the most modern services and conveniences. The new Custom House was to combine an architectural style that embodied the tradition of the customs service, the federal government, and the United States with the latest building technology.

The architect, Cass Gilbert (who later designed the Woolworth Building), was selected in competition (required by a new law, the Tarnsey Act, 1897). Even though conflicts of interest were suggested, because the government's supervising architect was a former partner of Gilbert, the selection could not have been better for everyone concerned, it was generally agreed later. Gilbert was from Minnesota, and by this time he had designed the state's capitol and had outstanding credentials in training and practical experience. He had studied at Massachusetts Institute of Technology, worked in New York with the highly prestigious architectural firm of McKim, Mead, and White, traveled through Europe on the Grand Tour, and had earned the respect of leading architects and influential patrons alike.

The site that the government selected for the new building was itself historically significant. It was the location of the original Fort Amsterdam, built in 1626. There had been nine forts on the site until 1790, when Fort George was demolished and Government House was built on the site by James Robinson and John McComb, Jr., as George Washington's official residence. When the nation's capital moved to Philadelphia, soon after, the Government House became the Governor's Mansion under George Clinton and John Jay. Then the state capital moved to Albany in 1797 and the mansion became a tavern, leased by John Avery from 1798 until 1799. From 1799 it served as the Custom House until it burned down in 1815. The building was replaced by a fashionable row of private residences which, by the end of the century, had been transformed into steamship offices called "Steamship Row." Customs business was conducted at various locations until the Greek Revival building by Town and Davis was completed at Wall and Nassau streets in 1842. In need of more space by 1863, the customs service moved across the street to Isaiah Rogers's Merchants' Exchange Building, and remained there until it moved back to Bowling Green in 1907.

A Modern Bond Between Tradition and Technology

Gilbert built a modern steel skeleton structure and clad it in the fashionable Beaux-Arts style uniting sophisticated technology with traditional forms in a building appropriate for a leading port of the world. The building is trapezoidal in plan, following the irregular shape of its site, with seven stories above the sidewalk and two below. It is bounded by Bowling Green, State, Whitehall, and Bridge streets. Begun in 1901, it was completed in 1907.

The central focus of the Custom House is the rotunda, a masterful mixture of a new vaulting system (system for covering an arched ceiling) with traditional European Beaux-Arts decoration. There is an elliptical marble counter shelf, whose shape is echoed by the room and its skylight, which is the center of negotiations where export notices and declarations were filed, and where foreign vessels were cleared and entered. The geometrically patterned floor, executed in variegated marbles and onyx, supported the busy traffic of customs and conveyed to the room the desired sense of richness and permanence. Above, one sees the 140-ton glass and metal skylight featuring ships' bows carved in high relief around the base of the drum which provided ever-changing natural light. Unfortunately during World War II, the skylight was painted and tarred over for "blackouts," when all lights were extinguished and windows were covered as a precaution against air raids, and remains blacked out.

The rotunda is covered with a timbrel or flat vault (also called a Catalan vault because of its popularity in Catalonia, Spain), constructed by the Guastavino Fireproof Construction Co. Although the origins of this system are obscure, examples have been found in such areas as ancient Egypt and Byzantium (today's Istanbul). The Spaniard Rafael Guastavino (and his son, Rafael) applied it to modern technology and brought it to the United States in 1881; therefore, it is sometimes called the Guastavino System.

Timbrel vaults are made of thin flat clay tiles laid next to each other in several layers and bound together by mortar, producing an eggshell-thin, laminated structure that is at once sturdy, light, and fireproof. Timbrel vaults can be built more rapidly and cheaply than traditional vaults which rely on gravity, friction, and lateral thrust for stability, and which also require a cumbersome centering apparatus for construction. Dramatic results were subsequently achieved with this timbrel vaulting system in New York—in the dome of St. John the Divine on Riverside Drive (1892–1916); St. Thomas Church on Fifth Avenue (1914); and, perhaps the most superb example of its use, in St. Paul's Chapel at Columbia University (1907).

Even though Gilbert had budgeted for murals to decorate his elliptical dome, they were not executed until 1937, when the American scene painter, illustrator, and printmaker Reginald Marsh was commissioned, as part of the government's WPA program, to paint a series of eight panels portraying scenes of the arrival of an ocean liner at New York Harbor (passing the Statue of Liberty, tugs working the ship into dock, etc.). Eight smaller panels separating these

257

U.S. Custom House: rotunda. Above the rich marbles and onyx of the floor, walls, columns, and the grand elliptical counter shelf hovers a 140-ton glass-and-metal skylight set in an egg-shell-thin timbrel, or flat, vault—highly innovative at the time.

scenes portray famous men connected with exploration of the New World and of the New York port region: Block, Verrazano, Columbus, Gomez, Cabot, Cortoreal, Vespucci, and Hudson.

The three principal offices, those of the collector, manager, and cashier, lie north of the rotunda across the main lobby and directly behind the main facade. Years of inadequate maintenance have left these offices in poor condition, but they are constructed of durable materials, and a federal program now underway to renovate the Custom House should restore these rooms to their original splendor. The collector's office was originally designed as the office of the U.S. Secretary of the Treasury and was lavishly decorated. It is oak paneled beneath a coffered wood ceiling covered with dark gold aluminum leaf which matches fourteen gilded light fixtures. Baseboards are in green marble, and the mantel and fireplace are bordered in Hauteville marble. An elaborate wood screen with hand-carved swags, masks, and maritime motifs, capped by the eagle of the customs service, separates the collector's office from his drawing room. A frieze of nautical designs along the cornice sets off ten oil paintings in gilded frames by Elmer E. Garnsey (c. 1911), each depicting a seventeenth-century port important to the discovery, set-

U.S. Custom House: cashier's office. Here, massive oak doors with stippled glass protected by bronze screens are framed by a carved marble doorway (carrying nautical motifs) set between grand pilasters.

tlement, and commerce of the Dutch and English colonies in the New World: Amsterdam, Netherlands; Curaçao, Dutch West Indies; Fort Orange, Albany; New Amsterdam, New York; La Rochelle, France; London, England; Port Royal, Jamaica; Plymouth, England; Cadiz, Spain; Genoa, Italy. Each view shows the port in 1644, the last year the Dutch flag flew over Fort Amsterdam, the site on which the Custom House was built. When cleaned, these paintings will once again brilliantly tell their story.

The manager's office is distinguished by the simplicity of its plain white plaster walls and Ionic cornice, and the design of the cashier's office expresses its function. A lightly veined white Vermont marble counter shelf supports a simple but massive bronze screen and the panels over the two doorways are carved with nautical motifs in high relief. The walls in front of the screen, where the public conducts its business, are sheathed in white marble; the walls behind the screen, not visible to the public, are plaster. The floor is white marble with a geometric border.

These offices have elaborate entrances from the main lobby. Varnished oak doors with stippled glass are protected by cast bronze screens bearing the "U.S." emblem above, supported by a Classical

259

lyre pattern, and a caravel below, all framed by a continuous rosette border with the custom eagle at the corners. Directly facing these offices, on the south wall, are carved marble fountains with Neptune-head spouts and conch-shell basins; original bronze tables with glass tops still flank the office entrances.

The main lobby is sheathed in marble from floor to ceiling. No less than sixteen different kinds of marble were used, from Vermont, Georgia, Alaska, Pennsylvania, and numerous European quarries, especially those in Italy; each marble has a distinctive color, grain, texture, and pattern. The lobby is divided into five bays by massive membrane arches supported by green cippolino marble (from the Italian word for onion because the pattern looks like the layers of a sliced onion) columns with white capitals. The lobby is flanked at either end by curved staircases rising to the seventh floor. The whole is illuminated by three gilded bronze lanterns suspended from the vaults at the third floor gallery, over a large disc of red Vermont marble and gilded bronze sconces at the first floor. Allegorical murals by Elmer Garnsey enhance the vaulting, while Classical and nautical motifs (such as the trident) decorate the marble and bronze details and incorporate U.S. government symbols.

Gilbert also employed Guastavino on the staircases that flank the lobby. The stairs are supported by timbrel arches that spring from landing to landing up to the seventh floor, where a skylight replicates a ship's cabin and is glazed with cathedral glass. The stairway ironwork complements the metalwork of the open cage elevators nearby. With matching bronze transom grilles, they were installed at either end of the lobby. Although new elevators replaced the open cages *c.* 1935, the original matching transom grilles above still remain, and they repeat the caravel (ship) design from the bronze screen of the office doors. The caravel is also found on the shield of Queen Isabella (referring to Columbus's ship and his discovery of America), standing at the attic level of the facade.

Beaux-Arts Cladding: The Exterior

Cass Gilbert was highly progressive in his use of modern steel-skeleton construction (first perfected in the early skyscrapers in Chicago), Guastavino vaulting, and the most modern technology throughout the Custom House—elevators, heating, water system, and the like—but he was equally conservative in the selection of an architectural style. He wrapped his modern structure in exuberant decoration and expansive forms on a grand scale, characteristic of the still-fashionable Second Empire style of the 1860s and 1870s in Europe and America (from France's Second Empire under Napoleon III), to satisfy the prevailing taste of the time for rich display and to convey the image of wealth and power his patrons desired. The style had become less curvacious and more eclectic by the end of the nineteenth and early part of the twentieth centuries in the United States, when the Custom House was built. It was then called the Beaux-Arts style, after the École des Beaux-Arts (School of Fine Arts) in Paris.

In addition to its lavish opulence and glitter, the quickly identifiable hallmark of the Beaux-Arts style is the mansard roof, named after its inventor, François Mansart, the French architect who introduced it in his first masterpiece, the Orléans wing of the château at Blois in 1635, never completed. The mansard roof has a double slope, which is very steep, allowing the richly textured and crested roof to serve as a decorative capping to the building, while at the same time allowing an additional floor or two of usable space, otherwise lost on the attic.

Alternation between paired and single columns to define a facade, extensive use of sculpture, elaborate window and door enframements, inventive dormers, and metal crestings at the roof also distinguish the style. Important, too, was the site of a Beaux-Arts building—it should be located at the end of a long boulevard as an appropriate terminal point, and it should enhance the site. In the nineteenth century, much of Paris was organized by Baron Georges-Eugène Haussmann according to this principle, and Charles Garnier's Opéra in Paris (1875) is considered by many to be the most splendid example embodying these ideas.

The column is the fundamental structural element that dictates the Custom House's organization, which is visually evident throughout. Resting upon a massive basement (base), the building is composed of three registers surrounded by a screen of forty-four Corinthian columns that unite the registers as one unit (shaft), with an attic story (capital) above, beneath a dormered mansard roof. This organization of base, shaft, and capital is effectively articulated on the main facade, facing Bowling Green. Columns (shaft) emerge from massive rectangular sculpture groups (base) at the basement level and culminate in vertical statuary (capital) at the attic just below the roof. The arrangement of these columns and the statuary at the attic level into paired and single units (ABBA) on either side of the great arched entrance creates a unifying screen. The resulting intersection of the vertical and horizontal elements produces a stable and symmetrical grid over the face of the building.

The Symbiosis of Sculpture and Architecture

At the time the Custom House was built, most people still believed that art was supposed to express a message and should therefore have a beneficial influence on people's thoughts and feelings. Cass Gilbert's three-fold sculpture program is an example of this conception of sculpture's role in a public building. The sculpture identifies the purpose of the building through nautical decoration; it illustrates the history of maritime power and commerce from antiquity to modern times through the figures at the attic level; and it describes the development—past, present, and future—of the human spirit through a selection of major human races and cultural types represented at the basement level and in some of the key-stones.

Decorations over the entire exterior weave maritime motifs: dolphins, shells, prows, rudders, masts, anchors, and waves; along with ancient forms: the acanthus, urns, and Classical mouldings. Races of man are portrayed in the keystones at the second floor (Caucasian, Hindu, Latin, Celtic, Mongolian, Eskimo, Slav, African); a wave pattern surmounts the lintels at the third floor; a shell motif embellishes the fourth floor lintels; and the head of Mercury replaces the customary rosette in the Corinthian capitals near the fifth floor, where a nautical frieze encircles the building.

Cass Gilbert described the four groups projecting from the basement of the facade, by Daniel Chester French, assisted by Adolph Weinman, for the *New York Sun:* Asia is a serene figure in Oriental costume seated on a throne supported by skulls; she holds an idol in her lap as the cross rises behind her right shoulder, symbolizing the victory of Christianity, born in the East, over paganism. Prostrate figures and a suppliant tiger personify the subordination of both man and beast to the superstition and tyranny of ancient beliefs.

Uniting the old and the new ideologically and geographically, Europe rests her left arm on a book, symbol of the law, supported by the globe it governs. Prows of Viking ships, the Roman eagle, reliefs from the Parthenon, and coats of arms embroidered on Europe's robe are united by the shrouded figure of Ancient History, who sits behind reading from a scroll of man's achievements and holding a laurel-crowned skull above the empty crowns of past rulers. The statue represents the perpetuity of tradition, custom, and law.

America holds a sheaf of Indian corn in her lap and rests her foot on a remnant of Aztec sculpture, showing her triumph over prehistoric civilizations. She thrusts the torch of progress forward as a modern Mercury sets the winged wheel of commerce into motion, and an Indian rises from behind to follow her gaze into the future.

Africa sleeps, her enormous potential to awaken anon. Her right arm on the silent sphinx and her left on a slumbering lion, she rests

U.S. Custom House: cartouche. Karl Bitter's sculpture group has two winged female figures supporting the shield of the United States, with the American Eagle above and horns of plenty below. The figures of Venice and Spain (at left) and Holland and Portugal (at right) below the cartouche are among others that stand for leading maritime nations in the history of commerce.

her foot on a desert rock shaped by ages of shifting sands. A draped and hooded figure behind contemplates the age when the sleeping continent will awake to write its history.

The massive groups by French and Weinman serve as a fitting and stable base for the columns and statues at the attic level above. Moreover, these attic figures suggest the column beneath them with their fluted shafts and richly carved capitals. Gilbert required the sculptors to give the lower part of the figures a vertical movement either by the pose of the limbs, the drapery, or an object such as a staff or sword to continue the vertical lines of the columns below. The upper parts of the statues were to be rich in detail, culminating in an appropriate resolution of the upward movement.

This careful design focuses attention visually on the figures at the attic level, which then tell the story of maritime commerce through the ages, from ancient times to the present. The narrative reads from left to right, beginning with Greece and Rome and ending with France and England. The United States is represented in the enormous cartouche by Karl Bitter that crowns the building, and New York City's coat of arms is carved above the main entrance by Andrew O'Connor. Moreover, the colossal head of Columbia, carved by Vicenzo Albani, forms the keystone of the main archway.

U.S. Cartouche

The national seal is placed on the building at the seventh story in the colossal cartouche by Karl Bitter, which identifies it as a building of the U.S. government. Two sinuous figures, thinly draped, support between them the shield of the United States with the American eagle above, a horn of plenty below. One figure holds the sheathed sword, symbol of peace, the other a bound bundle of reeds, symbol of strength in unity.

Karl Bitter came to America from Vienna in 1888 at the age of twenty-one and first distinguished himself in 1891 by winning the design competition for the set of bronze doors at the main entrance of Trinity Church on Broadway, a few blocks north at the head of Wall Street. Many commissions followed, including the personifications of Architecture, Sculpture, Painting, and Music, and medallion portraits of some of the old masters on the facade of the Metropolitan Museum of Art. One of his best-known, and alas, his last sculptures, Pomona (1915), stands in front of the Plaza Hotel atop the Pulitzer Fountain.

Since the customs service moved to its new headquarters in the World Trade Center in the early 1970s, the old Custom House building has remained empty and through lack of maintenance has deteriorated. However, its exterior was cleaned during the Bicentennial, and Congress has alotted funds for a full restoration of the building, which is now underway. When completed, the building will house federal offices, and space will be set aside for public use as well.

GRAND CENTRAL STATION*

As Cass Gilbert's great temple of commerce, the U.S. Custom House, was going up at the lower tip of Manhattan, celebrating this country's leading role in maritime trade, another Beaux-Arts palace was rising uptown at Forty-second Street, a monument to the country's preeminence in overland transportation: Grand Central Sta-

---

* The entire complex is properly Grand Central Terminal (because routes terminate here), but the designation "Grand Central Station," describing the depot building, has come to replace the more precise term.

tion, which, like the Custom House, celebrated the compatibility of the steel skeleton with the Beaux-Arts architectural style.

It stands on the site of the first Grand Central Station, built by Cornelius Vanderbilt in 1871 as a monument to his railroad empire. It was designed in an elegant Second Empire style to fit in with the mansions of the wealthy along Madison and Fifth avenues. Vanderbilt's first Grand Central Station was the product of the transportation boom in New York which had begun in the early nineteenth century. With its steady advance northward in the early nineteenth century, New York became less and less a walking city, and by the late 1820s the omnibus (a four-wheeled horse-drawn coach) had appeared to carry passengers short distances and along fixed routes over bumpy streets. Then, iron tracks were laid, making possible smoother and faster travel and larger cars to accommodate more passengers.

Public Transportation

By 1832 America's first horse-drawn streetcar line was carrying passengers from Prince Street to Union Square at Fourteenth Street. The line was introduced by New York's first railroad, the New York and Harlem Railroad Company. The railroad's main, and more ambitious purpose, however, was to link the markets of Manhattan with the village of Harlem, some five miles farther north, and its tracks followed the Commissioners' Plan of 1811 along Fourth Avenue due north, establishing a route still traveled today.

In lower Manhattan at this time, as many as 250 horse-drawn cars carried passengers along established routes, while almost 200 hackney coaches and over 220 cabs contributed to the traffic congestion of lower Manhattan. When the horse-drawn streetcars got uptown to the less populous areas, they were connected to locomotives (noisy, smoke-belching locomotives frightened horses and pedestrians and caused accidents; therefore they were prohibited in populous areas) at what were called "transfer points." These transfer points followed the population growth northward.

Meanwhile, many railroad lines were springing up in various parts of the country connecting inland markets and principal waterways with the eastern seaboard, and New York became a busy rail center. "Commodore" Cornelius Vanderbilt, who had built an enormous steamboat empire, was the first to recognize the inevitable shift in transportation from steamboats to locomotives, and in 1863 he began consolidating such major lines as the New York Central, the Harlem, and the Hudson River Railroad. He established a monopoly in rail transportation from New York to Chicago and amassed the largest personal fortune yet in the United States.

265

The First Grand Central Station

By the end of the decade, Vanderbilt's main transfer point, located at Forty-second Street and Fourth Avenue, was equipped with a blacksmith shop, sheds for engines and cars, and stables for the horses; nonetheless, the rapidly increasing train and passenger traffic demanded more elaborate facilities. A depot was clearly needed. Furthermore, it was imperative that the depot be elegant, because the Commodore's trains were close to a fashionable residential area. New York's wealthy members of high society were building along Fifth Avenue and Madison Avenue between Thirty-fourth and Forty-second streets, and the residents of the socially prominent Murray Hill area, south of Forty-second Street, were protective of their peace and quiet as well.

Vanderbilt then commissioned architect John B. Snook, a highly respected practitioner of cast-iron architecture in New York and the man who had built America's first great department store. Vanderbilt wanted him to build the biggest railroad station in the world, combining the most advanced technology with palatial grandeur. Snook's creation was not only enormous, it was also elegant and efficient. The train shed was designed by engineer-architect Robert Griffith Hatfield and engineer Joseph Duclos for Architectural Iron Works, fabricators of the shed. Influenced by innovations in ferrovitreous train-shed construction in England, France, Germany, and Holland, their design was a broadly sweeping, simple semicircular metal-and-glass arch spanning the train yard. This single-span shed, which allowed more usable space than multiple-span structures, followed the design of engineers W. H. Barlow and R. M. Ordish for St. Pancras Station in London. Even though smaller than St. Pancras Station, historians have noted that Grand Central Station's shed (100 feet high, 200 feet wide, and 600 feet long) was the largest interior in America at the time, and it set the style for most of the single-span sheds in this country for the next twenty years.

To accommodate the structure to the palatial mansions of the wealthy west of the station, the three-story west and south facades —erected in handsome red brick with cast-iron mansard roof, crestings, and detailing—were constructed to conceal the train shed and were modeled after the Louvre in Paris. Because immigrant tenements, squatters' shacks, breweries, and slaughter houses made up the area east of the station, the east side of the yard was left open. Snook's building was hailed as a great success, and even though Vanderbilt had been ridiculed for building too far north, elevated rapid transit systems were soon uniting the city to the south with Grand Central Station. The city also continued expanding north and ultimately proved Vanderbilt's judgment correct.

Grand Central Terminal, Forty-second Street and Park Avenue; 1903–13.
Reed and Stem, Warren and Wetmore, architects. The main facade in
Bedford limestone symbolizes the gateway to New York; the creation of a
"Terminal City" was an innovation in urban planning.

Fashionable hotels enhanced the neighborhood. For example,
the Grand Union came in 1874, absorbing the Reunion and Riggs
House across from Grand Central Station (thus its name). Dark
mansards and handsome cresting related it to the architecture of
Snook's elegant depot. Its seven hundred rooms catered to a fashionable clientele and its proprietors, Samuel T. Shaw and his
brother-in-law and law partner, Simeon Ford, complemented each

267

other superbly. Besides being law partners, they had the concession for table water for the better New York hotels. Ford, a well-known wit and popular after-dinner speaker of the day, made it a point to know all the hotel's regular guests and their tastes. Samuel Shaw, U.S. fencing champion turned art collector, had one of the finest collections of original prints in New York, which he displayed on the walls of the hotel. The collection remained there until the Grand Union was razed in 1914 for the construction of subway connections to Grand Central. The Bowery Savings Bank stands on the site now.

Strain and Tragedy: Catalysts for Change

With the death of Cornelius Vanderbilt (1877), his son William H. Vanderbilt trebled his father's empire during the following decade, and the great rail palace Cornelius Vanderbilt had erected showed the strain. By the 1890s Grand Central Station was handling three times the traffic it had in 1871, and the city pressed relentlessly north. It was fast becoming apparent that Grand Central Station was a bottleneck at the intersection of one of the city's major crosstown thoroughfares, Forty-second Street, and a busy north-south traffic artery, Park Avenue, so the building was enlarged. Between 1898 and 1900 the depot's three stories became six, and the waiting rooms were consolidated into one large main space. But these measures would neither satisfy the increased rail requirements within the structure nor alleviate the traffic bind around it.

The increasing stresses of crowding also made the entire train system unsafe. This was tragically underscored on the cold morning of January 8, 1902, when, vision obscured by excessive smoke and steam in the tunnel approach to Grand Central Terminal, two trains collided, killing fifteen people instantly. Consequent legistation prohibiting steam trains south of the Harlem River hastened the electrification of the entire rail system.

This modernization became part of a much larger master plan, conceived by William J. Wilgus, chief engineer in charge of all bridge and terminal construction for the railroad, that produced today's Grand Central Station. Wilgus's revolutionary plan solved the traffic and real estate problems of the railroad and the area around the depot and train shed and established a model of multiuse architecture that inspired such complexes as Rockefeller Center —the most successful venture of its kind—and the Chanin Building across the street.

Innovation in Urban Planning

Wilgus began his career with the railroad as a draftsman with a background in civil engineering. By the time the new Grand Central

Station was to be built, he had already designed and supervised the construction of major terminals and stations in the country and had been involved in the changeover from steam locomotives to electrically powered engines. Capitalizing on the elimination of smoke and noise through electrification, Wilgus enlarged the Grand Central train yard and established two levels of underground track. The lower bed for suburban trains had an uninterrupted loop allowing incoming trains from the north to unload passengers, and follow the loop around to the opposite side to board outgoing passengers. Locomotives, therefore, did not have to uncouple, which saved time and maintenance costs, and made a safer system.

Wilgus covered over the tracks down Park Avenue to promote fashionable apartments, hotels, and commercial structures to extend from Madison to Lexington avenues and from Forty-fourth to Fifty-ninth streets. Through special engineering, a unique system of insulation between the ground and the building's foundations was developed to absorb the vibration created by the rail traffic beneath. Moreover, to eliminate the bottleneck in traffic the terminal had caused, Wilgus introduced the idea of an elevated drive, called a circumferential plaza, to wrap around the terminal and to extend over Forty-second Street, leaving the east-west movement unimpeded as well.

From a limited competition of leading architects, which included McKim, Mead, and White—whose Penn Station created during the same period (1910) alas stands no more—Wilgus's brother-in-law's (Charles Reed) firm, Reed and Stem of St. Paul, was selected. This was a logical choice in spite of the criticism of nepotism, for Wilgus had employed the firm before for the station in Troy, New York, for example. However, after the competition was closed, Warren and Wetmore was appointed to collaborate with Reed and Stem. Whitney Warren was a cousin of William K. Vanderbilt II, the last of the Vanderbilts to be actively involved in the railroad. Because of political, financial, and public pressures that came with increased social awareness at the end of the nineteenth century, the Vanderbilts had methodically divested themselves of their railroad holdings. By the time of the new Grand Central Station project, they were minor stockholders, although not without influence, to which the appointment of Warren and Wetmore attests.

Reed and Stem handled the large-scale planning and technical aspects of the complex and devised the ingenious system of multi-level elevations—connected by ramps, concourses, and stairs—for pedestrian and vehicular traffic and designed the plaza around the terminal that at once allowed traffic to flow freely north and south around the terminal and set the building back, rising on a high stylobate (platform). Light, space, and air surround the structure

269

and allow it to be seen easily from below. And now, even with high-rise buildings around it, Grand Central Station stands as a solid and radiating icon of innovative urban design.

Warren and Wetmore, on the other hand, was responsible for the *parti,* that is, the architectural conception, and the elegant detailing that distinguishes the structure. Whitney Warren was educated at the École des Beaux-Arts and formed a partnership with lawyer Charles Wetmore in 1896. They came to national attention with their New York Yacht Club (1899)—37 West Forty-fourth Street, an ingenious example of *architecture parlante*—a yacht club whose exterior windows resemble those of a ship's. The facade is composed of windows duplicating sterns of seventeenth-century Spanish galleons, set between colossal columns and amongst nautical deities, sea life, and splashing waves—all carved in limestone. Warren was one of the organizers of the Society of Beaux-Arts Architects in 1895 (later Beaux-Arts Institute of Design, 1911), whose purpose was to perpetuate the teaching of the École and the French atelier system in this country. Architects would train students in their studios, or ateliers. Toward that end, he also organized the annual Beaux-Arts Ball in 1913 to raise funds for scholarships to the École. The ball was held for twenty-four years.

The station's main facade, a Roman triumphal arch, faces south, and symbolizes the gateway to the city. This became a popular design for railroad stations throughout the country after Charles Atwood used it for the railroad station in the Columbian Exposition in 1893, the great World's Fair in Chicago. Paired Corinthian columns flank three colossal, arched windows and support a massive entablature surmounted at the center by a grand sculpture group. The group is by Jules-Alexis Coutan, is sixty feet wide by fifty feet high, and depicts Mercury, symbol of commerce, supported by the American eagle. Mercury is flanked by Hercules, symbol of moral strength, and Minerva, symbol of mental energy. A glazed clock is beneath Mercury (the window behind each numeral can be opened to facilitate maintenance).

One of Reed and Stem's early plans repeated the triumphal arch from the south facade on the north facade and had a grand plaza—simulating ancient Rome—extending northward for an arts center, where the Metropolitan Opera and National Academy of Design could be housed. The executed design, however, eliminated the northern court, but retained the great triumphal arch. Moreover, an urban design of office buildings and apartments resulted in a complex called Terminal City. Park Avenue's landscaped strip covered the tracks and widened the thoroughfare, creating an unusually large open space for the city.

Park Avenue then became lined with apartment houses, but the office buildings of the 1950s all but destroyed the effect of unity and continuity expressed in the uniform building heights and cornice lines of the apartment houses. A powerful reminder of this unity remains majestically in the New York Central Building (now Helmsley), built by Warren and Wetmore in 1929. Its giant flanking arches frame the ramps to the elevated circumferential plaza. And the corners of the New York Central Building at the basement level curve out slightly to meet the facades of the buildings on the east and west sides of Park Avenue. This curve creates the effect of a continuous wall interrupted by the crosstown street. The cornices of the apartment houses that once stood along Park Avenue were on the same level with the New York Central Building's cornice, further enhancing the continuity. The commercial buildings to the west of Grand Central Station still echo the cornice line and color of the terminal building clad in Bedford limestone. The different colored materials above the cornice line in the surrounding buildings simply emphasize their unity with Grand Central.

A City Within a City

In addition to its power as a symbol of welcome, the architectural design of Grand Central Station relates the many functions housed in the building to the street and pedestrian traffic around it. The terminal building accommodates people from all walks of life: commuters from the suburbs, subway riders, and pedestrians taking a shortcut through the station. At one time it housed an art gallery and a movie theater. Its many shops, restaurants, and fast-food stands located along the various concourses lend an atmosphere to the station that its architect, Whitney Warren, likened to a bazaar.

Beneath Mercury and the circumferential plaza at the street level are entrances into the station and into shops from the sidewalk. Ramps lead down through tunnels and low groin-vaulted concourses into the main waiting room with its high, coffered ceiling and bronze chandeliers. The room is parallel to the street; its walls of smooth limestone are detailed with elaborately carved Botticino marble, and the floors are of Tennessee marble. All these materials are warm in tone. Above the coffered ceiling of this room is a large open loft space used in the 1960s for some of the popular studio television shows. It is now used for a tennis club.

A still wider ramp leads through a low arch into the main concourse, parallel to the waiting room. Higher than the nave of St. John the Divine and larger than the nave of Notre Dame Cathedral in Paris, the room is 470 feet long, 160 feet wide, and 150 feet high. One of the models for this remarkable space was the Roman baths. The great scale of the concourse recalls the visionary designs for

271

Grand Central Terminal: grand concourse. Larger than the nave of Notre Dame Cathedral in Paris, the room is 470 feet long, 160 feet wide, and 150 feet high.

cultural temples by Claude-Nicolas Ledoux and Étienne-Louis Boullée, and the great vault has much in common with the atmospheric theater that was introduced by John Eberson in the 1920s. This vault is not a true vault; it is of plaster and suspended from the building's steel skeleton. Painted blue with constellations (inadvertently reversed when painted) designed by French artist Paul Helleu, it is picked out with small electric lights simulating the stars and the firmament.

The natural light that once flooded into the concourse through the skylight is blocked out because the windows were painted over during World War II for blackouts. However, light streams down from the clerestory windows in great shafts during certain hours of the day, and the triad of colossal arched windows at the Vanderbilt entrance afford an abundance of natural light. From the Lexington Avenue entrance, a low groin-vaulted tunnel leads into the great concourse. From the Vanderbilt entrance, opposite, the passenger enters at the plaza level and beholds the great space from above the main floor. A gallery at the same level along the north and south walls provides a view of the concourse traffic below and the firmament above, as if suspended between the two. Here a grand staircase leads down to the concourse floor and to the lower level. The lower treads of the staircase fan out in ceremonious fashion.

From the main concourse, ramps lead to the upper level tracks, and stairs lead to the lower level. From the Forty-second Street entrance, ramps also lead to the lower level and the Oyster Bar and Restaurant, shops, and boarding platforms. The vaulting above these ramps and the vaulting of the oyster bar is all Guastavino tile.

Exquisitely detailed carving marks the ornament throughout the building, and the tie to Commodore Vanderbilt is evident in the Vanderbilt coat of arms above the entrance to the lower level tracks and in the stairways to the upper floors. By the third generation of Vanderbilts in the United States, the family had acquired the coat of arms, consisting of three acorns, oak leaves, and a motto: Great oaks from little acorns grow. Its appearance here recalls the association of Whitney Warren and William K. Vanderbilt II.

A further reminder of the Commodore is his colossal-sized bronze portrait statue that stands facing the automobile traffic coming from the south over the viaduct. The statue is also a reminder of Vanderbilt's three-story, cast-iron terminal building of 1869 that he built at St. John's Park south of Canal Street to accommodate freight. The statue was part of Vanderbilt's sculpture program, which included scenes of his life executed in bronze relief in a narrative style.

Today, even though the skyscrapers soar around it, Grand Central Station is set back enough and elevated sufficiently above its great basement level that it refuses to be dwarfed. The width of Forty-second Street allows it to be seen clearly when approaching from east and west. Moreover, even though the Pan Am Building diminished its impact (from the south) as the great welcoming gateway it once was, nonetheless, it can still be seen, and Mercury and the other deities are still vigilant atop the great triumphal arch.

12

Art Deco Skyscrapers

THE CHANIN BUILDING:
BEACON OF PROGRESS

Almost two decades after the Woolworth Building opened, two major Art Deco skyscrapers rose practically side by side, and almost at the same time: the Chanin Building (1929) was located at the southwest corner of Lexington Avenue and Forty-second Street, and the Chrysler Building of 1930 is on the northeast corner of the same intersection. Both were built as monuments to the American dream realized in the lives of two self-made men, not unlike F. W. Woolworth.

In 1918 Irwin S. Chanin, who had studied engineering at Cooper Union and had worked on the construction of New York's subways as a young man, returned from World War I with $200 and a dream. Assisted by his fiancée, who raised additional capital, he built two one-bedroom frame houses in Bensonhurst for $7,000 and was thereby launched in the construction business.

From building middle-income houses in Brooklyn in the early 1920s to building a skyscraper in Manhattan at the end of the decade, Chanin expanded into the construction of hotels (Lincoln Hotel at Forty-fourth Street and Eighth Avenue), theaters (the legendary Roxy, largest motion picture theater in the world, 6,000 seats), apartment houses (the Majestic in 1930, at 115 Central Park West), and modern suburban developments (Green Acres in Valley Stream, Long Island, 1936). During World War II he received a number of U.S. government commissions, and by the 1950s his

Chanin Building, 122 East Forty-second Street (*facing page*); 1929. Sloan and Robertson, architects. The Chanin Building is a monument to the principles and ideals of its construction magnate builder, Irwin S. Chanin, who created here a structure of peerless efficiency and beauty.

organization had grown to encompass a complex network of real estate operations that far exceeded Chanin's early expectations. Nonetheless, his great skyscraper at Forty-second Street and Lexington Avenue remains the building that best embodies his principles and ideals.

Chanin's staff, headed by Jacques Delamarre, worked with architects Sloan and Robertson in designing the building. John Sloan, who studied architecture at New York University, and T. Markoe Robertson, who attended the École des Beaux-Arts after completing his studies at Yale, became partners in 1924, the year that Raymond Hood's American Radiator Building (40 West Fortieth Street) was built. This was a significant coincidence because Hood's building and the Chanin Building have a common model—Eliel Saarinen's competing design for the Chicago Tribune Building in 1922. Hood won the competition with a medieval design, which also influenced Sloan and Robertson's Chanin Building.

The Chanin Building is composed of a central rectangular tower of brick, trimmed with terra-cotta and limestone, rising from a series of staggered setbacks between the fourth and thirtieth stories. It is capped by a square-topped tower rising to the fifty-fourth floor. The setbacks are uniform above the north entrance on Forty-second Street and the south entrance on Forty-first Street, which frame the main entrance on the Lexington Avenue side. The first setback on Lexington Avenue is at the fourth floor over the main entrance. This gives the Lexington Avenue front of the building the appearance of a giant medieval two-towered facade.

During the day the faces of the piers at the top of the building read as projecting solids, and the dark spaces between them as receding voids. At night, however, the dark spaces between the piers were originally illuminated with powerful floodlights that could be seen for forty-five miles (although the fixtures are still in place, they are no longer used). This dramatic lighting had the effect of turning the cresting of the building inside out: the lighted recesses advanced and the dark piers receded. At the fifty-fourth floor, an observation promenade, once open to the public, surrounds the building and is open to the air but covered by an ambulatory created by the buttresses.

Chanin's private suite of offices and reception areas on the fifty-second floor are decorated in wrought iron and brass, etched glass, imported marbles, natural woods, and various leathers, including pigskin and walrus hide in brown, black, and tan. His furniture is coordinated with the overall decoration. Moreover, the wall paneling and furniture of his executive reception room are also coordinated, and a cove-lighted elliptical recess of pastel blue covers the entire ceiling.

Chanin Building (illuminated). In daylight the piers at the top seem to project; at night, their illumination was originally visible forty-five miles away.

Because of the innovative use of tile, brass, ornament, and lighting, Chanin's private bathroom was awarded the first prize of $500 as "America's finest bathroom" at the National Convention of Tile and Marble Manufacturers in 1929 (the Fisher family of Detroit, famous for the Fisher automobile bodies, won the second prize of $250), the *New York Sun* reported. Chanin's bathroom then became the model for all the bathrooms installed in his Majestic apartments, which he built in 1930 at 115 Central Park West, between Seventy-first and Seventy-second streets.

A City Within a City

At the street level of the Chanin Building, storefronts face both the sidewalk on the outside and the main lobby corridor on the inside, with entrances on both thoroughfares. The windows facing the sidewalk are framed in thin bronze strips set in Belgian black marble and are two bays wide to provide ample space for display.

Those facing the lobby are the same, except more elaborately framed. Sculptural decoration on the outside further embellishes the building at the lower floors which are visible to pedestrian traffic. A bronze frieze in low relief above the first story extends around three sides of the building and carries images of marine plant life, fish, and birds representing the evolution of life from the sea. At the fourth floor, motifs of stylized plants cast in terra-cotta form a continuous band around the building parallel to the bronze frieze below. The evolutionary theme is carried into the interior as well. For example, the elevator doors in the lobby, in alternating textures of etched bronze and black enamel, portray the waterfowl in flight, echoing the themes of the exterior friezes.

The construction of Grand Central Station had stimulated economic growth in the area, and demand for more offices close to centralized transportation and apartments inspired Irwin Chanin to build more than simply a skyscraper. Chanin built a skyscraper that offered business people the most up-to-date facilities and services available anywhere, which he promoted as a "city within a city." The nearby Chrysler, Daily News, RCA Victor (now General Electric), and Graybar buildings would soon follow Chanin's lead.

From Park Avenue, Murray Hill, and Tudor City, H. Douglas Ives's newly created complex of 3,000 apartments and 600 hotel rooms, people could now walk to work; those coming by subway or commuting from Westchester and Connecticut need never see the light of day (especially appealing in bad weather). An underground passage connected the subways, shuttle, and trains of Grand Central Station with the Chanin Building, and a bus depot (no longer extant) accommodated surface traffic from the West Side. Moreover, a train to Montreal, Palm Beach, or Chicago was only a few steps away. These conveniences and the Chanin Building's proximity to principal hotels, the Racquet and Yacht clubs, as well as the Harvard, Princeton, and Yale clubs, made the Chanin Building's "city within a city" concept credible and appealing to prestigious tenants. It was an idea that would be more fully realized in Rockefeller Center in 1931.

The Chanin Building was the last word in efficiency and service. Twenty-one Otis elevators spirited tenants to their offices without delay, traveling every twenty-four hours the distance covered by the Twentieth Century Limited between New York and Chicago, its brochures proudly noted. An auditorium for tenants' use (now removed to make room for more offices) occupied the fiftieth and fifty-first floors and had a seating capacity of two hundred in an orchestra and mezzanine. Its stage and projection booth were fully equipped for film and live presentations. Concerts, film previews, plays, and popular radio shows were staged there and the space served conventions, conferences, institutes, and tenants' general meetings.

Besides being the most efficient and appealing office building in town, Chanin intended his skyscraper to be a work of art expressing the modern American age of business—"architectural beauty wedded to business efficiency" was the way he advertised it.

Beauty and Symbol

In addition to building a structure peerless in efficiency and beauty, Chanin also wanted to create a modern landmark that would be a monument to New York, city of opportunity, and to the spirit of modern industry that sustains it. Chanin wished his building to convey the message he learned early in life: that any individual in New York City may rise from humble beginnings to wealth and influence through the use of his mind and hands. For Chanin, the building itself embodies these principles, but he had them translated into narrative and symbolic language through a program of sculpture and decorative detail that enriches the building throughout. Sculptor René Chambellan and Jacques Delamarre, head of Chanin's architecture department, designed and executed the sculpture program. The formal inspiration was derived from the prevailing Art Deco style, whose roots in Cubism, Expressionism, and Futurism are evident in the translation of multiple views of three-dimensional forms into flattened images, and in the use of strident, active shapes and energetic compositions.

A series of eight plaster reliefs painted with a dark bronze patina, showing powerful, animated figures above polished bronze convector grilles, greet the visitor at the three entrances to the building. Six of these represent the physical (effort, activity, endurance) and mental (enlightenment, vision, courage) means by which the other two are gained (achievement and success). Each personification is set against a geometric pattern of coils, rays, or blocks that is repeated in the grille below it. Scrolls represent the birth of ideas, rays stand for the emanation of the spark of genius, and the block-like forms signify the act of building.

The metalwork mirrors the variety of moods of the different spaces. For example, "the spirit of modern industry" is expressed in the wrought-iron gates at the entrance to the general reception room on the fifty-second floor. Its cog wheels signify the interdependence of component parts necessary to any smooth-running machine, and its stacks of coins symbolize the financial rewards of hard work and one of the foundations of industry.

In the executive reception room on the fifty-second floor, hammered bronze plaques, illuminated from below each panel, repre-

279

Chanin Building: lobby. Plaster reliefs painted with bronze patina above the bronze convector grilles represent figures symbolizing the spirit of modern industry.

sent some of the enterprises in which Chanin was active: the theater, rapid transit system, bridges, and skyscrapers. The convector grilles in Irwin Chanin's private office include a stylized view of downtown New York, a tribute to the age of the skyscraper, as well as personalized symbols, such as intertwined drafting triangles, implements of his craft as an engineer, builder, and architect.

THE CHRYSLER BUILDING:
AUTOMOTIVE MONUMENT

While the Chanin Building turned its top into a great torch at night, William Van Alen was commissioned to build the Reynolds Building across the street, which was to have a great glass dome lighted from within, atop a tall tower. William H. Reynolds, a real estate developer and former New York senator who had leased the property at Forty-second Street and Lexington Avenue from Cooper Union in 1921, commissioned Van Alen to build a modern office building in 1927. In 1928 Walter Percy Chrysler bought the lease as a real estate investment and retained Van Alen to build the tower, but now it was to be called the Chrysler Building and was to have a peak instead of a dome. Chrysler had been a key executive officer with General Motors, then the Willys-Overland Co., and finally the Maxwell Motor Company, which became the Chrysler Corporation in 1925, the year after he introduced the Chrysler automobile. As a fitting monument to his own achievement and to world commerce and industry, he decided to, erect the Chrysler Building.

William Van Alen had studied architecture at Pratt Institute, the Beaux-Arts Institute of Design (where he was later director of sculpture) in New York, and at the École des Beaux-Arts in Paris. He worked first for the builder Clarence True, then as a designer for Clinton and Russell architects, and later as an associate of H. Craig Severance. At the time Van Alen was building the Chrysler Building, Severance was no longer associated with him and was building the Bank of the Manhattan Co. at 40 Wall Street; both had the same aim—to build the tallest skyscraper in the world.

The Chrysler Building followed the high standards of efficiency and convenience set by the Chanin Building across the street, and it became the center of attention when it soared above the Woolworth Building (793.5 feet high), the world's tallest office building since 1913, and even above the Eiffel Tower, the world's tallest metal skeleton. The race to build to unprecedented heights gained excitement when the Bank of the Manhattan Co. Building entered the competition and briefly challenged Chrysler's race for dominance of the skies. Severance added a flagpole to his building, making it 927 feet high—two feet taller than the Chrysler Building was originally planned.

William Van Alen countered this flagpole with what he called the "vertex"—a high spire that made the Chrysler Building 1,046 feet tall when it was completed in August 1930. Van Alen assembled the vertex within the top of the building and once H. Craig Severance's building was completed, Van Alen raised the giant spire up into position through a specially prepared opening in the top of the tower. As a result, the Chrysler Building became the tallest office building in the world. But the victory was short-lived. The Empire State Building rose above it the next year in 1931.

Chrysler's private club on the sixty-sixth floor celebrated the building's great height. Appropriately dubbed the Cloud Club, it commanded a unique view of New York and its skyline. The club featured dining areas and meeting rooms designed for Chrysler executives and their clients. It later served as a public restaurant until 1979, when it was closed.

From the checkroom just off the elevators a wide, carpeted hall leads into the main dining room of the Cloud Club. Its ceiling is executed in white textured stucco to approximate real clouds that appear to settle picturesquely around the windows which look out through the actual natural clouds over New York's skyline. Opposite the actual view is a hand-painted mural showing lower Manhattan

281

Chrysler Building, 405 Lexington Avenue, at Forty-second Street *(facing page);* 1930. William Van Alen, architect. A dramatic monument to the automotive industry and to Walter Percy Chrysler's achievement; through its high spire, it became the tallest building in the world in 1930. Decoration: stylized automobiles *(above)* executed in light-and-dark brick with hubcaps in actual chrome race toward the buttressed corner, where colossal Chrysler radiator caps emerge from the automobile hood.

from the Chrysler Building. Cove lighting, with chevron fixtures repeating the building's major design motif, illuminates the stucco clouds from the polished marble piers that support the ceiling.

On the mezzanine an open bar is paneled in dark wood with matching wooden tables and chairs. Adjoining it is a reminder of the Prohibition era: a small tavern room in dark wood. Its bar is an oversize beer keg and there are private lockers with owners' initials carved on the locker doors. Small, private dining rooms for Chrysler and his clients are also located on the mezzanine, and the decorations in each carry a theme related to the client's business. In Chrysler's dining room, for example, there is an engraved glass mural that extends around three sides of the room. Life-size figures of Chrysler's auto workers in their work clothes and with their tools are engraved in black relief against a blue ground. The dining room for Chrysler's Texaco clients has a hand-painted mural along two walls, showing a typical New England town with a Colonial church, rolling countryside, and a convenient Texaco service station; facing on the opposite wall is an oil refinery with a fully rigged Texaco truck, its logo prominently displayed.

A library opens off the mezzanine hall. Its wood-paneled book-lined walls, marble wood-burning fireplace, and engaged fluted pilasters with their gilded capitals enhance the quiet mood of the library. The south wall of windows provides an unbroken view of lower Manhattan.

The Lobby: Mise-en-scène *for Business*

The lobby of the Chrysler Building is shaped in an enormous "Y," and its unusual shape works successfully as a grand entrance to service the building's many tenants and to move them toward the elevators and stairs to offices, stores, and underground transportation. The travertine lobby floor is designed with a pathlike pattern of chevrons, here serving the function of guiding pedestrians to the various access routes of the lobby.

Chrysler wanted his lobby to give a "mental lift" to those who entered. Van Alen achieved this transformation through a *mise-en-scène* of rich materials, theatrical illusion, and dramatic lighting, the kind of design that explained why he was called the "Ziegfeld" of architecture. Natural light pours into the lobby through high panels of the etched glass over the three entrances. The lobby walls and the octagonal piers are faced with rouge flamme, a variegated red Moroccan marble with light accents of beige. Cove lighting from fixtures of inverted chevron design illuminate the lobby from the walls and the piers. There is stainless steel framing around the shop fronts that flank the entrances and the directories in the lobby, as well as around the panel behind the red marble information desk and the doors throughout the lobby. It was manufactured specifically for the Chrysler Building, and its surface reflects a soft glow and complements the subdued tone of the marble of the lobby and the woods used in the elevators.

The elevator doors are of imported inlaid woods and each has a stylized lotus pattern. Each of the elevator cabs is of a different geometric design, to offer variety and to break the monotony of this space for the tenants who travel them every day. Over the entrances to the four elevator banks are vertical panels of polished Mexican onyx in an overlapped ziggurat pattern. In approaching the elevator banks from the adjacent corridors, these overlapping panels—lighted from behind—look like the curtains over the proscenium in a theater.

The ziggurat design is continued throughout the building; for example, it appears in the stainless-steel railing and beveled brackets supporting the tubular handrails in the stairways. The beveled pattern is repeated in the silhouette of the etched-glass chandelier frames that hang above the stairways running up to the mezzanine and down to the basement and subway passage. The ceiling of aluminum leaf and the etched-glass chandelier framed in stainless steel make a striking contrast to the highly polished black marble walls of the stairway, which mirror the soft forms and the red marble newel posts at the ground level.

Edward Trumbull, one of America's leading muralists of the day, executed the lobby ceiling decoration. He was a student of Frank Brangwyn, a well-known Welsh muralist who is best remembered in New York for his murals at Rockefeller Center, which replaced Diego Rivera's. Trumbull's portrait of the Chrysler Building extends along the ceiling of the main arm of the Y-shaped lobby. Over the rest of the ceiling, images emanate from a colossal personification of Power, embodying man's vision, energy, and engineering, the human attributes that made the building possible. In addition to abstract patterns that symbolize the primitive forces of nature, there are also such figures as construction workers and airplanes, representing modern society and technology.

While the Chrysler Building but briefly enjoyed the reputation of the tallest building in the world, the Empire State Building, which succeeded to that title, became the embodiment of height and a nationally recognized symbol. The Empire State Building was produced by many of the same realities that produced the Chanin and Chrysler buildings—the need for better and more convenient office space in the midtown area, and the grand ambitions of a self-made man. But the Empire State Building became symbolically identified with New York, which epitomized to most people superlative achievement, wealth, and power. It soon became successful and a legend, at a time when New York and the nation needed legends: the Great Depression.

THE EMPIRE STATE BUILDING: SYMBOL OF THE METROPOLIS

When William Backhouse Astor bought the Thomson-Lawton farmland in 1827 as an investment in Manhattan's northward expansion, even the second son of the founder of the Astor dynasty in America could not have anticipated the fame that site would enjoy, nor the legends that would be born there.

Astor mansions were built on the site, then razed to make way for the two hotels the family built: the Waldorf (named after the village in Germany where John Jacob Astor came from) in 1893, and the Astoria (named after the fur trading post John Jacob Astor founded in Oregon), which was joined to it in 1897, to become the famous Waldorf-Astoria. The Waldorf was built by William Waldorf Astor and the Astoria by his cousin, the former Caroline Schermerhorn, known for establishing the list of the Four Hundred, New York's most fashionable residents (four hundred was said to be the number of guests who would fit into her ballroom for New York's main social event of the year).

Waldorf-Astoria; 1893–97. Henry J. Hardenbergh, architect. This postcard shows the original Waldorf-Astoria at Thirty-fourth Street and Fifth Avenue; its conspicuous elegance set standards of taste, and its innovative conveniences established new trends in the hotel industry.

Because relations between the two Waldorfs were strained, Caroline required the architect, Henry J. Hardenbergh, who had also built the Waldorf, to make provision at each floor to seal off the buildings from each other, if the need to do so ever arose.

The Waldorf-Astoria's procession of guests included nobility, dignitaries, and the most famous people from all over the world. Its conspicuous elegance set standards of taste, and its practical approach to innovative conveniences such as room telephones and modernized room service established new trends in the hotel industry.

The aura of the Waldorf-Astoria continued to dominate New York's social world well into the 1920s, when socioeconomic factors began to change the character of the midtown neighborhood around it. The demise of the Waldorf-Astoria at the end of the decade was part of the new look that had taken over the area. Department stores had moved into the area: Altman's, Gorham's, and Tiffany's in 1906; Lord and Taylor's in 1914; and Franklin and Simon, later W & J Sloane, in 1922. And office buildings pushed northward: the Fuller Building, called the Flatiron because of its shape, came in 1902; the Metropolitan Life Insurance Co. added its Tower in 1909; and the New York Life Insurance Co. came in 1928.

Combined with rising real estate costs, the institution of the personal income tax in 1913, and the competition of the new money from copper, coal, and railroads—these factors forced old money like the Astors to new and quieter quarters uptown. The Thirty-fourth Street area was thus transformed into a progressive industrial and commercial center.

The Waldorf-Astoria closed its doors on May 1, 1929, and demolition began on October 1 to make way for a fifty-story office building, as the newspapers reported. The Waldorf-Astoria was rebuilt two years later at Park Avenue between Forty-ninth and Fiftieth streets by Schultze and Weaver in the then popular Art Deco style. It was also the style of the new office building that was built on its old site—the Empire State Building.

The Making of an Icon

The Empire State Building was the inspiration of John Jacob Raskob, a self-made man, who had risen from economically deprived circumstances in Lockport, New York—by way of a series of successful ventures with Pierre DuPont, his mentor (who had discovered him)—to enormous wealth and positions of influence as an officer and shareholder in General Motors. Active in politics, Raskob supported Al Smith for governor of New York and was Smith's campaign manager in his presidential race against Herbert Hoover in 1928. The friendship grew, and when Al Smith left public office, he played a major role in Raskob's success story with the Empire State Building.

From his automotive experience Raskob understood the importance of producing a superior product, the complexities of merchandising it, and the necessity of having the right people to achieve these ends. He applied his formula for success to the new building at Thirty-fourth Street and Fifth Avenue at a time when the country was experiencing its worst financial crisis, and he produced not only the tallest building in the world, but the most famous and revered skyscraper yet to be built. Even now that other commercial structures have reached far greater heights, the Empire State Building remains an icon that refuses to relinquish its special meaning.

Raskob produced the perfect skyscraper with the perfect image for its time and place: it was a building that did exactly what an executive office building ought to do with maximum efficiency and economy, and it was executed with superb artistry and superlative engineering in a tastefully modern style. Although the Empire State Building did what any office building was supposed to do for its tenants, it did it better and in a bigger way. At least that was Raskob's message, and people believed it.

287

Unlike the Woolworth, Chrysler, and Chanin buildings, named for men of remarkable achievement, Raskob's building was to be identified with the very embodiment of superlative achievement—New York. It was to become a symbol of the city. Being the tallest building in the world meant more than winning a race for Raskob; height was symbolically identified with the essential concept of the building.

It is the interdependence of the building's architectural preeminence and its symbolic content that relates the Empire State Building conceptually to such landmarks as the Eiffel Tower and that establishes it as a major image of modernity in the twentieth century. This successful confluence of form and content is also what has made the building an enduring symbol. What it looked like, what it was, and what it stood for all became identified in the minds of the public and the building's tenants.

Selection of the Architects

To produce this superior product, Raskob selected the architectural firm of Shreve, Lamb, and Harmon. A fairly new partnership, the group had good credentials and a practical approach to building that appealed to him. William Frederick Lamb was the designer of the building. The son of a New York builder, he had studied architecture at Columbia University in New York and the École des Beaux-Arts in Paris and had been a partner with Richmond Harold Shreve in Carrère and Hastings, Shreve, and Lamb. Shreve had studied architecture at Cornell and had taught there, before joining Carrère and Hastings. Arthur Loomis Harmon joined them in 1929 to form Shreve, Lamb, and Harmon. Harmon studied architecture at Columbia University and had been a designer with McKim, Mead, and White before practicing independently.

The Significance of the Design

Lamb's natural propensity was toward simplicity, and he preferred functional architecture, which was why the contemporary architect Raymond Hood's Daily News Building, built a year before the Empire State Building, appealed to him and influenced him. So Lamb envisioned a building shaped essentially by the practical factors of budget, time, zoning regulations, and technological necessities. Raskob wanted 36 million cubic feet of space on a lot 200 feet (Fifth Avenue) by 425 feet (Thirty-third and Thirty-fourth streets) for a construction budget of approximately $60 million. The building was to be completed by May 1, 1931, in order to make rental space available immediately (the day for signing commercial leases).

The Empire State Building, 350 Fifth Avenue; 1931. Shreve, Lamb, and Harmon, architects. The inspiration of John Jacob Raskob, the building's architectural preeminence and its symbolic content have made it an enduring major image of modernity.

That gave the architect a year and a half to complete the plans and erect the building.

Lamb reduced these requirements to their bare essentials for his design. A central core rising up the height of the building accommodates service and utility rooms, corridors, and shafts for four elevator banks of low and high-rise elevators. Around this core is a perimeter of rentable office space twenty-eight feet deep from window to corridor—at that time, the accepted formula for sufficient natural light. As the low-rise elevators drop away, the core space is reduced, which is expressed in the facades as setbacks.

The vertical composition of the building conforms to the traditional organization of skyscraper mass into base, shaft, and capital—the design, based on the divisions of the Classical column, that has its origins in New York's earliest elevator buildings of Post (Western Union Building) and Hunt (Tribune Building) in the 1870s.

A limestone tower rises from a 5-story base to the 86th floor observatory and is capped by a monumental spire, a "mooring mast" of metal and glass for dirigibles (which proved too dangerous to be used as such), and the television antenna added much later. Atop the 5th-story base is a 60-foot-wide terrace created by setting the tower back to fulfill the zoning requirements. This terrace setback emphasizes the tower and its unprecedented height of 1,250 feet. Although it has 86 floors of offices, the Empire State Building is often described as being 102 stories high, because the mooring mast is equivalent in height to 14 stories and when the building's two basements are also counted, the total comes to 102 stories.

The grandeur of the Empire State Building—its height, materials, and design, and the technological skills that produced it—immediately captured the minds and hearts of all Americans. To watch the building's steel skeleton rise 102 stories into the sky in just over eight months was even startling to the construction workers who put it up, as Harold L. McClain wrote in his "Recollections of Working on the Empire State Building."

At the opening ceremonies, May 1, 1931, former New York Governor Al Smith hailed the Empire State Building as the world's greatest monument to man's ingenuity, skill, mind, and muscle. Three weeks later, Earl Musselman stood on the platform of the Empire State Building's observation tower. Looking at the tall buildings around him, he said, "I keep wanting to put out my hand to feel them—so that I can tell what they really look like." Born blind, the twenty-two-year-old Musselman had only two months before undergone an operation that gave him sight. His uncle brought him to New York from Philadelphia to see the view from the top of the Empire State Building, a view of sea and land that only three weeks before was beyond the earth's horizon.

The great height of the Empire State Building has been celebrated in such movie myths as *King Kong* and *Tarzan's New York Adventure*, and it was the source of tragedy when Lt. Col. William F. Smith's B-25 Mitchell bomber, with a crew member and a passenger aboard, crashed into the north side of the fog-shrouded building at the seventy-ninth-floor level on the morning of July 28, 1945. Fortunately, because it was a Saturday, there were few people in the building; nonetheless, at least fourteen people perished along with the pilot and his crewman.

Now, through a modern lighting system, the top of the Empire State Building is a great beacon honoring special events that was inaugurated on October 12, 1977, when blue and white lights announced that the Yankees had won the World Series. From the seventy-second floor to the top of the TV antenna, colored lights in various combinations celebrate such significant days as St. Valentine's Day (red and white), Washington's Birthday (red, white, and blue), St. Patrick's Day (green), and Columbus Day (red, white, and green). And from Christmas to New Year's Day, festive combinations of red and green illuminate the top of the building.

The New Symbol

The main entrance on Fifth Avenue echoes the building's tripartite design. Grand columns flank the entrance doors, and great black stone bases at the ground level support reeded shafts which terminate in capitals of stylized American eagles that frame the massive attic on which is engraved "EMPIRE STATE." At ground level, broad shop fronts of moulded aluminum and glass are set within black marble beneath a three-story screen of masonry piers.

The time and budget within which the building had to be completed dictated a system of fenestration and a method of handling the stonework that eliminated traditional, but time-consuming, practices and fortuitously resulted in enhancing the vertical emphasis of the building. By setting the windows in framed strips of stainless steel, and projecting them in front of the Indiana limestone cladding, the stone finishing usually needed at the juncture of wall and window was eliminated, saving time and money. Furthermore, by using aluminum for the spandrels, instead of masonry, cross bonding was avoided and resulted in a further economy.

The projected window units, grouped in bays of one, two, and three, were visually united to read as continuous, slender, vertical units capped by geometric crowns. The masonry cladding read as a skeleton of slender alternating piers, reflecting the building's internal structure. Lamb's solution, which unifies the building's almost 6,500 windows into a coherent design, was probably influenced by the way his friend Raymond Hood handled the Daily News Build-

291

Empire State Building: lobby. The grand entrance hall, made of marble, stainless steel, and glass, features a portrait of the building superimposed over a map of New York State.

ing. Hood de-emphasized the windows by an innovative recessed vertical strip and a continuous pier unbroken up to the cresting.

The hubris that informs the design and ornamentation of New York's Art Deco skyscrapers is uniquely expressed in the Empire State Building's scale and the decorative features that enhance it, which are geometric and carry almost no narrative content. The architects avoided didactic ornamentation except in the main lobby at the ground floor, where they celebrate the concept and image of the building in a program of restrained symbolism coordinated with rich materials and dramatic lighting.

The design of the lobby was dictated by the same realities that guided the general massing of the building. Here, the four banks of elevators in the central core of the building are subdivided by three east-west concourses and connecting lateral corridors to facilitate traffic flow from the main Fifth Avenue entrance and the side entrances at Thirty-third and Thirty-fourth streets.

Moreover, the elevator banks are surrounded by shops with entrances from both the lobby and the street and aluminum bridges (originally open, now enclosed) over the east-west concourses connect offices at the second story. Stairs led down (now escalators) from the ends of the concourses to the lower level.

A grand entrance hall in gray marble, stainless steel, and glass extends from the main entrance to a wall of polished black granite, which is the backdrop for a portrait of the building above the information desk. The aluminum image of the building, emanating rays symbolic of man's creative energy which merge with the rays of the sun—nature's energy—is superimposed over a map of New York. The building's location is marked, and at the lower left the dates of construction, March 17, 1930–March 1, 1931, are inscribed in a medallion. At the right is a clock set in a compass, symbolic of the coordinates of time and space that define the position of the Empire State Building in the mural and in the modern world. The panel, beneath the clock and over the aluminum information desk, lists those responsible for constructing the building and includes Pierre S. DuPont, Raskob's mentor and associate. South of the information desk is a scale model of the building in a display vitrine with base, made in the Empire State Cabinet Shop by Oliver J. Brown and painted by J. M. Rossi (1938).

Natural light pours into the great ceremonial space through the three glazed and traceried vertical panels over the main entrance. Beneath each panel and above the three doors is a round medallion with a stylized representation of Electricity (north), Masonry (middle), and Heating (south). These are three of the eighteen medallions placed throughout the lobby that identify the industries involved in producing the Empire State Building.

To merchandise the building properly, Raskob sought to give it a strong identity with New York and with an image of integrity associated with high purpose. Raskob hired Al Smith to be the president of the Empire State Company and to give his superior product a superior image. As the building and its function were inseparable, so Al Smith became identified with the building, and his personal popularity and reputation for integrity imparted a sense of high purpose to the building, which was totally believable. Moreover, through his lifelong connection with public affairs and the Democratic party, Smith had consistent visibility at the public level; he was always news. Thus, the Empire State Building had much greater exposure through the press and news media than any building before it.

Raskob's judgment proved sound. Even though his building opened during the Great Depression, it flourished, and by the 1940s it had 98 percent occupancy.

13

Rockefeller Center: Innovation in Urban Planning

Rockefeller Center began as a search for a new home for the Metropolitan Opera. On January 21, 1926, the Metropolitan Opera and Real Estate Company voted to build a new opera house. Increased traffic congestion around the old building at Thirty-ninth Street and Broadway, deterioration of the site, poor building maintenance, and insufficient space led to the board's decision to construct a new building.

They considered many alternatives, which included purchasing the elegant but unprofitable Century Theater at Sixty-third Street and Central Park West. The theater was eventually razed to make way for Irwin Chanin's Century Apartments in 1931. Naming a new building for a famous one that it replaced was common practice. Another example is the Stewart Apartments on the site of the old A. T. Stewart Department Store, 70 East Tenth Street, between Broadway and Fourth Avenue. Finally, the opera board decided on a block of land then owned by Columbia University, that extended from West Forty-eighth Street to West Fifty-first Street between Fifth Avenue and a line about one hundred feet east of Sixth Avenue—an area accessible to public transportation, near the theater district, and where rents were low.

The area had been the site of the well-known Elgin Botanic Garden, a pioneering experiment in medical research that Dr. David Hosack, Professor of Botany and Medicine, developed for his Columbia students. Dr. Hosack (famed also as the physician who attended Alexander Hamilton after his fatal duel with Aaron Burr, July 11, 1804) named the garden after Elgin, Scotland, which was

Rockefeller Center (*facing page*). This view (*c.* 1936) across Fifth Avenue shows the RCA building before the high-rise buildings along Sixth Avenue were built. The downward slope of the promenade and other design devices draw the stroller into the Center.

his family home. He purchased the land for $5,000, but the garden proved so costly (he invested over $100,000) that he sold it to the state of New York in 1810 for $75,000. In 1814 the state gave the land to Columbia University along with $10,000 as part of an assistance program for schools. Columbia rented the property in 1823 for $125 a year to John R. Driver to farm; the lease is part of the university's Columbiana Collection.

Following the Civil War, New York's building boom transformed the Columbia area property into a fashionable residential neighborhood of genteel brownstones leavened with some elegant mansions in limestone and granite. Some of the finer houses faced on Fifth Avenue, the first thoroughfare to be surfaced with asphalt (the "soundless pavement") and the main artery to the fast-growing and wealthy neighborhood around Central Park north of Fifty-ninth Street.

The area retained its character until about 1900, in spite of strains on property values exerted from time to time by such neighbors as Madame Restell, noted abortionist and central figure in a sensational murder trial. But during the first decade of the twentieth century, the business community pressed northward and the well-to-do moved on. By 1928 the university was collecting $300,000 annually from a rundown residential area of row houses, speakeasies, and shops. Therefore, any plan such as a cultural center that promised to increase and improve the value of the land would naturally have appealed to Columbia.

A CULTURAL COMPLEX

While the site was being selected, the opera board retained the fashionable architect Benjamin Wistar Morris, whose works included the Cunard Building at 25 Broadway, the addition to the Morgan Library at 29 East Thirty-sixth Street, and the American Women's Association Clubhouse, 353 West Fifty-seventh Street, to develop recommendations for the new opera house. In additon to the opera house, Morris's plan included a landscaped plaza to enhance the cultural atmosphere and to produce revenue to support the enterprise. This more ambitious project was influenced by the successful Grand Central Station complex, and it was planned to involve tall commercial buildings, fashionable shops, gardens, and terraces; and to allow for efficient circulation of traffic, a street, covered parking, open and underground walkways, and bridges.

Even though it was costlier than the original plan for a new opera house building, the board liked this more elaborate idea and sought the assistance of John D. Rockefeller, Jr., to finance it. Then in his early fifties, a vital individual with enormous resources, John D. Rockefeller was in charge of the Rockefeller affairs. He was also known for his philanthropic building programs, such as the restoration of Versailles (begun 1924) after World War I and that of Colonial Williamsburg (begun 1926), and for his support of humanitarian projects, most notably the Rockefeller Institute, founded by his father in 1901 and, under the direction of his son, David, destined to become a modern university. And with this project, too, John D. Rockefeller agreed to help.

Rockefeller's advisers included architects, builders, and real estate specialists, who believed in the project's potential. Furthermore, the Rockefellers already had property north of the Columbia site, and John D. believed, as did the Sixth Avenue Association, that shoddy, old Sixth Avenue, darkened by the El, had a brighter future than its dingy appearance suggested.

Consequently, on October 1, 1928, Rockefeller leased the Columbia University property with options for renewal. The rent paid between 1928 and 1973 ranged from $3.6 to $3.8 million a year, according to Carole Herselle Krinsky in her penetrating and informative study of Rockefeller Center. To connect Fifth and Sixth avenues as the east and west boundaries of the plot, Rockefeller purchased the strip of land, west of the Columbia property, to Sixth Avenue. He made the purchase through a holding company he called Underel, because the land was under the El. After he merged Underel with Rockefeller Center in 1951, Rockefeller sold the strip to Columbia for $5.5 million and leased it back on a twenty-year lease. In 1973 Rockefeller Center and Columbia renegotiated the Rockefeller Center lease at an annual base rent of $9 million, rising in periodic increments of $200,000 up to $13 million over twenty-one years.

To circumvent a municipal statute under which property used as a public thoroughfare eventually belongs to the city, small bronze tablets are set into the pavement of the Center at various points, with the inscription "Property line of the Trustees of Columbia University, crossing is by permission only, which permission is revocable at will." For the same purpose, Columbia must close the private street, Rockefeller Plaza, for twelve hours between sunrise and sunset one day in July each year to demonstrate that the street is not publicly owned.

ROCKEFELLER'S NEW ROLE

Rockefeller's involvement in the opera scheme coincided with the advent of the Great Depression of 1929, along with a growing

297

Rockefeller Center, West Forty-eighth to West Fifty-first streets, Fifth to Sixth avenues; 1931–40. Reinhard and Hofmeister; Corbett, Harrison, and Macmurray; Raymond Hood, Godley and Fouilhoux.

This aerial view shows the RCA Building, tallest in the complex, and the
International Building, which repeats its shape and design of setbacks.

disharmony among the opera board members and its associates concerning the lease, revenues, and administration of the project. This finally led to the board's decision in December 1929 not to pursue the opera house program further.

By this time, Rockefeller and his battery of professionals were enthusiastically committed to an urban project they believed had unprecedented potential as a commercial, as well as a cultural, center. With the withdrawal of the opera board, their aim shifted from producing a cultural center to developing a profitable business and commercial complex that would be architecturally and aesthetically of the highest order, to attract prestigious clients.

Rockefeller had assembled a team of distinguished and accomplished architects, diverse but complementary and compatible, whose individual contributions were coordinated and administered by the management and real estate specialist, John R. Todd. L. Andrew Reinhard and Henry Hofmeister had been Todd's associates. Raymond Hood's American Radiator Company Building and Daily News Building and his winning design for the Chicago Tribune Tower (1922) competition demonstrated his ability to blend European modernism with the historical tradition. Harvey Wiley Corbett was progressive but practical, and he had experience in urban design. Wallace K. Harrison, Corbett's partner, had a solid foundation in traditional academic training.

Rockefeller initially expected to attract tenants who would build and finance their own buildings. That failing, he financed the entire project through the Metropolitan Life Insurance Co.; estimated at $120 million, it was the largest transaction the company had ever made. The project, which had been called Metropolitan Square after the opera project, was then rechristened Rockefeller Center (upon consideration of other names, including Rockefeller City and Radio City) and was promoted as a "city within a city."

A CITY WITHIN A CITY

Rockefeller Center is composed of twenty-one buildings. The original buildings, bounded by Forty-eighth and Fifty-first streets and by Fifth and Sixth avenues, were built between 1931 and 1940; the Esso Building (now Warner Communications) was added north of Fifty-first Street in 1945, and 600 Fifth Avenue (Sinclair Oil) in 1950. Additions on the west side of Sixth Avenue, beginning with the second Time and Life Building in 1957, and followed by Exxon, McGraw-Hill, Celanese, and Sperry-Rand, make up a common facade of slabs set back from the street with surrounding, extensive open plazas, in accordance with later zoning regulations.

The buildings that make up Rockefeller Center form several groups. The RCA Building is at the heart of the Center, approached from Fifth Avenue by a symmetrical composition of buildings, plazas, walkways, and a private street, Rockefeller Plaza, which unites another group of buildings along its north-south axis. The three international buildings facing Fifth Avenue echo the RCA Building composition, and a facade of buildings along Sixth Avenue makes up the final group of original buildings. The latest additions west of Sixth Avenue constitute the final group.

Building began in 1931, and the last rivet in the original block of buildings was driven by Rockefeller in 1939. The decade of the 1930s was beleaguered by the depression, and it required the utmost resourcefulness to make the Center work financially—that is, to fill the Center with buildings and to fill the buildings with desirable tenants. Even though the site was generally desirable, Sixth Avenue was an eyesore at the time with its deteriorating four-story buildings and noisy El that polluted the air and kept the sunshine out; consequently, the land near it held little appeal for potential clients. Therefore, a principal feature of the plan for Rockefeller Center was to capitalize on the distinction of Fifth Avenue and the growing business and building activity on the East Side, in order to make the property near Sixth Avenue more potentially attractive to prospective tenants.

To connect Fifth and Sixth avenues, a system of intersecting axes, multilevel surfaces, and connecting thoroughfares were designed around the RCA Building, which was conceived as a long, rectangular slab in three parts; a low-rise office tower with an imposing facade on Sixth Avenue, called RCA West (a dramatic move to upgrade shoddy Sixth Avenue), the much lower NBC studios behind it to the east, and the seventy-story main office tower which faces Fifth Avenue across a plaza and promenade to the east and steps down to RCA West, visually relating the two towers and establishing an east-west axis connecting Fifth and Sixth avenues.

Rockefeller Plaza, the private street, runs in front of the RCA Building north and south from Forty-eighth to Fifty-first streets, dividing the Center into two sections, approximately one-third lying west of the street to Sixth Avenue, and two-thirds lying east of it to Fifth Avenue. The RCA Building is the focal point of the Center; as the tallest building of the original complex—850 feet high—all the others step down from it north, south, east, and west, and are oriented toward it, an innovative idea that permitted maximum access to natural light and air.

Hood also introduced roof gardens, a feature he borrowed from luxury apartments, so that the employees in the Center would have beautiful landscape views from their offices high above the city streets. Spectators too could enjoy viewing the gardens, seeing them from the seventieth floor observatory. Sky-high dining is still an attraction in the center's Rainbow Room and Rainbow Grill, situated on the sixty-fifth floor of the RCA Building.

It has been noted that the organizational ideas of Rockefeller Center had their origins in antiquity, traditional European academic principles, European modernism, and the practical exigencies of building commercial spaces in conformity with the contemporary New York zoning regulations and building codes. The symmetry of the great Roman forums influenced the logic and organization of the Center, and the order of priority assigned to individual buildings was taught in the École des Beaux-Arts, which Rockefeller's architects knew well. Proper light and air, subterranean trucking depots, a pedestrian concourse linking all the buildings of the Center, as well as high-rise office space—all had to be supplied according to New York's structural and zoning guidelines. Together the historical and practical helped shape Rockefeller Center.

THE ARCHITECTURAL STYLE

As the first building erected, the RCA Building also set the architectural style to be followed by the others in the Center. Its imposing Indiana limestone walls are broken only by the windows and low-toned aluminum spandrels recessed from the slab, which create long vertical lines that extend unchecked to the flat roof, a design inspired by Hood's Daily News Building, which had also influenced the fenestration of the Empire State Building.

As in the Empire State Building, a perimeter of rentable space surrounds the centrally grouped elevators and service rooms on the office floors; in the lobby corridors, traffic patterns permit easy access to the elevators in the center and to the shops that also open onto the street. Twenty-eight feet between window and corridor allowed the proper amount of natural light and ventilation, and reduction of permanent partitions, as in the Chrysler Building, made the internal organization of space more flexible.

Three setbacks on the north and south walls step the building back from the east facade, reflecting the reduction of the number of elevator shafts within, a pattern that is echoed in the International Building to the northeast. Legislation of 1931 allowed the use of new high-speed elevators, reducing the number required, and fewer elevators meant less unrentable space taken up by elevator shafts. The three setbacks on the east facade are functionally unnecessary, but they continue the setback lines of the north and south walls around the front of the tower slab, presenting a unified surface and a visually coherent exterior.

The limestone cladding is textured in a shot-saw pattern, that is, a weft of thin and irregular linear indentations across the surface of the stone. The architects achieved additional variety in the stonework by laying up the individual limestone blocks irregularly so that, occasionally, the striations of the shot-saw pattern meet at right angles. A panel of darker Deer Island granite runs around the building from the sidewalk up about four feet and makes a visually pleasing transition from the pavement to the limestone slab.

The west face of the tower rises sheer from the NBC Studios, which needed broad open spaces incompatible with a forest of closely spaced vertical supports that tall buildings require. Therefore, the low-rise NBC Studios, which could also do without natural light while the tall office buildings could not, were logically placed between the tall east tower and RCA West.

The studios were designed to accommodate the radio needs of the 1930s and to anticipate the radio and television needs of the future. In addition to four of the most modern broadcast studios serviced by a central control room, there were two- and three-story spaces for stage plays, large studio audiences, and exhibitions. These were equipped with ramps, stairs, balconies, and elevators. The studios are still in use today, using updated equipment.

THE INVISIBLE GUIDE

The main access to the Center is the visually and physically magnetic approach off Fifth Avenue between Forty-ninth and Fiftieth streets, across from Saks Fifth Avenue and along the east-west axis of the Center established by the RCA Building. The east facade of the building is framed symmetrically by the Maison Française on the south and by the British Empire Building on the north—twin, seven-story buildings that step up to nine stories, echoing the RCA tower setbacks. Horizontal mouldings on both buildings above the shop windows at the ground-floor level, and their cornices above the sixth and seventh stories, create uninterrupted perspective lines that converge like pointers at the entrance of the RCA Building. These devices create a logical and coherent space, as in a realistic painting, into which the spectator is immediately drawn. Moreover, everything in that space conforms to human scale; that is, the width of the walkways, the size of the display windows, and the distances —all are manageable and comfortable for the stroller, as if he were being conducted through the Center by an invisible guide.

Between these lower buildings, a promenade with beautiful gardens is dedicated and inscribed in marble to Dr. Hosack. Elegant shops and convenient benches gradually slope downward to gravi-

303

Rockefeller Center: The lower plaza is popular as an ice-skating rink in the winter and as an outdoor cafe in warm weather. Paul Manship's statue of Prometheus overlooks the skaters.

tationally and visually entice the visitor to enter and pause to look. Nicknamed the "Channel Gardens," because they separate the French and British buildings as the English Channel separates the two countries, the gardens divide the wide promenade into two walkways, taking passersby closer to the displays in the shop windows of the Maison Française and the British Empire Building. Impeccably manicured beds of seasonal flowers surround six rectangular glass-bottom pools of polished Deer Island granite (the same material used in the base of the RCA Building), which are guarded by fountainheads of tritons and nereids.

Sculptor René Chambellan, who executed the sculpture program for the Chanin Building, used these six bronze tritons and nereids riding dolphins to symbolize modern man's conquest of new frontiers through his spiritual and physical energies, as expressed in leadership, will, thought, imagination, energy, and alertness. Chambellan's signature is legible on some of the dolphin tails.

The promenade's noticeable downward slope leads the stroller westward along the walk to a great open space in front of the RCA Building with sunken plaza, called the lower plaza, where ample sidewalks, stairs, and streets with low curbs link the other buildings of the Center and underground access routes.

THE LOWER PLAZA

The lower plaza was originally flanked on the north and south by shops, but it is now used as an ice-skating rink in the winter and as a restaurant the remainder of the year. It was first opened on Christmas Day 1936, as an experiment to infuse economic life into the plaza, which had been a financial failure. The rink was so successful that it became a permanent feature of the Center and still is the Center's most popular attraction.

An enormous fountain at the basin of the lower plaza against the west wall is surmounted by a bronze-gilded flying figure of Prometheus, whose mission is described in a quotation from Aeschylus's *Prometheus Bound* on the Balmoral granite wall behind Prometheus. Eighteen feet high, weighing eight tons, the figure by sculptor Paul Manship was unveiled in 1934. Surrounded by a ring bearing the signs of the Zodiac, representing the Cosmos, Prometheus delivers the stolen fire to mankind. The earth below is symbolized by the gigantic convex base that supports the sculpture. Prometheus was originally flanked by two smaller figures, a male and a female, symbolizing the people of the earth, but these have been pressed into service on the roof garden of the Palazzo d'Italia. The fourteen-foot-high sheet of water behind Prometheus and the electronically controlled lighting were designed by artist and lighting designer Abe Ferber in 1958. Demonstrations of changing light patterns synchronized with music are presented regularly from dusk to 1:00 A.M. during the summertime.

Doorways at the left and right of the fountain lead the stroller to the underground pedestrian street lined with shops, restaurants, and service areas. The street radiates from the RCA Building and connects all the buildings and the subway system in the Center.

ART AND ARCHITECTURE

From the top of the stairs facing the lower plaza, great red, green, and gold reliefs by sculptor Lee Lawrie appear over the RCA Building's east entrance, rising behind Prometheus, and eclipsed only at Christmas time by the giant spruce Christmas tree. The figure of Genius over the center door was inspired by William Blake's teaching figure of Urizen (Blake's combination of the biblical Jehovah and the god of the deists). The colorful low-relief figures above the doorways on either side of Genius symbolize light and sound—the foundations of radio, television, and motion pictures.

As the RCA Building established the architectural style for the Center, it also established the Center's carefully coordinated art program, to which Rockefeller attached great importance. The entrance reliefs express the principal underlying theme of the art program. Through wisdom and knowledge of the universe, man will find security and fulfillment. The motivating spirit behind the theme is man's search for spiritual significance through material conquest.

Almost thirty artists were employed as mural painters and sculptors for the Center, and craftsmen in mural and enamel work, and mosaicists worked to execute an art program that was conceptually and stylistically allied to the architecture. For example, José María Sert's ceiling mural for the RCA Building lobby symbolizes man's progress in his quest for immortality through the conquest of space and time. Then, the relief sculpture on the facades of the Maison Française and British Empire buildings carry international themes of peace, commerce, and the arts.

The sculpture program of the International Building, 630 Fifth Avenue, carries the theme of cooperation among nations for world peace and prosperity. The stability of such a world in harmony with the universe is symbolized in the seven-ton, fifteen-foot-high cast bronze statue of Atlas by sculptor Lee Lawrie, holding an armillary sphere in the courtyard at the main entrance, facing St. Patrick's Cathedral. On the horizon band surrounding the interlaced celestial

Rockefeller Center. Located in the sunken plaza of the McGraw-Hill Building on Sixth Avenue is Athelstan Spilhaus's 50-foot-high stainless steel triangle sculpture that marks the summer and winter solstices.

circles are the signs of the Zodiac, linking the Atlas sculpture to that of his brother Prometheus, executed three years earlier (1934) in the sunken plaza, by Paul Manship. Its axis points to the North Star, which at once symbolizes universal harmony, consonant with the theme, and relates the International Building to the cosmic order, a common device used by architects. Other examples include the compass in the lobby dome of the Woolworth Building, and the McGraw-Hill sculpture by Athelstan Spilhaus that relates the building to the seasons.

The Center's Eastern Airlines Building characteristically unites art and architecture. It enjoys particular significance, however, because it stands on the site originally intended for the new Metropolitan Opera House, and its lobby uniquely relates it to the underground world of Rockefeller Center. The Eastern Airlines Building at 10 Rockefeller Plaza is a sixteen-story office tower facing One Rockefeller Plaza. It has a four-story base for shops, exhibition

Rockefeller Center: Associated Press Building. Isamu Noguchi's 10-ton stainless-steel relief illustrates the network of the Associated Press's news services.

and meeting areas, and an adjoining garage, which supports a twelve-story slab tower of offices with one setback, like its neighbor One Rockefeller Plaza. The center of the lobby floor opens up toward the underground shopping concourse by means of a broad, curved staircase. Lobby murals by Dean Cornwell portray the story of transportation from the time of covered wagons and clipper ships to the airplane. Centered on the west wall facing the entrance and overlooking the stairwell, heroic personifications of North and South America holding an airplane between them symbolize unity through air travel. The use of gold leaf (earthbound subjects) and silver leaf (airborne subjects) lends a textured surface to the walls that animates them and gives the images a three-dimensional quality that further enriches the lobby decoration.

Isamu Noguchi's ten-ton stainless steel relief over the main entrance to the Associated Press Building, at the opposite end of the street, is one of the Center's most outstanding pieces of sculpture. Five compressed and animated clothed and semi-nude male figures using camera, telephone, wirephoto, teletype, and pad and pencil symbolize the AP network of news services. The four narrow bands behind the figures, which sharply converge at a vanishing point at the left center background, suggesting infinity, represent the wires that transmit news worldwide. The building also houses a movie theater—originally the Newsreel, now the Guild.

Sidewalk Superintendent's Club

The New York custom of the peephole in fences around construction sites was institutionalized by none other than John D. Rockefeller, Jr. Because he was prohibited from watching the work in progress at the Eastern Airlines Building by an overly protective construction worker, he went ahead and formed the Sidewalk Superintendents Club, to which anyone could get a membership card just to watch construction from a specially erected bleecher for that purpose. The idea caught on and no self-respecting construction site today is without its proscenium peephole—through which can be viewed New York's ever-new and ever-changing drama of construction.

RADIO CITY MUSIC HALL

Art and architecture were also superlatively united in Rockefeller Center's two theaters, Radio City Music Hall and the Center Theater. RCA built two theaters on the recommendation of Samuel Lionel Rothafel, better known as Roxy. The two theaters faced on Sixth Avenue and flanked the RCA building. The largest, the International Music Hall, which became Radio City Music Hall (Radio City was the term invented by David Sarnoff), was to feature live entertainment and to seat 6,200 persons. The smaller theater, the RKO Roxy (later changed to the Center Theater after a law suit by the Roxy Theater) was to show movies with vaudeville acts.

Roxy, a legend of the 1920s, had built an empire by combining movies with vaudeville acts. In 1927 he erected the world's largest movie theater (seating almost 6,000): the Roxy, on Fiftieth Street between Sixth and Seventh avenues. One of its main features was the Roxyettes, precursors of the Rockettes, Radio City Music Hall's still-famous precision dancers.

Radio City Music Hall combines Roxy's blend of the practical and the spectacular with Art Deco design and decoration—by architect/designer Donald Desky—on a scale never before tried. The auditorium is not based on any one model, and in scale and technical capabilities it was unique for its time. It reflected the influence of the latest contemporary theater design and technology. One source of inspiration, for example, was the Grosses Schauspielhaus in Berlin, which seated 5,000 persons. It was a round circus building redesigned by the Expressionist architect Hans Poelzig in 1919. He did the work for Max Reinhardt (1873–1943), the Austrian director who gave the Salzburg Music Festival a worldwide reputation and

309

Rockefeller Center: Radio City Music Hall. Seating 6,200 people, the largest of its kind when it opened in 1932, the theater, with its movable stage and huge organ, was an instant success.

who became known to American audiences through his productions of such works as *Everyman* and *A Midsummer Night's Dream.* Poelzig's cavernous vaulting over a circular stage, which noted architectural historian Henry Russell Hitchcock has likened to an Expressionist stage-set itself, and his dramatically illuminated corridors and lobby embody a visionary aspect of Expressionism that Radio City Music Hall has captured.

THE CENTER THEATER

The Center Theater was designed for movies and was richly decorated in the Art Deco style by Eugene Schoen. Its lobby was 158 feet long, the width of the theater, and 22 feet deep. Elevators and stairs serviced the three balconies and the lounge below. Floor-to-ceiling windows were framed by beige draperies and wall panels on one side of the lobby and by a low, light wood-paneled wall echoing the curve of the proscenium of the auditorium on the other side. The walls were pierced by the doors into the auditorium. The auditorium ceiling was approximately 65 feet high, and supported a chandelier 25 feet in diameter and weighing six tons. More than 400 floodlights offered ample and flexible illumination, and the interior was decorated with Classical figures by René Chambellan and Oronzio Maldarelli.

All furniture, drapery, carpets, lamps, and fixtures were coordinated with the architecture and art. The story of aviation was rendered by Edward Steichen in photomurals installed on the walls of the men's lounge, and a glass relief by Maurice Heaton hung in the women's powder room with a tribute to Amelia Earhart, the first woman to fly the Atlantic; the relief showed the last leg of the flight.

When the two theaters opened in 1932, RCA Music Hall did not attract enough audience to be profitable; therefore, Roxy instituted his earlier success formula of movies with live entertainment, which in turn hurt the Center Theater's business.

Efforts to make the Center Theater pay its way included enlarging the stage for live shows and Sonja Henie's famous ice show, renting the roof to Simon & Schuster for office space (they now have the U.S. Rubber Co. Building renamed for them), and alterations in the auditorium to accommodate television productions. But nothing succeeded in making it profitable. In 1954 it was razed to make way for the U.S. Rubber Co. to build on the site. The U.S. Rubber Co. Building is an office slab on a base with a two-story exhibition space that echoes its model—the nearby Eastern Airlines Building.

THE CHANGING FACE OF SIXTH AVENUE

The Center Theater, Radio City Music Hall, RCA West, the RKO Building, and the U.S. Rubber Co. Building formed an impressive continuous facade for Rockefeller Center and proved a boon to Sixth Avenue, when the U.S. Rubber, Co. Building was completed. On November 1, 1939, John D. Rockefeller, Jr., officially united the components of that facade when he drove a silver rivet in the steel skeleton of the U.S. Rubber Co. Building to celebrate the official completion of Rockefeller Center's original construction.

The buildings added in the 1960s and 1970s on the west side of Sixth Avenue complete the Center: the skyscrapers named after Time-Life, Sperry-Rand, McGraw-Hill, Exxon, and Celanese. These constitute a unified facade of stone and glass that respects the lines established by the original group of buildings, but they depart from the principles of scale and proportion. Fountains, flower beds, benches, and vine-covered walkways enhance the large plazas, but the comforts and diversions they offer are not related to one another, affording little relationship to the other buildings of the Center. Even though the Sperry-Rand Building to the north is part of the Center and connected to it by the underground concourse, its pre-cast concrete facade breaks with the stone cladding of its neighbors, and it does not appear to be part of the group.

311

14

Graves, Gardens, and Parks

Graves, gardens, and parks have a common origin that goes back to ancient times. The American park tradition reflects these origins and began in colonial times with a small, family burial place set aside in a remote area of the farm. These are called homestead graves or cemeteries and were held in reverence by our forefathers, a fact to which their wills and deeds attest. These documents, historians have noted, carefully stipulate provisions for the family's remains. Those remains were either never to be moved, or, if the family moved, they, too, were to be relocated to the new family homestead.

As the family grew, so did the cemetery. New names appeared on the tombstones, reflecting the growing genealogy. This can be seen at the Lent Homestead in Queens, where the cemetery is adjacent to the family house. That one, called the Riker-Lent cemetery, dates from 1667 and predates the present house. It was enlarged in the nineteenth century by a later owner, Isaac Rapelye, who added an adjoining strip of land. In all sales of the property, the graveyard has been duly preserved, so that some of the earliest settlers who farmed this land and who established the Dutch Reformed Church are buried here.

Two other examples of the few homestead cemeteries to survive to modern times are in Staten Island and Far Rockaway. Along Arthur Kill Road at Rossville Avenue on Staten Island, a low retaining wall encloses one of the first homestead burial grounds on Sta-

Soldiers and Sailors Memorial Arch *(facing page),* Grand Army Plaza, Prospect Park, Brooklyn; 1892. Designed by John H. Duncan after French models, it commemorates the triumph of Union forces in the Civil War.

ten Island, the Sleight Family Graveyard, named for one of the families that owned it. Peter Winant, one of the first settlers of Staten Island, is buried here, and his house once stood nearby. The cemetery is also known as the Blazing Star Graveyard because the mooring slip of the Blazing Star Ferry to New Jersey was located nearby.

Master ironworker Richard Cornell, who came from England as a child, settled in Flushing. In 1687 he bought most of today's Far Rockaway and lived on the site of today's Hartman YM-YWHA at 257 Beach Seventeenth Street. The family cemetery at 1457 Greenport Road is seventy-five feet wide by sixty-seven feet deep and is enclosed by an iron fence. The plot was used by the family through the nineteenth century. Cornell's descendants include Ezra Cornell, founder of Cornell University, and his son Alonzo B. Cornell, governor of New York 1879–82.

COMMUNITY CEMETERIES

Another type of cemetery was planned as part of a community, in accordance with common interests. Old Gravesend Cemetery, on Gravesend Neck Road near McDonald Avenue in Brooklyn, is important both as such an early burial site and also as the only surviving remnant of a sophisticated system of town planning. Gravesend was settled by Lady Deborah Moody from England, who headed a group of Anabaptists (against infant baptism). In 1645 she secured a charter from Governor William Kieft for Gravesend, named either for a town in England or Kieft's hometown, historians have noted. The charter was the earliest document for land in the New York area to be written in English, it was the first town charter in the New World to list a woman patentee, and one of the earliest to allow religious freedom. The nearby Dutch communities, today's Maspeth (Maspet, 1642) and Flushing (Vlissingen, 1643), were founded shortly before.

Originally encompassing some sixteen acres, the town was enclosed by palisades, walls of sharpened wood poles, for protection and was divided into quadrants by north-south (McDonald Avenue, formerly Gravesend Road) and east-west (Gravesend Neck Road) axes. Houses were built surrounding each quadrant, creating an enclosure that was first used to contain animals at night, and later provided space for schools, town hall, church, and burial ground. Radiating from the palisades were individual wedge-shaped farming strips. Even though most of the original boundaries have been obliterated, some of the present streets reflect the early pie-shaped plots. This plan was not unique in the New World, but it was uncommon. It derived from Renaissance and Baroque town planning ideas, also applied in Philadelphia and New Haven, and provided a practical plan for a community intending to expand.

Part of today's Gravesend Cemetery occupied the open ground of the southwest quadrant. Subsequent additions, however, have changed the shape and size of the original configuration. Although most of the seventeenth-century gravestones have disappeared or have become illegible, the earliest grave dates from probably 1650. Some of the headstones (mostly brownstone) that can be read carry both English and Dutch inscriptions.

First Sheareth Israel Graveyard

One of the oldest burial sites in Manhattan is the First Sheareth Israel Graveyard, 55 St. James Place. It became obscured by the buildings constructed around its small site. But in the 1950s Bernard Baruch, whose ancestor Rachel Rodriguez Marques was buried there in 1733, bought a triangular plot of land adjacent to it. He razed the buildings around it and made a park to once again open up the area to the light of day (he then donated the park to the city).

The cemetery had served the oldest Jewish congregation in New York and the first permanent settlement of Jews in North America, historians have noted. Burials date from 1683 to 1825. According to Sephardic custom, the stones are flat slabs set flush with the ground. However, some are raised on supports to appear as sarcophagi, and there is one modified obelisk set on a square pedestal. The inscriptions are in Hebrew, Spanish, Portuguese, and after 1719, in English. Consistent with the Jewish aversion to graven images, decoration is limited to such stylized motifs as floral scrolls, rosettes, hands raised in benediction, or a hand cutting off a flower, symbolic of the interruption of life. An exception, however, is a relief of the angel of destruction brandishing a flaming sword over the city, whose silhouette is clearly depicted, while an ax, wielded by a hand emerging from a cloud, hews down the tree of life. The stones are of sandstone, limestone, marble, and bluestone granite. The 1683 tombstone of Benjamin Buero de Mesquita is still legible because it was probably carved from the same durable Westchester County marble used in the Sub-Treasury Building on Wall and Nassau streets.

With the northward expansion of the city, the congregation bought land on Milligan Street in Greenwich Village (now 72–6 West Eleventh Street). This served them until 1830, when West Eleventh Street—following the Commissioners' Plan—was cut through and left the cemetery in its present truncated form. The remains were removed to the congregation's third cemetery on West

315

Twenty-first Street between Sixth and Seventh avenues in Chelsea. When city legislation in 1851 forbade burial within Manhattan, the congregation selected a site in Cypress Hills, Long Island.

THE RURAL CEMETERY:
MAN'S UNION WITH NATURE

As cities expanded and the small community and churchyard cemeteries could no longer accommodate the increased number of burials, a new kind of burial place emerged: the rural cemetery. Rural cemeteries had roots in the English landscape garden movement of the early eighteenth century. This movement had developed around the ideas and projects of such figures as Lord Burlington, a major force in the Classical Revival in England and his protégé, William Kent, the versatile and gifted architect, painter, landscape gardener, and designer.

Drawing from models of republican Rome, Renaissance Italy, and eighteenth-century China, Burlington and Kent popularized a new and spontaneous naturalism in landscape gardening, diametrically opposed to the geometric gardens of France, which they maintained forced nature into a straitjacket. Expansive vistas of greenery, water, and sky, great trees with overhanging boughs, and winding paths and streams were the hallmarks of the English landscape garden. These were also the components of the great Baroque landscape paintings of Claude Lorrain, so well known and loved by English collectors of the period.

Under the influence of Burlington and Kent and the popular Baroque tradition, the landscape gardeners altered and tamed the wild countryside of English estates to look like Lorrain's paintings. From any view, they insisted, the landscape should be "picturesque" —that is, look like a picture.

The leading protagonists in this drama of the landscape, who believed that nature should have a salutary effect upon man, and who also debated among themselves about aesthetics, included "Capability" Brown, Humphrey Repton, William Gilpin, Richard Payne Knight, and Uvedale Price. On seeing the great gardens of Chiswick, Stowe, and Richmond, English poet James Thomson described the landscape as ". . . sylvan scenes, where art alone pretends/ To dress her mistress and disclose her charms. . . ."

The idea of the picturesque came to embody a feeling for the countryside through which man could identify his moods and aesthetic sense with nature. This implication of man's essential integration with nature is the basis of the appeal of the rural cemetery. This type of cemetery began in America first with Mount Auburn Cem-

316

etery in Cambridge, Massachusetts, in 1831, then with Green-Wood Cemetery in Brooklyn, and Laurel Hill Cemetery in Philadelphia. These three were the models for all those that followed in the United States.

These rural cemeteries were not just final resting places for the dead, but they were also America's first urban parks. They were indeed places where man could commune with God, but they also became popular places for family outings; after all, they were beautiful spaces, were well tended, and offered a welcome relief from the congestion of the city. Moreover, they had beautiful architecture and outdoor sculpture.

Green-Wood Cemetery

Green-Wood Cemetery was the largest and most sophisticated of these rural cemeteries, and it, along with the distinguished European parks and landscape gardens, set the standards for the great urban parks of Frederick Law Olmsted and Calvert Vaux, including Central Park in Manhattan and Prospect Park in Brooklyn. Green-Wood was laid out in 1838 by David Bates Douglass, a surveyor and engineer by training and experience, and one who enjoyed great prestige. Douglass taught at West Point, was involved in establishing the border between the United States and Canada, worked with leading railroads and canals, and taught engineering and architecture at New York University (where he contributed to the design of the Washington Square campus). Green-Wood was his first commission in landscape architecture, and it was a *tour de force* in the picturesque tradition.

Originally 178 acres, Green-Wood now encompasses 478 acres of landscaped terrain in the heart of Brooklyn, and it still retains its picturesque beauty. Douglass objected to the suggestion that the cemetery be called the Necropolis, because he said that name emphasized its role as a repository for the dead rather than as a place of quiet repose, which accommodated also the living. The names of the various sites on the grounds also stressed the vital and picturesque aspect of the park: Halcyon Lake, Vista Hill, Camelia Path, and Sylvan Cliff.

A remarkable monument to the picturesque landscape in America, Green-Wood was designed by Douglass with a variety of traditional features, including winding paths, lawns, forests, hills, valleys, lakes, and scenic views; he composed them, however, to take advantage of the urban scenes of New York, Brooklyn, and the harbor. A virtual architectural encyclopedia, Green-Wood contains some of America's outstanding mortuary architecture and sculpture. Tombs and monuments include all styles: Egyptian, Classical, Gothic, Ro-

Green-Wood Cemetery, Brooklyn, Fifth Avenue to MacDonald Avenue
and Fort Hamilton Parkway; 1838. David Bates Douglass, designer. The
largest, most sophisticated of the early "rural" cemeteries, Green-Wood
set standards of architecture, landscape design, and planning for
America's great urban parks.

manesque, as well as ingenious combinations of styles. Moreover,
many were designed by the leading architects of the period, designers including Richard Upjohn, Minard Lafever, and Warren and
Wetmore.

The original buildings, which were numerous shelters, were designed by Richard Upjohn and coordinated with Douglass's plan.
The shelters were constructed in wood in various styles—Gothic
Revival, Italian Villa, and Swiss Chalet—and they all have long since
deteriorated, except for the ladies' rain shelter. However, Upjohn's
rusticated gates and office (1861–65) still stand and are in superb
condition. Two gate portals flank a Flamboyant Gothic clock and
bell tower 106 feet tall. Administration offices on one side of the
entrance and the chapel and reception area on the opposite side are
connected to the gates as a coherent architectural unit.

Green-Wood is the final resting place for many of New York's
and the country's best-known figures from all walks of life. Artists
include the painter George Catlin, the famous print-makers Na-

thaniel Currier and James Ives, the successful designer Louis Comfort Tiffany, and Hudson River painter Asher B. Durand. Among New York's most successful architects buried here are Richard Upjohn, whose many monuments are an eternal vigil to his memory, and James Renwick, whose Grace Church on Eleventh Street and Broadway, and St. Patrick's Cathedral on Fifth Avenue remain leading monuments to his work and to the Gothic Revival in New York. Those in public life include De Witt Clinton, Henry Ward Beecher, Horace Greeley, and "Boss" Tweed. Among America's commercial leaders who lie here are William Colgate, Charles Pfizer, and Edward Squibb.

Green-Wood steadily became more and more popular with the public as a place for family leisure. By the 1840s the cemetery was attracting as many as 30,000 persons who came by carriage or ferry during the spring and fall seasons. Publications of all kinds became popular for strollers and visitors. Maps and small guide books were common. A description of the cemetery plan was published in 1839, an illustrated guide in 1847, a directory in 1849, a history of the cemetery in 1866, and a handbook in 1867.

The rural cemetery pointed the way for the public park. It also served as a model for the private monument of the affluent. One of the most spectacular funerary designs inspired by this tradition is the Vanderbilt Cemetery and Mausoleum.

Vanderbilt Cemetery and Mausoleum

The rural cemetery and the picturesque tradition were the origins of the Vanderbilt Cemetery and Mausoleum at New Dorp, on Staten Island. When William Henry Vanderbilt, America's wealthiest man at the time, retired in 1883 at the age of sixty-two, he was ill and anxious to prepare his final resting place. The Vanderbilts had settled on Staten Island in the eighteenth century, and had been members of the Moravian sect there. William Vanderbilt was baptized in the little church at New Dorp, and even though he had become an Episcopalian, he continued to contribute to the Moravian Church, which held special meaning for him all of his life.

Vanderbilt had planned to enlarge the family plot in the Moravian cemetery, but because the land was too expensive, he built his own cemetery of twenty-one acres, adjoining the Moravian cemetery and overlooking New York Harbor. He commissioned America's leading architect, Richard Morris Hunt, to design his mausoleum and Frederick Law Olmsted, the country's leading landscape gardener, to design the grounds.

In keeping with Vanderbilt's desire for his mausoleum to be simple but substantial, Hunt built it in Indiana limestone in the

319

Romanesque Revival style. Hunt knew the great French Romanesque buildings from his studies and travels in France, and he was fond of the modern French buildings that were indebted to the Romanesque tradition, such as the Basilica of Sacré-Coeur in Paris of the 1870s.

Hunt's design for Vanderbilt's mausoleum is a restrained combination of the old and the new, historians have analyzed. The facade is composed of the main entrance: a large barrel arch, flanked by two smaller barrel-arched side entrances. Over the central portal, Christ in majesty is surrounded by the symbols of the Evangelists, the tetramorph; the flanking tympanums contain angels and winged souls symbolic of the Second Coming. Acanthus leaves, vines, and grotesque heads surround the portals. Seven slender vertical round-arched windows in the massive gable above the main entrance permit natural illumination into the narthex. Beyond the narthex, the crypt is in Indiana limestone, sparsely decorated and illuminated beneath two domes on pendentives.

The building is sited on the crest of a hill surrounded by forest land and overlooking a panoramic view of the Lower Bay. Olmsted chose plants and trees that blend well with the surrounding natural growth in order to frame certain aspects of the landscape and to create suitable backdrops for others. Olmsted was especially well suited for this task. He had owned an experimental fruit tree farm on Staten Island at mid-century, and he was perhaps the most knowledgeable person alive on the subject. The approach to the mausoleum begins at the lowest point on the hill through a large stone arch, and a winding road leads to the mausoleum, which is set within a large terrace and parapet walls. Unfortunately, now Olmsted's work is all overgrown, and the concept behind the plan for the cemetery is obscured through lack of maintenance.

This was the first collaboration of Hunt and Olmsted, but it was not the last. They went on to design Biltmore, George Washington Vanderbilt's great estate near Asheville, North Carolina, for example.

CENTRAL PARK

The growth of commercial production in the nineteenth century fostered immigration and the consequent crowding in the major cities, especially in New York, underscoring the limitations of the Commissioners' Plan of 1811 and the need for squares, promenades, and parks. The pressures of urban life left less time and opportunity for people to enjoy the countryside. The promise, then, of a great urban park would be most appealing. As early as 1844, William Cullen Bryant in his *New York Evening Post* called for a great public park in the European tradition and the following year suggested a "central" reservation as in London, a city which had felt the scourge of the industrial revolution early. Then A. J. Downing, in *The Horticulturist* in 1851, advocated the creation of a "central" park of at least five hundred acres. These pleas apparently reflected the public's voice, because a public park for New York City was promised by each candidate in the mayor's race in 1850.

So Central Park, New York's first great urban park, was the result of a combination of forces: man's attitudes toward nature, the landscape tradition, the press of urban life, and the aesthetic climate of the times. People could once again renew their sense of integration with nature, which had been a meaningful part of their lives since colonial times. The leading figures in its development were Frederick Law Olmsted, Calvert Vaux, and Andrew Jackson Downing. Olmsted and Vaux were the designers of the nation's first urban park, and Downing was the major force in paving the way toward its realization.

In a public competition in 1856 Olmsted and Vaux won with their design for a great park first called "Greensward," which later became known as Central Park. On the site of some 300 squatters' hovels and marshy land, they created hills and lakes, mounds and valleys with winding paths and picturesque views over an area that grew to 840 acres. A drainage system ninety-five miles long channeled underground streams, carried off excess surface water, and allowed fresh water to flow. Footpaths, bridle paths, carriage drives, and waterways were laid out. An ingenious system of transverse roads to carry east-west traffic through the park were depressed beneath ground level, which makes the traffic unnoticeable to those in the park even today. Bridges cover waterways, and springs emerge as if miraculously. For example, at the southeast corner of the park below the dairy, where youngsters could once watch cattle tethered and grazing, such a spring flowed from the slope in front of, and below, the dairy into a stream that ran under the rusticated stone bridge and into the duck pond. The stream continues southeast under Corning Glass Co., supplying their fountain on Fifth Avenue, and empties out into Turtle Bay near the United Nations. The ice-skating rink now located below the dairy has destroyed the original picturesque view and the sight of the emerging spring.

Central Park is divided into a natural section—the northern part —and a pastoral section—the southern end. The natural section is more rugged with dramatic scenery characterized by sudden shifts in terrain and mysterious shaded areas, as in the Ramble. Steep hills, rocky outcroppings, thick woods, and bodies of water linked by brooks create a sense of raw wilderness.

321

The Picturesque

In the southern part, the park abounds in a variety of picturesque devices drawn from the English landscape garden and from the rural cemetery. The duck pond, for example, winds around to the west and is surrounded by full overhanging trees. These trees and the tall hedges nearby are reflected off the mirrorlike surface of the water. The reflective properties of water were an important aspect of the picturesque tradition. The natural rock formations that jut out from promontories, and which were carved by nature thousands of years ago, also contribute to the picturesque.

The principal formal element in the park is the treelined mall and the terrace, called the esplanade, from Sixty-fifth to Seventy-third streets, planned so that the Belvedere (a small lookout tower with a view) at the north terminates a view from the south looking north. The terrace is divided into two levels and is reached by taking stairways and going through a gallery, lined with Minton tiles, beneath Seventy-second Street, or by crossing the street and descending two flights of stairs, which have carved rails. The dominant feature of the lower terrace is Emma Stebbins's Bethesda Fountain. The Angel of the Waters, a colossal bronze figure, rises above a giant basin and is supported by four youthful figures representing Health, Purity, Temperance, and Peace. The inspiration is from the Gospel of St. John, 5:2–4.

The terrace was designed by Calvert Vaux, but the decoration for the stairways was designed by Jacob Wrey Mould, an English architect who had studied with Owen Jones, best remembered for his *Grammar of Ornament*. Mould had come to America in 1853 with a commission to design and build All Souls Unitarian Church on Lexington Avenue and Twentieth Street (demolished). He became an associate architect on Central Park in 1857.

Terrace Sculpture

The theme of the carving around the terrace is the seasons, reflecting the tradition of calendar illustrations popular in medieval illuminated manuscripts, and features imagery and pictorial ideas that go back to ancient times. On the three sides of the newel posts, animals and fruit that belong to the various seasons are carved: lambs' heads symbolic of early spring; firewood for winter; butterflies and berries of summer; and birds on branches above pine cones, pine boughs, and holly leaves representing autumn. The balustrades have panels filled with these symbols.

Central Park: Seventy-second Street transverse. The terrace, or esplanade, was designed by Calvert Vaux, and the sculpture for the Bethesda Fountain *(above)*, depicting the Angel of the Waters, was by Emma Stebbins. Designed by Jacob Wrey Mould, the carving around the terrace *(below)* illustrates the seasons of the year, expressed through birds, berries, and foliage.

Central Park: This terrace relief *(above)* of a bird in its nest hatching its eggs celebrates the cycle of life and the changing seasons. The arsenal *(left)*, Fifth Avenue and Sixty-fourth Street; 1851. Martin E. Thompson, architect. The front-stairs railing, made of casts of inverted rifles, and the newel post, the cast of a cannon, are examples of *architecture parlante.*

But there are others as well. In one panel there is a pair of skates. Still other images symbolize the effect of the changing seasons on the home. The rooster heralds an early dawn of longer spring and summer days. Gathered grain of the harvest stands for early autumn, a book and lamp are reminders that autumn's long nights are spent inside. Halloween is symbolized by a witch on a broomstick. Along the ramps flanking the stairs, scrolls are formed by branches of flowering plants with birds. Originally, the terrace was to be ornamented with marble and bronze figures representing the seasons, the ages of man, and the times of day. But those figures were never commissioned.

Olmsted and Vaux designed the architectural structures of the park to be subservient to its landscape, and a variety of structures in numerous styles were designed to complement the picturesque aspects of the park. Bridges, for example, are in stone, wood, and cast iron, and are in Romanesque Revival and Gothic Revival styles. Many of the gazebos, shelters, and the original bandstand on the esplanade have been demolished. But the recent trend to save the park has led to such projects as the restoration of the dairy with its porte-cochère, recently completed. Another optimistic sign is the ladies pavilion. Originally for lady passengers waiting for horsecars at Columbus Circle, it was designed by Calvert Vaux. It was badly vandalized, and then in 1973 the pavilion was restored at the Hermshead.

The arsenal stands in the park at Sixty-fourth Street just west of Fifth Avenue. Designed by Martin E. Thompson (1851) to house all the arms and munitions of the state that were not in use, it replaced the old arsenal at Franklin and Centre streets, built in 1808. Thompson's building looks like a great medieval fortress, complete with crenellations for crossbows. Remodeled by Richard Morris Hunt in 1862, the building has housed the Seventh Regiment Armory, the Eleventh Precinct Police Station, the Weather Bureau, the American Museum of Natural History, and since 1934, the New York City Parks Department.

Its main-entrance stairway is flanked by railings composed of casts of rifles and its newel posts are casts of cannon barrels. Above these picturesque touches of *architecture parlante,* a carved American eagle spreads its wings over two stacks of cannon balls above the main doorway.

The building is two hundred feet wide, fifty feet deep, and five stories high. Its massive redbrick walls and towers above a granite faced basement are opened by large vertical double-hung windows in the four bays on either side of the central bays and by the narrow windows in the faces of the great towers. Its east facade facing the park is a mirror image of the west facade facing Fifth Avenue.

PROSPECT PARK

The enormous appeal of Green-Wood Cemetery, the enthusiasm for the new Central Park in Manhattan, and the need for a large urban recreational area in Brooklyn, voiced loudly by William Cullen Bryant and A. J. Downing, led to the development of Prospect Park. Legislation was passed in 1859 and 1860 establishing Mount Prospect Park, and Egbert L. Viele, chief engineer for Central Park, was commissioned to design it. The Civil War interrupted implementation of Viele's plan and by the time the war was over, it was totally rejected.

325

A revised scheme by Olmsted and Vaux, approved on May 29, 1866, consisted of a large open meadow and playground; a hilly district of groves and shrubbery, shaded rambles and broad views; and a lake district, providing ice skating in the winter and rowing the rest of the year. These three principal districts and their components were to be connected by rides, drives, and rambles. Work began in 1866 and most of the plan was completed by 1873. It is noteworthy that Olmsted and Vaux's revised plan eliminated the hill, Mount Prospect, which gave the park its name. Often to make a park look "natural," nature was violated.

Olmsted and Vaux designed a vast waterworks and drainage system, coordinated with an elaborate network of roads, bridle paths, and walks that conformed to or modified the natural topography of the site. The traffic circulation system was based upon the experience they had had with Central Park. It differs mainly in that Prospect Park has no transverse arteries. Instead, the park is surrounded by drives connected to parkways leading from one section of Brooklyn to another. Pedestrian and vehicular traffic are separated by means of arched overpasses to carry vehicles over walks. For example, Eastwood Arch allows pedestrians to pass beneath the East Drive, and Nethermead Arches incorporates three arches combining a pedestrian walkway, stream, and bridle path beneath the Central Drive. To blend the arches picturesquely into the setting, they were built in heavily wooded areas so that vines and creepers would overgrow them.

Among the many and varied picturesque effects in Prospect Park is the entrance from Grand Army Plaza, which looks over the vast expanse of Long Meadow, giving a sense of infinite space. Long Meadow is over a mile long, covering seventy-five acres with high lookouts alternating with rolling hills and valleys, and the sloping vistas so popular for picnics in the nineteenth century. One of the most spectacular picturesque features is the meandering water system that begins at Swan Boat Lake and flows through a deep secluded ravine into Mid-Wood, finally emptying over a waterfall into the Lullwater. The Lullwater winds its way into the fifty-seven-acre lake, especially popular for ice skating in the nineteenth century.

Olmsted and Vaux planned a number of formal spaces. The concert grove (now flower garden) was laid out on the eastern shore of the lake to allow visitors to enjoy promenade concerts. The musicians were located on a small island while the audience faced them from seats beneath a grove of plane trees. The terrace area is divided and lined by handsome stone railings, walls, and parapets. Flower planters and fountain basins complete the decoration and all are richly carved with Gothic Revival ornament of flowers, plants, animals, and birds. The designs were by Calvert Vaux, assisted by

Jacob Wrey Mould, and are similar to those by Mould on the terrace in Central Park.

The Architecture

Olmsted and Vaux designed the architecture to complement their landscape. Unfortunately, few of those early structures remain standing. Rustic shelters provided cover from the rain and snow, but they are long since gone, although some were reconstructed along the lake in the early 1970s. A rustic dairy built in the Mid-Wood in 1868–69 is gone, and a refreshment house of 1871–72 in the concert grove is also gone. Even though Olmsted and Vaux's plans for a lookout tower and refectory atop Lookout Hill were never carried out, part of Vaux's Oriental pavilion built in 1874 as an open-air cafe can still be seen in the flower garden. Partly destroyed by fire in 1974, some of the cast-iron elements of the original structure remain. The Music Pagoda (1888), recently restored, retains its exotic Chinese character.

There are two residential buildings within the park boundaries that have historical and architectural significance: the Lefferts Home-stead on Flatbush Avenue—an example of Dutch Colonial architecture—and Litchfield Villa near Prospect Park West, now headquarters of the Park, Recreation, and Cultural Affairs Department.

Litchfield Villa is one of the finest Italian Villa–style houses in the country and was the home of Edward C. Litchfield, a lawyer who made a fortune in midwestern railroads. Designed by A. J. Davis, the house is a romantic mansion atop a small hill in Prospect Park. When it was first built, it commanded the view to the harbor from the hill. By the mid-1880s, however, other mansions began to appear. The lavish homes that clustered along Plaza Street and Prospect Park West became known as the Gold Coast. The many post–World War I apartment houses now concentrated along Grand Army Plaza contrast with the earlier row houses.

Even though Litchfield Villa is the best surviving example of Davis's Italianate style, its over eighty years of service as a public office have eroded much of the villa's original richness. The original exterior stucco, simulating cut stone, has been stripped off, exposing the common brick behind. The two irregularly shaped towers of the villa and its tall slender turret are all attached to the main building and create a picturesque silhouette. A colonnade, in wood painted white and carved to simulate marble, supports the roof over the side porch and extends beyond the rear of the house, connecting it with the annex in the rear. This was a later addition by architects Helmle and Huberty. An expansive terrace retained by a low

Litchfield Villa, Prospect Park West, between Fourth and Fifth streets; 1857. This Italian Villa-style mansion was designed by Alexander Jackson Davis, a leading New York architect in the picturesque tradition.

wall sets off the villa. The capitals of the columns are ears of corn indigenous to the United States and symbolic of the country's early agricultural foundations. These capitals were inspired by Benjamin Henry Latrobe's so-called corncob capitals for the U.S. Capitol Building in Washington, D.C.

A spirit of formal Classicism that animates some aspects of the park was introduced in the latter part of the nineteenth century and at the beginning of this century. It resulted from the pervasive influence of the Chicago Exposition of 1893, which led to a wide use of Classical elements in urban design.

The Classical works tend to dominate rather than complement the landscape, such as the Soldiers and Sailors Memorial Arch does at Grand Army Plaza (by John H. Duncan, 1892, architect for Grants' Tomb, 1895). The arch has sculpture by some of America's leading artists of the time. The Quadriga atop is by Frederick MacMonnies (1898), and inside the arch itself are bas-reliefs of Abraham Lincoln and U. S. Grant by Thomas Eakins, and William O. Donovan, 1895. On the south pedestal are Army and Navy, groups by MacMonnies, 1901. Among the other outstanding Classical Revival additions are those of McKim, Mead, and White. The pedestals at the Third Street entrance (1895), ornamented with bronze panthers by Alexander Phimister Proctor (1898), are good examples.

The union of sculpture and architecture within the landscape setting has always been an integral part of the urban park tradition.

One of the most successful examples of this union existing today is to be found in the Farragut Monument in Madison Square Park, between Fifth and Madison avenues, extending from Twenty-third Street to Twenty-sixth Street.

FARRAGUT MONUMENT

The death in 1870 of America's first admiral, David Glasgow Farragut, sparked a succession of tributes to the Civil War hero who at the battle of Mobile Bay, uttered the famous command "Damn the torpedoes. Four bells Captain Drayton. Go ahead full speed," which has been edited for posterity as "Damn the torpedoes, full speed ahead."

Soon after Farragut's burial in picturesque Woodlawn Cemetery, a bronze-relief portrait was commissioned for the Church of the Incarnation at Thirty-seventh Street and Madison Avenue, where he worshiped, and Congress appropriated funds for a statue in Washington, D.C., which was cast from one of the propellers of Farragut's ship, the *Hartford*.

The Farragut Monument in Madison Square Park, commissioned in 1876 and unveiled in 1881, is important not only as perhaps the most successful public monument to this war hero, but also because it introduced a new kind of memorial in America—one in which sculpture and architecture were integrated. Instead of a statue with a pedestal, the Farragut Monument was designed as a memorial in which the portrait figure and the base were conceived as a single entity. Furthermore, the monument was conceived within an appropriate urban landscape setting—a small park that provided the statue and its base an attractive setting. It became a model for many other memorials that followed.

Sculptor Augustus Saint-Gaudens and architect Stanford White set a precedent with this design which they themselves followed in such famous monuments as the Lincoln Memorial (1887) in Chicago, the "Puritan" (1887) in Springfield, Massachusetts, and the Adams Memorial (1891) in Washington, D.C.

Saint-Gaudens's figure portrays the sixty-three-year-old admiral as being of medium height, having a stout build, finely proportioned head, and clean shaven face. Farragut is wearing the uniform prescribed by Congress for the first admiral of the United States Navy: a double-breasted frock-coat with straps on the shoulders and three wide stripes on the sleeves. His sword hangs at the left side from the belt; the buckle is ornamented with the American eagle encircled with a wreath. He stands with head turned slightly to the left and eyes glancing to the side, a portrait technique popularized by the

329

Farragut Monument, Madison Square Park, Madison Avenue at Twenty-third Street; 1881. Stanford White, architect; Augustus Saint-Gaudens, sculptor. The base of the monument, from the back, approximates the bow of Farragut's ship, the *Hartford.*

famous French sculptor J. A. Houdon to lend a sense of "life" to a portrait. While he is holding his binoculars in his left hand close to his body, his right foot is advanced and the wind has tossed the skirt of his coat free of the upper part of his right leg. This is a device which further enlivens the figure. Naturalistic modeling of the head, clothing, and accessories help to animate Farragut's vital stance.

White's pedestal is a Classical exedra—a semicircular base with bench above three stairs and surrounding it a floor of pebbles approximating a beach. In the center a bronze crab contains the names of Saint-Gaudens and White, their signatures on the monument. Across the face of the elliptical pedestal, personifications of Loyalty (left) and Courage (right) flank the central prism which bears an upright sword. A single dolphin terminates the exedra at each side, and waves and foam course along the stone surface and across the inscriptions, which are in low relief and which salute Farragut's achievements and heroism. From the back of the monument, the exedra approximates the bow of the *Hartford,* with Farragut silhouetted against the sky, as if surveying his fleet. Nautical motifs are disposed along its surface.

The monument originally stood at the northwest corner of the park where it faced the fashionable Delmonico's—a favorite oasis of Stanford White—and the fashionable Fifth Avenue Hotel next door. The park served as a picturesque backdrop to the monument and a neatly manicured walkway with blue pebbles made an inviting approach to the exedra. Moreover, the position of the statue allowed marchers in each parade down Fifth Avenue to pass in review before the admiral. Farragut could also survey New York's first experiment with "noiseless pavement" (asphalt) which was done along Fifth Avenue between Twenty-sixth and Twenty-seventh streets. Before the monument was erected, Saint-Gaudens and White had first selected the site at the southwest of the park, but Saint-Gaudens noted that the glare of the morning sun, reflected off the windows of the Fifth Avenue Hotel, would impede a favorable view of the monument during the morning and early-afternoon hours.

The monument was unveiled before 10,000 persons, with leading dignitaries participating. One observer, expressing the exuberance of the event, opined that these artists' monument preached a small sermon in truth, honor, courage, and loyalty that touched the universal heart of man and assured its longevity. In spite of the blush of the moment, the fact that the monument has survived at all is a miracle. Neglect and weathering by the elements combined to destroy the original bluestone pedestal, whose marine color blended well with the nautical motifs and subject.

Restoration

In 1933 Lawrence White, Stanford's son, advised the parks department of the appalling condition of the monument and the city assured him a speedy solution. Subsequently, the city was redesigning its parks and this included moving the Farragut Monument. At that point, Lawrence enlisted the aid of Homer Saint-Gaudens, the sculptor's son, and although they failed to keep the monument in its original location, they did manage to get it restored. A new pedestal, exactly replicated from the original (but in more permanent material) was made because the original was too badly deteriorated to save.

The original pedestal was moved to Aspet, Saint-Gaudens's studio (a national landmark) in Cornish, New Hampshire, and a reproduction of Farragut's statue stands atop it there. As for the restored monument, its new location in the park divorces it from its proper context, since it is no longer backed by the park but by a deteriorating commercial facade across the street from the park.

The new base was placed upon an ingeniously devised cradle-type foundation that absorbs the traffic vibrations, reducing that destructive force. Unfortunately, other forces, vandalism and neglect, have increased in the park and its monuments are being systematically destroyed.

331

15

The Picturesque Point of View: Fonthill Castle, Firehouses, and the Seventh Regiment Armory

FONTHILL CASTLE

Fonthill Castle, located between the Hudson River and Riverdale Avenue just south of Yonkers, today surveys the Hudson as it did when the American Shakespearean actor Edwin Forrest built it in 1852. Forrest intended to live there with his wife Catherine and provided that after their deaths, it would be maintained as a home for indigent American actors. The castle is a remarkably well-preserved example of Gothic Revival architecture, and its site was laid out according to the picturesque tradition based on the English landscape garden.

Forrest bought the land—fifty-five acres—in 1847, intending to build his castle on a natural promontory extending into the Hudson. Angered on finding that the Hudson River Railroad commanded a narrow strip of land close to the river, which cut across the promontory on which he planned to build, Forrest then selected the present site, which is on a high knoll affording a handsome view of the Hudson and an imposing silhouette for the building.

The Design

Named after Fonthill Abbey in England, the castle's design, which may have been largely Forrest's own, was influenced to some extent by Lismore Castle in Ireland; Forrest kept a model of Lismore on his mantel for many years. Fonthill consists of five octago-

Fonthill Castle rotunda, 262nd Street and Riverdale Avenue *(facing page)*; 1852. This picturesque Gothic Revival castle is situated along the Hudson River; the rotunda's floor is laid with encaustic tile in a tessellated pattern.

nal towers of differing heights and dimensions radiating from a central tower, which encloses an octagonal rotunda with a glazed skylight.

The castle is built of dark hammer-dressed fieldstone, quarried on the estate only a quarter of a mile southeast of the site. The castle's crenellated towers are laid up in random coursing, and the slender and tallest stair tower reaches almost seventy feet in the air. Round-arched and pointed-arched windows are arranged to complement the varying dimensions of the towers, whose interiors they illuminate.

Forrest had wanted the highest tower of his castle to reach down to the water's edge, as does the keep of Lismore Castle, which is situated on the banks of the River Blackwater. During the Middle Ages, castle keeps were designed to spring directly from the water, making access more difficult. Consequently, the castle was safer from enemy attack. Forrest, however, had not been interested in defense but in aesthetics. He had wanted his tower to create a bold vertical silhouette, readily seen from far up or down river, and also providing the inhabitants with a good view of the Hudson.

Fonthill Abbey (1796–1807) in England, after which Forrest named his castle, was built for William Beckford by the architect James Wyatt. Forrest had *The Delineations of Fonthill Abbey* in his library, which fully illustrated the famous castle, and he and Catherine obviously were guided by it in their interior design. Several details come directly from Fonthill Abbey. The fan vaulting of Forrest's drawing-room ceiling is closely modeled on the abbey's St. Michael's Gallery; and the proportions and designs of the moulded pendants are strikingly parallel in the two buildings. Moreover, the corbels from which the vaulting springs in the rotunda in the Riverdale castle are very close to those in the Abbey.

Forrest and Catherine may have seen the ruins of Fonthill Abbey in their travels. The great tower had collapsed in 1825, but the ruins were highly celebrated. Forrest traveled to England and the continent in 1834. In the tradition of the Grand Tour, he spent two years there as a private gentleman, visiting the important points of interest, which were carefully described in the many travel journals of the mid-century and even interpreted for the traveler in such works as Byron's *Childe Harold* and Madame de Staël's *Corinne*.

In 1837 Forrest sailed a second time for Europe, this time to perform there. He enjoyed enormous success and was hailed as a great American actor. It was during this trip to Europe that he married Catherine Norton Sinclair, the daughter of an English musician, and for whom he built his castle on the Hudson.

The Rotunda

The rotunda, or great hall, opening from the vaulted entrance vestibules, has eight massive oak brackets supporting a gallery approximately sixteen feet above the rotunda floor, which Forrest planned to use to exhibit paintings. A glazed skylight in the center of the rotunda ceiling repeats the octagonal shape of the room, and its mirror image vault light below, in the center of the rotunda floor, admits light to the basement rooms. The rotunda floor is laid with encaustic tile of different colors arranged in a tesselated pattern resembling a cross.

The drawing room, library, and dining room all open off the rotunda through round-arched doorways. Their entrances are surrounded by simply carved colonnettes and plain chevron and billet moulding in the arches. Each room is lighted by its own ample bay window, the illumination constantly changing with the light of day. The dining room, northeast of the rotunda, is rectangular with a chair rail, and its bay window lies at the eastern end of the castle, catching the morning sun directly, appropriate for the breakfast meal. A fireplace mantel in the south wall is carved of a light-colored wood, which the hearth, in light marble, matches.

The drawing room, southwest of the rotunda, repeats the octagonal plan of the rotunda, and a magnificent pendant, similar to Beckford's, is the most immediately striking feature of the room. Modeled of plaster, it is finished to give the appearance of wood, a popular practice in the nineteenth century. The bay window to the west and a rectangular window in the south wall afford less direct, and softer natural light than in the dining room. A fireplace in the northwest wall of the room is very simply carved in black marble. The floor is parquet with an eight-pointed star design in the center, beneath the massive pendant. Ogee arches over the two doorways in the room complement the rich line of the elaborate ceiling. The door to the south opens onto a broad terrace, enclosed by a low parapet wall along the southern line of the building, which faces the rich, natural landscape to the east. The lower Hudson River to the south can also be seen.

The library lies to the northwest of the rotunda and, as in the drawing room, repeats the octagon theme established by the rotunda. Even the window tracery subtly echoes this geometric shape. Perhaps the most exciting feature of the room is the floor, which is inlaid with five different types of wood (hickory, walnut, maple, pine, and oak) in an eight-pointed star pattern radiating from a small central octagon. The various floor woods contrast dramatically with the rich dark woodwork of the walls to lend an air of unique vivacity. The fireplace, now encased, has a flue that is adjusted with a turnscrew on the wall—a modern luxury in the 1850s.

To the north is the room designed to be Catherine Forrest's own special room, and a delicate charm is reflected in the fireplace of rose-colored, white-veined marble, and in the windows made of intertwining tracery, a delicate arrangement of small geometric panes.

The second floor of Fonthill Castle was designed for the bedrooms and the gallery. The rooms are generally simpler in decoration. The northwest tower room is distinct in its floor, which is composed of three different kinds of wood, and in its vaulting with rich lathed webbing. Otherwise, the decoration is similar to the other rooms, and the carved or moulded capitals repeat the decoration of the colonnettes and corbels in the rotunda.

The Architect

Although Forrest and Catherine were the main forces behind Fonthill, and Thomas C. Smith was the builder, it is unclear who the architect was. Even though it has been suggested that the well-known New York architect A. J. Davis may have had something to do with the building, there is nothing definite to identify him as the architect. Davis and Forrest knew each other, and Davis visited the site on numerous occasions while it was being constructed. Moreover, Davis included the ground plan of Fonthill Castle and its facade in his unpublished "Rural Residences." But there is no conclusive proof that Davis was the architect.

Fonthill Castle was finished in 1852, but Edwin and Catherine never shared their castle on the Hudson River together. Disagreements arose revolving around Edwin's accusations of Catherine's infidelity; these resulted in the couple's separation and finally in their divorce.

Meanwhile, in 1856, the northward expansion of Central Park was forcing the Academy of Mount Saint Vincent, then at 109th Street and Fifth Avenue (at McGown's Pass), to find a new home. Forrest, interested in selling the castle and some of the grounds, and the Sisters of Charity, interested in relocating the academy to this area, came to an agreement. The Sisters purchased the ground and the castle on December 20, 1856.

A tragic irony connects Fonthill Castle in a special way with the picturesque tradition in America. The year this fine example of a building in the picturesque tradition was completed, Andrew Jackson Downing, the major pioneer of the picturesque in America, was drowned only a short distance from Fonthill's shoreline in a senseless steamboat accident.

FIREHOUSES

Fire was a constant threat to the early settlers of New York, and the threat mounted as the city grew in density. The colonists took various steps to protect themselves; the first fire ordinance in 1648 outlawed wooden chimneys and thatched roofs from Fort Amsterdam to Fresh Water Pond, and fire wardens were appointed to enforce the law. Moreover, fines were levied for every chimney that was not swept.

One hundred and fifty fire buckets were imported from Holland in 1657, and the following year the first fire company—called the "Prowlers" or "Rattle Watch"—was formed, consisting of eight men (soon the number grew to fifty) who walked the streets from 9:00 A.M. to sunrise, watching for fires. Their equipment consisted of 250 buckets, and hooks and ladders. Citizens were required to leave three fire buckets by their doors, and there were to be ten buckets at all public wells. The first public well was in front of Fort Amsterdam, where the U.S. Custom House now stands.

In 1731 hand engines, invented by Richard Newsham, were imported from London; these produced an uninterrupted stream of water, greatly improving fire-fighting power. By the end of the eighteenth century, the Volunteer Fire Department had been established, and it was incorporated March 20, 1798, as the Fire Department of the City of New York. Also in that year, the city's first fire insurance companies were founded.

Growing competition among the numerous volunteer firehouses began to create a threat to the safety of the city, for territorial disputes arose when fires broke out, and these delayed prompt action. Therefore in 1865 the Metropolitan Fire District, made up of New York and Brooklyn, was established to be served by a paid professional fire department under the jurisdiction of the state. Five years later, under the Tweed Charter of 1870, control passed to the city, and separate fire departments in New York and Brooklyn were set up.

Fireman's Hall

The first Fireman's Hall, which served as both a social center and a headquarters, was built *c.* 1824 on the north side of Fair (Fulton) Street, just east of Gold Street. In 1854 enlarged quarters were built, and these still stand at 153–157 Mercer Street. As the city grew, fire detection became increasingly more difficult. The cupola of City Hall served as a fire watchtower beginning in 1830, and a salaried fire watchman was employed there in 1835. Cast-iron watchtowers sprang up; the last extant example is in Marcus Garvey Park in Harlem, interrupting Fifth Avenue between 120th and 125th streets.

By 1851 a telegraph system connected eight watchtowers at strategic places all over the city with the central relay station at City Hall —a system the police used also. Twenty years later as buildings got taller, the watchtower system became ineffective. The fire telegraph was installed in Fireman's Hall, and later, box alarms were constructed to give broader coverage. Finally by the 1890s, telephones were installed to provide instant communication with fire fighters.

The Firehouse

Early firehouses were little more than meeting halls. With the formation of a department, however, new firehouses were built to provide proper storage of equipment, suitable dormitory and kitchen facilities for the men, and adequate stables for the horses. However, with no uniform guidelines, taste and efficiency became confused, and the lavish furnishings of some of the houses generated dissension among the others. Those who could not afford crystal chandeliers resented those who could; in addition, the angered public doubted the need for such furnishings.

Since 1862 the police department had successfully employed an architect, Nathaniel D. Bush, to design its buildings and supervise their maintenance. Recognizing the advantages of standardization, the fire department commissioned the renowned architect Napoleon LeBrun to build approximately thirty firehouses between 1879 and the 1890s.

LeBrun was from Philadelphia, where he studied with Thomas U. Walter, architect of the U.S. Capitol Building, and where he had achieved prominence with such commissions as the new Cathedral of Saints Peter and Paul (1846–64) and the Academy of Music (1852–57). Relocating to New York in 1864, LeBrun distinguished himself first as a church builder. His St. John the Baptist Church at 211 West Thirtieth Street (1872), which is still standing, is an exquisite Gothic Revival union of a brownstone exterior with a radiant white marble interior. LeBrun's last building—the Metropolitan Life Insurance Company tower at One Madison Avenue between Twenty-third and Twenty-fifth streets—was completed by his sons Pierre and Michel after his death in 1909 and was specially honored for its excellence of design by the American Institute of Architects.

All Alike but Each Different

LeBrun standardized the main components of the firehouse, but he used different architectural styles for each one, so that the firehouses could retain their individuality. The early firehouses were usually brownstone, with the horses stabled behind the house. When the alarm was sounded, the horses would be brought through the back door and hitched up to the apparatus, which was then brought out the front door into the street. LeBrun's first task was to make this system more efficient. By extending the ground floor through to the rear of the lot, LeBrun incorporated the stables into the building, thereby eliminating the need to pass through two sets of doors and saving valuable time. By connecting the dormitory above with the garage by a sliding pole, an 1870s innovation, LeBrun saved additional time. (The firepole was later adopted by the parking garage in Rockefeller Center in the 1930s, and throughout the country by the parking industry.)

Engine Company No. 31

In Engine Co. No. 31 of 1895 at 87 Lafayette Street, LeBrun placed the horses' stalls along the rear of the apparatus space and equipped them with automatic doors. At the sound of the bell, the

Engine Company No. 31, 87 Lafayette Street; 1895. Napoleon LeBrun, architect. Called the "French Chateau," this firehouse was designed in the Loire Chateau style popularized in the United States by architect Richard Morris Hunt.

doors opened and the horses came forward from their stalls directly underneath their harnesses, ready for immediate hitching. A large fire house, Engine Co. No. 31 accommodated four engines, seventeen horses, twenty-five firemen, four engineers, and four officers.

Engine Co. No. 31 became a popular tourist attraction in New York, and sightseeing buses included the "French Chateau" fire station in their tours. It was based on the Loire Chateau style which was popularized by R. M. Hunt. Hunt designed great mansions for the wealthy in this style, which subsequently became very popular and influenced architecture of all kinds—residential, commercial, and civic as well. The style combined Gothic and Renaissance elements. LeBrun's building is structurally modern and visually historical, with a roof of slate and copper resting on a steel frame clothed with masonry and brick in the popular decorative style.

Four central piers frame three stone-arched doorways at the ground floor. The floors above are faced with brick, banded in stone, and the main cornice carries a balustrade of scrolled strapwork. A steeply pitched slate roof rises behind, with copper cresting. Renaissance capitals flank the windows, Renaissance-inspired pilasters and entablatures combine with Gothic forms to make up the dormers. Volutes of dolphin forms and balusters of attenuated flame-bearing lamps crown the building.

New Headquarters

In 1884 the fire department moved its headquarters from the congested Mercer Street location to a new site at 157–159 East Sixty-seventh Street, where LeBrun combined Engine Co. 30 and Ladder Co. 16 in the first two stories, with the fire department headquarters above.

This building has a two-story basement of rusticated granite. Headquarters and administrative offices rise above, faced in red-brick with brownstone. The large round-arched windows at the third story mark the fire commissioner's offices. The building is capped by a black slate mansard roof above a brick cornice. Two dormers of brownstone with paired round-arch windows are set under triangular pediments, carved with Romanesque ornament and circular medallions. A brownstone chimney terminates the roof at the left. The original cresting at the ridge line is no longer extant, but it served as a decorative foil to the tower at the right. The main entrance at the base of the tower has a porch with paired columns of polished granite shafts, brownstone bases, and basket capitals, supporting a massive pediment.

Double iron garage doors are framed in red, symbolic of the building, as are the salamander heads on the lintels—firemen in the nineteenth century were nicknamed "salamanders." The building's round-arched form, its columns and capitals, and its moulding reflect the influence of the Romanesque Revival. However, the tower is indebted for its design to the first skyscrapers in New York, Richard Morris Hunt's Tribune Building and George B. Post's Western Union Building (both 1873). The fire department's watch-tower on Sixty-seventh Street originally had a belfry and lookout stage. The fire department telegraph was housed on the sixth floor.

Times Change

In 1912 the fire department changed from horses to motorized vehicles, and this required alterations in the apparatus floor and renovating the stables area to accommodate new vehicles. Changes extended to the department's organization as well. In 1914 the department returned downtown, but the fire telegraph remained uptown until 1922, when it was moved to Central Park. However, the building on East Sixty-seventh Street still serves the engine and ladder companies.

SEVENTH REGIMENT ARMORY

The National Guard traces its origins to the seventeenth century, when merchants, doctors, lawyers, and journalists banded together to protect themselves from hostile Indians. However, it was in 1824 when the Marquis de Lafayette visited the United States, that the volunteers were inspired to call themselves the National Guard, after Lafayette's celebrated National Guard of Paris. In recognition of the National Guard's debt to Lafayette, his portrait hangs in the Seventh Regiment Armory reception room.

The Seventh Regiment itself began in 1806, when the United States resisted Britain's insistence on searching American ships for British deserters. Helmsman John Pierce was killed during a search by the British, and when his body arrived in port, a mass rally called for reprisals, and the Seventh was formed.

Before the Civil War, the different companies of the regiment occupied separate quarters, but from 1853 to 1857, the central headquarters was the arsenal in Central Park at Sixty-fourth Street and Fifth Avenue. In 1860 the regiment moved into a new cast-iron armory above Tompkins Market on Third Avenue between Sixth and Seventh streets, which remained their headquarters until their present building was completed in 1880.

When the regiment recognized it needed new quarters, Colonel Emmons Clark raised the funds for the building and established the general requirements of the structure. Architect Charles W. Clinton then designed the building, and Charles MacDonald, head of the

Seventh Regiment Armory, Park Avenue and Sixty-eighth Street; 1880. Charles W. Clinton, architect. The regimental drill room, pictured here, was designed by engineer Charles MacDonald, who employed the latest technology in steel skeletal construction to create this enormous space.

Delaware Bridge Co., designed the drill room according to the latest technological developments in steel skeletal construction. The cornerstone was laid in October 1877, and on April 26, 1880, the regiment moved into the new building.

Two Buildings in One

The Seventh Regiment Armory blends the architecture of history and function, which marks much of the progressive architecture of the nineteenth century. The building covers the block bounded by Sixty-sixth and Sixty-seventh streets and Park and Lexington avenues. It is sited on a lot two hundred by four hundred feet and is composed of two buildings under one roof. The administration building with regimental meeting rooms is a big brick and stone fort that runs parallel to Park Avenue, while the drill hall is a giant steel skeleton that parallels Lexington Avenue.

342

The building is laid out like a giant fortress. A central tower with the main entrance at its base is flanked at the corners by projecting square towers crowned with crenellated parapets. The main entrance, reached by low stairs and a massive stoop, is an archway with a great oak door, protected by a colossal bronze gate with the regimental coat of arms above. Recessed fortress walls connect the three towers, and the redbrick structure, with light granite trim above the rock-faced granite basement, creates an imposing facade along Park Avenue.

The central tower was originally crowned with a steeply pitched belfry, rising high above the three stories of the administration building, and this created a more animated silhouette. The site itself is high, and because the avenue is wide, the building can be seen from a great distance down Park Avenue. But in 1909 the belfry was removed and another floor was added, which diminished the bold silhouettes of the parapets and created the more uniform rectangle of the Park Avenue facade. A fifth floor was added in 1930, further suppressing the original design and conforming to modern taste.

The regimental drill room, east of the administration building and behind the Lexington Avenue facade, is a grand open space two stories high and two hundred by three hundred feet, with balconies to seat 1,100 spectators. Two staggered tiers of windows offer abundant illumination, which sifts through the skeletal train-shed construction that vaults the space. Massive piers buttress the thrust of the low broad-iron arches that majestically span the drill area. The floor is constructed of narrow planks of thick Georgia pine, set in concrete and asphalt for dryness, durability, and solidity. In addition to drills and reviews, the space is used for fairs, balls, antique shows, and sporting events.

The Regimental Rooms

The regimental rooms parallel to Park Avenue are organized along a north-south axis on each floor. On the ground floor, the halls, reception area, and ceremonial rooms that house the regiment's traditional materials and memorabilia are grand in scale and richly restrained in decoration.

Congressional Medal of Honor winners are commemorated in both the north and the south halls. The south hall contains trophies of war, portraits of key officers in the regiment's history, and the Book of Remembrance, listing the regiment's casualties beginning with the War of 1812; a page is turned each day.

The board of officers room, also called the Clark room for Colonel Emmens Clark (who was responsible for funding and building

Seventh Regiment Armory: veterans room. Elaborate wood-carved ceiling, inlaid walls, and stained-glass windows were designed by Stanford White and Louis Comfort Tiffany.

the armory building), is finished in dark mahogany and has a grand fireplace seven feet high. The reception room off the Clark room, paneled in maple, is called the Mary Divver room, for the daughter of Major Joseph A. Divver. Killed in the Mexican War, he left the ten-year-old orphan Mary, whom the regiment then adopted.

The veterans room and the library were designed by Louis Comfort Tiffany and Stanford White. Oak wainscoting surrounds the veterans room beneath a pattern of iron panels picked out in silver bolt heads. Antique tile and brick distinguish the immense fireplace, and the mosaic above the great oak mantel portrays a sea dragon attacked by an eagle; thus it symbolizes the theme of survival and complements the colorful execution of the fireplace. Iron columns wrapped round with massive chains portray strength and security and act as an impressive foil to the subtle tones of Tiffany's remarkable variegated stained glass.

Beneath the library's pink vaulted ceiling, a light stone fireplace, mahogany paneling, and rich ironwork combine to create the sense of stability and calm appropriate to a library. A gallery and alcoves are protected by iron gates, and the stairway is equipped with handsome iron railings. Grand wrought-iron chandeliers illuminate the room along with the natural light coming through the Tiffany glass windows. The room was originally designed for a valuable military library, which is now housed in the New York Historical Society.

A grand staircase of solid oak on an iron base leads off the entrance hall to the basement and upper floors. The offices and clubrooms of the Tennis Club and Rifle Club are in the basement, which also houses the indoor shooting range. Company rooms, simply constructed and appointed, occupy the second floor; administrative offices the third floor; and the lounge bar occupies the fourth floor (designed in 1930). Its bronze entrance gates were donated by the Union Club, where they hung on Fifty-first Street at Fifth Avenue at the old club house. The fifth floor houses the gymnasium and squash courts.

16

"O Harp and Altar":
The Brooklyn Bridge

Curiously, the three most important architectural achievements in the nineteenth century, according to many historians, were not produced by architects: The Crystal Palace in London of 1851 was the creation of one of England's leading landscape gardeners, Sir Joseph Paxton, the Eiffel Tower of 1889 was conceived by an engineer, Gustave Eiffel, and the Brooklyn Bridge of 1883 was done by an engineer, inventor, and intellectual.

John Augustus Roebling, German immigrant, thinker, engineer, and inventor, designed the Brooklyn Bridge, the longest suspension bridge in the world when it was built—1,595 feet long—and the first suspension bridge to be constructed of steel. Roebling was a student and admirer of Georg Hegel, the philosopher, and he conceived of the bridge in philosophical terms—a materialization in steel, stone, and concrete of the union of man's creative spirit and nature. His intention was to create a national monument, as well as a practical thoroughfare to link the communities on either side of the East River. Roebling wanted his two great Gothic Revival towers, his "giant brothers," as Walt Whitman would call them, to be landmarks to both New York and Brooklyn. Hart Crane, in his epic poem on the bridge, saw Roebling's two landmarks and his materialization as a modern icon, a symbol of scientific progress united with poetry.

The Brooklyn Bridge: "O Harp and Altar" *(facing page)*. The poet Hart Crane saw the towers of the bridge as a giant altar, the wires and cables as the strings of a harp—a modern icon combining science and poetry.

347

A BETTER LINK BETWEEN BROOKLYN
AND MANHATTAN

The need for improving transportation between New York and Brooklyn was becoming acute as the harbor became the leading maritime center in the world. Not only was ferry service slow but it was unpredictable, especially in winter when ferry schedules were affected by ice. In fact, Roebling probably conceived the idea for the Brooklyn Bridge in the winter of 1852, when ice in the East River suspended ferryboat service, paralyzing transportation and leaving Roebling stranded for hours on a ferryboat in the middle of the East River. In 1857 John Roebling proposed to cross the East River with a suspension bridge, the most efficient means to link the communities. Suspension could satisfy the height requirements of the naval ships nearby (135 feet) and at the same time keep the river free of enormous supporting piers of traditional types of bridges, which would interfere with the navigation of large vessels.

John Roebling had earned a wide reputation through his ingenious solutions to suspension construction and his system of steel cable manufacturing. He was a strange fellow but he could work miracles. Consequently, in 1867 he was given the commission to erect the East River Bridge, better known now as the Brooklyn Bridge.

Before coming to America, Roebling had been a bridge and road builder for the Prussian government. He immigrated to the United States from Germany in the 1830s, along with a small group that wanted to set up a utopian community called Saxonburgh, near Pittsburgh. For a while, he farmed and built houses. By 1837 he was a U.S. citizen and was working as an engineer on the canal system in Pennsylvania; then later he surveyed a prospective railroad route east of Pittsburgh, which took him to Johnstown. There, he saw how the new portage railroads hauled the canalboats up and over the Alleghenies. He also saw that the large hemp ropes used to pull the canalboats were expensive, and they often broke, causing loss of valuable loads. And workers were even killed in such accidents. Inspired by a kind of iron rope being manufactured in Europe, Roebling developed his own design for an iron rope to pull the canalboats. It was stronger and longer-lasting than the great hemp hawsers and a fraction of the diameter and weight of the rope, which made it more manageable. Roebling's iron rope was not only accepted by the portage railroads and other canal systems but by other industries, as well, and it launched him full-scale in the manufacturing business.

Roebling developed new ideas for stronger cables in suspension bridges and proved his new ideas in designing suspended aqueducts for canalboats over the Allegheny River. The one at Lackawaxen, Pennsylvania, still stands and is used today for automobile traffic. He established the Roebling Works in Trenton, New Jersey, to manufacture steel wire and cable, the nucleus of his success. By 1867 Roebling was a successful engineer who enjoyed wide acclaim for the Niagara Suspension Bridge and the Covington Bridge across the Ohio River at Cincinnati (linking Ohio and Kentucky).

THE BRIDGE

In spanning the East River, Roebling proposed five lanes: two outer lanes for horse-drawn carriages, two middle lanes for cable trains with terminals at either end, and a fifth lane, an "elevated promenade" for pedestrians, dramatically suspended eighteen feet above the traffic, to stroll across the bridge on nice days. A toll of five cents was to be charged for the cable train ride, which would pay for the bridge and its maintenance.

In preparation for construction Roebling familiarized himself with the latest advances in steel manufacture. He sent his son, Colonel Washington Roebling, to study the manufacture of steel at the Krupp and Essen works in Germany and to study the latest developments in caisson foundation, a method of construction Roebling was to use in building the great towers that support the bridge. Tragically, during the first weeks of construction, John Roebling's toes were crushed in an accident. After his toes were amputated, Roebling refused conventional medical treatment, insisting on his own method of bandaging and water treatment. Consequently, he soon died of lockjaw. His son, who was serving as chief engineer, succeeded him and with Emily completed the bridge.

THE CAISSONS

The first major project was to sink the caissons. These were like giant inverted boxes to create dry space under water. Then the "sand hogs" (the laborers) could work inside them, dig down to rock, and lay the foundations for the towers to support the bridge. Compressed air kept the water out of the caissons. As the sand hogs dug deeper, the tower was being constructed above them, the weight of which forced the caisson down to the river bottom. When the caisson reached firm ground, it was filled with concrete. Many workers suffered caisson disease, called "the bends," which caused cramps, paralysis, and sometimes even death. Work shifts were

349

shortened which seemed to reduce the problem. There were over one hundred cases of the bends. Washington Roebling himself was partially crippled from the bends for the rest of his life. In fact, his wife, Emily, had to take over supervision of construction at one point. It was not until after the foundations were built that medical researchers found that it was the rate of decompression that determined whether of not one got the bends.

The Brooklyn caisson was constructed first, 168 feet long and 102 feet wide; it was over 14 feet high. The foundation was 90 feet below the river bed, and it took a year and a half to sink the caisson and secure it in position. The New York caisson went down 70 feet, but the irregularity of the rock formations required blasting, and the soft river bottom presented additional problems in digging. It went much slower therefore—a total of three years. In all, it took five years to build the two main towers and construct the anchorages for the cables. It is perhaps noteworthy that the site of the New York anchorage is located near where George and Martha Washington stayed on Cherry Street, just before Washington's inauguration as first president in 1789. The Brooklyn tower was completed in May 1875 and the Manhattan tower in July 1876. Two years later, on October 5, the last of the cables that would support the great roadbed was drawn across the river.

STRONG AND SAFE

Roebling had designed a bridge that looked impregnable to the elements and as it turned out, the finished bridge really was. His pioneering use of steel in a long suspension bridge and his innovative method of weaving support cables, which uniquely increased their strength, combined to produce a bridge of uncommon stability. Moreover, Roebling developed a system of iron trusses to prevent excessive movement in the structure caused by strong winds and storms. Four cables eleven inches in diameter, each cable containing 3,515 miles of wire, support the bridge and its roadbed. Hundreds of stays fan out diagonally downward from the great Gothic towers for additional strength. If the four giant cables were all removed, this fanwork of stays would nevertheless prevent the bridge from collapsing.

The great cables that stretch from one side of the bridge to the other are anchored deep in the ground beneath the inclined roadways leading up to the bridge. Beneath these roadways are giant vaults of brick and granite from one to three stories high inside. They are called anchorages, because the cables that support the bridge are anchored here.

Washington Roebling designed these spaces to be used; he was convinced they were secure enough to house the U.S. Treasury. They were used commercially until the 1930s, when business moved away from the area beneath the bridge on both the Manhattan and Brooklyn sides. These spaces (115,000 square feet on the Manhattan side) are being offered once again for lease by the city of New York, as part of its rejuvenation of lower Manhattan. The city has already created a pedestrian mall around the anchorage on the Manhattan side, bounded by Frankfort, Pearl, and Rose streets and the Avenue of the Finest. Sidewalks, benches, and lighting have been installed, and trees were planted at a cost of $2 million. A pedestrian esplanade parallel to Frankfort Street constitutes Phase II, budgeted at an additional $1 million.

The city hopes the space in the anchorages will be converted to gift shops, restaurants, bookstores, and a theater to appeal to the almost four million tourists a year who visit the South Street Seaport, Chinatown, Little Italy, the Civic Center, and City Hall—all nearby. On the Brooklyn side, a museum, aptly called the Anchorage, is fully operational.

STRUCTURE AND SYMBOL

The Brooklyn Bridge became the most famous bridge in the world, both as a structure and as a symbol. As an engineering feat, nothing on that scale had ever been attempted. Roebling's innovative diagonal stays, his use of steel for the first time in a suspension bridge, and his system of trusses distinguish it further as an engineering marvel. Long before he designed the Brooklyn Bridge, Roebling had become a recognized master of suspension-bridge construction through his many aqueducts and bridges in Pennsylvania, New York, Kentucky, and Ohio. His bridge over the Niagara gorge of 1855 was the first iron wire-cable suspension bridge for railroads, and his Cincinnati-Covington Bridge of 1867, the longest in the world then (1,057 feet), included his innovative diagonal stays and incorporated wrought-iron beams in place of wooden ones for the roadbed. In the Brooklyn Bridge, Washington Roebling used steel wire for the cables and constructed a bridge floor entirely of steel, the first time steel was used in a structure of this size.

John Roebling predicted that the bridge's most conspicuous features, the great towers, would become landmarks to Manhattan and Brooklyn, and he boasted that they would be entitled to be ranked as national monuments. The U.S. government later agreed, and in 1964 proclaimed the bridge a national monument.

Brooklyn Bridge; 1883. John Augustus Roebling, designer of the Bridge, intended the two towers —"giant brothers," as Walt Whitman called them—to be national monuments to New York and Brooklyn.

Terrific threshold of the prophet's pledge
(Hart Crane, *The Bridge*)

In uniting Brooklyn and Manhattan, Roebling linked Long Island with the mainland and thereby supplied the final link between the East and West that historians have related symbolically to Columbus's quest for a passage to India, an idea that is as old as America. Roebling's two monolithic towers have become symbols of this notion of the threshold to America and have inspired artists and writers to paint the bridge and to write about it.

The "grand obelisk-like towers," as Walt Whitman described them, rise 276 feet and have captured the imagination of many artists including John Marin and Joseph Stella, who painted them, and poet Hart Crane, who proclaimed the bridge a modern icon, a symbol of scientific progress united with poetry. Whitman himself saw Roebling's two great landmarks as "giant brothers twain, throwing free graceful interlinking loops high across the tumbled tumultuous current below. . . ."

Under thy shadow by the piers I waited.
(Hart Crane, *The Bridge*)

The Brooklyn Bridge is a remarkable example of the power of a symbol. While the bridge brought an end to commerical life at the Fulton Ferry Landing by providing a new and modern transportation link, it is now playing a significant role as a symbol in the rejuvenation of that very area. Hart Crane's line quoted above seems almost prophetic if applied to the Fulton Ferry Landing. That district is now being revived, and the image of the Brooklyn Bridge, in whose shadow it lies, is very much a part of that rejuvenation. But to appreciate that, we have to review its past.

AN ARCHITECTURAL RENASCENCE
WHERE BROOKLYN WAS BORN

The growing prosperity of the New York port gradually transformed life along the harbor, and that was nowhere more evident than at the ferry village, which the Dutch first settled in the seventeenth century when Brooklyn ("Breuckelen") was born. The changes were apparent in the ferry service itself, which linked Manhattan and Long Island, and in the increasingly substantial buildings at the ferry landing, which reflected the growth of an important commercial center.

The ferry service grew from a makeshift system in the seventeenth century to a sophisticated and lucrative service, in the nineteenth century, of numerous entrepreneurs and shipping lines competing for business and linking major cities and ports along the eastern seaboard. At first, "ferries" were thought of as anything that floated, from rowboats to sailboats, and they departed only when they had a full load and weather permitted. Schedules were unheard-of then. As commerce expanded, the ferries got bigger and better; by the early nineteenth century these "floating bridges" as they were called were some thirty by eighty feet and could carry horses, several hundred passengers, and even entire wagons.

When Robert Fulton, inventor of the steamboat, introduced steamboat service on his ferry line (the line served such points as Brooklyn, New York, New Jersey, and Albany) in 1814, Ferry Road (the old Indian trail) was renamed Fulton Street in his honor. Two years later, the village of Brooklyn was incorporated.

Fulton Street got a new name in this century—Cadman Plaza West, named for the popular divine, S. Parkes Cadman, Brooklyn pastor and first of the great radio preachers in America. It was the Reverend S. Parkes Cadman who proclaimed the Woolworth Building as "the Cathedral of Commerce," the name it has been known by ever since. Fittingly, the gleaming ivory-colored terra-cotta tower of Mr. Woolworth's "cathedral" can be seen against the Manhattan skyline directly west across the East River from Cadman Plaza West.

Among the first buildings on the landing, but now no longer standing, were a succession of ferry house taverns. They were built of wood or stone; were rectangular in plan; and were two or three

353

stories high with stepped gables at either end, similar to the Vechte-Cortelyou House. Gradually, however, the seventeenth- and eighteenth-century buildings were razed, and landfill extended the shoreline, providing additional real estate for the commercial expansion there that produced some of the nineteenth-century buildings still standing. These buildings record the wide variety of commercial activity at the Brooklyn ferry landing during the nineteenth century. There are a number of well-preserved examples of the dominant architectural styles and types of the nineteenth century. For example, an office building (some historians say it is the oldest office building in New York) that stands at No. 5–7 Water Street was built in 1834, in the Federal style. Erected as the office of the Long Island Insurance Co., it is three stories high with stone sills and lintels, three bays wide with elevated entrance, stoop, and original handrailings featuring a scroll and acorn motif. The facade is red brick laid up in Flemish bond and has a projecting cornice over a simple fascia. The building now houses a restaurant. From the year 1835, the fashionable Franklin House at No. 1–5 Cadman Plaza West, a leading hotel of the period (now occupied by a restaurant and apartments above), was built in the Greek Revival style and forms part of a handsome row. In the 1860s it was modernized through the addition of popular Italianate forms, such as pedimented lintels above the windows and a paneled roof cornice, all supported by elaborate brackets. The bold cornice supported by large brackets at No. 17 reflects the same Italianate trend. In spite of modifications, there is enough intact in this row, such as the stepped cornices following the street incline, to preserve the appearance of what the block was like.

A variety of businesses occupied the row, historians have noted, including saddleries, taverns, coopers, grocers, ship agents, warehouses, an oyster house, a boarding house, a publisher, and numerous small craftsmen. East of the Franklin House, No. 13 is an example of the new type of commercial building, similar to the counting house, discussed at Coenties Slip. At one time, this was a livery stable, and then in the 1840s, it became a hotel. The transformation at the street level was simple and illustrates the flexibility of this building type that had appealed to the practical-minded businessman. The wide opening required by a stable was divided in two for the hotel by installing an additional pier, this time of more economical wood, painted to look like stone.

The Fulton Ferry area flourished until the Brooklyn Bridge opened in 1883. Then the ferry service became obsolete and commercial life on Fulton Street began to move elsewhere. The area was permanently bypassed in 1909, when the Manhattan Bridge was opened to traffic. For the next fifty years, the area saw a variety of

Cadman Plaza West: In this view *(top)* from the roof of No. 7 Everit Street, the Franklin House at No. 1–5 Cadman Plaza West is visible at the right. At No. 17 Cadman Plaza West, this Italianate cornice *(center, right)* has elaborate brackets, dentil moulding, fascia with diamond motif, and richly carved acanthus patterns, all still intact and surveyed by one of New York's ever vigilant pigeons. No. 13 Cadman Plaza West *(bottom, right)* was converted from a livery stable to a hotel in the 1840s, demonstrating its flexibility and obvious commercial appeal.

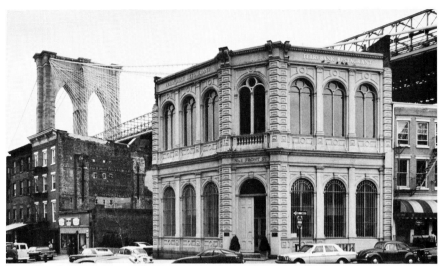

Ferrybank Restaurant, formerly the Long Island Safe Deposit Company, No. 1 Front Street, Brooklyn; 1868–69. William Mundell, architect. This was the site where Indians landed in the seventeenth century; all structures left of the cast-iron building are built on landfill. The Franklin House, not pictured, is to the left.

manufacturing operations and small industries come and go, finally leaving the area almost deserted.

Then in the 1960s several enlightened investors, acting independently of each other, began what became a complicated process to convert some abandoned buildings and barges at the Fulton Ferry Landing to residential, commercial, and cultural use. Their perseverance sparked a revived interest in the Fulton Ferry, which was designated a Historic District by the New York Landmarks Preservation Commission in 1977. The Fulton Ferry Historic District is bounded by the East River, the eastern tower of the Brooklyn Bridge, and Main and Doughty streets. The buildings these investors selected to restore are each as particularly noteworthy as their revitalizations were successful.

THE LONG ISLAND SAFE DEPOSIT COMPANY

The two-story Long Island Safe Deposit Company Building, designed by William Mundell in a palazzo style and erected in 1868–69 at No. 1 Front Street, is the area's only cast-iron structure. It stands on the site of the printing company of Isaac Van Anden, cofounder in 1841 of the *Brooklyn Eagle and Kings County Democrat*, which he first printed there and which later moved across the street to the site of the Eagle Warehouse and Storage Company. In the earliest days, a farm stood on this site, close to the shoreline.

The main entrance to No. 1 Front Street is placed diagonally across the corner of the building, and it is flanked by identical facades to the south and east. Thin tracery echoes the enframements of the great arched windows on both floors, and massive diamond-pointed piers outline the two facades and entrance. Dentil coursing and acanthus leaf scrollwork enhance the twin facades and entrance beneath a boldly projecting cornice. Originally, a balustrade and pediment, now missing, dramatically capped the building.

With the decline of commercial activity in the area following the opening of the Brooklyn Bridge, the Safe Deposit Company moved to new offices at Fulton and Clinton streets in the 1890s, and this building was subsequently converted to small manufacturing and warehousing. In 1966 Brooklyn contractor Salvator Bommarito, whose affection for the building dates from when he played there as a child (he was born a few blocks away at 120 Adams Street, and grew up in the neighborhood), purchased No. 1 Front Street. In the late 1960s and early 1970s, Bommarito leased the building as an experimental theater and movie set, and it appeared in scenes from *The Valachi Papers* and *Mortadella*, a movie starring Sophia Loren (whose favorite view of the bridge and Manhattan skyline is from the roof of this building). (See pages 358–359.)

More recently, the building housed a flea market, and then Bommarito leased it to James A. Strawder in 1976, who converted it into the Ferrybank Restaurant, which opened on July 4, 1981. Strawder's forty years in the food business began on the Brooklyn waterfront in the 1930s, where he served on the *Henry Hudson* flagship. His son James A. Strawder, Jr., a practicing architect in Brooklyn, was commissioned as the architect and general contractor to restore the building and convert it to the new use. The structural system of the building is brick arch and steel with brick walls sheathed in cast iron and cast-iron Corinthian columns and pilasters within.

Conversion has posed both structural and decorative challenges. For example, to satisfy a building department code, two doorways on the west facade affording additional exits involved cutting through a twenty-inch-thick wall. Moreover, replacing missing cast-iron scroll brackets below the cornices, as well as Corinthian capitals and diamond-point panels on the exterior surface, was impossible within the available budget. To solve this problem, a master mould-maker and sculptor, Santo Matarrazo, was commissioned to make moulds of the existing original decorative details, and F. Lombardi and Sons of Brooklyn made the replacement pieces in fiberglass.

The visual difference between the cast iron and the fiberglass is imperceptible, but the fiberglass pieces cost a tenth of the cast iron, making the restoration financially possible. Each of the twenty-foot-high windows has been restored with ½-inch-thick plate glass consisting of two pieces each, the arched top and the rectangular panel below. The original metal tracery lies over the plate glass, retaining

357

The Manhattan skyline from the top
of the Ferrybank Restaurant.
Walt Whitman proclaimed that such views
were "the best, most effective
medicine my soul has yet partaken."

No. 1 Front Street.
Fiberglass replacement of
cast-iron decoration *(top,
right)* is made in rubber
moulds, such as the one
lying at left; its plaster casing
and the finished bracket are
on the right. In conversion,
the architect retained many
original features including
the cast-iron Corinthian
capitals and window
mouldings *(below)*.

Brooklyn City Railroad
Company Building, No. 8
Cadman Plaza West *(bottom,
right);* 1861. Now converted
to apartments, it was
originally the office of the
Brooklyn City Railroad
Company.

360

the original appearance. The first floor and mezzanine accommodate 128 people. The second floor is reached by the original cast-iron stairway.

THE BROOKLYN CITY RAILROAD COMPANY BUILDING

In the spring of 1972 the *Fulton Ferry*, a study of the architectural and historical significance of buildings in the area, was published by the Office of Downtown Brooklyn Development and Brooklyn City Planning Office. The study recommended that the city encourage private investment through such means as revised zoning regulations to develop the abandoned properties as residences.

That summer, architect David Morton bought the Brooklyn City Railroad Company Building, No. 8 Cadman Plaza West, to convert it into loft apartments. Since few guidelines existed, procedures had to be established and these became a model for succeeding conversions. Following its designation as a landmark building in February 1973, a section of the zoning resolution permitted conversion, provided the owner restored and maintained the structure according to guidelines of the Landmarks Preservation Commission, which included the installation of roof cornices and the repair of exterior cast iron and stonework. With the Board of Estimate's approval, the Brooklyn Building Department issued the permit necessary for conversion, and construction was accomplished from October 1973 to November 1974. Morton financed the entire project through personal loans, and acted as his own general contractor.

This five-story building is constructed of brick above cast-iron piers at the street level on Fulton Street. Granite quoins define the wall surface, which is distinguished by stone sills, lintels, and pediments. Carved console brackets, corbels, dentil moulding, and paneled pilasters in the Italianate style further enrich the stonework.

The building was erected in 1861 as the office of the Brooklyn City Railroad Company, which had replaced the former stagecoach line in 1853 to provide modern transportation linking the ferry with principal points on Long Island. Remnants of the old railroad's tracks are still visible behind the building, just off Furman Street. The street takes its name from William Furman, one of Brooklyn's leading businessmen and politicians (he served as a judge and state legislator), whose house was built on this site in the late eighteenth century. At that time, the house was at the river's edge and the entrance to the ferry.

361

Brooklyn City Railroad Company: railroad track remnants *(top)*, reminiscent of the Railroad Company Building's original use, are still visible behind it just off Furman Street. The original brick, cast-iron columns, oak beams, and joists have been retained in this converted loft apartment *(bottom)*. A view from the loft apartment *(facing page)* frames the Brooklyn Bridge, Manhattan, and the top of the Municipal Building.

With the demise of the ferry, the Railroad Company Building was converted to manufacturing and warehousing. Later, it was occupied by the Berglas Manufacturing Co., makers of toilet seats (Morton discovered in the old files a letter of commendation from the secretary of war for a special toilet unit the company designed for use in the trenches during World War I).

In converting the structure to lofts, the architect retained the interior organization of the building as it was when he purchased it. It is rectangular in plan and divided by a stairwell into north and south units, each unit now an apartment (excepting the first floor, whose north side is further divided into two apartments). A modern steel stairway replaces the original, whose profile may be seen on the exposed brick. Modern doorways at each floor, beneath original relieved-brick arches, replace windows in the brick wall of a light shaft and open onto a vestibule common to the north and south apartments.

The structural system is cast-iron columns supporting oak beams and joists, which form the ceilings of the lofts. Over the wood floors, Morton poured 2½-inch-thick steel-reinforced concrete slabs (for soundproofing) anchored to the exterior walls by tie rods at each floor and on all sides for structural support. Storm windows, new gas lines, and modern kitchens and baths were installed throughout, and the steel staircase entering from the west facade provides access to the apartments. Modern planters enhance the natural brick stairwell.

A CARRIAGE HOUSE AND
ITS ENVIRONMENT

David Morton also converted the carriage house (*c.* 1900) at No. 7 Everit Street between 1978 and 1981 (the building also follows the configuration of a firehouse). This building and its adjacent lot belonged to Edward Gardiner, owner of the Eagle Warehouse and Storage Company, behind it. He was using it as another warehouse. In early 1978 a couple looking to buy a home discovered the carriage house while crossing the Brooklyn Bridge, and by that summer, they had bought it in conjunction with David Morton and his partner Thomas Cordell. The carriage entrance at the ground floor provided access to the building, and a ramp led up to nineteen stalls on the second floor, which were still intact when the developers discovered the building. The third floor was used for storing feed, and an apartment above that housed a caretaker.

In converting the building to apartments Morton retained the structural integrity of the original building, which he tastefully in-

No. 7 Everit Street, originally a carriage house *(top, left); c. 1900.* In converting to apartments, the architect added square panels of windows and masonry in a Mondrian-like pattern; their panorama features the Brooklyn Bridge. The ceiling *(bottom, left)* is the exposed structure of the floor above; the architect retained such unique features in conversion.

No. 7 Everit Street *(above).* Each apartment has its own unique view of the Brooklyn Bridge, like a framed picture.

corporated into his interior design. For example, the reinforced concrete ceilings are the exposed structure of the floor above. The building houses three garden apartments on the first floor, two each on the second and the third floors, and a penthouse with deck.

Morton introduced new windows to visually unite the individual apartments to their neighborhood and to their unique relationship with the Brooklyn Bridge. He opened up the wall between the piers facing the bridge with square panels of windows and masonry in a Mondrian-like pattern viewed from the outside. From the inside of each apartment the wall takes on the appearance of a crystal screen flanking the fireplaces, through which a panorama featuring the bridge appears. The view of the bridge and the Manhattan skyline is different from every vantage point; therefore, each apartment has a set of unique images, each one like a framed picture.

With this device, Morton introduced a sophisticated variation on a nineteenth-century theme. During the second half of the nineteenth century, when New York's elevator buildings, the nation's first skyscrapers, reached higher and higher, artists were attracted to the Manhattan skyline as valid subject matter for pictures, prose, and poetry. Coincidentally, exactly a century before Morton framed his views from the old carriage house with glass and masonry, one of America's greatest poets was framing his with pad and pencil in a little boat nearby. Sailing up the East River in June 1878, Walt Whitman was inspired by Manhattan's "cloud-touching edifices" to proclaim that such views were "the best, most effective medicine my soul has yet partaken."

A FORTRESS AND SYMBOL PRESERVED

East of the old carriage house is the Eagle Warehouse and Storage Company of Brooklyn, No. 28 Cadman Plaza West, which has been converted into an apartment house of eighty-five units. The building was designed and erected by Frank Freeman in 1893–94, who came to New York from Canada in 1885 when he was twenty-four years old and who became one of Brooklyn's foremost architects.

The Eagle Warehouse took its name from the *Brooklyn Eagle* (where Walt Whitman had been an editor), because two of its directors had been affiliated with the newspaper, whose offices and plant stood on this site from the early 1840s until 1892, when they were almost entirely demolished. A three-story pressroom, added by the newspaper in 1882 at the rear of the building, was preserved and incorporated into the present building.

The Eagle Warehouse,
No. 28 Cadman Plaza
West *(right);* 1893–94.
Frank Freeman, architect.
In the Romanesque
Revival style, this former
warehouse has been
converted into an
apartment house of
eighty-five units. A metal
eagle *(below)* from the
newspaper *Brooklyn Eagle,*
originally on this site, ties
present uses to the past.

In the Eagle Warehouse and Storage Company, as in Freeman's old Brooklyn Fire Headquarters on Jay Street of the previous year (1892), the architect employed the fashionable Romanesque Revival style popularized by Henry Hobson Richardson.

The style is characterized by massive round-arched doors and windows, a generous use of exterior pilasters, medieval motifs, and corbels. Rusticated stonework and red brick distinguish this style, which became very popular especially for civic buildings, warehouses, and churches.

Although the Romanesque Revival extends from the 1840s to the 1890s, its greatest period dates from *c.* 1870, when Henry Hobson Richardson, its most able and imaginative practitioner, returned from his studies at the École des Beaux-Arts in France (1859–62) and gave the style a life and sophistication that appealed to many architects and builders.

Strength, solidity, and permanence are expressed in the Eagle Warehouse's compact cube of great redbrick walls, medieval parapet, and colossal barrel-arched entrance, which is flanked by square openings with densely woven iron grilles protecting them. This warehouse, designed for storing household furnishings and personal possessions, appropriately conveyed an image of impregnability, reassuring to those whose valuables were stored within.

Through the central archway, a drive led to the storage area; vaults and a stone stairway rose to the mezzanine. Paired iron gates with decorated finials still share a common rectangular goosenecked shutting post, which terminates in a fire-breathing dragon's head (behind the stair the archway is now attractively glassed in to enclose the building's main lobby).

Freeman's three-part design embodies symmetry and stability. The ground floor and mezzanine are unified by the great central archway to make up the basement, or lower register. Four floors above are contained by an undecorated wall and simple rectangular windows (subtly relieved by decorative high-splayed lintels a tone lighter in the center, darker in the pavilions) cut into the thick walls; they are widely spaced across the redbrick surface and reinforce the enormous mass of the building. This central cube is capped by a projecting horizontal band with massive cornice and high attic story punctuated by an eleven-foot clock, added later, which repeats the round shapes of the main arch below.

Freeman added a third building (after his first building and the original press building) to the east of this main structure in the same style in 1906. The metal eagle, with wings outspread, now unlocated, that projects from the line where these two buildings meet came from a later *Brooklyn Eagle* building. It is a vigilant reminder of the newspaper's origins and the historical significance of this site.

The Eagle Warehouse. Lobby mural *(above)* by Tom Loepp realistically portrays Cadman Plaza West from a vantage point east of the Warehouse building entrance. Actual view outside *(below)*, from the same vantage point as in the lobby mural.

In 1978 builder and real estate developer Ben Fishbein was looking for property along the waterfront when he discovered the Eagle Warehouse. He liked it, started talks with the owner, and bought it in 1979. Architect Bernard Rothzeid (Rothzeid, Kaiserman, and Thomson) began the conversion that summer. It was difficult to satisfy the complex requirements of the official agencies involved, while at the same time retaining the spirit of Freeman's original structure and creating attractive and comfortable apartments. One of Rothzeid's main challenges was the west wall facing Manhattan.

Above the basement level, Freeman's building had no windows in that wall. The apartments needed light and a proper view of the Manhattan skyline and the Brooklyn Bridge, so windows had to be cut into the massive brick fabric—forty-two inches thick at the bottom and thirty-two inches thick at the top (contemporary building regulations had required that load-bearing walls be thicker at the bottom and taper upward). These sturdy brick walls and the cast-iron columns that have been retained throughout the building account for much of the charm and character of the apartments.

Modern window fixtures were sensitively adapted to contemporary proportions consistent with the fenestration on the Cadman Plaza West facade. For additional light and air, Rothzeid built an atrium into the center of the structure; it opens off the lobby where a gazebo and plantings afford a light contrast to the massive Romanesque forms. The lobby is decorated with stone masks, an eagle, and cast-iron columns, and a large mural by realist painter Tom Loepp, portraying Cadman Plaza West from east of the warehouse building entrance. The mural not only relates the building to its site, but relates itself to the lobby space by *trompe l'oeil* means. To the left of the Eagle Warehouse's arched entrance in the mural is the actual door, stoop, and railing of a ground floor apartment and to the right, the atrium projects into the lobby, following the row of commercial buildings on the north side of Cadman Plaza West in the mural.

CONVERTED BARGES

As advanced maritime technology developed new methods of shipping, one of the familiar structures to be replaced on the waterfront was the old coffee barge. As more sophisticated loading systems were introduced, the shipyards bought the obsolete barges from the railroads and sold them to individual buyers. The music barge at the Fulton Ferry Landing came from the Erie-Lackawanna Railroad and was sold by the Mowbray Shipyards to Olga Bloom, founder and operator of Bargemusic, Ltd.

370

Olga Bloom and her husband lived on the south shore of Long Island for many years, where they often gathered with fellow musicians to play waterfront concerts for their own enjoyment. Tobias Bloom played violin with the NBC Orchestra under Toscanini, and Olga Bloom played violin and viola with numerous ballets, symphonies, studios, and opera companies. In thirty-five years as a professional musician, Olga Bloom became increasingly aware of the abundance of outstanding musical talent that relatively few people ever heard. When she saw an ad in the *Village Voice* in 1970 offering a barge for sale, her long experience with music on the waterfront connected with her concern for young talent, and she got the idea of a floating concert hall offering chamber music year-round at reasonable prices.

She had her barge towed to Far Rockaway, where she learned how to restore it from tugboat captains, artisans, and shipyard owners. Then she found a permanent berth at the Fulton Ferry Landing, where she opened the Bargemusic, Ltd. in 1977. To establish concert hall acoustics and to seal out the drone of the bridge, she paneled the interior with wood from the old *American Legion,* a Staten Island ferry boat that had been retired to John Witte's shipyard on Staten Island.

The Bargemusic, Ltd., funded by many public and private sources, features a year-round resident string quartet (the only residency in the world that does) whose members are graduates of Juilliard and trained by the Juilliard String Quartet. A resident pianist adds variety to the weekly programs of chamber music (Thursday evenings and Sunday afternoons). Moreover, in addition to performing, the residents also teach children to perform duets, trios, and quartets, modes which develop individual talent through working in concert with others.

Another converted coffee barge from the Mowbray Shipyards (this one from the B & O Railroad) houses the River Café. The River Café was also born of a dream that went back to its proprietor's childhood. Michael O'Keefe grew up on the waterfront of Silver Beach in the Bronx, a place on the southwest edge of the peninsula at the tip of Throgs Neck. The barges coming down from the sand pits at Port Washington loaded with sand for construction in Manhattan used to stand off shore from Silver Beach. Michael and his friends would swim or paddle out to them, feeling like modern-day Marco Polos as they explored the great mountains of sand and listened to the tales of the old barge captains. A connection between the waterfront and the restaurant business was also established in those early years. The O'Keefes' housekeeper had run an elegant avant-garde supper club on the Harlem River, and Michael never forgot the tales she told of great food and famous people.

371

In 1963 O'Keefe approached the city government to lease waterfront land for a restaurant. Guidelines (which did not exist) in the building code had to be formulated and implemented through the appropriate city agencies. Eleven years later (and with the success of his Pear Tree Restaurant, founded in 1969) O'Keefe signed a lease with the Department of Ports and Terminals for the property at the foot of Cadman Plaza West. He opened the River Café in June 1977. O'Keefe designed the conversion himself, which was executed by C. Benvenga, architect of record. He tastefully terraced and planted the entrance area with stone excavated from the East River, and he installed brass lighting fixtures to enhance the illumination at night.

The small waterfront park nearby, a gift of Michael O'Keefe to the city, was designed by David Hirsch, Office of Downtown Brooklyn Development, and Edward Weinstein, New York City Department of Ports and Terminals, which administers the park. Weinstein directed the execution of the park, and landscape architect J. Turofsky was in charge of the planting.

The River Café has not only been a business success, it has attracted many new and notable visitors to the historic district (over 95 percent of his business comes from outside of Brooklyn). Encouraged by the city, O'Keefe opened the Water Club, another barge restaurant, in Manhattan in September 1983, at 500 East Thirtieth Street at the shore adjacent to the FDR Drive in an old waterfront warehouse.

Remove not the ancient landmark . . .
(Proverbs 22:28)

The continuing story of the restorations and conversions at the Fulton Ferry Landing is an eloquent response to the historical imperative "Remove not the ancient landmark . . ." It demonstrates, through a small group of converted and restored buildings—united by the Brooklyn Bridge—how the city's historical and cultural interests can be served through the cooperative efforts of city agencies and the owners and developers of historic structures.

372

GLOSSARY

Acanthus. A plant whose scalloped leaves are represented in the Corinthian capital and other decorations.

American bond. A method of laying brick so that a row of headers (short sides) alternates with from four to six rows of stretchers (long sides).

Anta. A pilaster usually placed at the end of a wall.

Anthemion. Ornament with honeysuckle design common in Greek and Roman art.

Architecture parlante. Revealing the purpose of a building mimetically so that the architecture and decorative forms express or imitate what the building is or is used for.

Architrave. The lowest part of the entablature.

Baffle. A plate for deflecting sound (as in a pulpit).

Balustrade. A series of short pillars or posts (balusters) supporting a railing.

Bay. A principal division of a structure or its parts, such as a wall.

Bead and reel moulding. A kind of decorative moulding that gets its name from the two forms that alternate in making its design; also called astragal.

Belt course. A continuous projecting horizontal band on the exterior of a building.

Billet moulding. Romanesque moulding consisting of bands of short cylinders or squares placed at regular intervals.

Blind arch. Arch applied to the surface of a wall.

Boss. An ornamental projection that covers the intersections of ribs in a vault or ceiling.

Caged newel. A cast-iron newel whose elaborated structure resembles a cage.

Cap mould. Moulding over a window or other opening.

Cartouche. An ornamental panel in the form of a scroll, paper, or parchment and usually bearing an inscription.

Chevron moulding. Romanesque moulding forming a zigzag design.

Coffer. Sunken geometrical panel, usually used to decorate a ceiling or a vault.

Colonnette. A small column.

Console (or console bracket). A small decorative support, often in the form of a scroll or volute (see Corbel).

Coping. Flat or sloped capping to a wall to throw off water.

Corbel. A projecting block (usually stone) to support a beam or other horizontal member.

Corinthian. One of the three orders of Greek architecture (Doric, Ionic, Corinthian) identified by its leafy capital (acanthus leaf).

Cross bonding. A masonry bond in which courses alternate or interconnect.

Crow steps (or corbie steps). Steps on the coping of a gable, used in Dutch houses.

Cupola. A small dome crowning a roof or tower.

Dentil moulding. Moulding composed of dentils, small square blocks, used in cornices.

Diaper pattern. Allover surface decoration composed of small repeated patterns.

Doric. One of the three orders of Greek architecture (Doric, Ionic, Corinthian) identified by its donutlike capital.

Dormer. A window in a sloping roof with its own roof.

Drum. Vertical wall supporting a dome.

Egg and dart moulding. A convex moulding decorated with a pattern of egg shapes and dart (or arrowhead) shapes, alternating with each other.

Elevation. The external face of a building or a drawing to show the vertical plane of a building.

Encaustic tile. Earthenware tile glazed and decorated.

Entablature. The upper part of a wall or story of a building usually supported by columns and composed of a frieze, architrave, and cornice.

Extruded brick. Brick shaped by being forced into a mould under pressure.

Facade. Face or front of a building.

FAR. Floor area ratio. The size of buildings is determined by the floor area ratio assigned by the zoning resolution to each zoning district. If a zoning district has an FAR of 8, for example, a building to be constructed on a lot of 10,000 square feet can contain up to 80,000 square feet. The lowest FAR is .5 (R1, single-family detached house) and the highest FAR is 15 (C6, high-bulk office building).

Fascia. Plain horizontal band in the architrave.

Finial. An ornament that crowns an architectural element.

Flemish bond. A method of laying brick so that headers (short sides) and stretchers (long sides) alternate in each course.

373

Frieze. Middle division of an entablature, the decorated band beneath the cornice.

Gable. Triangular part of a wall under the end of a pitched roof.

Gallery. An upper story often over an aisle, but also found as an exterior feature as well.

Glazed. Furnished or fitted with glass.

Hipped roof. A roof with sloped instead of vertical ends.

Ionic. One of the three Greek orders in architecture (Ionic, Doric, Corinthian) identified by its scroll-like capital, called a volute.

Italianate style. Having characteristics of Italian Renaissance architecture.

Leaf and dart moulding. A convex moulding decorated with a pattern of leaf shapes and dart (or arrowhead) shapes, alternating with each other.

Lintel. A horizontal member over an opening, as in a window or door; lintels are often decorated and are often different shapes, as in the shape of a pediment.

Metope. The square space between two triglyphs in the frieze of a Doric order.

Modillion. A small console used in series to support a cornice.

Moulding. A decorative surface either recessed or relieved.

Newel. The post at the foot of a stairway.

Ogee arch. An arch consisting of a double curved line (a concave and a convex part).

Paneled pilaster. A pilaster whose face is paneled.

Parapet. A low wall used in houses, bridges, monuments, and the like.

Party wall. A wall dividing two adjoining properties.

Pediment. A low-pitched gable above a portico.

Pendant. A boss, elongated so that it hangs down.

Pier. A solid vertical support, usually masonry.

Pilaster. A shallow pier rectangular in profile projecting slightly from a wall and in Classical architecture conforming with the base, shaft, and capital of one of the orders.

Portico. A porch with columns and pediment.

Proscenium. The arch and frontispiece of the stage facing the audience.

Quoins. The stones at the corner of a building that alternate in size.

Random bond. Method of laying stone in a wall that creates a random pattern (random coursing).

Rib vault. A vault with diagonal arched ribs.

Rotunda. A circular building or room, usually with a dome.

Row house. One of a series of houses connected to other houses by common sidewalls and forming a continuous group.

Rustication. Masonry composed of large blocks with beveled edges to emphasize the joints.

Shed dormer. A dormer with a roof parallel to the roof from which it projects.

Spandrel. The surface between two arches in an arcade; also, the wall panel beneath a windowsill extending to the top of the window of the story below.

Strapwork. Decoration consisting of interlaced bands having an appearance similar to leather straps.

Temple front. Having the components of a Classical temple: portico with entablature and pediment supported by Classical columns.

Tesselated. A surface in which tesserae (small cubes of glass, stone, marble, and the like, used in mosaics) are embedded.

Trabeated. A term applied to a system of construction based upon the post and lintel principle.

Triglyph. Vertically grooved block in a Doric frieze separating metopes.

Tuscan pier. Pier with base, shaft, and capital that conform to the Tuscan order, similar to but simpler than the Doric order.

Vault. Arched ceiling or roof usually of stone, brick, wood, or plaster.

Volute. A spiral scroll as on an Ionic capital.

Zoning. Zoning is the means by which a city controls building size, population density, and land use, and the mechanism by which a city carries out planning policy. New York City's first comprehensive zoning resolution (a model for the rest of the United States) was passed in 1916. It established height and introduced setback controls, and it separated incompatible uses (e.g., factories could not be built in residential neighborhoods). Among other things, the zoning resolution establishes zoning districts and size of buildings permitted within each district. Zoning Districts: Residential (R), Commercial (C), and Manufacturing (M) (they are further broken down by density).

BIBLIOGRAPHY

Adams, Rayne. "The Reliefs and Grilles of the Chanin Building Vestibules." *Architectural Forum* 1 (May 1929): 693–698.

Albion, Robert Greenhalgh. *The Rise of New York Port, 1815–1860.* New York: Charles Scribner's Sons, 1939.

Alexander, James Waddell. *A History of the Union Club of New York, 1865–1915.* New York: Charles Scribner's Sons, 1915.

Alpern, Andrew. *Apartments for the Affluent: A Historical Survey of Buildings in New York.* New York: McGraw-Hill, 1975.

Andrews, Wayne. *The Vanderbilt Legend; the Story of the Vanderbilt Family, 1794–1940.* New York: Harcourt Brace and Company, 1941.

Armbruster, Eugene L. *Bruijkleen Colonie.* Limited edition by E. L. Armbruster. New York, 1918.

———. *The Ferry Road on Long Island.* Limited edition by E. L. Armbruster. New York, 1919.

"Art Program of Rockefeller Center and Its Contributing Artists, The." New York: Rockefeller Center, 1972. (Revised September, 1972.)

"Art to Embellish Corporate Complex." *Art in America* (November 1984): 24.

"At Home in the Dakota." *Interiors* 123 (June 1964): 58–64.

Bach, Richard F. "Henry Janeway Hardenbergh." *The Architectural Record* 44 (July 1918): 91–93.

"Back to Ground Zero for MOMA." *New York Times* (July 16, 1978): 18E.

Bailey, Rosalie Fellows. *Pre-Revolutionary Dutch Houses and Families in Northern New Jersey and Southern New York.* New York: William Morrow and Co., 1936.

Bailey, Vernon Howe. *Magical City: Intimate Sketches of New York.* New York: Charles Scribner's Sons, 1939.

———. *Skyscrapers of New York.* With an introduction by Cass Gilbert. New York: W. E. Rudge, 1928.

Baker, Paul R. *Richard Morris Hunt.* Cambridge: MIT Press, 1980.

Ballen, Kate. "People to Watch: Pari S. Choate." *Fortune* (October 27, 1986): 31.

Bannister, Turpin C. "Bogardus Revisited; Part I: The Iron Fronts." *Journal of the Society of Architectural Historians* 15 (December 1956): 12–22.

Barlow, Elizabeth. *Frederick Law Olmsted's New York.* New York: Praeger Publishers, 1972.

Barrington, Lewis. *Historic Restorations of the DAR.* New York: Richard R. Smith, 1941.

Baugher-Perlin, Sherene. "Analyzing Glass Bottles for Chronology, Function, and Trade Networks." *Archaeology of Urban America.* New York: Academic Press, 1982.

"Bayard-Condict Building, The." A paper by Margaret Tuft in the files of the New York City Landmarks Preservation Commission.

Belden, Ezekiel Porter. *New York—as It Is: Being the Counterpart of the Metropolis of America.* New York: J. P. Prall, 1849.

———. *New York Past, Present, and Future.* New York: G. P. Putnam, 1849.

Bernard, Michael M. "Case Study: Air-Rights Development at 'Museum Tower'." *The Journal of Real Estate Development.* 1, no. 3 (Winter 1986): 48–54.

Bhatia, Arun, developer. Interviews with author. October–November 1993.

"Big Business and Art." *Visual Arts Newsletter* 5, no. 5 (August/September 1985): 4.

Bletter, Rosemarie Haag, and Cervin Robinson. *Skyscraper Style: Art Deco New York.* New York: Oxford University Press, 1975.

Bliven, Bruce, Jr. *New York, a Bicentennial History.* New York: W. W. Norton and Company, 1981.

Brenson, Michael. "Museum and Corporation—A Delicate Balance." *New York Times* (February 23, 1986) Arts and Leisure Sect.: 1–4.

Brewster, Todd. "The Big Money in High Art." *Life* (April 1986): 52–58.

Brooks, Andree. "Brooklyn Theater Becomes Housing." *New York Times* (July 28, 1988): B8.

———. "Luxury Tower at 10th Avenue and 42nd Street." *New York Times* (June 3, 1989): A20.

_____. "Troubles Beset Housing Plan for Clinton." *New York Times* (July 3, 1988): 26.

Brouwer, Norman. "The Late Clipper of Them All—Snow Squall." *Seaport* 15 (Summer 1981): 28–30.

_____. "Ships In Our Cellar." *Seaport* 14 (Fall 1980): 20–23.

Brown, Eve (Mary Eudora Nichols). *The Plaza: Its Life and Times*. New York: Meredith Press, 1967.

Brown, Frederick, *Père Lachaise: Elyseum as Real Estate*. New York: Viking Press, 1973.

Brown, Glenn. *History of the U.S. Capitol*. Washington, D.C.: U.S. Government Printing Office, 1900–03.

Brumbaugh, T. B. *Horatio and Richard Greenough*. Ann Arbor: University Microfilm, 1969.

Burnham, Alan, ed. *New York Landmarks*. Middletown, Conn.: Wesleyan University Press, 1963.

Callow, Alexander B., Jr. *The Tweed Ring*. New York: Oxford University Press, 1966.

"Cass Gilbert's New York Custom House Design." *The Inland Architect and News Record* 35 (February 1900): 6–7.

Castro, Janice. "New Jewel for the West Side." *Real Estate* (Spring 1986): 1–3.

Chira, Susan. "Battery Park City Rousing From a 2-Year Fiscal Sleep." *New York Times* (November 7, 1989): B1, B6.

_____. "New Designs for Times Square Try to Reflect Neon Atmosphere." *New York Times* (August 31, 1989): B1, B4.

"Chrysler Building, The." *Architecture and Building* 62 (August 1930): 222–224.

Clavan, Irwin. "The Empire State Building, Shreve, Lamb, and Harmon, Architects; IX: The Mooring Mast." *The Architectural Forum* 54 (February 1931): 229–234.

Clute, Eugene. "The Chrysler Building." *Architectural Forum* 53 (October 1930): 406.

_____. "The Story of Rockefeller Center; X: The Allied Artist." *Architectural Forum* 57 (October 1932): 353–358.

Clute, John J. *Annals of Staten Island from Its Discovery to the Present*. New York: Press of G. Vogt, 1877.

Collins, George R. "The Transfer to Thin Masonry Vaulting from Spain to America." *Journal of the Society of Architectural Historians* 27 (October 1968): 176–201.

Condit, Carl. *American Building Art—the Nineteenth Century*. New York: Oxford University Press, 1960.

Cooper, Jerry. "At Equitable Center." *Interior Design* (September 1986): 254–267.

Corbett, Harvey Wiley. "The Problem of Traffic Congestion, and a Solution." *Architectural Forum* 46 (March 1927): 201–208.

"Correspondence. The Buildings in City Hall Square." *American Architect and Building News* 1 (June 24, 1876): 206–207.

"Correspondence. The Buildings in City Hall Square." *American Architecture and Building News* 3 (March 16, 1878): 94.

Crane, Hart. *The Bridge*. New York: Liveright Publications, 1970.

Craven, Wayne. *Sculpture in America*. New York: Thomas Y. Crowell Co., 1968.

"Criticism of the Chrysler Building." *Architectural Forum* 53 (October 1930): 410.

Crosby, Theo. *The Necessary Monument*. Greenwich, Conn.: New York Graphic Society, 1970.

Cummings, Judith. "Tower Over Museum to Rise in Expensive Luxury." *New York Times* (June 10, 1979): 59.

Curl, James Stevens. *The Victorian Celebration of Death*. London: (Newton Abbot) David and Charles, 1972.

David, A. C. "The New Theaters of New York." *The Architectural Record* 15 (January 1904): 39–54.

Davidson, Marshall B., with biographical essays by Margot P. Brill. *The American Heritage History of Notable American Houses*. New York: American Heritage Publishing Co., 1971.

Davis, Douglas. "MOMA Lets the Sunshine In." *Newsweek* (May 21, 1984): 88–89.

Dawson, Henry B. *Reminiscences of the Park and Its Vicinity*. New York, 1855. Excerpts in the files of the New York City Landmarks Preservation Commission.

Dean, Andrea Oppenheimer, and Allen Freeman. "The Rockefeller Center of the 80s?" (reprinted from) *Architecture* (December 1986).

Dennis, James M. *Karl Bitter, Architectural Sculptor*. Madison: University of Wisconsin Press, 1967.

Dilliard, Maud Esther. *Old Dutch Houses of Brooklyn*. New York: Richard R. Smith, 1945.

Doubilet, Susan. "Big City Builders Olympia & York." *Progressive Architecture* (July 1985): 79–86.

Doyle, Margaret Anne. "The Preservation of Municipally Owned Buildings: The Tweed Courthouse, A Case Study." Master's Thesis, School of Architecture, Columbia University, 1978. Excerpts in the files of the New York City Landmarks Preservation Commission.

Dunlap, David W. "At Lincoln Center, A New Building Big Enough for All." *New York Times* (November 25, 1989): 13.

———. "Board to Review 63rd Street Tower Plan." *New York Times* (March 9, 1989): B2.

———. "Demolition Plays the Palace (But the Theater Plays On)." *New York Times* (May 13, 1988): B3.

———. "New Dispute Involves Plan on Times Square." *New York Times* (May 18, 1989): B1, B4.

Eisen, Gustave A. *Portraits of Washington.* 3 volumes. New York: Robert Hamilton and Associates, 1932.

Embury, Aymar, II. *The Dutch Colonial House: Its Origin, Design, Modern Plan and Construction.* New York: McBride, Nast, and Co., 1913.

Emmanuel, Muriel. *Contemporary Architects.* New York: St. Martin's Press, 1980.

Farrell, James J. *Inventing the American Way of Death.* Philadelphia: Temple University Press, 1980.

Fein, Albert. *Frederick Law Olmsted and the American Environmental Tradition.* New York: George Braziller, 1972.

Finch, J. Kip. "Seven Modern Wonders Named." *Civil Engineering* (November 1955). Copy in Empire State Building files.

Fire Houses. New York City Landmarks Preservation Commission files (survey), n.d.

"First Shearith Israel Graveyard." Nomination Report for National Register of Historic Places Inventory, 1966. New York City Landmarks Preservation Commission.

Fitch, James Marston, and Diana S. Waite. *Grand Central Terminal and Rockefeller Center.* New York State Parks and Recreation Division for Historic Preservation. Albany, 1974.

Fleming, Robins. "A Half Century of the Skyscraper." *Civil Engineering* (December 1934): 634–638 (reprint in Avery Library).

———. "Whence the Skyscraper." *Civil Engineering* (October 1934): 505–509 (reprint in Avery Library).

Frary, J. T. *They Built the Capitol.* Richmond: Garrett and Massie, 1940.

———. *Thomas Jefferson, Architect and Builder.* Richmond: Garrett and Massie, 1939.

Frazier, George. "Elegance Entrenched." *Esquire* (January 1956).

Frohne, H. W. "Designing a Metropolitan Hotel, The Plaza." *Architectural Record* 22 (November 1907): 349–364.

Fulton Ferry. Report prepared by Office of Downtown Brooklyn Development. Housing and Development Administration. City of New York. April, 1972.

Gardner, Deborah S. "The Architecture of Commercial Capitalism: John Kellum and the Development of New York, 1840–1875." Unpublished Ph.D. dissertation, Graduate School of Arts and Sciences, Columbia University, 1979.

Gayle, Margot. *Cast-Iron Architecture in New York: A Photographic Survey.* New York: Dover Publications, 1974.

Gebhard, David, and Deborah Nevins. *Two Hundred Years of American Architectural Drawing.* New York: Watson-Guptill Publications, 1977.

Geismar, Joan H. "Archaeological Investigation of 175 Water Street Block for Soil Systems, Inc." New York Landmarks Preservation Commission files, 1982.

Gimelson, Deborah. "The Tower of Art." *Art & Auction* VIII, no. 4 (October 4, 1985): 150–155.

Glueck, Grace. "Modern Museum Head Hopeful Despite Setback from Court." *New York Times* (August 7, 1978): 22–23.

———. "Modern Museum Will Get $17 Million for Air Rights." *New York Times* (June 10, 1979): 1, 59.

———. "Museum Tower Delayed by Rift." *New York Times* (May 31, 1978): 14.

Gold, Jack. Public Affairs, Cesar Pelli Associates. Interviews with author. November–December 1993.

Goldberger, Paul. "The New MOMA." *New York Times Magazine* (April 15, 1984): 37–49, 68–74.

———. *The Skyscraper.* New York: Alfred A. Knopf, 1981.

Gottlieb, Martin. "Equitable Life Will Mix Art and Commerce." *New York Times* (September 20, 1984): 21.

Gray, Christopher. "A Conversation to Serve Another Generation's Needy." *New York Times* (April 16, 1989) Real Estate Sect.: 12.

———. "A New Life—and Mission—for a Bronx Residence." *New York Times* (January 8, 1989) Real Estate Sect.: 6.

———. "From Rentals to Cooperatives: Reconverting a Grand Palazzo." *New York Times* (May 8, 1988) Real Estate Sect.: 12.

Gray, Erin Drake. "The Schermerhorn Row Block

Preservation Project: It's Begun!" *Seaport* 15 (Winter 1982): 10–17.

Great East River Bridge, The. Exhibition Catalogue. Brooklyn: Brooklyn Museum, 1983.

Green-Wood Cemetery Nomination Report for National Register of Historical Places Inventory, 1966.

Grove, Harold E. *St. Thomas Church.* New York: St. Thomas Church, 1965.

Gwathmey, Charles. Gwathmey Siegel & Associates Architects. Interview with author. December 1993.

Haaga, Claire. President, Housing & Services, Inc. Interview with author. November 1993.

Hall, Ben M. *The Best Remaining Seats: The Story of the Golden Age of the Movie Palace.* New York: Bramhall House, 1961.

Hall, Edward Hagaman. "An Appeal for the Preservation of City Hall Park with a Brief History of the Park." American Scenic and Historical Preservation Society Annual Report, vol. 8, no. 10. Albany, 1910.

Hamilton, George Heard. "Education and Scholarship in the American Museum." *On Understanding Art Museums,* edited by Sherman E. Lee. Englewood Cliffs, N.J.: Prentice-Hall, 1975, 98–100.

Hamlin, Talbot. *Greek Revival Architecture in America.* New York: Dover Publications, 1944.

———. *The American Spirit in Architecture.* New Haven: Yale University Press, 1926.

Hardenbergh, Henry Janeway. Obituary. *Journal of the Society of Architectural Historians* 6 (April 1918): 199.

Harlow, Alvin Fay. *The Road of the Century: The Story of the New York Central.* New York: Creative Age Press, 1947.

Hartman, William Jay. "Politics and Patronage: The New York Custom House, 1852–1902." Columbia University Thesis. New York, 1952.

Henderson, Helen Weston. *A Loiterer in New York.* New York: George H. Doran Company, 1917.

Henderson, Mary C. "The New Theatre." *Marquee* 7 (Fourth Quarter, 1975): 14–17.

Hershkowitz, Leo. *Tweed's New York—Another Look.* Garden City, New York: Anchor Press, 1977.

History of Real Estate, Building, and Architecture in New York City During the Last Quarter of a Century. New York, 1898 (reprinted by Arno Press, Inc., New York, in 1967).

Hitchcock, Henry-Russell. *Architecture: Nineteenth and Twentieth Centuries.* The Pelican History of

Art series, edited by Nikolaus Pevsner. Baltimore: Penguin Books, 1958.

Holloway, Emory, ed. *The Uncollected Poetry and Prose of Walt Whitman.* Garden City, New York: Doubleday, Page and Co., 1921 and 1932.

Horsley, Carter B. "Museum Tower Plan Runs Into Obstacles." *New York Times* (August 6, 1977): 21.

"Houdon's Washington." *Harper's Weekly,* vol. 12. Harper and Brothers. New York, 1868.

Hoyt, Charles K., A.I.A. "Letters." *New York Times* (July 28, 1977) Home Sect.: 14.

Hughes, Robert. "Revelation on 53rd Street." *Time* (May 14, 1984): 78–80.

Humphreys, Hugh Campbell, ed. *Gateway to America: The Alice Austen House and Esplanade.* Friends of the Alice Austen House and Esplanade, 1968.

Huxtable, Ada Louise. *Classic New York.* New York: Doubleday and Company, 1964.

———. "Progressive Architecture in America: Grand Central Depot—1869–71." *Progressive Architecture* 37 (October 1956): 135–138.

———. "A Dubious Survival Plan for the Modern." *New York Times* (August 7, 1977) Arts and Leisure Sect.: 1–20.

———. "Times Square Renewal (Act II), Farce." *New York Times* (October 14, 1989): 25.

Illes, Jack. Kahn Company. Interview with author. December 1993.

Illustrations of Iron Architecture Made by the Architecture Iron Works of the City of New York. New York: Baker and Godwin Printers, 1965.

"It's Been a Long Journey from Traveling Salesman's Blend." *Candid.* White Plains, New York: General Foods, 1970.

James, Theodore. *The Empire State Building.* New York: Harper and Row, 1975.

———. *Fifth Avenue.* New York: Walker and Co., 1971.

Kaiser, Charles. "Court Invalidates Law for Apartment Tower Over Modern Museum." *New York Times* (July 14, 1978): A1, A13.

Kardas, Susan, and Edward Larrabee. Report on excavations at Schermerhorn Row. Excerpts in files of New York City Landmarks Preservation Commission.

Karson, Robin. "Winter Garden." *Landscape Architecture* (January–February 1986): 76–77.

Kennedy, Shawn G. "A Mixed-Use Project for Times Square." *New York Times* (July 12, 1989): 20.

_____. "Offices in a Former Industrial Area." *New York Times* (September 17, 1989): 23.

_____. "Offices Near Grand Central Are Renewed." *New York Times* (May 31, 1989): D16.

_____. "Theater-Hotel Partnership in Times Square." *New York Times* (March 1, 1989): D22.

Kimball, Roger. "Art and Architecture at the Equitable Center." *The New Criterion* (November 1986): 24–32.

King's Handbook of New York City. Boston: Moses King, 1892 and 2nd revised edition, 1893.

King's Photographic Views of New York. Boston: Moses King, 1895.

Klein, Claire. "Columbia and the Elgin Botanic Garden." *Columbia University Quarterly 31* (December 1939): 272–297.

_____. "The Rockefeller Center Property." *Columbia University Quarterly 33* (February 1941): 59–75.

Klein, Dan. "The Chanin Building, New York." *The Connoisseur* 186 (July 1974): 162–169.

Koch, Robert. "The Medieval Castle Revival: New York Armories." *Journal of the Society of Architectural Historians* 14 (October 1955): 23–29.

Krinsky, Carol Herselle. "Rockefeller Center." *Antiques* 107 (March 1975): 478–486.

_____. *Rockefeller Center.* New York: Oxford University Press, 1978.

Lafever, Minard. *The Architectural Instructor.* New York: G. P. Putnam and Co., 1856.

_____. *The Beauties of Modern Architecture.* New York: D. Appleton and Co., 1835·(republished by Da Capo Press, 1968).

_____. *The Modern Builder's Guide.* New York: Henry C. Sleight, Collins and Hannay, 1833.

_____. *The Young Builder's General Instructor.* Newark, New Jersey: W. Tuttle and Co., 1829.

Kondylis, Costas. Costas Kondylis Associates, Architects. Interviews with author. October–November 1993.

Kutner, Janet. "Equitable Assembles Impressive Collection of Murals and Marble." *The Dallas Morning News* (July 24, 1986) Art Review: 1.

Lampert, Hope. "Master Builders, the Reichmann Brothers." *Quest* (October 1989): 58–61.

Lancaster, Clay. "Central Park, 1851–1951." *Magazine of Art* 44 (April 1951): 123–128.

Landau, Sarah Bradford. "The Row Houses of New York's West Side." *Journal of the Society of Architectural Historians* 34 (March 1975): 19–36.

Laning, Edward. *The Sketchbooks of Reginald Marsh.* Greenwich, Conn.: New York Graphic Society, 1973.

Lee, Felicia R. "Gentrification and Crime Lay Siege to Clinton." *New York Times* (July 8, 1989): 25–26.

Leonard, Don. Project Manager on 485 Lexington Avenue, Skidmore Owings and Merrill. Interview with author. November 1993.

Lewittes, Esther. "The Terrace in New York's Central Park." *Antiques Magazine* 106 (October 1974): 649–657.

Limpus, Lowell M. *History of the New York Fire Department.* New York: E. P. Dutton and Co., 1940.

Lockwood, Charles. *Bricks and Brownstones; the New York Row House: A Social and·Architectural History, 1783–1929.* New York: McGraw-Hill, 1972.

Loercher, Diana. "Apartment House Atop a Museum?" *The Christian Science Monitor* (August 16, 1977): 15.

Lueck, Thomas J. "Key Step Taken in Times Square Redevelopment." *New York Times* (June 22, 1988): A1, B4.

_____. "Reprieve for a Famed Tower on Times Square." *New York Times* (July 2, 1988): 25.

Lyman, Susan E. *The Face of New York: The City as It Was and as It Is.* New York: Crown Publishers, 1954.

_____. *The Story of New York, an Informal History of the City.* New York: Crown Publishers, 1964.

Lynch, Denis Tilden. *"Boss" Tweed: The Story of a Grim Generation.* New York: Boni and Liveright, 1927.

Lyons, Richard D. "All of a Pattern." *New York Times* (August 21, 1987) Real Estate Sect.: 1.

_____. "Carriage Houses: New Homes for Ballet." *New York Times* (November 12, 1989) Real Estate Sect.: 1.

_____. "Condos Atop a Jewelry Exchange." *New York Times* (June 4, 1989) Real Estate Sect.: 1.

_____. "Factory Renovation: Ping Pong Apartments." *New York Times* (September 17, 1989) Real Estate Sect.: 1.

_____. "555 Broadway: 3 Sisters Renovate." *New York Times* (September 17, 1989) Real Estate Sect.: 1.

_____. "Historic Archive Building Restored for Rental Use." *New York Times* (June 10, 1988): A29.

_____. "New Look in Lobbies." *New York Times* (July 24, 1983) Real Estate Sect.: 1, 14.

_____. "SoHo Renovation: 24 Cast-Iron Condominiums." *New York Times* (September 10, 1989) Real Estate Sect.: 1.

——. "Vertical Mall Rises in Old Gimbel's Store." *New York Times* (June 28, 1989): D18.

——. "Watch Out! New Rentals for Woodside." *New York Times* (September 3, 1989) Real Estate Sect.: 1.

McCullough, David. *The Great Bridge.* New York: Simon and Schuster, 1972.

Maiorana, Ron. MC Communications. Interview with author. July 1989.

Malone, Dumas, ed. *Dictionary of American Biography.* New York: Charles Scribner's Sons, 1936.

Mandelbaum, Seymour J. *Boss Tweed's New York.* New York: John Wiley, 1965.

"Marvelous MOMA." *New York Times* (May 13, 1984): editorial.

Marxer, Bonnie, and Evelyn Ortner. "The Vander Ende-Onderdonck House." A Historic Structure Report prepared by the office of Giorgio Cavaglieri for the Greater Ridgewood Historical Society. New York, 1979.

McCain, Mark. "A Mandated Comeback for the Great White Way." *New York Times* (April 9, 1989): 23.

——. "Law Firms Expand Their Presence in Midtown." *New York Times* (July 16, 1989) Real Estate Sect.: 15.

McGill, Douglas. "Art Complex Planned in New Tower." *New York Times* (May 14, 1985): 14.

——. "Battery to Get Four More Artworks." *New York Times* (April 25, 1985): C21.

McGuigan, Cathleen with Maggie Malone. "A Word From Our Sponsor." *Newsweek* (November 25, 1985): 96–98.

Meeks, Carroll L. V. *The Railroad Station.* New Haven: Yale University Press, 1975.

Middleton, William D. *Grand Central, the World's Greatest Railway Terminal.* San Marino, California: Golden West Books, 1977.

Miller, John; Donald Anderle; and Julia van Haaften Schick. *The American Idea.* New York: New York Public Ligrary, 1976.

Mitchell, Joseph. *The Bottom of the Harbor.* Boston: Little, Brown, 1959.

——. "Mr. Hunter's Grave." *New Yorker* 32 (September 22, 1956).

Mitchell, Joseph Brady. *Decisive Battles of the American Revolution.* New York: G. P. Putnam's Sons, 1962.

"MOMA." *The New Yorker* (May 23, 1977): 44–45.

Moore, Abbot Halstead. "Individualism in Architecture—the Works of Herts and Tallant." *Architectural Record* 15 (January 1904): 55–91.

Morris, Ira K. *Memorial History of Staten Island.* 2 vols. New York, 1898–1900.

Morrison, Hugh Sinclair. *Early American Architecture: From the First Colonial Settlements to the National Period.* New York: Oxford University Press, 1952.

Mujica, Francisco. *History of the Skyscraper.* Paris: Archaeology and Architecture Press, 1929 (New York, 1936). Reprinted by Da Capo Press, 1977.

Mumford, Lewis. *The Brown Decades: A Study of the Arts in America, 1865–1895.* New York: Harcourt, Brace, and Company, 1931.

Muschamp, Herbert. "42nd Street Plan: Be Bold or Begone!" *New York Times* (September 19, 1993) Arts and Leisure Sect.: 33.

Museum Of Modern Art. Cesar Pelli and Associates. Design statement. August 22, 1989.

The Museum of Modern Art. Statement to the New Construction Committee of Community Board 5 in Support of the Museum's Application to the Trust for Cultural Resources of the City of New York, the New York City Planning Commission, and the New York City Board of Standards and Appeals. May 23, 1977.

Nakamura, Toshio, ed. *Cesar Pelli.* Tokyo: Yoshio Hoshida, 1985, 176–199.

Naylor, David. *American Picture Palaces: The Architecture of Fantasy.* New York: Van Nostrand Reinhold Co., 1981.

Nevins, Deborah, gen. ed. *Grand Central Terminal, City Within the City.* New York: The Municipal Arts Society of New York, 1982.

"New Lyceum Theater." Landmark Ceremony brochure. Tuesday, May 16, 1978. Copy in files of New York City Landmarks Preservation Commission.

"New Tribune Building, The." *The American Builder* 9 (October 1873): 235.

New York City Board of Aldermen. Report of the Special Committee Appointed to Investigate the "Ring" Frauds, Docket No. 8, January 4, 1878, p. 43. Excerpts on file in the New York City Landmarks Preservation Commission.

New York State Cultural Resources Act. Article 13-E, General Municipal Law (July 27, 1976): 50–65.

"Nineteenth Century Dwelling Houses of Greenwich Village." Association of Village Homeowners. New York, 1969. Sources and references selected by Regina Kellerman. Excerpts in files of the New York City Landmarks Preservation Commission.

O'Brien, Lucy. Public Affairs, Museum of Modern Art. Interview with author. December 1993.

Oldenburg, Richard E., Director of The Museum of Modern Art. Statement presented at the Joint Hearing held by Community Board 5 and the Trust for Cultural Resources of the City of New York. June 23, 1977.

Olmsted, Frederick Law, Jr., and Theodora Kimball, eds. *Forty Years of Landscape Architecture: Central Park.* Cambridge: MIT Press, 1973.

———. *Frederick Law Olmsted, Landscape Architect, 1822–1902.* 2 vols. New York: G. P. Putnam's Sons, 1922–1928.

Onderdonck, Elmer, and Andrew J. Onderdonck. *Genealogy of the Onderdonck Family in America.* New York: Long Island Historical Society, 1910.

"Opening of the New Grand Central Terminal, New York City." *Engineering Record* 67 (February 8, 1913): 144–148.

"Origin of Breuckelen." Harrington Putnam *Half Moon Series,* vol. II, no. 11, November 1898. New York: G. P. Putnam's Sons, 1898.

Owen, Dick. "Famous Churches of Our City: The Mariners' Temple." *Sunday News,* May 17, 1959.

"Pacing the Tribune." *Progressive Architecture* 47 (July 1966): 57–58.

Pagan, David. Administrator, Southside United Housing Development Fund Corporation. Interview with author. November 1993.

Peterson, Iver. "Eighth Avenue Goes from Grit to Glitter." *New York Times* (January 29, 1989) Real Estate Sect.: 1.

———"A New Manhattan Office Tower Awaits First Tenant." *New York Times* (June 22, 1988): A24.

———"Union Square: Gritty Past, Bright Future." *New York Times* (November 26, 1989) Real Estate Sect.: 1.

Pike, Martha V., and Janice Gray Armstrong, eds. *A Time to Mourn.* Museums at Stony Brook. New York, 1980.

Placzek, Adolf K. *Inventory of the Alexander Jackson Davis Collection.* Avery Architectural and Fine Arts Library. Compiled by Adolf K. Placzek (1955) with additions by Jane B. Davies (1974).

———, ed. *Macmillan Encyclopedia of Architects.* 4 vols. New York: The Free Press, Macmillan, 1982.

———, ed. *The Origins of Cast-Iron Architecture in America.* With an introduction by Walter Knight Sturges. New York: Da Capo Press, 1970.

Plaza Hotel. National Register of Historic Places Inventory Nomination Report. Draft, n.d.

Porzelt, Paul. *The Metropolitan Club of New York.* New York: Rizzoli International Publications, 1982.

Price, Matlock. "The Chanin Building." *Architectural Forum* 50 (May 1929): 699–731.

Prudon, Theodore H., and Timothy Burditt. "The Coenties Slip Buildings. An Historic Structures Report." Prepared for the New York Landmarks Conservancy. New York: The Ehrenkrantz Group, 1979.

Real Estate Record and Builders Guide. Real Estate Board. New York, 1898. Excerpts in the files of the New York City Landmarks Preservation Commission.

Reed, Henry Hope, and Sophia Duckworth. *Central Park: A History and a Guide.* New York: Clarkson N. Potter, 1967.

"Reinstalled Third-Floor Painting and Sculpture Galleries Feature Renovated and Expanded Galleries for Contemporary Art." Museum of Modern Art press release. July 1993.

Reni, Albert Christian. *American Cut and Engraved Glass.* New York: Thomas Nelson and Sons, 1965. Excerpts on file in the New York City Landmarks Preservation Commission.

Reynolds, Donald Martin. "Custom House Sculpture Expresses Maritime History." *The Bridge* 5 (December-February 1970–1971): 11.

———. *Hiram Powers and His Ideal Sculpture.* New York: Garland Publishing. 1977.

———. "The Origins of the Skyscraper." *Immovable Objects Exhibition* (June–August 1975). Cooper Hewitt Museum.

———. "The Sculpture Program for the Facade of the United States Custom House: 'A Great Temple of Commerce.'" MA Paper. Columbia University, New York, 1970.

———. "The Tallest Building in the World, 1913–1930." *Immovable Objects Exhibition* (June–August 1975). Cooper Hewitt Museum.

Reynolds, Donald Martin; Mary David Barry; and Jane Nobes Brennan. *Fonthill Castle: Paradigm of Hudson-River Gothic.* Riverdale, New York: College of Mount Saint Vincent-on-Hudson, 1976.

Reynolds, Helen Wilkinson. *Dutch Houses in the Hudson Valley Before 1776.* New York: Holland Society of New York, 1929.

Reynolds, John B. *The Chrysler Building.* Compiled and published by John B. Reynolds. New York, c. 1930.

Richards, T. Addison. "The Central Park." *New Monthly Magazine* 23 (August 1861): 289–305.

"Rockefeller Touch in Building, The." *Architectural Forum* 108 (March 1958): 86–91.

Rojo, Rick. Public Affairs, Museum of Modern Art. Interview with author. December 1993.

Roper, Laura Wood. *FLO: A Biography of Frederick Law Olmsted.* Baltimore: Johns Hopkins University Press, 1973.

Rosenbaum, Lee. "MOMA's Construction Project: Reflections on a Glass Tower." *Art in America* (November/December 1977): 10–16, 21–25.

Roth, Leland M. *A Concise History of American Architecture.* New York: Harper and Row, Publishers, 1980.

———. "McKim, Mead, and White Reappraised." *McKim, Mead, and White, 1879–1915.* New York: Arno Press, 1977.

Rothschild, Nan A., and Diana di Zerega Rockman. "Excavated New York: The Big Apple." *Archaeology* 33 (November/December 1980): 56–58.

Rudofsky, Bernard. *Streets for People.* Garden City, New York: Doubleday and Company, 1969.

Scardino, Albert. "New Offices Changing the Theater District." *New York Times* (June 13, 1987): 29, 32.

Schuyler, Montgomery, "The New Custom House at New York." *The Architectural Record* 20 (July 1906): 1–14.

———. "The Small City House in New York." *Architectural Record* 8 (April–June 1899): 357–388.

———. "Two New Armories." *Architectural Record* 19 (April 1906): 259–264.

———. "The Work of Napoleon LeBrun and Sons." *Architectural Record* 27 (1910): 365–381.

———. "The Works of Henry Janeway Hardenbergh." *Architectural Record* 6 (January–March 1897): 335–375.

Sclare, Donald. Donald & Lisa Sclare Architects. Interview with author. December 1993.

Semsch, Otto Francis. *A History of the Singer Building Construction.* New York: The Trow Press, 1908.

"750 Seventh Avenue." Architects' design statement. July 1989.

Shaman, Diana. "Condos Top 6th Building to Rise at Lincoln Center." *New York Times* (June 9, 1989): B6.

Sheehan, Arthur, and Elizabeth Sheehan. *Pierre Toussaint.* New York: The Candle Press, 1953.

Shopsin, William C., and Mosette Glaser Broderick. *The Villard Houses.* New York: Viking Press, 1980.

Shultz, Earl, and Walter Simmons. *Offices in the Sky.* New York: Bobbs-Merrill Co., 1959.

Shumway, Floyd M. *Seaport City: New York in 1775.* New York: South Street Seaport Museum, 1975.

Smith, John F. X. *St. James Parish: 150 Years, 1827–1977.* New York: Park Publishing Co., 1977.

Smith, Thomas E. V. *The City of New York in the Year of Washington's Inauguration, 1789.* Riverside. Connecticut: Chatham Press, 1972 (first edition 1889 privately printed).

SoHo Cast-Iron District Designation Report. New York City Landmarks Preservation Commission. 1973: 44, 93.

Solomon, Jean. Solomon Equities. Interviews with author. July 1989, December 1993.

Solovioff, Nicholas. "Vanishing Glory in Business Buildings." *Fortune* (September 1963): 119–126. Reprint in Avery Library.

Starrett, William A. *Skyscrapers and the Men Who Build Them.* New York: Charles Scribner's Sons, 1928.

Stave, Pari. Curator of Collections, Equitable Life Assurance Society. Interviews with author. 1989–1990, 1993.

Stephens, Suzanne. "An Equitable Relationship." *Art in America* (May 1986): 117–123.

Stiles, Henry Reed. *A History of the City of Brooklyn.* 3 vols. Published by subscription. Brooklyn, 1867–70.

Still, Bayrd. *Mirror for Gotham: New York as Seen by Contemporaries from Dutch Days to the Present.* New York: New York University Press, 1956.

Stokes, Isaac Newton Phelps. *The Iconography of Manhattan Island, 1498–1909.* 6 vols. New York: R. H. Dodd, 1915–1928.

Stone, William Leete. *Centennial History of New York City from the Discovery to the Present.* New York: E. Clève, 1876.

———. *History of New York City from the Discovery to the Present Day.* New York: Virtue and Yorston, 1872.

Story, W. W. "The Mask of Washington." *Harper's Weekly* 31. New York: Harper Brothers, 1887.

Stuart, James, and Nicholas Revett. *The Antiquities of Athens,* 2 vols. London: Priestley and Wale, 1825.

Sturges, W. Knight. "Cast-Iron in New York." *Architectural Review* 114 (October 1953): 233.

"Themes of Rockefeller Center in Painting and Sculpture." Rockefeller Family Archives, n.d.

"Times Square Crossroads." *New York Times* (November 14, 1993) Neighborhood Report: 6.

Todd, Frederick P., and Kenneth C. Miller. *Pro-Patria.* Hartsdale, New York: Rampart House, 1956.

Too, Patrick. New York City Planning Commission. Interview with author. November 1993.

Trachtenberg, Alan. *Brooklyn Bridge: Fact and Symbol.* Chicago: Chicago University Press, 1965.

"The Treasures of the University Club." In-house exhibition brochure. New York: University Club, April 1980.

Tunnard, Christopher, and Henry Hope Reed. *American Skyline.* New York: The New American Library, 1956.

Valentine, David Thomas. *Manual of the Corporation of the City of New York for 1858.* New York: C. W. Baker, 1858.

Van Alen, William. "The Structure and Metal Work of the Chrysler Building." *The Architectural Forum* 53 (October 1930): 493–498.

"Venerable Dakota, The." *Architectural Forum* 110 (March 1959): 122–129.

Vlack, Don. *Art Deco Architecture in New York, 1920–1940.* New York: Harper and Row, Publishers, 1974.

Waite, Diana S. "The Dakota." *Selections from the Historic American Buildings Survey,* no. 7. U.S. Department of the Interior. National Park Service, Washington, D.C.: 55–67.

———. "Tribune Building." *Selections from the Historic American Buildings Survey,* no. 7. U.S. Department of the Interior. National Park Service, Washington, D.C.: 30–44.

Waite, John Graves. "The Development of the New York City Firehouse 1731–1910." Student paper, May 1966. Avery Library. Excerpts quoted in files in New York City Landmarks Preservation Commission.

Walker, Lester. *American Shelter.* Woodstock, New York: The Overlook Press, 1981.

Walker, Tom. "Business, art mesh at Equitable." *Crain's New York Business* (May 20, 1985): 1.

Wallach, Amei. "Lobbying for Art." *New York Newsday* (February 9, 1986) Part II: 4–6.

Webster, J. Carson. "The Skyscraper: Logical and Historical Considerations." *Journal of the Society of Architectural Historians* 18 (December 1959): 126–139.

Weisman, Winston. "The Anatomy and Significance of the Laing Store by James Bogardus." *Journal of the Society of Architectural Historians* 31 (October 1972): 221–222.

———. "The Architectural Significance of Rockefeller Center." Thesis, Ohio State University, 1942.

———. "The Commercial Architecture of George B. Post," *Journal of the Society of Architectural Historians* 31 (October 1972): 176–203.

———. "Commercial Palaces of New York." *Art Bulletin* 36 (December 1954): 285–302.

———. "A New View of Skyscraper History." *The Rise of an American Architecture.* New York: Praeger Publishers, 1970.

———. "New York and the Problem of the First Skyscraper." *Journal of the Society of Architectural Historians* 12 (March 1953): 13–21.

Wertenbaker, Thomas Jefferson. *Father Knickerbocker Rebels: New York City During the Revolution.* New York: Charles Scribner's Sons, 1948.

———. *The First Americans, 1607–1690.* New York: The Macmillan Company, 1927.

———. *The Founding of American Civilization: The Middle Colonies.* New York: Cooper Square Publishers, 1963.

White, Norval, and Elliot Willensky. *AIA Guide to New York City.* New York: Collier Books, Macmillan, 1978.

Whitman, Walt. *Specimen Days.* Philadelphia: R. Welsh and Co., 1882–83.

Wilentz, Elias. *City Hall: A Guide to Its Art and Architecture.* New York: New York City Art Commission, 1977.

Willensky, Elliot, and Norval White. *AIA Guide to New York City.* New York: Harcourt Brace Jovanovich, 1988, 292, 330–331.

Williams, Frank. "Grand Central City." *The Architectural Forum* 128 (January–February 1968): 48–55.

Withey, Henry F., and Elsie Rathburn Withey. *Biographical Dictionary of American Architects, Deceased.* Los Angeles: New Age Publishing Co., 1956.

WPA Guide to New York City, The, with a new introduction by William H. Whyte. New York: Pantheon Books, Random House, 1982.

Zermuhlen, Frederick H. *The Renascence of City Hall.* Department of Public Works and Downtown Manhattan Association, Inc. New York, 1956.

Zurier, Rebecca. *The American Firehouse: An Architectural and Social History.* New York: Abbeville Press, 1982.

I have found the New York City Landmarks Preservation Commission's designation reports particularly useful, especially the following:

Church of the Incarnation (Marjorie Pearson, 1979), Chrysler Building (Marjorie Pearson, 1978), Empire State Building (Anthony Robins, 1981), RKO Keith's Flushing Theater (Anthony Robins, 1981), Vanderbilt Cemetery and Mausoleum (Nancy Goeschel, 1982), Racquet and Tennis Club (Marjorie Pearson, 1979), Fulton Ferry Historic District (Lea Roberts, 1977), Metropolitan Club (1979), Trinity Church and Cemetery (1966), South Street Seaport (1977), Prospect Park (1975), Chelsea (1970), SoHo Cast-Iron District (1973), U.S. Custom House (1979), Central Park (1974), Park Slope (1973), Greenwich Village Historic District (1969).

INDEX